BRITAIN'S GREATEST WARSHIP
HMS ARK ROYAL IV

Ark Royal at speed during the trials of the DH110 in April 1956 at the close of the ship's first commission.
(British Aerospace plc (Farnborough))

BRITAIN'S GREATEST WARSHIP
HMS ARK ROYAL IV

RICHARD JOHNSTONE-BRYDEN

FOREWORD BY ADMIRAL OF THE FLEET
SIR MICHAEL POLLOCK GCB, LVO, DSC

SUTTON PUBLISHING

First published in 1999 by
Sutton Publishing Limited · Phoenix Mill
Thrupp · Stroud · Gloucestershire · GL5 2BU

Paperback edition first published in 2000

British Library Cataloguing in Publication Data
A catalogue record for this book is available from the British Library.

ISBN 0-7509-2504-3

Typeset in 11/14pt Perpetua.
Typesetting and origination by
Sutton Publishing Limited.
Printed in Great Britain by
Butler & Tanner, Frome, Somerset.

CONTENTS

ACKNOWLEDGEMENTS   vii

FOREWORD   ix

1.   CHANGING TIMES   1

2.   PASSING THE BATON   15

3.   IN SEARCH OF THE PILGRIMS   43

4.   ICEBERGS AHEAD!   60

5.   A GLIMPSE INTO THE FUTURE?   76

6.   THE BATTLE OF BEIRA   107

7.   THE WIND OF CHANGE   124

8.   THE KOTLIN INCIDENT   132

9.   FAME AT LAST   161

10.   THE FINAL CURTAIN   191

11.   A STAY OF EXECUTION?   225

12.   THE *ARK*'S AIRCRAFT   234

13.   *ARK ROYAL* – THE DETAILS   243

14.   THE *ARK ROYAL* LEGEND   246

15.   DINOSAUR OR PHOENIX?   253

BIBLIOGRAPHY   255

INDEX   257

ACKNOWLEDGEMENTS

A book of this nature would not have been possible without the kind help and assistance given to me by some of the people who served in *Ark Royal* and have given up their time to talk about their memories of this great ship and check through the drafts of their quotes to ensure the highest level of accuracy. I would also like to thank each of the surviving Captains for checking the chapters covering their time in command and offering useful advice. I would especially like to thank Admiral of the Fleet Sir Michael Pollock GCB, LVO, DSC for writing the Foreword to this book. Although it is not possible to cover the stories of everyone who served in *Ark Royal* I hope the following account gives some insight into life on board an active fixed-wing aircraft carrier.

In particular I would like to thank the following former Flag Officers, Captains and members of the ship's company and Air Group: Admiral of the Fleet Lord Hill-Norton GCB, Admiral of the Fleet Sir Michael Pollock GCB, LVO, DSC, Admiral of the Fleet Sir Henry Leach GCB, DL; Admiral Sir Raymond Lygo KCB, Admiral Sir Desmond Cassidi GCB, Admiral Sir Michael Layard KCB, CBE; Vice Admiral Sir Edward Anson KCB, FRAeS, Vice Admiral Sir Donald Gibson KCB, DSC, JP, Vice Admiral Sir James Weatherall KBE, Vice Admiral Sir David Dobson KBE; Rear Admiral D.R.F. Cambell CB, DSC, Rear Admiral J.O. Roberts CB, Rear Admiral J.R.S. Gerard-Pearse CB, Rear Admiral W.J. Graham CB, FNI, Rear Admiral T.R. Cruddas CB, Rear Admiral Harkness CB, Rear Admiral A.R. Rawbone CB, AFC, Rear Admiral R.H. Burn CB, AFC, Rear Admiral Sir Ronald Forrest KCVO, DL, Rear Admiral Sir Robert Woodard KCVO; Commodore P.A. Fish CBE; Captain G.V.P. Crowden OBE, RN, Captain A. Skinner RN, Captain T.R. Lee RN, Captain J.G.H. O'Donnell RN, Captain C. Lawrence RN, Captain A. Morton DSC, RN, Captain F. Hefford OBE, DSC, AFC, RN, Captain M. Rotheram RN, Captain W.A. Tofts CBE, AFC, RN, Captain P.M.C. Vincent CBE, RN, Captain C. Waite RN; Cdr C.W.S. Dreyer DSO, DSC, RN, Cdr M. Cudmore OBE, RN, Cdr D. Hobbs MBE, RN, Cdr B. Peppe OBE, RN, Cdr D. Macdonald RN, Cdr A. Mancais OBE, RN, Cdr D. Dawson-Taylor RN, Cdr W.J. Woolley OBE, RN, Cdr P. Bell OBE, RN, Cdr D. Monsell RN, Cdr G. Wilcock RN, Cdr G. Kinch RN, Lt Cdr B. Chilcott RN; Lt Cdr P. Wreford RN, Lt Cdr S. Farquhar RN, Lt Cdr Sir Michael Richardson-Bunbury RN, Lt Cdr C. Brazendale MBE, RN, Lt Cdr R. Edward RN, Lt Cdr P. Hardy RN, Lt Cdr B. Bevans MBE, DSC, RN, Lt Cdr T. Martins RN; Major A.S. Hughes; Steve Riley, Grant Eustace, Revd Mike Pennington; T. Wilkinson MBE, BEM, W. Harwood, B. Ahern, R. Amphlett, R. Lampen, R.H. Booth, R. Dear, O. Roberts, C.E. Clapham, R. Fleming, B. Whitworth, J. Downing, A. Eliss, B. Salter, M. Smith, J. Woollen, J. Taylor, B.M. Davies, K. Moore, Lady Griffin, Captain Sir Alaistair Aird GCVO, Private Secretary to Queen Elizabeth the Queen Mother, D. Shepherd OBE, J. Purdie, R. Holme, D. McColm, D. Nelson, D. Philips and J. Reeve. Acknowledgement is also due to the following official archives and associations: Jan Keohane and Gerry Shore of the Fleet Air Arm Museum, Yeovilton, Cdr D. Macdonald RN of the Fleet Air Arm Officers Association, Cammell Laird Shipbuilders, Ernie Ruffler of the Metropolitan Borough of Wirral Cammell Laird Archives (Wirral Museum), Lt Cdr M. Coombe RN of the Association of Royal Naval Officers, HMS *Ark Royal V*, Stan Field and the British Aerospace Heritage Centre at Brough, Pam Guess of British

Aerospace Heritage Centre at Farnborough, Phil Boydon of British Aerospace Dunsfold, Steve Zalokoski of Rolls-Royce at Bristol, Anne Gleave of the E. Chambré Hardman Trust, Air Commodore Graham Pitchfork MBE, Buccaneer Aircrew Association, Cdr Mike Mullane RN, Editor *Broadsheet*, Cdr M.J. Reeves OBE, RN, Paul Cowpe, Chief Photographer/DPRN, Mr D. Ashby, Naval Historical Branch, Mr D. Holyland, Martin-Baker Aircraft Company Ltd, M. Lennon, GKN Westland Helicopters (Photographic Department), and D. Waller.

Sadly, it has not been possible to identify the numerous skilled ship's photographers who took many of the official photographs that appear throughout this book. However, I would like to highlight the important work which they have left behind so that future generations will be able to see as well as read about the events that make up the story of this great ship.

Sadly, with the passage of time since I began my research for this book some of the people who have contributed to the book are no longer with us. In particular two people who gave me a lot of encouragement and assistance in the early stages of the book were the late Admiral Sir Anthony Griffin GCB and the late Mr Frank Lindstrom (formerly of Cammell Laird).

Last and by no means least I would like to thank my father for patiently reading through the draft of the book and to acknowledge the support given to me by my parents and my grandmother throughout my writing and photographic career. I would also like to thank Jonathan Falconer of Sutton Publishing for his help, guidance and patience through this, my first book.

FOREWORD

When, in my long and happy retirement, I have been asked by the people of this less than maritime area [Powys] to describe what I did in my forty-four years of active naval service ending as the professional head of it, from a whole list of distinguished appointments they all pick out one and exclaim: 'Oh, were you actually the Captain of the *Ark Royal?*' Perhaps a surprising choice, perhaps not.

This minutely detailed record of the fourth *Ark Royal* and the men who kept her running, of her aircraft and air department crews, of the near superhuman efforts which had to be made to keep this formidable weapon system effective at a level of intensity in peacetime that could hardly have been exceeded in war, goes far towards explaining the position of strategic importance, public recognition and professional prestige which was held by *Ark Royal IV* from the time of her launch to the time, twenty-five years later, when various heritage preservation societies were squabbling, fortunately unsuccessfully, over her worn out structure with a view to long-term display. It is largely addressed to the professionals involved in the great enterprise of her twenty-five-year life and will be eagerly read as an extended 'Report of Proceedings' not otherwise easily available.

For myself, the appointment – out of the blue and at three weeks' notice – to the most prestigious ship command in the Royal Navy came as a great shock: the last time I had served in an aircraft carrier was as a midshipman in HMS *Furious* in 1934 when the aircraft were Blackburn Baffins, Hawker Ospreys and Fairey 3Fs, no sights, no catapults, no radar, no voice radio! I had a lot to learn, very quickly! I found, when I got there, that I had the most wonderful support on all sides and a ship's company totally dedicated to keeping the squadrons operational at whatever personal cost in spite of the operating conditions for which the ship had not been designed, the intensity of operations, the age of the machinery and the endemic shortage of aircraft spares which doubled the load on the air maintenance department.

It was a most demanding, exciting and frequently nail-biting appointment and I would not have missed it for the world. The sadness of 'Ring off main engines' at the end of the commission was only offset by the sense of achievement which I, and everyone else associated with the ship and her squadrons, felt at having successfully completed what was, in some cases, a most remarkable triumph of mind over matter.

The ethos of a 'Happy Ship' is well known to all seagoers and, when achieved, is a pearl without price. In some totally inexplicable way, in the Royal Navy the ethos becomes linked to the name of the ship and transfers to the next similarly named one in a succeeding generation. May the fifth *Ark Royal*, now in service, inherit the unconquerable spirit of her predecessors and carry that lustre forward to successive generations for as long as it remains necessary for aircraft to operate from ships at sea.

Michael Pollock
Montgomery, Powys
January 1999

CHANGING TIMES

On 13 November 1941 a single torpedo fired from the submarine *U-81* ended the illustrious wartime career of the third HMS *Ark Royal* while she was returning to Gibraltar. Despite valiant efforts by Captain Maund and the ship's company, who had worked through the night to save the ship and get her into Gibraltar under tow, the end came just after 6.15 a.m. on the 14th. As she slipped from sight below the still waters of the Mediterranean, watched by her Captain and crew, the Royal Navy lost one of its most famous warships. The year 1941 had already witnessed the loss of the *Hood*, sunk by the *Bismarck* in May; now *Ark Royal*, which had played an important part in the sinking of the *Bismarck*, was itself the victim of a U-boat attack. For its role in sinking the *Bismarck, Ark Royal* had become famous, and this battle played a part in establishing the aircraft carrier as the dominant type of warship, thus leading to the demise of the battleship. Her successor would prove equally worthy of the name *Ark Royal* and was to play a significant part in the continued development of the aircraft carrier. When she was eventually commissioned in 1955 she was the first aircraft carrier in RN service to be fitted with all the major postwar developments in aircraft carrier design, namely the angled flight deck, steam catapults and the mirror landing sight. These ideas, which were to revolutionize the design of all future aircraft carriers, had been tried out separately on other RN carriers but *Ark Royal* was the first to be fitted with all three.

Originally, *Ark Royal* was to have been built as HMS *Irresistible*, but her name was changed, as the following extract from the minutes of the Ships' Names Committee meeting held on 11 February 1942 illustrates: 'The secretary reported that Captain L.E.H. Maund RN, late of HMS *Ark Royal*, had informed him that he was holding the sum of £750 on behalf of his ship's company for the purchase of a bell and other trophies for a new *Ark Royal*. He had informed Captain Maund that the King had approved the proposal to change the name of the new aircraft carrier *Irresistible* to *Ark Royal*.' A major factor in ensuring the revival of *Ark Royal*'s name was the part played by the people of Leeds. During the Second World War the Government tried to encourage people to save in support of the war effort. One of the Government-sponsored schemes was the holding of 'Warship Weeks' around the country. The city of Leeds adopted *Ark Royal III* on 4 November 1941 to provide a focus and incentive for their Warship Week which was due to be held between 30 January and 7 February 1942. The initial fund-raising target was set at £3 million. The tragic news of the 14th led to the target being increased to £5 million but even this was surpassed and the final total was £9,301,293. As a result of this goodwill the Admiralty confirmed the city's adoption of the next *Ark Royal* at a ceremony held in Leeds on 19 September 1942.

The story of *Ark Royal*'s construction began when Contract CPBR.8/29887/42 was placed with Cammell Laird on 18 March 1942 to build Vessel number 1119. Cammell Laird had already gained useful experience in building aircraft carriers during the construction of the third *Ark Royal* in the 1930s. The keel was laid without ceremony on 3 May 1943 but HRH Princess Marina, the Duchess of Kent, presided over the official keel-laying ceremony on 11 May 1943, when a plate was lifted and laid. Because of the war and the need for secrecy, the keel-laying ceremony was not turned into a major occasion as it would have been in peacetime.

In the January 1979 issue of *Shipbuilding News* a number of the men who had helped build *Ark Royal* recalled their experiences. Joe Jemitus, a draughtsman at Cammell Laird, had been involved in the latter stages of building the third *Ark Royal* and throughout the fourth *Ark Royal*. He said: 'I remember there were constant stops and starts on the ship during the war because other vessels became priority jobs depending on the circumstances of the time. After the war ended it was a similar situation because the merchant fleet needed building up. It was a joke at the time about which would be finished first, the *Ark Royal*, or Liverpool Cathedral. At the time we looked at it as just another job, but looking back I feel a sense of pride about being involved in building what was truly a wonderful ship.'

Neville Lear was the head foreman fitter in *Ark Royal*. 'I was involved with the *Ark Royal* right through the twelve years during which she was built. In that period we built about 130 vessels, so we were always very busy. The delays, caused by transfers to other buildings and because of technological changes, were frustrating, but owing to the amount of other work we never had the time to sit and brood about it!' he recalled.

Jack Wilson, the manager of Cammell Laird's south yard during *Ark Royal*'s construction, talked about his memories of *Ark Royal*. 'There was a good atmosphere in the yard in those days – a strong camaraderie among the workers in all trades, everybody worked hard and there was a genuine interest in the job among all employees from the top of the scale down to the bottom. Obviously *Ark Royal* was a prestige project and we

The official keel-laying ceremony, presided over by the Duchess of Kent on 11 May 1943. (Cammell Laird Archives)

The great ship slowly begins to take shape. (Cammell Laird Archives)

were aware of that but there was no sense of awe about it. At the time it was just one of many jobs we were working on.'

Wilf Lowey was shop foreman plater when *Ark Royal* was launched. He recalled: 'Technology kept catching up with the ship and there were times when it seemed as if she would never be finished. In those days there were very few industrial disputes which was just as well in the circumstances. There was a strong discipline in the yard and missing a completion deadline was unthinkable – you got the sack if you did.'

As *Ark Royal* took shape on the slipway she 'hosted' her first broadcast, as Geoff Moore, who worked in the cost department of Cammell Laird, recalled: 'I went on board *Ark Royal* as part of the audience to watch the recording of Wilfred Pickle's "Have A Go" radio programme. It was held in her hangar deck and Wilfred was given a specially built stage to host the programme from. The programme was well attended by those working in the yard.'

In April 1950 the Liverpool-based photographer E. Chambré Hardman took perhaps one of the best known images of *Ark Royal*. It took him at least twenty trial shots before he found the right time and place on Holt Hill, Birkenhead. Over the years this stunning photograph has come to symbolize the glory years of shipbuilding on the Mersey. In the photograph, the freshly painted *Ark Royal*, resplendent in her white undercoat, sits on the

This is perhaps the most famous photograph of *Ark Royal*. It was taken by the Liverpool photographer E. Chambré Hardman shortly before *Ark Royal*'s launching in 1950. (E. Chambré Hardman Trust)

slipway prior to launching, with the cranes of the shipyard towering above her, while she in turn dominates the surrounding housing. To ensure that the eye is drawn to *Ark Royal*, Chambré Hardman retouched the negative to darken the white gable end of the central house in the foreground. Chambré Hardman's attention to detail also led to the removal of a lamp-post and the retouching of one of the schoolboy's socks so that it was no longer halfway down his ankle. Chambré Hardman died at the age of 89 in 1988. Since then, his photographs have been preserved by the E. Chambré Hardman Trust which is currently undertaking the massive task of archiving his entire collection of photographs. Sadly, the collection is not yet open to the public but the Trust does allow people with a serious interest access to the archive.

Finally the great day arrived. Seven years to the day after her keel was laid, *Ark Royal* was ready to be launched by HM Queen Elizabeth (now HM Queen Elizabeth the Queen Mother), who was to maintain an active involvement with the ship throughout its service. In 1940 the Queen made a surprise visit to Cammell Laird along with King George VI. Just as the royal couple were leaving, Sir Robert Johnson, who was Cammell Laird's Chairman and Managing Director, asked the Queen if she would name a ship in the yard on a future occasion. She told him that she would be very pleased to do so if the yard had a suitable ship and times were more settled.

The sheer size of *Ark Royal* can be gauged from this photo of her towering above the crowds gathered for her launching. (Cammell Laird Archives)

Queen Elizabeth sends the great ship on her way down the slipway. (Cammell Laird Archives)

The launching of *Ark Royal* was the fulfilment of that promise. She was the heaviest ship that Cammell Laird had ever built, with a launching weight of 24,800 tons, only 1,000 tons less than Britain's last battleship HMS *Vanguard*, launched in 1944. In sharp contrast to her keel-laying, *Ark Royal*'s launching was turned into a great occasion. A crowd of more than 50,000 people turned out to watch her take to the waters of the Mersey for the first time. The Navy contributed to the event by mooring the wartime aircraft carrier HMS *Illustrious* nearby to act as a floating grandstand for the C-in-C Plymouth, Admiral Sir Rhoderick McGrigor, and a thousand guests. A guard of honour was sent to Birkenhead from *Ark Royal*'s future home port, Devonport. One of the sailors in that guard was Owen Roberts. 'We travelled up from HMS *Drake* by train to HMS *Illustrious* in Birkenhead. We drew bedding from the stores and we slept in the hangar. The following day we marched to the slipway and formed up just to port of *Ark Royal*'s bow. The Queen Mother inspected the guard and then went to perform the launching ceremony,' he recalled. Shortly after midday, at the top of the spring tide, the Queen pressed the button to signal *Ark Royal*'s launch. Within a few moments the great ship began to slide gracefully down the slipway into the waters of the Mersey. To commemorate the launching, a signal was sent from *Ark Royal*'s sister ship *Eagle* which was fitting out in the Belfast yard of Harland & Wolf. It read: 'Your elder sister, who has the honour of being the first of the *Ark Royal* class, sends you all good wishes on this happy and auspicious occasion. Be a good girl and you will soon be big enough to come and play with us.' As part of the ceremony *Illustrious* fired a 21-gun salute to welcome the Royal Navy's newest ship. The FAA staged a flypast from RNAS Stretton, which consisted of Sea Furies and Sea Hornets.

24,800 tons of ship makes its way down the slipway as *Ark Royal* enters the water for the first time. (Cammell Laird Archives)

Tugs take the hull in tow to move it round to Cammell Laird's fitting-out basin. (Cammell Laird Archives)

When she was launched part of the bow was missing, according to Mr William Howard in an interview for the *News* in April 1978. He said, 'We had to take about 40ft off, otherwise the sill at the bottom of the slipway would have crushed it. We cut the bow out, patched it up and replaced it afterwards.'

With the festivities completed, *Ark Royal* was secured alongside Cammell Laird's basin to begin nearly five years of fitting-out work. During this period her intended date of commissioning was postponed a number of times to allow for the inclusion of advances in carrier design. For example, two months after launching it was decided to fit *Ark Royal* with a deck edge lift, while further upheaval was caused in November 1950 when the decision was made to fit steam catapults. On 1 June 1953 Cdr C.W.S. Dreyer DSO, DSC, RN joined *Ark Royal* as her Senior Executive Officer to oversee the remaining fitting-out period and start the preparations for her entry into service. When she was commissioned, Cdr Dreyer was due to become her Commander and second-in-command. At the time of his appointment it was intended to commission *Ark Royal* within twelve to thirteen months, but further delays resulted in the process taking twenty-one months. Cdr Dreyer had never before served with the Fleet Air Arm or in an aircraft carrier, except for a six-week air course as a Sub-Lieutenant in the previous HMS *Ark Royal*, so one of his high priority jobs was to learn about the running of an aircraft carrier and the Fleet Air Arm. Starting in June he made visits to all the RN aircraft carriers in commission. He spent ten days at sea in HMS *Eagle*, the *Ark*'s sister ship. Dreyer recalled: 'Out of all this, and especially the *Eagle*, I acquired a lot of knowledge of what I didn't want for *Ark Royal*, and some ideas and thoughts for modifications which we might manage to achieve before she was completed. The *Eagle* was not a happy ship and I was determined that the *Ark Royal* would be entirely different. Happiness in a warship is a strange and distinctive characteristic made up of many strands – the ship must be efficient, good at work and play; she must be as comfortable as is possible in a warship and the food must be good; the routine must be well run, without niggling irritations; the ship must be clean and look good; the sailors must trust their officers; everyone must know the programmes and plans and the maximum possible leave must be available; the mail must come and go efficiently.'

Over the coming months Cdr Dreyer began the task of planning *Ark Royal*'s routines. The *Eagle* had two Commanders because the Admiralty thought that a complement of nearly 2,500 men was far too many for one man to manage. The senior Commander was the second-in-command and was responsible for discipline, morale and leave, while the second Commander was the head of the Seaman Department. Discussing the background to the decision to have just one Commander for *Ark Royal*, Dreyer said, 'I was determined that we should have only one Commander, and I told the Admiralty that if they wanted two then it must be two other chaps – but I must have five able helpers to run the ship. These would be the First Lieutenant, who would run the mess decks and accommodation; the Mate of the Upper Deck, who would run the outside – the seamanlike part of the ship; the Routine Officer, who would run my office and produce the Daily Orders and all the ship's special parties and orders, etc.; the Damage Control Officer; and the Dining Halls Officer, to oversee this vital function.' Admiral Sir Anthony Griffin, who served as the senior Commander in HMS *Eagle* and later as Captain of *Ark Royal* in the fifth commission, said: 'Although I felt the system of two Commanders worked well during my time in HMS *Eagle*, the decision to have just one Commander in *Ark Royal* stood the test of time as she got through her entire service with only one Commander.'

As the summer of 1953 progressed Lt Cdr George Sievewright joined *Ark Royal*. His job was to run Cdr Dreyer's office and when she commissioned, he would become her Gunnery Officer. During the final months of fitting out he was given the unenviable task of writing the ship's Standing Orders. Another important arrival was the future Commander (S) Cdr John Watkins. Dreyer recalled: 'He went off to spend time in *Eagle* and came back to us bubbling with ideas. He and I had a series of long discussions and then produced a big paper on the improvements we wanted to see incorporated into the living and feeding arrangements for the main dining halls and the Wardroom. The ship was running late on programme anyway and a little further delay was acceptable. I was also determined to improve the quarterdeck arrangements, so that we had a properly dignified ceremonial area. This involved removing boat stowages for two ship's boats and placing them elsewhere, and fitting

Despite the sheds on deck and part of the flight deck yet to be completed, *Ark Royal* is beginning to take shape with the superstructure now complete and her radars in place. (Cammell Laird Archives)

accommodation ladders on the quarterdeck, rather than further forward. There was also to be a ladder fitted aft on the quarterdeck up to the Admiral's and Captain's quarters.'

Dreyer continued: 'As the number of crew standing by *Ark Royal* continued to grow, further improvements were thought of. One of our major achievements was an idea which came from the electrical department, when Lieutenant Commander May suggested that we buy and install our own internal television system – a camera and transmitter and television sets in each mess deck. This was a tremendous and unheard-of innovation, paid for by Lloyds, who had adopted the ship. It enabled us to show television programmes or movies or our own shows direct to every mess. Of course, the whole thing took quite a bit of organizing.' This was a great step forward because it enabled instructional films as well as movies and announcements to be shown at any time of the day without having to clear a hangar deck and specially rig a large projection screen. To begin with there were only five television sets spread around the ship, with two for the ship's company, one for the Wardroom, one for the CPOs and one for the POs.

In addition to organizing the future routines for *Ark Royal* and looking for improvements within the ship itself, Cdr Dreyer was also responsible for establishing links with the outside world. Cdr Dreyer renewed the wartime links with Leeds and visited the city's Mayor and Corporation. On the sporting front, 'We arranged that the ship would use Leeds United football colours and the club supplied us with a lot of gear. Also Waddingtons, the well-known playing cards and games maker, supplied every mess with a whole outfit of cards and games – a most valuable present', Dreyer recalled.

During the winter of 1953/4 Cdr Dreyer became convinced, after long talks with the future Commander (Air), Cdr Michael Fell DSO, DSC, that the unhappiness in *Eagle* was due to one main reason. 'She had too many aircraft, with the result that about 100 junior ratings never had a permanent hammock billet. I wrote a number of letters and lobbied hard in the Admiralty to have the ship's allocation of aircraft reduced by one squadron and thereby achieve two extra mess decks', he said.

Early in 1954 Cdr Dreyer learned that the future Captain of *Ark Royal* was going to be Captain Dennis Cambell DSC (now Rear Admiral Cambell CB, DSC). Summing up his time in command Cambell said, 'The next eighteen months were to be the high point of my time in the Navy. Although I reached a higher rank later on, nothing could ever equal the extraordinary feeling of power and responsibility which lay with me while I was in command of this Behemoth. Whether I achieved all that I set out to do, I cannot know for sure. All I do know is that when I finally left I felt pretty good about it, very unlike some other posts I had held.' Prior to his appointment to *Ark Royal* Cambell had had little experience of commanding ships: 'My only other experience of sea command had been as Captain of the training corvette *Tintagel Castle* working for the Anti Submarine School at Portland. As such, I gained a superficial skill at single-screw ship handling, for we were in and out of the harbour on a 9 to 5 basis every working day of the week. Being by then a Commander, I was in charge of four other ships, half the training flotilla. But it was not much of a preparation for taking over the *Ark*. So my qualifications for the task of turning that monstrous ship into a fully trained and efficient fighting carrier were not very obvious, to say the least, and I can't help suspecting that the publicity given to my part in inventing the angled deck had something to do with my being selected.' Coincidentally Captain Cambell had commanded 803 Squadron in *Ark Royal III* from the end of 1938 through to February 1940, flying Skua fighters.

As Cambell recalled, the search for extra space in *Ark Royal* was assisted by the angled flight deck which he had invented with Mr Bodington in 1951. 'One big bonus of the angled deck was that it freed some valuable space which could be used for accommodation because she only required six arrester wires as opposed to the fourteen in a conventional carrier. Therefore, the space used for all of the associated gear that came with the extra wires could be used for extra accommodation.' Although *Ark Royal* was fitted with six wires of the latest

Ark Royal alongside in Cammell Laird's fitting-out basin shortly before her first sea trials in 1954. (Cammell Laird Archives)

Mark 13 arrester gear she was normally only rigged with four wires to avoid pulling out the No. 1 wire by tractor while ranging aircraft on the after lift. No. 2 was also left unrigged because it was on the same unit as No. 1 wire.

At the beginning of May 1954 *Ark Royal* was moved across the Mersey for docking in the Gladstone dock, as *Ark Royal*'s first Navigating Officer Lt Cdr W.J. Woolley (now Cdr W.J. Woolley OBE) recalled: 'I detached myself from HMS *Dryad* and went to Birkenhead to familiarize myself with the layout and communications around the bridge. I always manned the conning intercom for all movements, the first of which was across the Mersey with two Mersey pilots in charge.' The passage across the Mersey was done on two engines under the command of the pilot, who handed over to the dockmaster once inside the basin. As the ship entered the Gladstone dock it became apparent that the overhang was going to foul the newly built dockmaster's office by the entry to the dock – and its roof disintegrated! Because of the time on passage some heads (toilets) had been commissioned, and just as the ship entered the gate of the dock, a flush was used and the 'product' fell among the riggers handling the wires. A furious chargeman looked up and caught sight of the pilot: 'Hey,' he shouted, 'The dockmaster will not have this.' The instant Merseyside reply was 'Well, share it among yourselves, then.'

By June 1954 *Ark Royal* was at long last ready to begin her first set of contractor's sea trials on the Clyde. Dreyer recalled: 'The whole standing-by team went in her but the ship was operated and run by Cammell Laird. A retired RN Captain called Larry Lentaigne was provided by the Admiralty and employed by the firm to act as Captain for the trials. He was supported by Captain Stewart who was the Clyde Pilot. We provided, on an informal basis, a number of officers and men to act as Officers of the Watch, Quartermasters and other watch duties, all under the firm's control. It was an odd, unofficial compromise arrangement which worked well in

To sea at long last! The view from the bridge as *Ark Royal* conducts her first set of sea trials in June 1954. (Commander Woolley)

practice. A firm of Liverpool caterers provided food for everyone and it was very good. I do remember that the steward who looked after the bridge was an elderly pansy – queer, but kindly and efficient, and called Ruby.' Describing the scene on board for the ratings during the trials Clapham said: 'Everybody was dossing down on camp beds in any convenient place. I was in one of the aircrew briefing rooms where I discovered that we had one or two rats for company. This became apparent when one night after having a shower and plastering my hair with hair cream, as was the fashion in those days, I woke, conscious of something tugging at my hair and, yes, it was one of the aforementioned members of the crew.'

Because *Ark Royal*'s size had made such a crewing arrangement necessary, the trials provided some of the ship's future officers with valuable experience which would be very useful for the commission ahead. As Woolley recalled: 'Once clear of the Bar light vessel I did everything an "N" would do under RN circumstances, under the guidance of these two officers. We learnt to handle the splendid vessel. The ship had two rudders and four independent shafts, and the rudders were nearly in line with the inner screws; so we decided to treat the ship as a three-screw ship, with the inner engines normally working together providing a flow of water past the rudders. We anchored for the night at the Tail of the Bank off Greenock, and ran speed trials off Lamlash on the Isle of Arran, where there is a two-mile measured distance (beacons in transit on shore). On the fourth day, we were working up to full power on the mile, and were heading south along the track, when the whole ship vibrated (as in a volcanic eruption) and black smoke massed from the funnel. The Pilot said, "Come away from

The Clyde Pilot Captain
J. Mitchell on board during
sea trials. (Commander
Woolley)

the land into the open Firth." We had just done so when we lost all power, electricity and steering – a dead ship! We were all safe, heading for Paddy's Milestone (Ailsa Craig). Captain Lentaigne was ringing for the engine room to enquire what was going on, the Pilot said, "I am sure they don't know themselves yet!"' It was three hours later that Cammell Laird's Engineering Manager came to the bridge, and asked to return to the Tail of the Bank – "We think we have stripped a turbine – but we can offer you three other engines soon!"' Cdr Cruddas (now Rear Admiral Cruddas CB) was the Air Engineering Officer during the first commission; explaining what caused the accident he said, 'They lost the water level in a boiler's gauge glass and the watchkeeper assumed that the water was too low and pumped more water into the boiler. What had actually happened was the water was above the top of the gauge glass and thus the extra water went over with the steam into the turbine and damaged the turbine blades.'

Despite stripping the turbine, *Ark Royal's* trials were not stopped. Woolley again: 'There were some gunnery trials to do in the next week, so it was decided to complete these, and then return to the Mersey. It was on arrival off the basin in Birkenhead that the next bit of fun occurred. The power pack for the conning intercom was fitted in the bridge wireless office. This space was manned during the trials by a radio contracting company. Seeing the ship nearly alongside, the operator bade his farewells on air, switched off all power and left the office

Left to right: Captain Lentaigne (Master), Mr White (Cammell Laird), Captain Mitchell (Clyde Pilot) and Mr Gillieland (Cammell Laird's Ship Manager). (Commander Woolley)

locked. On the bridge the pilot had just asked for slow ahead on one engine to nudge the vessel round the knuckle of the basin. Feeling the movement he asked for "Stop her". There was no feedback on the conning intercom, and we speedily resorted to the sound powered telephone. Dead ahead was a caisson covering the entrance to the graving dock in which there were men working on a tanker. There was great relief on the bridge when the engine room telegraph was responded to by the engine room!'

Following her return to Cammell Laird the shipyard opened up the ship's side to exchange the stripped turbine for a spare turbine. The work was completed within three months so that by September *Ark Royal* was once more ready for contractor's sea trials. For this second batch of trials Captain Cambell joined the crew as an observer because she was still under the Red Ensign and the control of Cammell Laird. During these trials John Woollen, who was a stoker, said, 'The whole ship reeked of foul water and paint. There were cables and rubbish all over the place.' Nevertheless, the trials passed without incident until the ship's return to the Mersey. As Clapham recalled: 'When we arrived back at the Mersey after the trials, the weather was too severe to enter the estuary and we were stuck out there for three days. The problem was we had run out of food but eventually a small amount of food was delivered to us.'

As winter approached, the small nucleus of officers and men who were standing by the *Ark Royal* began to increase in numbers, with Captain Cambell finally joining his new command before Christmas 1954. As the New Year dawned it seemed as though the great ship was at last on course for completion. 'George Sievewright planned the commissioning and arranged an office in Devonport barracks to prepare the details and all the

Ark Royal running sea trials in September 1954. Note she is still under the Red Ensign. (Cammell Laird Archives)

ratings' joining cards. All was gradually falling into place,' said Dreyer. The long job of drafting the Standing Orders for the individual departments and the ship as a whole was completed by the end of 1954. Dreyer continued, 'I had wanted to call the *Ark Royal* Standing Orders by the short title ARSOs, but George said it was vulgar and people would laugh at the defaulters' table when it was used, so we agreed to ARKOs which was dull but safer.'

According to Woolley: 'There had been so many changes to the ship that we decided to hang pieces of rope between all the slinging davits around the ship and we counted them all up and found that we were some 600 slinging billets short for sailors who were due to join the ship in three months' time. We informed the Admiralty design department of this and changes were made to accommodate the sailors. The cause of this shortage was the fact that the ship was built to an essentially pre-war design which had been extensively updated to cope with the challenges of the postwar era.'

In the New Year Cdr Dreyer and Captain Cambell began the process of interviewing all the prospective ship's company in Devonport and Lee-on-Solent. 'The effort of doing this was well worth while – a photograph and detail card was prepared for each man, and from these it was possible to make preliminary arrangements for all sorts of things: games teams, the band, the choir, special duties, etc.; and all sorts of special capabilities came to light: the cartoonist who enlivened my daily orders and *Noah's News*; a ferret handler to help prevent rat problems; an apprentice printer from our Royal Marines; a shoemaker or two and many other useful people,' said Dreyer.

By the beginning of February the final countdown to commissioning had begun. There was just under a month to go before twelve years of hard work would be completed and the great ship would finally be handed over to the Royal Navy.

Chapter Two

PASSING THE BATON

FIRST COMMISSION,

FEBRUARY 1955–APRIL 1956

After twelve years under construction at Cammell Laird, the day was coming ever closer when *Ark Royal* would exchange her Red Ensign for the White Ensign and take her place as the Royal Navy's most modern aircraft carrier and pride of the fleet. On 14 February the standing-by team finally moved on board. Until then they had been living in local accommodation, including the Liverpool Racquets Club which had been home to the Captain and his senior officers. On 20 February two special trains from Devonport brought the rest of the ship's company to join their new ship. They stayed in local service establishments overnight and the process of ferrying them to Cammell Laird's yard to join the ship began the following day. A fleet of buses was used and carefully planned to arrive at ten minute intervals to maintain an even flow of arrivals. The whole process passed off very smoothly with only a few problems. Dreyer recalled: 'I remember that one cook came up the gangway fully adorned with powder and lipstick. After a quick inspection of his ditty bag he was turned straight round, given an escort of two Petty Officers and sent back to barracks. I rang the barracks' Drafting Commander, who laughed and said, "Statistically, out of your 1,800 ship's company, there must be at least nineteen more." In fact, over the coming months we did find several (mainly officers' stewards and a strong team in the NAAFI barbers' shop) and sent them back to base.'

Ken Moore joined *Ark Royal* as a Leading Stoker, having previously served in *Eagle* for six months. Talking about his first impressions of *Ark Royal*, and some of the differences between the two ships, he said: 'It was a nice-looking ship and I thought it looked bigger than the *Eagle*. Before I joined *Ark Royal* everything was organized. I knew exactly what job I would be doing, which mess I would be in and which watches I would be doing. This was in marked contrast to when I joined *Eagle*.'

Once the ship's company had embarked in *Ark Royal*, there followed five days of preparations before she sailed on her final acceptance trials. The ship's company was mustered in the hangar deck to be addressed by both Captain Cambell and Cdr Dreyer prior to the next day's Commissioning ceremony which was to be held in the hangar deck. The purpose of this muster was for the senior officers to set the tone for the forthcoming commission with a few words on how they expected things to be done. Cdr Dreyer felt it was important to keep the ship's company informed of the future programme and, at this muster, he promised that the men would always be kept informed as far as security would permit. This was a promise that he was able to keep fairly well during his time as the Commander.

A press conference was held on board two days before the Commissioning ceremony at which Cambell 'was allowed to disclose the fact that the *Ark* was fitted with remote control of the engines in the event of an atomic attack. The minute I mentioned this the press went bananas. The following day headlines such as "Atomic Age

Aircraft Carrier" appeared: it was an absolute non-starter but that is the way it came out. It always plagued every press conference thereafter.'

The Commissioning ceremony was held on board on 22 February 1955, and was broadcast on the BBC's Home Service. The ceremony was attended by Viscount Leverhulme, the Lord Lieutenant of Cheshire, most of the area's Mayors and other local dignitaries. At the beginning of the service a recorded message was played from Vice Admiral Sir John Eccles, who had been the Commander of *Ark Royal III*. In it he spoke about the role of a modern carrier and included some personal reminiscences of *Ark Royal III*. The service itself was conducted by another former member of *Ark Royal III*'s ship's company, Chaplain of the Fleet the Revd J.W.B. Moore. A series of four cocktail parties were held on the four days following the Commissioning ceremony, hosted by the officers on the quarterdeck; these provided an excellent opportunity for this most important of social events held by the ship to be perfected, and making the most of the ship's facilities, including her television system which had five sets on trials at this time with a view to a wider permanent installation.

Cambell also had to cope with the anti-Fleet Air Arm campaign which was launched by the Beaverbrook papers. 'Prior to her commissioning there had been a lot of bad press building up against the *Ark Royal*, most notably fuelled by the *Daily Express* and *Sunday Express* who had seized on what would usually have been classed as trivial matters and blown them out of proportion to make them front page headline news. A good example was when the *Ark Royal*, still in the builders' hands, was moved from Cammell Laird's yard to the Gladstone dock in Liverpool in May 1954. To get the *Ark Royal* into the dock was quite a tight fit and as she was gently eased into the dock with only a few feet to spare on each side one of the gash chutes* was slightly bent. The *Sunday Express* seized upon this immediately and produced the headline "*Ark Royal* Hits Dock; Unlucky *Ark Royal* Is Unlucky Again", and the editorial started off with "Waste, waste, waste, why is this enormous ship being commissioned when what we need is bombers", and so it continued. It is likely that an *Express* reporter sent in his account of the proceedings, giving credit to the pilot for completing such a delicate manoeuvre with so little damage, but our *Ark* was on the Beaverbrook black list – as indeed was Mountbatten, coincidentally then First Sea Lord. So we were pilloried in good company.'

Ark Royal left Cammell Laird for the last time on Friday 25 February. Cambell described the scene: 'At about noon the ship was warped out of the basin ready for her final acceptance trial. After anchoring off the Isle of Man for the night, the full power trial was begun during the forenoon of Saturday 26th. Various defects were disclosed but were overcome, and at 18:00 the engines were pronounced acceptable by the E-in-C representatives aboard, including Rear Admiral Weston. Sir Robert Johnson, Chairman and Managing Director of Cammell Laird, and I jointly signed the form of turnover and acceptance.' Thus at 6.30 p.m. a bugle sounded the alert, which was followed by the lowering of the Red Ensign for the last time. In its place the White Ensign was hoisted as *Ark Royal IV* formally took her place at the head of the Royal Navy. With the formalities complete she sailed past the Cumbraes to anchor off Greenock for the night. The next day the 500 men from Cammell Laird and the Admiralty were disembarked while the ship was fuelled up before she left that night bound for Loch Ewe for four days' shakedown. 'This was a valuable period to clean up the accumulation of rubbish from storing, completion and trials; and to try out our routines and to practise the main seamanship exercises – towing forward and aft, hoisting and lowering boats, fire drills, oiling and supplying by jackstay, go to action stations and other defence stations; and above all to find one's way around the ship,' Dreyer said.

While the crew were getting used to living and working in *Ark Royal*, it was soon discovered that while some of the mess halls and other accommodation were likely to be crowded at times, especially when the squadrons

---

* Gash chutes were tubes strung over the side of the ship to pass the rubbish from on board down to skips on the quayside.

Watched by representatives from Cammell Laird, Captain Cambell signs the document to accept *Ark Royal* into the RN. (Rear Admiral Cambell via the author)

were embarked, *Ark Royal* had a rather large number of heads, particularly the main heads which stretched from one side of the ship to the other. Captain Cambell decided to send a signal to the Admiralty about the situation, suggesting that some of the space could be adapted for extra accommodation. The wording of the signal was later to haunt him: 'I used some words that I bitterly regret. I said that the ship's company spirit and morale start on a high note and remain high but if overcrowded conditions are allowed to continue to persist they may come down. The Third Sea Lord got this signal and flew into a temper, thinking that I was threatening mutiny. I was sent for by the C-in-C Portsmouth, Admiral Sir George Creasey, and told about his complaints. Creasey said that I had better write a letter of apology or else I would lose my command, so I did. The sequel to this was that the Third Sea Lord sent down his deputy, a Rear Admiral, to come on board the ship and I was instructed to receive him with full honours when he came to inspect what I was complaining about. He refused all offers of hospitality and it was the coldest visit I ever received. The moral of the story can best be summed up in Hopwood's *Law of the Navy*: "They prosper, who burn in the morning the letter they wrote overnight", and it is so true.'

On the voyage to Portsmouth, the *Ark* encountered moderately rough weather. This presented no real challenge to the new ship, although Dreyer recalled one young sailor remarking to a Chief Petty Officer, 'Cor, ain't it rough, Chief', to which the CPO replied tersely, 'I've seen bigger ripples on me tot!' The only real casualty of the trip was the first White Ensign which was ripped to shreds during the gale.

On 7 March 1955, following her arrival off Southsea, Captain Cambell left *Ark Royal* by boat for Gosport. He returned later by helicopter, landing his Dragonfly on *Ark Royal* and thus claiming the privilege of being the first pilot to land on the deck. Cambell had been checked out to fly the Dragonfly while he was waiting for *Ark Royal* to be completed and this was the start of a long association with helicopters which continued after he left the RN in 1960.

A number of problems were encountered during *Ark Royal*'s first visit to Portsmouth. Dreyer recalled three in particular. 'While off Portsmouth *Ark Royal* was given a real man overboard drill when a cook decided to commit suicide. He had been waiting outside the Regulating Office to be charged with "urinating in an improper place". He jumped over the side but changed his mind halfway down and cried for help. Thanks to the quick action of the sentry on the quarterdeck, who threw him a lifebelt, and the bridge crew, he was safely back on board within twenty minutes. The second incident occurred one evening when a CPO came to see me. After I had sat him down with a cigarette he said to me abruptly, "The thing is, Sir, I rather think that I may have committed bigamy." After about two minutes' discussion it was abundantly clear that he had indeed done exactly that. I sent him off with his Divisional Officer to see the Legal Aid and Welfare Officers in the barracks, and they sorted things out for him excellently, although he had to stay on board rather a lot for a bit, till it was safe.' On the third occasion Dreyer recalled, 'I remember one night going to have a bath before turning in and hearing, to my surprise, a small noise from the Admiral's bathroom next door. When I'd finished my bath I walked through the flat and went into the empty Admiral's quarters, and on into the sleeping cabin, where, to my considerable amazement, I saw a totally naked Petty Officer sitting up in bed. I told him to go immediately, and to see me on the quarterdeck at 08:15 the next day. I like to think he spent an anxious night for, apart from a hell of a blast from me, that was the only punishment he got. I decided that, since the man worked for the Captain, it would be a distraction for the Captain to have to deal with it, which he would have to do if I made the matter official.'

Dreyer tried hard to be accessible as the ship's Commander. He said: 'I made it an absolute rule in harbour that I sat on the quarterdeck from 08:15 till 08:45, smoking my pipe and available for anyone to come and talk to. I tried very hard throughout my time in the ship not to become involved with the routine running, and this generally worked pretty well. My team did it all for me so that I was always free to see people and make myself available for whatever was needed. I had to see Requestmen and Defaulters every day at 09:00, and I told the

The Admiral's dining cabin. (Cammell Laird Archives)

ship's company that it was my aim and object to be nice to Requestmen and horrid to Defaulters. In fact, throughout my time, everyone behaved remarkably well with very few exceptions, and out of our large crew I usually had no more than three or four Defaulters and quite often none at all.'

Dreyer recalled that the Commanders in *Ark Royal* had a novel form of transport. 'Rennie Cruddas, who was the Air Engineer Officer, was the instigator of the Sergeants' taxi. The nine Commanders (including the padre) in the first commission had a jointly owned landau taxi, which we carried about in the ship. We were referred to as "the Sergeants" because of our three stripes. The taxi was a happy, and occasionally useful joke.' Cruddas said: 'We paid £230 for the taxi. Petty Officer McGibben was the man responsible for the flight deck mobile equipment and he was also responsible for lifting the taxi on and off the ship. I remember one occasion when the ship was actually moving away from the quayside just as the taxi was being craned back on board. When at sea the taxi was stowed out of the way at the end of the hangar.'

During *Ark Royal*'s trials in the Solent she became the centre of attention for all the wrong reasons, as Cambell recalled. 'During the severe gales which followed and when the ship was heeled over at anchor at Spithead (due to a strong cross-current), a leak developed in a main fuel tank. A very large blob of oil was disgorged and carried into Portsmouth Harbour, where the wind and tide spattered it all over houses, cars, streets and so on. A very indignant tone was taken by the local press and later by MPs in Parliament, calling for the Captain to be disciplined. However, C-in-C Portsmouth promptly convened a Board of Inquiry at which the facts were established, and the ship, though found guilty in fact, was absolved of intent.' There was a nice sequel to the story: as *Ark Royal* returned to the Solent after her shakedown cruise to Gibraltar a sizeable oil slick was sighted off the port bow and Cambell sent a tongue-in-cheek 'not guilty this time' signal to the C-in-C.

On 25 March *Ark Royal IV* picked up the mantle of her famous predecessor when she was presented with her silver bell. It was given to *Ark Royal IV* by Mr Vatcher, the Chief Cook of *Ark Royal III*. The belfry was then presented by *Ark Royal III*'s Commander, Vice Admiral Sir John Eccles. The story of the silver bell began after the sinking of *Ark Royal III* when survivors met in a street in Gibraltar Dockyard, close to the main wharf, on 16 November 1941 to hold an informal meeting of the Canteen Committee. They decided to make donations from the ship's fund to the ships which had taken off the survivors and to give £100 to the next-of-kin of the only sailor to be lost, Able Seaman Edward Mitchell. It was agreed that the remaining money – about £500 – should be used to purchase a silver bell for the next *Ark Royal*. Messrs Gillett and Johnston of Croydon agreed to cast a flat-topped bell measuring 19 inches in diameter at the mouth for £597. A casting ceremony was held on 10 December 1943 and attended by the First Lord of the Admiralty, Mr A.V. Alexander, and fifteen officers and fifteen men from *Ark Royal III*. The First Lord stepped forward while the silver was poured into the mould and threw a sixpence into it saying 'Here's luck to the Ark'. The bell, having survived the bombing of Croydon, was moved to the barracks at Lee-on-Solent in accordance with the dedication agreement which stated that when no *Ark Royal* was in commission it was to be held by the Commodore of the FAA barracks at Lee-on-Solent (or by the Commanding Officer of any such other establishment that might become the headquarters of Fleet Air Arm personnel). And there it was to stay until it was presented to the *Ark Royal IV*. Led by *Ark Royal III*'s first Captain, later Admiral of the Fleet Sir Arthur Power GBE, KCB, CVO, the surviving officers paid for a wooden belfry to house the bell. It was built by the craftsmen at Cammell Laird but was subsequently lost when it was swept overboard during *Ark Royal*'s encounter with the remnants of Hurricane Flossie in September 1978.

At the end of March *Ark Royal* left the Solent for eight weeks of catapult deadload trials in her home port of Devonport. While in Devonport, *Ark Royal*'s sister ship *Eagle* came into port on 29 April and moored with her stern end towards *Ark Royal*'s. On the following Saturday both crews were surprised when Captain Cambell and Cdr Dreyer conducted rounds in the *Eagle* and *Eagle*'s Captain Lewin and her senior Commander, Cdr A.

Ark Royal enters her home port of Devonport for the first time on 30 March 1955. (Commander Woolley via the author)

Griffin, destined to become *Ark Royal*'s sixth Captain in 1964, conducted rounds in *Ark Royal*. No doubt there were a few sailors wondering for a split second if they were on the right carrier!

Dreyer described some of the modifications carried out to *Ark Royal* while she was in Devonport during April. 'The ship, like her sister ship *Eagle*, was designed and built with two Wardroom ante-rooms and two dining rooms, adjacent to each other. The ante-rooms each had a bar. We feared that the separated units would become stylized, either one for ship's officers, one for air department; or, worse still, Commissioned Officers and Branch Officers. During our time in Devonport in April we achieved one long bar in the bigger ante-room and the removal of the other bar in the other room. This was a great improvement and the bar was a truly impressive fitting, which must have been 40ft long or more.'

Ark Royal made her debut at Plymouth's Navy Days during that year's Whitsun Bank Holiday event. She played host to some 26,226 people out of a total of 33,296 people who visited the Naval Base. Highlights for visitors to the ship included a trip on the hangar lifts and the electrical department's display, featuring a model plane which, at the press of a button, released a bomb on the model ships in the tank.

Ark Royal slipped her moorings in Devonport on 31 May bound for a shakedown cruise to Gibraltar without any of the squadrons embarked. Dreyer described her departure: 'We sailed out of Devonport in a snowstorm. It was the same depression which caused such devastation in the Bordeaux vineyards. The 1955 claret was, in fact, excellent but there was very little of it.' As she left, Captain Cambell was to learn a very valuable lesson about how to handle *Ark Royal*. 'The ship was stopped off Mountbatten Cliffs to disembark the pilot and to carry out a brief gunnery radar calibration. On attempting to go ahead again and turn through south to south-west, the ship refused to respond to the rudder and/or the turning effect of the engines. With only four to eight feet under her keel she would only turn into wind and the bow tug had to be recalled to hold her head, and turn and tow her out past the breakwater.' The incident was caused by the so-called shallow-water effect and the lesson was strongly impressed on both the Captain and the Navigator, Lt Cdr James Woolley. Cambell later said: 'You have a very experienced team with you, all experts in every department, so you do have to rely on them and you really learn it all the hard way. The shallow-water effect was a good example of this.'

Cdr Dreyer was particularly concerned about two aspects of the ship's company's welfare when they arrived at Gibraltar. On the voyage out there both he and the doctor had made a broadcast over the ship's television warning the men of the dangers of sunburn and dodgy women. These points were especially important because a large proportion of the ship's company comprised young sailors who had never been to sea before. He was also concerned about the conduct of the ship's company while they were out there. This was prompted by previous visits by other carriers whose large ships' companies had caused drunken brawls and other trouble. The Captain had also received a concerned message from the Port Admiral at Gibraltar, Rear Admiral P. Curry, on the subject. Curry had been disappointed by the conduct of previous RN ships' companies, especially when the ships' companies of American carriers had behaved well during their visits to Gibraltar. Cambell and Dreyer were both anxious that *Ark Royal's* ship's company did not follow the poor example of previous RN carriers! Instead, they hoped to create a very different impression during their stay. During the voyage out both officers gave the ship's company a pep talk on the ship's television about how to behave in Gibraltar. Throughout the three weeks the ship spent there, a board was kept at the bottom of the gangway with a cumulative total of the number of people who had gone on shore leave and the number who had misbehaved. This worked well as a means of focusing the ship's company's pride in their personal conduct ashore, with the total number of offenders for the period remaining in single figures, despite the thousands who had taken shore leave. 'The success of this policy could be measured by the story of one Petty Officer who was on leave in Gibraltar and bumped into one of the locals. Thinking he was from the *Eagle* the local said "Why can't you chaps be more like the *Ark*? They look after their own. If one of their number gets into trouble they take them back on board. Very fine ship, the *Ark*." The Petty Officer was proud to be able to say that he *was* from the *Ark Royal*. This gave me a good tale to tell the crew to illustrate that their good behaviour was in fact noticed,' said Cambell.

During the work up the Captain was faced with some tense moments. 'We had one anxious moment when we had to do eight hours of refuelling with RFA *Wave Sovereign*. We did it by going into the Mediterranean from Gibraltar and then slowly turning round and coming back again. We did a slow turn and it took us about two hours to do the complete 180 degree turn. While we were turning a Norwegian tanker came towards us and showed no signs of giving way.' Luckily the tanker realized at the last moment what was going on and the Captain avoided having to order the messy operation of an emergency separation from the RFA.

An incident like this illustrates some of the pressures of the job. 'The complications boiling up on the Captain were many and sometimes almost disabling. You could get an awful lot of problems bubbling up at the same time. The pressure of a job like that is quite something when you know that it's new, and there is no guidance as no one has done it before, but I enjoyed it and I look back on it as the best time of my naval life,' said Cambell.

On 6 June the *Ark Royal* passed over the spot where her predecessor had sunk nearly fourteen years previously. The lower deck was cleared and a short service of remembrance was held. The Governor of Gibraltar sent a message on behalf of the local people saying, 'All our wishes and affection go with you today in paying respect to your gallant predecessor.' A wreath was then dropped over the side followed by the sounding of the Last Post by the buglers.

At the end of June, following her return from Gibraltar, *Ark Royal* carried out a series of flying trials to test both the arrester gear and the steam catapults. The privilege of landing the first jet on *Ark Royal* went to Cdr M.F. Fell DSO, DSC, who brought a Sea Hawk on board. Cdr Fell later became the seventh Captain of *Ark Royal* during the fifth commission. He was also the pilot of the first jet aircraft to be launched using a steam catapult. He described it as the fastest launch he had ever made. The following four days saw the arrival of the other types of aircraft that would soon make up the first air group, and the ship saw take-offs and landings by Gannets, Skyraiders, Wyverns, Sea Venoms, and of course Sea Hawks. These trials also witnessed another first when *Ark Royal* became the first ship to anchor while running the engine rooms by remote control. However, the trials did not pass without an element of drama as Cambell recalled: 'While *Ark Royal* was at anchor in Sandown Bay on Friday 1 July, a floating mine was reported in the vicinity by C-in-C Portsmouth; it was spotted from the flag deck and the motor cutter, with James Woolley aboard, guided by helicopter, located it and sank it by rifle fire.'

When the *Ark Royal* returned to Plymouth in July 1955, Cdr Dreyer became ill with a recurrence of undulant fever; he had suffered three outbreaks of it on previous occasions in the Mediterranean. During his absence of seven weeks he is sure that, on the organizational side, he was hardly missed because the routines he had spent so much time devising before the ship was commissioned worked well in practice. While in Plymouth, *Ark Royal* spent a week at a buoy to 'ammunition ship'. To compensate for missing some of the summer's finest weather ashore members of the ship's company volunteered to participate in helicopter rescue exercises and thus enjoyed a quick cool dunking before they were picked up in the rescue net.

The next destination for *Ark Royal* was Lyme Bay where she was to conduct various performance trials to see how much room she needed to turn at different speeds. *Ark Royal* also proved to be an extra attraction for holiday-makers staying in Portland and Weymouth and many of them came out in small craft to have a look at the great ship. Cambell recalled Sub Lieutenant Lord's appropriate description of *Ark Royal* undergoing turning trials in Lyme Bay: 'She went rushing aimlessly about the calm sea at very high speed, thrusting a great mass of spray ahead of her, belching black smoke and hooting incessantly – for all the world like a monster gone mad.' The following week there were more flying trials which were completed in four days allowing *Ark Royal* to return to Devonport for shore leave.

On the morning of 25 July *Ark Royal* entered Devonport. She was dry docked the following day to correct some of the faults which had been found during her work up period, and most of the ship's company left to take

The deadweight 'Noah' is loaded on to the starboard catapult prior to firing during the eight weeks of catapult trials in Devonport during April and May. (Rear Admiral Cambell via the author)

their leave. Those few who remained on board described her as very hot and airless. A welcome change of routine was brought by Navy Days. She could only play a small part in the events owing to the small number of ship's company left. Despite this the NAAFI made a tea garden on the flight deck and the upper hangar deck was opened. As work progressed over the following months Captain Cambell was faced with a major challenge: 'Being a new ship, with the first angled flight deck, and more importantly the first to use steam catapults, we were involved in the first few months with getting the catapults to work. This may sound like a minor detail but if you didn't have working catapults you weren't an aircraft carrier.' Two other factors came into play to make the Captain's job with the catapults more complicated: 'The Admiral in charge of carriers was out in the Mediterranean and he got very annoyed with me for not getting out to the Mediterranean more quickly. I had to call for high level help from the C-in-C Plymouth, Admiral Sir Alec Madden, because we were very busy getting the catapults ready and nothing else could be done before they were finished. The Flag Officer Aircraft Carriers was very brusque about the whole matter, sending signals such as, "There is no point hanging around the Channel, you won't get any work done there." It was an added complication I didn't need and the C-in-C advised the Admiral concerned to allow me more time to complete the work. The other problem was that at the time there was a spate of saboteurs in the Navy. They were mostly fellows who did not want to leave their girlfriends so they would wreck engine room gauges and that sort of thing. There came a time when we had all the bits of the starboard catapult laid out on deck. It only needed one disaffected rating to pick up a component and throw it over the side in the middle of the night and we would be back to the beginning again. I asked the Heads of Departments to draw up lists of those most likely to do that. They each named about three men and we went through them again. We finished up with about five potential trouble-makers who might well do such a thing. I then spoke to the PMO and asked him to have these men psychometrically examined to coincide with the ship's departure and then they could join the ship in Gibraltar. This was done and out they came to Gibraltar with no harm done. I don't know if it did any good but it was a precautionary measure.'

At the beginning of September Midshipman Colin Lawrance (now Captain Colin Lawrance) joined the ship. He said: 'I wondered if I would ever find my way about a ship as large as her. Even if I could, she really looked vast, towering above every other ship moored in the Dockyard, including the battleship *Vanguard*.' In his journal he compared his previous experience in the training carrier *Triumph* with his first days in *Ark Royal*. 'I went on board and reported to the Officer of the Watch who was the senior Midshipman. I was shown to the chest flat and found an empty chest and started unpacking my trunk. I found the chests are much larger than the ones we had in *Triumph* and there is generally more room to move about in the chest flat as a whole. By the time I had unpacked my kit it was time for supper so I changed into my best uniform and set out to find the Gunroom. I had been told it was down the starboard side and down a hatch which, as I soon found out, could be one of a hundred different places. Eventually, I discovered it was 5 tango 3, using the 1950 method of markings. I have never come across this method before, only in the seamanship manual, but I found it much easier to say go to 6 uniform than go to the flat containing the Wardroom. If anyone had wanted to describe a compartment in *Triumph* they had to pick the nearest landmark and then carry on from there. There is a great difference between the food and service that we get in the Gunroom and that which we had in *Triumph* where the food was just about thrown at one and there was no choice and it wasn't particularly good, plentiful, or hot.'

Before long the *Ark Royal* was ready to leave England again for Gibraltar, following the cleaning and storing which always follows a period alongside. Cdr Dreyer had by this time rejoined the ship, having recovered from the fever which had forced him temporarily to leave the ship in July. *Ark Royal*'s departure provided yet another 'first' to add to the already impressive list that she had acquired, when the Pilot was returned to the shore by Whirlwind helicopter, thereby saving him transit time.

The squadrons joined *Ark Royal* for the first time, thus making her a proper aircraft carrier, off the Isle of Wight at the end of September. During embarkation a new tradition came to light. The pilots of 898 Squadron climbed out of their Sea Hawks wearing bowler hats, except for the Squadron's CO, Lt Cdr J.H.S. Pearce, who was wearing a top hat. Individuality was not confined to 898 Squadron as Admiral Sir Raymond Lygo recalled. As Lt Cdr Lygo he was the CO of 800 Squadron, and said: 'We were the first squadron to start painting our aircraft. No one had dared do it before that and so we didn't ask because we knew we would be told no! We painted all the fins and the tanks red. This was what we believed to be the original colours used by 800 Squadron in the 1930s and we wanted to preserve this tradition.' After the squadrons had got used to the ship, *Ark Royal* paid a visit to Portsmouth where she received visits from three high-ranking RN officers. To prove that the problems had been solved and the catapults were fully operational, Captain Cambell organized a demonstration of their effectiveness as the ship headed out to sea on Tuesday 4 October. Four Sea Hawk fighters were launched while she was leaving Portsmouth Harbour and if nothing else it certainly livened up the day of those who were crossing the harbour on the Gosport ferry. One of the fighters was piloted by a future Captain of the *Ark Royal*, the CO of 800 Squadron, Lt Cdr Ray Lygo. Talking about the launch Lygo said: 'As the ship was turned into wind to face Priddy's Hard, which was the ammunition dump, I remember thinking if I go in there it will be the largest bang Portsmouth has ever heard!' As Lawrance recalled: 'The tugs were showered with the strops but that was the only hit that was made, although the last aircraft looked for a moment as though it had a sudden desire to be a submarine!'

One of 849 Squadron B Flight's Skyraider AEW1s about to catch a wire. (FAA Museum)

To prove the effectiveness of the new steam catapults Captain Cambell organized the launching of four Sea Hawks as *Ark Royal* left Portsmouth on 4 October 1955. (Rear Admiral Cambell via the author)

After a weekend at Spithead, which included a visit from the last Captain of *Ark Royal III*, Rear Admiral Maud, and members of the press, to see the aerobatics team of 800 Squadron put through their paces and to inspect the ship's television system, *Ark Royal* left home waters destined once more for Gibraltar. With the Beaverbrook campaign in full swing it was a very important part of the Captain's job to get on good terms with the press. At the press conference held on board prior to 800 Squadron's air display he was able to use some of the ship's new facilities to good effect: 'The journalists were taken to a guest room fitted with a television set and I welcomed them on the TV and appeared to see them. It was only a gimmick but it went down quite well, although of course some of them missed the point!'

During October, 898 Squadron decided to launch their own rival to the ship's monthly newsletter *Noah's News* which had by now become an established part of the ship's life and kept the ship's company in touch with events on the ship. This led to an offer in the November issue of *Noah's News* to print views from the other squadrons in retaliation for any comments which appeared in 898 Squadron's newsletter. In addition to the regular features in *Noah's News*, the first issue started off with a message of goodwill from HM Queen Elizabeth the Queen Mother, while the Christmas 1955 and end of commission editions had messages from the Captain. A summary of the major events of the previous month was given in 'Archives' (a story of west country folk). This was supplemented by reports from specific branches of the ship, such as squadron news. Each month the spotlight was focused on a few key people in a 'Who's who' section. The newsletter was put together by a team of five people, headed by Cdr Bellamy as the editor. Illustrations were provided by the most senior commissioned photographer in the RN at the time, Mr Ronald Little, who worked from his headquarters below the laundry issue room on deck 7. Cartoons were supplied by Mechanic (E) 1st class Gordon Tew, who also drew the cartoons that accompanied the ship's daily orders. Their typographic expert was Chief Airman Fitter (E) John Long who ran the Air Engineering department office and typed the various draft pages in the run-up to publication each month. The printer was Marine Robert Pike who, prior to his RN service, had served as a boy trainee in the Merchant Navy, including a tour in the Cunard–White Star liner *Mauritania*.

In October Midshipman Lawrance spent some time in the Engineering department. He recalled: 'I wrote in my midshipman's journal the following entry. "It appears we are just reaching a time in the boiler room when a

The spectacular sight of two squadrons of Sea Hawks starting up. (Captain Lee)

great number of fittings are starting to fall over at once." I could have said exactly the same thing during my time as the Direction Officer in 1975.'

Prior to joining the rest of the fleet at Malta, *Ark Royal* worked up off Gibraltar giving both the squadrons and the ship's company time to get used to working together. During the first commission aircraft were embarked for about a year and there were over 4,136 landings without any breakages. Unfortunately there were two fatal launching accidents and one aircraft went missing. Describing the launching accident involving a Sea Hawk on 14 October Cambell said, 'We were catapulting Sea Hawks off both catapults. As the starboard catapult fired I was watching the aircraft as it went along, and it went slower and slower until it just fell off the bow and sank and the ship went over it. We quickly discovered what had gone wrong: it was caused by extra zeal on the part of one of the operators down below who worked the levers. Essentially, having worked the lever to the fire position, he had quickly retracted it for the next aircraft.' Vice Admiral Sir Edward Anson, who as Lt Anson was a pilot in 800 Squadron at the time, explained: 'While this was how the previous type of catapults worked, it had the effect of slowing the aircraft down which nobody had predicted and thus there is no blame attached to the man concerned. Modifications were made in Gibraltar to ensure that it could not happen again.' The second and third accidents both happened in the early hours of 8 March 1956 during Exercise Cascade. Cambell recalled: 'A Sea Venom was involved in an exercise following a RAF Shackleton, but it disappeared never to be seen again. Two Gannets were launched to try to find the Sea Venom. To my horror the first Gannet went straight over the side into the water. No one knew why; perhaps he took off with his controls locked, or maybe he got disorientated.' Despite extensive searches by both *Ark Royal*'s aircraft and land-based aircraft there was no trace of the crew and no wreckage from either aircraft was ever found.

One of 824 Squadron's Gannet AS1s shortly after being launched. (Captain Lawrance via the author)

The lower level of the Operations Room. (Cammell Laird Archives)

At the end of October 1955 *Ark Royal* arrived at Malta to spend the winter there. Cambell recalled: 'They wanted us to go alongside Parlatorio Wharf. In the winter Malta suffers from storms called *gregale*. I therefore thought that mooring *Ark Royal* alongside the wall would not be very clever during the *gregale* season so we secured to one of the buoys. Even so we had quite a time when a storm struck on Boxing Day. I was ashore at the time and had to go on a MFV to get back on board as it was too rough to use the ship's boat.' Sadly, Cdr Dreyer was taken ill again on the way out to Malta and this time had to leave the ship for good, and left the service in the following year. His ceremonial departure from the ship took place on 22 November 1955 when he left in a motorboat manned by the other Commanders. In *Noah's News* the following item marked his departure: 'Saddest blow of all has been the departure of Cdr Dreyer, invalided off the station on account of a "bug" which he picked up here some twenty years ago. Pages would be needed to describe all he has done for the ship; suffice to say that *Ark* will not seem the same without him.' His successor was Cdr J. Roxburgh (now Vice Admiral Sir John Roxburgh KCB, CBE, DSO, DSC*), who was due to have relieved him in February 1956.

On Saturday 29 October 1955 *Ark Royal* made her first entry into Malta. As she entered Grand Harbour she fired a 17-gun salute to the C-in-C, Admiral Sir Guy Grantham. Once the ship was secured to head and stern buoys in Bighi Bay Admiral Grantham and his number two paid her a visit. (Although *Ark Royal* was visited by many Admirals during her first commission she was a private ship; as Cambell recalls, 'I never had a permanent Admiral on board *Ark Royal*. They came on board for an exercise and left again afterwards. A very nice Admiral came on board with his staff to supervise the exercise we were going to do. In the beginning he occupied my bridge when he had his own bridge above. He looked over my shoulder and worst of all sat in my seat! So I tried psychology on him. I was extremely polite to him when he was on his bridge, and boot-faced and hardly answered him when he was down on my bridge and gave him the cold shoulder. We parted on good terms but he did not seem to understand that a Captain's bridge is not to be treated like that! But that was the sort of silly trivial thing which could upset you and you couldn't stop thinking about it.') During *Ark Royal*'s stay in Malta the ship's company took shore leave to explore the historic island. All too soon it was back to work and *Ark Royal* left harbour to work up in local waters, principally so that the ship's aircraft could make use of the target ranges located in the Malta area.

Ark Royal enters Malta for the first time at the end of October 1955. (B. Whitworth via the author)

The compass platform.
(Cammell Laird Archives)

December saw another change of scenery for the ship's company when *Ark Royal* deployed to the French port of Toulon. The former Royal Navy light fleet aircraft carrier *Colossus*, which was the first ship of its type to be built and had since been renamed the *Arromanches* in French naval service, berthed quite close to *Ark Royal* during her visit. 'One of the first British representatives to go ashore in Toulon was the ship's cat Arko,' recalled Lawrance. Large numbers of the ship's company took the opportunity to visit the local shops and restaurants leading to a few sailors adopting different drinking habits during their stay due to the lower cost of wine compared with beer in France. The ship's bag meals came to be valued by the ship's company because of the price of French food in restaurants. Those who felt a little more adventurous, and entered restaurants which they thought were going to serve reasonably priced meals, ended up wishing that they had stayed with the other sailors eating bag meals outside when they discovered the cover and service charges on their bills. For some of the ship's company there was also a chance to look at the rows of expensive yachts moored at Cannes while they were given two free hours during a visit organized by the Padre. Despite some of them looking around for Sir Bernard and Lady Docker it was not their day for free champagne or invitations on board these exclusive vessels. 'When we slipped from Toulon we left behind a large number of our cats, because they were becoming too numerous for one ship, but we held on to Arko who had been presented to the ship and was as much a part of the ship as the ship's bell,' Lawrance recalled.

After more exercises on the way back to Malta from Toulon, it was time for Christmas in Grand Harbour. Of Christmas Day on board *Ark Royal*, Cambell said: 'Began badly with news that the catapult pistons had cracked; the ship is non-operational until put right, heaven knows when. Church on the quarterdeck was somewhat hot

Ark Royal entering Toulon in December 1955. (Commander Woolley via the author)

and stuffy with all side-awnings up and a full congregation. Eight carols, and ten lessons of which I read the ninth. And then a most fantastic tour of one-third of the messes, Roxburgh and Fell leading two other parties round the rest. Some mess decks were cold and formal and stood at attention, some weren't even decorated – others were very warm and jolly.' Of course rounds were a normal part of the ship's routine as Ray Amphlett, who served in *Ark Royal* during the first commission as a Stoker, recalled: 'We had a real character in our mess deck. He had been ashore the night before and had quite a bit to drink. In the morning no sign could be found of him. The doors of the mess deck burst open as the Captain accompanied by the Commander walked into the mess deck. The Commander said "Right, we will open those cupboard doors and see what you have hidden away in there" and as he opened the doors out rolled the sailor in question and he stood up and said "Coat locker ready for rounds, Sir". They of course marched him off to the quarterdeck to be dealt with.' Talking about another Christmas Day incident Lawrance said, 'I went down to the quarterdeck and saw a Lieutenant with a big bushy beard whom I thought I recognized, but I didn't recognize him as a Lieutenant. It was discovered shortly afterwards that he was in fact an Able Seaman who had gone along to his Divisional Officer's cabin and "borrowed" his set of No. 5s and then appeared on the quarterdeck to attend the official cocktail party. He appeared before the Captain and because it was Christmas was only fined one Lieutenant's share of the cocktail party, which was generous to say the least!'

Midshipman Tim Lee (now Captain Tim Lee) joined *Ark Royal* at the beginning of January 1956 in Malta as he recalled: 'I joined *Ark Royal* as one of a group of seven Midshipmen straight from the training carrier HMS *Triumph*. We knew what an aircraft carrier was like although the *Triumph* had neither the size nor complexity of *Ark Royal*. The purpose of being in *Ark Royal* as a Midshipman was to learn how to be an officer without having any of the responsibility. It was an eighteen-month period where one was somewhere between the lower deck and the Wardroom. We developed a tremendous relationship with the Leading Hands and Senior Rates who taught us our basic skills in a wide variety of activities as diverse as boathandling, firefighting and semaphore, all of which were vital if we were to pass our Midshipman's Board. In the Gunroom we had a separate mess which was presided over by the Sub-Lieutenant, who taught us within our own surroundings how to behave once we moved to the Wardroom. The Gunroom was out of bounds to officers, who could only enter by invitation. I think I was very lucky to be in one of the last terms of Midshipmen to go to sea in the Gunroom of *Ark Royal*.'

When Tim Lee joined *Ark Royal* the Sub-Lieutenant was Mike Forrest who had replaced Sub-Lieutenant James Lord in November 1955. Sub-Lieutenant Lord had joined Dartmouth in one of the last intakes which entered at the age of thirteen. He was known for his ownership of a grey Rolls-Royce called Angela which was eleven years older than him and had accompanied the ship on some of its travels.

Describing the influences and aspects of life on board *Ark Royal* for a Midshipman, Lee said: 'One of the main influences on our lives was the "Snotties' Nurse", who was usually the Navigating Officer on the basis that as soon as the ship was in port he would have nothing to do and therefore have more time to look after the Midshipmen . . . The "Snotties' Nurse" was meant to guide us in almost every aspect of our lives including the moral aspects, and so he would give us lectures from time to time about who we should, or should not even attempt to go to bed with. During my time in Flying Control Position I remember some very wise words which Cdr Fell had abbreviated into a set of initials in flyco. The initials were OGGMSTKMBMSUIKWIATA which stands for "Oh God Give Me Strength To Keep My Big Mouth Shut Until I Know What I Am Talking About!" Boat running was an essential part of a Midshipman's life. The ship was based in Malta for most of the period that I was in *Ark Royal* and you soon learnt what you should and should not do when in charge of the pinnace loaded with forty-five drunken matelots returning from shore. Another important part of a Midshipman's life was trophy hunting when other ships with Gunrooms were in harbour. All these Gunrooms took considerable pride in their collections of trophies "acquired" during runs ashore, and went to great lengths to protect the more valuable and historical ones, such as the famed barber's pole which had been with the fleet so long that few, if any, knew where it originally came from. Our prize trophy at that time was a lavatory seat beautifully inscribed with the names of its many temporary owners. During a Gunroom run ashore to La Linea (where we took due note, of course, of the advice given to us by the Snotties' Nurse) we were raided by a *Bulwark* Midshipman who calmly walked down the forward brow (or gangway) with the seat under his arm. The officer on the brow at the time was a short service commission aviator Sub-Lieutenant, who had never served in a Gunroom, so we should perhaps not have been surprised! It took many raids thereafter to regain our pride!'

On Friday 13 January *Ark Royal* slipped her mooring buoys for the first time since the Christmas break, leaving Malta for a week of exercises in the area off the island. The first exercise on leaving Malta was to conduct some catapult trials off the coast. Lee recalled: 'We had two retired Sea Hornets from Hal Far Air Station which were filled with water to make them heavier and they were shot off the catapults into the sea. They actually glided quite well!'

During the week of flying trials *Ark Royal* embarked the long awaited 891 Squadron flying the Sea Venom FAW21. 'Hook trouble' during a previous deployment to *Bulwark* in the summer of 1955 had led to the aircraft being grounded until they were modified, so as a result they were late in joining the ship. Lee noted in his Midshipman's Journal the preparations before his flight in a Sea Venom and the launching: 'I was told of the various techniques used when baling out and ditching – these hardly made me feel elated at the prospect. Nobody has yet baled out of a Sea Venom, so we lack first hand advice. The Sea Venom is one of the few jet aircraft which from necessity has no ejection seats. Therefore the advised, but as yet untried, procedure is to turn the aircraft upside down, if one still can, blow off the canopy, undo the safety harness, cross one's fingers and drop out, hoping that nothing will get caught on the way! The most impressive part of the flight was the take-off. After a succession of hand signals from the director, we halted with a jerk against the chocks, and then moved bodily sideways till we were centred. Having watched the operation from flyco so frequently, I could visualise exactly what was going on, the strop being attached forward, the hold back aft, then the chocks being

Friday 13 January 1956 was certainly an unlucky day for this redundant Sea Hornet from Hal Far which was sent to a watery grave after fulfilling its last role as a deadweight for catapult trials. (FAA Museum)

lowered and the aircraft moving forward till it was pulling at the hold-back like a hound at the leash. I rested my head back and as I did so saw the director's green flag drop. The three second wait seemed interminable, then suddenly there was a jolt in my back which spread over my body until I was powerless in the grip of a force that was accelerating me at something like three times the acceleration due to gravity. Just when it seemed that something was about to give, the pressure came off as suddenly as it had been applied and we were airborne.'

On 19 January *Ark Royal* returned to Malta. The following day FOAC, Rear Admiral A.R. Pedder and his staff embarked in *Ark Royal* making her a flagship for the first time. On Saturday 21 January 1956 *Ark Royal* disembarked eleven Sea Hawks to Hal Far while she was still moored in Bighi Bay. Cruddas recalled: 'I always went up to the flight deck before the start of flying to make sure that everything which came under my part of ship was serviceable. When I went up to the flight deck on that morning, I saw the COs of the two Sea Hawk Squadrons, Ray Lygo and Jimmy Pearse, walking up and down the flight deck. They came up to me and said "We don't like this at all, Sir." I replied "You will be launched at 10 knots above your stalling speed." However, I thought that their sentiments needed transmitting to Cdr (Air) Mike Fell, so I went to see him. I told him the boys aren't happy about this launch to which he replied "Get me an aircraft and I will be the first one to be launched!" He was, which I thought showed great leadership.'

The Sea Hawk was one of the most elegant aircraft ever flown by the Fleet Air Arm. Anson remembered: 'Having just come to the Sea Hawk from flying Sea Furies, where you couldn't see where you were going in the landing attitude, the Sea Hawk was a very nice aeroplane to fly. In a Sea Fury you would taxi out and take off with the hood open. As soon as you had taken off, you would bring up the undercarriage, shut the hood, close the gills, bring up the flaps and then check the instruments. On the other hand the Sea Hawk was much simpler. You took off with the hood closed and no flaps, so about the only thing you had to do after take off was bring up the undercarriage. The other major step forward with the Sea Hawk was that you could actually see where you were going which made deck landing much easier.'

On 31 January *Ark Royal* once more slipped her moorings for further flying exercises off Malta. Lee recalled from his Midshipman's Journal the evolution of fuelling from a RFA while anchored in the fleet anchorage at Marsaxlokk on Saturday 4 February 1956: 'This morning we started fuelling astern from RFA *Eddycliff*. At anchor this evolution is far more difficult than when at sea. The yaw of the ship, in spite of comparatively calm weather, did nothing to help the operation. The first phase is to pass two hurricane or spring hawsers to the oiler by the usual gun line messenger method. They are led out through the port and starboard stern fairleads and made fast to bollards. When all is secured, another gun line is used and the oiler passes the hose to us, up to a connection on the flight deck. Pumping was started at a rate of only 40 tons per hour, but this was then increased to 150. The oiler finally cast off at 17:23.' In addition to taking on fuel, FOAC and his staff were disembarked to *Albion* in five helicopters. Two days later *Ark Royal* sailed west from the Malta area to rendezvous with the cruiser *Birmingham* and collect her next Flag Officer, Vice Admiral Richmond. Originally, it had been planned to transfer the Admiral by jackstay, but bad weather forced a change of plan so the ships anchored in the relative lee of the Bay of Bone in Algeria to enable the Admiral and his staff to transfer by boat. The embarkation completed, it was time to sail for Exercise Febex which was to be a 48-hour intensive exercise, including air attacks, gun firing and replenishment at sea, followed by a fast entry into harbour. However, the weather dictated otherwise and disrupted the flying programme and replenishment at sea, and also ruled out the fast entry into port, so that *Ark Royal* was able to enter Grand Harbour at her normal speed for the start of a ten-day visit.

On 14 February *Ark Royal* was visited by a group of Labour MPs, including the future Prime Minister Jim Callaghan and Roy Jenkins. Cambell recalled: 'Of course being Labour MPs they wanted to distance themselves

The cramped living conditions endured by the ratings in their mess decks. (Rear Admiral Cambell via the author)

from the Wardroom. To get round this the Chief Petty Officers held a lunch for them and the Officers attended just to show *Ark*'s democracy so to speak.' One of the things which most interested the MPs was the living conditions on board for the ratings. Amphlett remembered: 'The mess deck which I lived on in *Ark Royal* during the first commission stretched across the width of the ship and consisted of about one hundred and twenty men, divided into four messes. At stand easy you had to get to the galley with the tea fanny and take it down to the mess. When you went up for your rum ration, one sailor would take the mess fanny, which was a metal pot, up to 4 deck to the Officer of the Day. You would give the officer your mess number, then a Chief would read out the number of people allowed rum, and the appropriate amount of rum was issued mixed with three parts of water. The rum had a very big bargaining power to get favours. For example, when the ship was in Plymouth a number of sailors with homes in Plymouth, who were known as "Janners", would trade their tot of rum with their fellow sailors to stand in for them during a watch. If you were watch keeping and you had the afternoon watch, and were thus about to go into a machinery compartment, you did not want rum inside you, so what we used to do was if you relieved the fellow who had the forenoon watch he would go down to the mess deck and have your tot and his. It would then work the other way when the watches were reversed. On special occasions, such as someone's birthday, the celebrating sailor would receive his rum in a half pint glass and there would be a note on the table to say that it was someone's birthday, or whatever, and you would each pour part of your rum ration into this half pint glass.'

On 21 February *Ark Royal* left Malta for the last time in this commission, bound for Naples; but first twenty-four hours of heeling trials had to be completed. The first batch took place at anchor off Delimara, while a second batch was carried out off the coast of Sicily, with the snow-capped Mount Etna forming an impressive backdrop. While heeling the ship 10 degrees may not sound a lot, the upper edge of the flight deck was some 25ft above the other side. Ken Moore, who served in *Ark Royal* during the first commission as part of the aviation party, said: 'We were told beforehand that we would be having listing trials. The ship was stopped and then went over to one side. We were told the point of the trials was to see how far she could go over. This worried us at the time because we wondered what would happen if they could not get her back up again, but we were assured that she would go over to a certain point and they would know not to take her any further.'

With the trials complete *Ark Royal* passed through the Straits of Messina with the challenge of passing under the high tension electricity cables across the Strait. The passage went without incident and *Ark Royal* arrived in the Naples area on the 23rd to embark an Italian film crew who were making a film about the ship and life on

A flight deck full of aircraft as *Ark Royal* leaves Malta. (Captain Lawrance via the author)

Don't panic! Heeling trials off Mount Etna on 22 February 1956. (Rear Admiral Cambell via the author)

board, to be shown on the Italian TV network. That night the ship anchored overnight in Puzzuoli Bay, before entering Naples the following morning. On her way into Naples, *Ark Royal* passed the American Essex class aircraft carrier USS *Ticonderoga* which was on her way out. The presence of the Italian film crew on board the previous day was to give 800 Squadron an idea 'to put one over' their great rivals in 898 Squadron. Anson described the background to this latest instalment in the continuing saga of friendly rivalry between the two Sea Hawk squadrons: 'We had a *Daily Express* reporter on board who talked to 898 Squadron. They told this reporter that 898 Squadron was the only real Sea Hawk squadron and 800 Squadron was only on board as a training squadron. This was published in the *Daily Express* so we thought up a suitable form of retaliation.' Lygo continued: '898 Squadron had this gimmick of embarking and disembarking wearing bowler hats, which sickened us in 800 Squadron. I therefore arranged for the Staff Officer to put together a letter purporting to be from an Italian TV company saying that they wanted to interview them because they had heard about these bowler hat chaps. 898 swallowed it hook, line and sinker, so I then sent Ted Anson and Alaistair Campbell ashore to grab a taxi to the nearest brothel and speak to the Madame, and tell her that we had these chaps arriving and we would like the girls to meet them outside. They thought they were going to a TV studio but they were in fact photographed outside this brothel being embraced by these ladies. The *Daily Express* published the picture under the headline "Navy's Bowler Boys Are Bowled".' Cruddas recalled another practical joke between the two squadrons: 'All of 898 Squadron's aircraft carried the squadron badge on both sides of the nose. The badge was a flying fish with the motto "Far and Wide" inscribed below. I was walking through the hangar early one morning when I noticed that all the aircrafts' insignia had been changed overnight from Far and Wide to Freshly Fried! It was beautifully done.'

On 29 February *Ark Royal* departed from Naples with fifty senior NATO officers on board to watch a demonstration of *Ark Royal*'s capabilities. Following a twenty-four hour War Routine Exercise *Ark Royal* headed back towards Malta, passing Mount Etna which was in the throes of its latest eruption. During the weekend of 3 and 4 March *Ark Royal* was at anchor off Malta. On the Sunday the first practice March Past was held in preparation for the visit later in the month of HM the Queen Mother. During the rehearsal Midshipmen stood in for the appropriate dignitaries with placards round their necks bearing the name of the person they were impersonating. Preparations began for *Ark Royal*'s second exercise of the year when she sailed on 5 March for the start of Exercise Cascade which was held between 7 and 12 March, when *Ark Royal* entered Gibraltar for an eight-day visit. Further rehearsals were held for the Queen Mother's visit before *Ark Royal* sailed on 20 March to participate in Exercise Dawn Breeze on her way home to the UK. Once again bad weather dictated the scope of the programme, as *Ark Royal* encountered a howling gale and heavy seas.

Having spent the previous night at anchor at Spithead *Ark Royal* made her way into Portsmouth, with her aircraft ranged on deck, to secure alongside South Railway Jetty at noon on 26 March. The following day was spent making sure that the ship was looking its best for the Queen Mother. Originally, the Queen Mother was due to have visited *Ark Royal* in May 1955 to coincide with the completion of her work up and commissioning trials, but due to *Ark Royal* undergoing maintenance on her catapults in Devonport the visit was postponed until the ship's return from the Mediterranean. Typically, for such a visit, an invitation would be issued by the Captain and a date would be set about three months ahead depending, obviously, on the operational commitments of the ship. Then there would be a reconnaissance trip to the ship by members of the Queen Mother's staff to check the planned route and make any alterations, such as avoiding vertical ladders. The key objective when the plans were drawn up for the Queen Mother's trips was to ensure that she saw as broad a cross-section of the ship as possible. For example, if the trip was held while the ship was at sea the Queen Mother would visit the bridge and flyco to view the flying display by the Carrier Air Group. However, if the visit was held while the ship was alongside, then special provision would be made for the Queen Mother to meet some of the ship's company's families. While the Queen Mother enjoyed all of her trips to the ship over the years, it is not known whether she had a preference for either sea trips or alongside visits. At 11.30 a.m. Divisions fell in on the flight deck just before the Queen Mother's Whirlwind landed at HMS *Vernon*. Cambell recalled: 'When coming down to the

HM Queen Elizabeth the Queen Mother made her first visit to 'her' ship in Portsmouth on 26 March 1956. She is seen coming up to the flight deck on the aft lift on board one of the ship's Land Rovers. Captain Cambell is seated in the passenger seat. (Rear Admiral Cambell via the author)

flight deck, in helping her through the island doorway, I found I was holding her handbag as we walked aft – which she quickly retrieved, saying "it doesn't look right for the Captain to be carrying a handbag!"' The whole visit passed off very smoothly and the Queen Mother left in her helicopter in the afternoon.

Over the Easter weekend *Ark Royal* was opened to the public as part of the Portsmouth Navy Days, receiving 6,000 visitors each day. On the following Wednesday, having being delayed twenty-four hours due to bad weather, *Ark Royal* slipped from South Railway Jetty to begin trials of the next generation of naval aircraft. Before those trials could begin *Ark Royal* had to disembark her squadrons for the last time to make way for the new aircraft. Lee recalled the aircraft trials of 5 April from his Midshipman's Journal: 'The first aircraft we saw was the semi-navalized version of the DH110. This proceeded to do a number of free take-offs, each time getting airborne by the time it had reached the forward lift. In the afternoon we saw the N113 through the mist, which landed on board after making several circuits round. The landing was done very near the round down, the hydraulic skid causing the tail to bounce upwards. On 6 April we received the third trials aircraft, a Sea Venom with blown flaps for supercirculation. This was struck down immediately and remained there until the DH110, landing rather heavily, broke its nose-wheel oleo. While this was being repaired, the Sea Venom was given trials and gave a very good display of slow flying when with flaps blowing it passed us at 86 knots. After a break for the weekend the trials resumed on 9 April. In the afternoon an incident happened that could have dashed our hopes of having the N113 in service in the near future. It had been the normal practice for the pilots, on taking off, to bring the engines to nearly full power, take off the brake and then put on full power. This time

The DH110 coming in to land during trials at the beginning of April 1956. (British Aerospace plc. (Farnborough))

The N113 is brought to a halt by the arrester wire during trials at the beginning of April 1956. (FAA Museum)

A Sea Venom fitted with experimental flap blowing during trials on board *Ark Royal* at the beginning of April 1956.
(British Aerospace plc. (Farnborough))

it was noticed that the aircraft did not gain speed as quickly as normal and after twenty yards white smoke started to rise from the tyres. Its progress along the flight deck was agonizingly slow and all onlookers held their breath as it reached the end of the deck with a speed of 100 knots. This was about 20 knots slower than normally required, but after dropping some 10 feet it remained airborne. After the white smoke had cleared, two parallel black lines were left on the flight deck as a lasting testimonial to what might have been the most tragic take-off. The cause of this mishap was that the parking brake had been left on, and when the pilot took the normal brakes off, this parking brake still locked the wheels. From his strapped-in position, the pilot was unable to reach the brake button. This incident demonstrates the immense thrust of the two Avon engines and the durability of the Dunlop tyres. Although they were both worn down to the cord, neither burst when the aircraft landed.'

On 11 April *Ark Royal* was to rendezvous with her sister *Eagle*, as Lee wrote in his journal: 'Before we weighed anchor this morning we saw HMS *Eagle* on the horizon and as soon as possible steamed towards her. Apparently, just before we arrived they broadcast that we would pass up the port side and fire the DH110 off the catapult as a demonstration: they were rather puzzled when we steamed up her starboard side and flew off a helicopter instead.' The following day the last catapult launch of the commission was made as Lee's journal continued, 'The flight deck engineers put an Emmettesque contraption of wood and iron on the catapult. It only resembled an aircraft by having wings and a revolving propeller. The acceleration of the catapult had quite an effect on it, as it performed half a loop before landing on its back in the sea.' The strange contraption was simply titled FDE1 WHAT. It was the start of an end-of-commission tradition in *Ark Royal* which included a lavatory and several pianos over the years. That evening *Ark Royal* made a radar-assisted approach to her night anchorage at Spithead, passing the Cunard liner *Queen Elizabeth* in the fog. Soon after the ship was anchored the second liner of the day, the American liner *United States*, passed under her stern. At 2 p.m. the following day *Ark Royal* weighed anchor bound for Devonport, arriving in Plymouth Sound early on the morning of 14 April to secure to a buoy for de-ammunitioning.

The de-ammunitioning was completed ahead of schedule at 7 p.m. on 19 April to enable *Ark Royal* to make her way up Plymouth Sound to secure alongside just after lunch on the following day. Once alongside, members

The start of an end-of-commission tradition on board *Ark Royal*, with strange things being fired off the catapult. FDE1WHAT was the last catapult launch of the commission. (Rear Admiral Cambell via the author)

This view of the DH110 landing clearly shows the angled flight deck. (British Aerospace plc. (Farnborough))

of the ship's company began to disperse to other ships over the coming weeks as she started her first refit. Lee's journal described the scene on board as the refit progressed during June 1956: 'The lower hangar appeared to be in an even worse state of shambles and bits of engines were scattered over the deck. Two access covers had been removed to reveal boiler rooms and in other places ventilation trunking was being moved or replaced. In the upper hangar most of the accumulators for operating side lifts, bomb lifts, sliding doors and arrester gear have been removed, and the side lift itself is not very recognizable. On the flight deck there is the usual activity, the catapults are in even more pieces, parts of the pistons now having been removed completely. The dent in the flight deck is being lifted by using long girders, and the deck now appears to be as convex as it was concave.'

Ark Royal at speed as she draws towards the close of her first commission. The Ship's Flight Dragonfly can be seen in the background while the DH110 is being moved forward. (British Aerospace plc. (Farnborough))

He recorded the dry docking of *Ark Royal* on 18 June, 'When I looked at the thousands of wires that connected the ship with the shore, it was hard to believe that it would only take two hours to have everything removed. Once inside the basin, everything was done by warping. The caisson was then put into position and flooded down and I then saw an interesting operation carried out by hand. After over a year of manoeuvring under steam, the *Ark* was finally placed centrally in the dock by a system of two-fold purchases which were hauled in at right angles to the head and stern ropes. Thus pure manpower was called upon to do one of the most exacting manoeuvres. The following day the ship was docked down. They started to pump the water out at 08:15, and as the level went down, men on catamarans attached hoses to ejector outlets, and put on flooding bonnets. With such a large ship it is very hard to remember where and at what level the next thing has to be done, so several times the pumping had to be stopped. We touched bottom at 09:30 and the dock was clear of water by 13:00.'

During the refit the murals that had been painted by Sir Peter Scott disappeared. Lt Cdr S.C. Farquhar, who was one of the pilots who conducted aircraft trials in *Ark Royal* during May 1955 and later became the CO of 831 Squadron during the second commission, remembered: 'Cdr Dreyer took me to see the main dining hall and asked if I had any suggestions as to how it could be brightened up for the ship's company. We came to the conclusion that it needed some pictures round the bulkheads and he told me that he was friendly with Peter Scott from his wartime days when they had both served together in MTBs. Cdr Dreyer was going to ask Peter Scott to come down to stay with him and come on board and have a look. This visit took place during the main ship's company leave. Peter Scott asked for five big canvas screens to be put on wooden frames and he then painted the five murals on them. The result was magnificent! Originally they had no protection and when Cdr Dreyer took me to see the finished result I said that they would need to be careful that no one spilt anything over them and as a result they were put behind perspex screens. They were all of wild ducks, geese and swans in estuary scenes. The paintings were removed at the end of the commission when the ship went into refit, and as far as I know they haven't been seen since. They must be worth a fortune as they were all signed.'

Chapter Three

IN SEARCH OF THE PILGRIMS

SECOND COMMISSION,

NOVEMBER 1956–JULY 1958

On 1 November 1956 *Ark Royal* was recommissioned at Devonport under the command of Captain F.H.E. Hopkins DSO, DSC (later Admiral Sir Frank Hopkins KCB, DSO, DSC). He had assumed command on 24 September 1956. The ceremony held on the upper hangar deck was conducted by the Chaplain of the Fleet and attended by both the C-in-C Home Fleet and C-in-C Devonport as well as the ship's company and many of their relatives. One of the officers to join prior to the recommissioning was Lieutenant Mike Pennington, who served in *Ark Royal* during the second commission as an Electrical Officer. When he was drafted to *Ark Royal* it was a strange twist of fate for him because as a schoolboy he had attended the launching of *Ark Royal* six years

Ark Royal at speed. Note how the angled flight deck enables aircraft to land safely while Fly 1 is still full of aircraft. (FAA Museum)

earlier. 'I was taken off the long electrical course to join *Ark Royal*. Part of the course I missed took place at the GPO telephone training centre at Leek in Derbyshire. The timing was ironic because when I joined *Ark Royal* the first job I was given was to look after the telephone exchange!' Pennington said.

After *Ark Royal* had recommissioned she spent the rest of the year in home waters working up prior to returning to Devonport for Christmas leave. The Carrier Air Group (CAG) during the second commission was somewhat fluid and consisted principally of 893 Squadron's Sea Venom FAW21s, 802 Squadron flying the Sea Hawk FB3, and later the FB5, 804 Squadron's Sea Hawk FGA6s, 815 Squadron flying the Gannet AS1, and later the Gannet AS4, 831 Squadron's Wyvern S4s, 849 Squadron B Flight's Skyraider AEW1s. In addition to these regular squadrons, the following squadrons made guest appearances during the commission: 898 Squadron flying, on their first appearance, the Sea Hawk FGA4, and during subsequent deployments to *Ark Royal* the Sea Hawk FGA6; 800 Squadron's Sea Hawk FGA6s; 701 Squadron B Flight's Whirlwind HAR3s, and a brief appearance by the Gannet AS4s of 824 Squadron.

The work up was a busy period for all of the ship's departments, including the electrical department. Pennington explained: 'The electrical department had eight officers, headed by a Commander. The Electrical Officers were distinguished by an "L" after their rank. During my first few months in the ship I worked as the number two Electrical Officer in the low power section, which looked after the low voltage internal communications equipment, such as batteries and telephones. I was then moved to the high power section which looked after the generators, the switch gear, the lifts, lighting and cranes. The third part of the electrical department looked after the main radios and radar. The electrical department did not look after any of the equipment on the aircraft, because that was the responsibility of the squadron maintainers.'

The New Year brought a further batch of Scimitar trials. With Commander P.C.S. Chilton at the controls, the third Scimitar prototype was embarked on 5 January 1957 for a series of landing and catapulting trials. Commander Chilton was the CO of the Naval Test Squadron at Boscombe Down. Mike Lithgow completed half the flying trials on 6 January, while the trials for 7 January were cancelled due to the unavailability of RNAS Culdrose as a diversion airfield because of poor weather. As a result, instead of remaining on board in the hope of an improvement in the weather, the prototype was fuelled up and flown back to Wisley airfield by Lt Cdr Whitehead. The poor weather and sea state during the three days meant that the trials were not as successful as they might have been.

A Gannet AS1 of 815 Squadron comes in to land on *Ark Royal*. (FAA Museum)

The second commission saw the addition of the Wyvern to *Ark Royal*'s CAG. 831 Squadron's CO, Lt Cdr S. Farquhar, described what the Wyvern was like to fly: 'It was an enjoyable aircraft to fly, although rather heavy, but an excellent weapon platform by day and night. The Wyvern was not popular in the service, being too large and cumbersome; most pilots were afraid of it at first because of its reputation and engine handling problems, however once they got used to it, they hadn't a bad word to say against it. It had three main problems: firstly the Python engine occasionally got excessive cooling of the oil system at altitude called "coring", which caused a fall in pressure and a rise in temperature leading to possible engine failure unless you descended to lower altitudes and warmer temperatures. Secondly, the variable pitch propellers automatically went into fully fine pitch if you were faced with engine failure, this was like hitting a brick wall and the aircraft went down vertically. Two pilots were killed this way until a stop was fitted to prevent it, but this only came into operation when the undercarriage was retracted, so for take-off and landing you played Russian roulette. Thirdly, one of the wing fuel transfer pumps had a habit of packing up, making the aircraft very one wing down. The Wyvern wasn't a difficult aircraft to deck land in spite of having slightly restricted forward vision.'

Each of the Wyverns had a mascot, as he continued, 'They all had Flooks on the side. It was our squadron mascot and one of our pilots was quite an artist so he actually painted them. When we adopted Flook as the mascot, the *Daily Mail* sponsored us so if we wanted anything like new sports gear for the squadron, the *Daily Mail* would give us some money towards the cost.'

On 29 May 1957 HM the Queen, accompanied by Prince Philip, left HMY *Britannia* by royal barge to make her way from Invergordon to *Ark Royal*, anchored off Cromarty. The purpose of the Queen's visit to *Ark Royal* was to watch a series of exercises and it was her first such visit to a warship since becoming the Sovereign. When she arrived, the Queen was greeted by FOAC, Vice Admiral M.L. Power CB, CBE, DSO and the Captain. Before sailing, the Queen and Prince Philip were driven round the upper hangar in the ship's ceremonial Land Rover to inspect Divisions consisting of two-thirds of the ship's company. The remaining third were preparing to take the ship to sea for a display by Sea Hawks and Wyverns engaged in firing practice on the splash target astern. After a small reception in the Admiral's quarters the Queen and Prince Philip left in the

All the Wyverns of 831 Squadron had a Flook painted on the side. Here one of the mascots is being painted on the side of a Wyvern by one of the squadron's pilots. (Lieutenant Commander Farquhar via the author)

royal barge to rejoin *Britannia*. 'It was a very happy occasion which was enjoyed by everyone. No press were allowed on board during the visit,' Farquhar recalled.

Following her visit the Queen sent the following signal, 'I thoroughly enjoyed this morning's carrier demonstration and I was impressed by the enthusiasm and efficiency of all hands. I send you all my best wishes for a happy and successful visit to the United States.'

With the royal visitors gone *Ark Royal* set sail for Norfolk, Virginia, in company with the destroyers *Diamond* and *Duchess*. The three ships would be representing the Royal Navy at the International Naval Review in Hampton Roads, part of a festival to celebrate the 350th anniversary of the founding in 1607 of Jamestown, the first North American settlement of English speaking people. During the voyage flying exercises continued, including a search launched on the morning of 7 June to find the *Mayflower II*. She had been built as a project to further Anglo-American relations and took the Brixham yard of J.W. & A. Upham Ltd two years to complete.

Ark Royal about to pass under the Forth Bridge in May 1957. (Lieutenant Commander Farquhar via the author)

Left to right: Prince Philip, Vice Admiral Power, Queen Elizabeth and Captain Hopkins during the royal visit to *Ark Royal* on 29 May 1957. (Revd Mike Pennington via the author)

HMY *Britannia* leads *Ark Royal* and *Apollo*. (Lieutenant Commander Farquhar via the author)

A plate was given to every officer who attended the banquet held on board *Ark Royal* during the Queen's visit to the Home Fleet at the end of May 1957. (Author)

She was the brainchild of Warwick Charlton and was funded by donations from British individuals and companies. On completion she left Plymouth Sound on 20 April 1957 to sail across the Atlantic to be presented to Plimoth Plantation inc. This company was rebuilding the original Pilgrim settlement in Plymouth, Massachusetts, and had agreed to berth and operate *Mayflower II* in perpetuity. *Mayflower II* was launched as a replica of the ship which had carried the Pilgrim Fathers, a group of Puritans originally from Yorkshire, who had fled from religious persecution in 1608. After twelve years in Holland they set sail in the *Speedwell* for England where their numbers were swelled by other pilgrims. At this point the *Speedwell* was joined by the *Mayflower* from Plymouth, which proved to be very fortunate because the *Speedwell* was forced to return to England after developing leaks. *Speedwell*'s pilgrims transferred to the *Mayflower*, originally intended only to carry their cargo, and reached America in November 1620. The *Mayflower II* was spotted by a Skyraider at 8.44 a.m. and the ship changed course to rendezvous with the replica. When the two ships met, *Ark Royal* sent over a few essentials,

Ark Royal meets up with *Mayflower II* in the Atlantic on 7 June 1957. (Revd Mike Pennington via the author)

such as freshly baked bread and fresh water, before resuming her voyage to Norfolk where she arrived the following day. During her stay *Ark Royal*'s host ship was the US Navy's newest aircraft carrier, the 78,509 ton USS *Saratoga*, which had only been in commission for two months. All the ships in Norfolk were opened to the public and *Ark Royal* was the joint favourite attraction with the Spanish sail training ship *Jean Sebastian de Elcano*.

Ark Royal slipped her moorings on 11 June to take up her position for the next day's fleet review in Hampton Roads. Over one hundred ships had gathered in the anchorage and they were split into two lines of anchored ships. The review itself was taken by the US Secretary of Defense Mr Charles Wilson, who was embarked in the Second World War heavy cruiser USS *Canberra* which had recently recommissioned after her conversion into a missile cruiser. The USS *Canberra* led her sister ship USS *Boston*, which had also been converted into a missile cruiser, and the command ship USS *Northampton*. They wore the flags of Admiral Arleigh Burke, US Chief of Naval Operations and Admiral Jerauld Wright, C-in-C US Atlantic Fleet. During the three-hour review a flypast of over two hundred aircraft from the US Navy was staged, culminating in a display by the US Navy's aerobatic display team, the Blue Angels, flying the F9F Cougar. With the ceremonies completed *Ark Royal* re-entered Norfolk for a period of static cross-operating deck trials in preparation for the exchange of aircraft during *Ark Royal*'s voyage north to New York. As part of these trials the Wyverns embarked in *Saratoga* in an unusual manner, as Farquhar explained: 'We flew two Wyverns to Petuxan River for catapult proving trials, while *Ark Royal* put into Norfolk. We then flew down to Norfolk and taxied the aircraft from the airfield to the USS *Saratoga* which was moored alongside with her side elevator down. We then taxied on to the side elevator and up on to the flight deck. It was quite incredible.' After both ships sailed from Norfolk on 17 June, *Ark Royal* successfully operated the 2TF1 Tracker, F2H Banshee, F9F Cougar, AD6 Skyraider, FJ3 Fury and F4D Skyray aircraft from *Saratoga*. While *Saratoga*'s aircrew were getting used to the smaller flight deck of *Ark Royal* the British pilots experienced operations from the world's newest and biggest aircraft carrier, as Farquhar said: 'There was very little difference between the two ships from a flying perspective other than a slightly larger angled flight deck.' At midday, after completing the day's liaison, the two ships went their separate ways, with *Ark Royal* heading north to New York and the *Saratoga* returning to her home port.

Ray Amphlett, who served in *Ark Royal* during both her first and second commissions as a Stoker Mechanic attached to the flight deck party, said of the catapults: 'You had three compartments which handled the operation of the catapult, with two below decks and one just off the flight deck. There was a main ram room with a PO stoker who operated the various levers to bring the grab backwards and forwards. A flight recorder would record about fourteen different readings for each aircraft launch, including steam pressure. There was a steam regulating room which, as the name would suggest, handled the regulation of the steam for the catapult. The compartment off the flight deck was called the howdah. You would determine the pressure of the steam according to the weight of the aircraft to be launched. The rollers on the catapult were operated by a handle in the howdah. If, for example, a Gannet was the next aircraft to be launched it needed two sets of rollers either side of the track, so that if the aircraft was slightly off track the rollers from the outside of the wheels would twist inwards and keep the aircraft in line with the track of the catapult. The Americans did not have this on their catapults which meant that we could launch more aircraft within a given time.'

Ark Royal's first visit to New York was brief, lasting only forty-five hours, yet the landmark that greeted the ship as it came alongside the French Line's pier 88 was very familiar because the famous Cunard liner *Queen Mary* was moored, on *Ark Royal*'s port side, at pier 90. The sight of these two great British ships moored close together was short-lived because the liner sailed the following morning. 'As we were coming in to make the turn for the pier the water was relatively shallow for a ship of *Ark Royal*'s draft, and we must have stirred up some mud, because mud was sucked into the cooling system for the turbo-generators. At that time we were

Ark Royal off Norfolk, Virginia, in June 1957. (Mike Lennon)

Ark Royal comes in to moor at Pier 88. On her port side is the famous Cunard liner *Queen Mary*. (Lieutenant Commander Farquhar via the author)

running six turbo-generators, three on each side of the ship, supplying power into the ring main, which was split fore and aft – the normal practice. One turbo-generator went down on the starboard side as the cooling system failed. The load on that generator was transferred to the other two generators on the starboard side, which had the effect of knocking both of them out on overload.

'The electrical distribution structure enabled vital equipment, such as the motors for the steering gear, to switch automatically from one side of the ring to the other, so that if one side of the ship lost power in battle, you could continue to operate using the other side. Lighting was not part of this automatic arrangement (individual compartments tended to have their lighting provided from two different sources anyway), but there was a large amount of equipment which could have its power supply fed from the other side of the ring main by a manual change-over switch.

'When we lost all the starboard side generators, all those automatic change-over switches flopped over to the port side. We then lost a generator on the port side because of overload, but we managed to save the other two generators on the port side. In the process we lost a lot of internal communication equipment, such as loud speaker systems, which was far from helpful as the ship was brought alongside,' Pennington recalled.

In the afternoon *Ark Royal* was opened to the public and 4,000 New Yorkers took the opportunity to look round. On 17 June *Ark Royal* set sail for the UK and was joined by the destroyers *Duchess* and *Diamond* which had visited Bermuda while she was in New York. On the voyage back across the Atlantic the ship suffered a potentially very dangerous situation, as Pennington recalled: 'There was always a danger from handling fuel, especially if any of it was spilt, and there was a series of levels of danger. The most extreme of these was the Grave Emergency Fuel Danger. When the damage control HQ piped "Grave Emergency Fuel Danger" on our way back from America, I was on 4 deck. I immediately shot down to the main switchboard, which was on 6 deck, and I was there within about ninety seconds. What we aimed to do was to isolate electricity from the area where the avgas was spilt by switching it off at a remote place which was preferably in an enclosure that was gas proof. There were very precise instructions for all of these eventualities and all the switchboard staff had been highly trained in these procedures. There were three stages of operation. The first stage would take about eight seconds to complete, while the second stage would have taken a further ten seconds, so within half a minute both stages should have been accomplished. So when I arrived at the switchboard I had expected them to be completed by the watchkeeper, who should have been getting on with the third stage, which was tedious because you had to go around the main switchboard turning off individual switches. As I arrived I picked up a checklist of these switches and went to the starboard side of the main switchboard and started there. As I got through to the middle of the board there was an illuminated diagram of the generators and the big switch gear. I looked at this diagram and realized to my horror that the first two stages had not been completed. I immediately performed the first two stages but, if I hadn't done this, there was the very real risk that we could have lost the ship due to a serious explosion and no one would have known why. One of the things this incident highlighted was the debate about whether we could get any power into the affected compartment to provide light and ventilation to the men who were having to deal with the problem.'

On 28 June *Ark Royal* recorded another first when 898 became the first squadron to be transferred at sea with all of its equipment. While Swordfish squadrons had transferred from one aircraft carrier to another at sea during the Second World War they were not able to transfer the squadron's mobile equipment. 898 Squadron were leaving to join *Bulwark* which was beginning its last commission as a fixed-wing carrier before its conversion to a commando carrier. Both carriers rendezvoused at midday so that the four Whirlwinds from the two ship's flights could transfer the complete ground party, baggage and squadron mobile equipment in less than an hour. Later in the day one of the Whirlwinds from the Ship's Flight, with a doctor on board, was sent to the assistance of a French trawler and flew one of the trawler's crew to Falmouth.

One of the two Ship's Flight Whirlwind HAS3 helicopters. (FAA Museum)

After two days at anchor in Falmouth Bay clearing customs, the ship spent ten days in Portsmouth for a self-maintenance period, before sailing on 10 July for exercises in the Channel prior to disembarking the squadrons to make room for further Sea Vixen and Scimitar trials. Prior to the disembarkation of the squadrons they participated in a TV programme called *The Navy Now* on 17 June. Sadly, bad weather meant that the intended flying display was restricted to the launching and recovery of two Sea Hawks. The following day saw the embarkation of two Scimitars and a Sea Vixen for intensive deck landing trials. Three Gannets were also embarked for the compressor-rub investigation, higher all-up weight, and prototype AEW undercarriage trials. Good weather prevailed for the week, which enabled the full programme of trials to be successfully completed, and enabled *Ark Royal* to enter Devonport on 26 July for the start of summer leave. During her month in Devonport the ship was docked to have her bottom scraped and maintenance and storing was completed. Over the August Bank Holiday the ship formed part of the attractions for Navy Days.

When *Ark Royal* slipped her moorings on 28 August her numbers on board had been increased by the families of the ship's company who had joined the ship for the trip down the Hamoaze and round to the Eddystone lighthouse. They were transferred to a tug for the voyage back from Cawsand Bay to Devonport.

With the long hot days of the summer leave fast becoming a distant memory, the ship sailed up the North Sea for a rendezvous with *Eagle* and *Bulwark* in the Moray Firth, prior to the work up for Exercise Strikeback. During the work up, 831 Squadron were disembarked because of problems with the Wyvern, as Farquhar

Sea Vixen and Scimitar trials, July 1957. (British Aerospace plc. (Farnborough))

Trials of the Sea Vixen from Boscombe Down, July 1957. (British Aerospace plc. (Farnborough))

recalled: 'The hook was too sharp; if it hit the arrester wire it would actually spear the wire, so we had to have a new hook to eliminate the problem.' In their place the recently departed 898 Squadron rejoined to increase *Ark Royal*'s complement of Sea Hawks to thirty-two. Bad weather greeted them soon after their return to the ship. Robert Dear served in *Ark Royal* as a Naval Airman Mechanic (E) in 898 Squadron. He reminisced: 'In a big ship it was amazing how much alone you could feel at times. I was called out one black and stormy night to help fix double lashings on our Sea Hawks parked in the starboard forward area of the flight deck. With the ship pitching madly, I was assigned to guarding the aircraft closest to the fore end of the flight deck. This involved sitting in the cockpit and, as the bows went down into the foaming sea, applying the brakes to stop the aircraft rolling forward. The strain on the steel ropes, lashed from the aircraft to ring bolts in the deck, was both audible and scary. When the ship settled for a while, never longer than a minute or so, I had to nip out of the cockpit, check and fix the lashings or call for help if any had come adrift. If the brake pressure had fallen off, I also had to give a few quick pumps on the hand pump for the brakes' hydraulic system, located in the port wheel well. You were wet through and could not see much, other than eerie shadows on the flight deck. The noise of the sea and the storm was deafening, but seeing the torch beam and hearing the brogue of PO Morrison in his frequent checks was very reassuring.'

Ark Royal managed to play her part in the exercise despite over eight hundred members of the ship's company being hit by Asian flu in the middle of the exercise. Describing the effects of the flu on board, Pennington said,

Ark Royal at speed in the North Sea in 1957.
(Revd Mike Pennington via the author)

'The Asian flu hit the junior mess decks first because they were more crowded. From a technical point of view it wasn't a complete disaster, because the senior rates could perform the jobs normally allocated to the junior rates, but of course the work was reduced to the bare essentials. However, the real problems set in when the senior rates were hit by the flu and there wasn't the skills base to cover for them. There was a genuine concern on board that the Soviets might have launched a biological attack to immobilize the Western forces participating in what was the biggest NATO exercise held up to that time.'

As a result of the illness the VIP demonstration, planned for the end of the exercise, was cancelled and the ship sailed for Spithead where she arrived on 29 September. After a period of recuperation spent at anchor in Spithead, it was time for *Ark Royal* to act as host to the American aircraft carrier USS *Forrestal* and her six escorting destroyers in Southampton. The locals, who were used to the impressive sight of the great liners, such as the *Queen Mary* and *Queen Elizabeth*, dominating their skyline, flocked to look at the two great carriers. 'I visited the *Forrestal* and I was astonished at the size because I thought *Ark Royal* was big. I think it was the vast open areas which amazed me,' Pennington remarked.

Soon it was time to head for warmer climes, when *Ark Royal* slipped her Southampton moorings on 11 October to participate in Exercise Pipedown, which provided another opportunity for her aircrew to complete a further two days of cross-deck operations with USS *Saratoga*. Perhaps one of the more memorable flying events on board *Ark Royal* at this time was the take-off of a F4D Skyray. The pilot had been among the batch of American pilots operating on board *Ark Royal* during June's encounter and he had wanted to perform a free take-off then. He was given his chance this time, because the Skyray had damaged its catapult hold-back attachment earlier in the day. By now the cross-operations between the two ships were becoming routine for both air groups and, as a result, the intervals between American aircraft landing on *Ark Royal* was coming down to twenty-five seconds between aircraft.

After a brief stopover in Gibraltar the ship sailed to Lisbon, passing Cape Trafalgar on 21 October. *Ark Royal* had been joined by *Albion* to participate in a memorial service to commemorate the Battle of Trafalgar, with each carrier steaming down the tracks taken by the two columns of the British Fleet at that historic battle. *Ark*

Royal hoisted the same signal ordered by Lord Nelson at Trafalgar and one of her Whirlwind helicopters dropped a wreath over the position where Lord Nelson received his fatal wound in *Victory*. *Ark Royal* sailed from Lisbon to work up in preparation for Exercise Phoenix. Prior to the work up *Albion* parted company with *Ark Royal* to return to the UK to begin her conversion into a commando carrier. In her place, *Ark Royal* was joined by *Eagle* but the work up was curtailed by bad weather, so *Ark Royal* set course for Falmouth Bay. Having perfected the art of transferring at sea, 898 Squadron were off on their travels back to *Bulwark*. The squadron's equipment was transferred by helicopter while the ship was at anchor in Falmouth Bay waiting for clearance from Customs.

Following eleven days in Devonport *Ark Royal* slipped her moorings and sailed north for Exercise Phoenix. One of the pilots serving in 831 Squadron at this time was Sub Lt R. Edward (now Lt Cdr Edward). Talking about his lucky escape from his crashed Wyvern on 11 November 1957, Edward recalled: 'We were actually doing a strike against Muckle Ossa, which is a small rock off the Orkneys. The weather was very rough and *Eagle* had stopped flying but on *Ark Royal* we had continued. While flying at low level, on the way back from Muckle Ossa I had an oil leak from the propeller which cluttered up the whole of the windscreen. With the salt spray which was coming up because we were at low level it smeared across the windscreen. The routine for such a situation if it occurred was, when you arrived back at the carrier to join the circuit, you checked if the windscreen wiper worked and, if it did, you pumped de-icing fluid across the windscreen which would make it opaque, then you turned the wiper on to clear the screen so that you could see again. I did this and the windscreen became opaque but when I turned the wiper on it didn't clear the screen. I landed with the canopy open so that I could see outside. The ship was corkscrewing and I caught the last wire, and ended up in the catwalk immediately aft of the deck-edge lift and bent the lift itself, which never worked again! The aircraft caught fire and a very brave man cut me free from the cockpit. The amusing part of it was when I got into the island a messenger came down from the Captain, at the same time that I was nobbled by the ship's Doctor. The messenger said, "The Captain wants to see you." So I brushed off the Doctor, who said, "No you don't have to do that, come with me." But I went up to the bridge and Captain Hopkins turned round in his chair and said, "I sent for you, Edward, to tell you I didn't think that the crash was your fault." The aircraft was subsequently

Sub Lieutenant R. Edward had a lucky escape, having been pulled clear from his Wyvern seconds before this photograph was taken on 11 November 1957. (Lieutenant Commander R. Edward via the author)

ditched over the side once all the useful remaining spares had been removed for use on the other embarked Wyverns.' A planned gathering of the Home Fleet was cancelled at the end of November, thus enabling *Ark Royal* to return to Devonport for Christmas leave.

Ark Royal's first port of call of 1958 was Gibraltar on 31 January, having spent Christmas and the New Year berthed in Devonport with *Eagle* astern. Over the New Year Vice Admiral A.N.C. Bingley CB, OBE had become the new FOAC and had hoisted his flag initially in *Eagle*, thus making *Ark Royal* a private ship once more. This new-found status was relatively short-lived because, once at Gibraltar, FOAC joined *Ark Royal*, while *Eagle* began her work up and the C-in-C Mediterranean embarked for a couple of days en route to Malta. While the New Year had brought a change of climate for the ship's company, the next few months were to be far from a holiday cruise, as *Ark Royal* participated in a number of exercises. The first of these was Exercise Marjex at the beginning of March with *Eagle* and the US Sixth Fleet. Once again, this exercise provided an opportunity for cross-deck operations with the Americans. Among the American aircraft to operate from *Ark Royal* were two new types, the A4D Skyhawk, and the F8U Crusader.

On 10 March *Ark Royal* arrived in Genoa for a week's visit which was memorable thanks to the wintry weather. Because of Genoa's busy commercial activities there wasn't a suitable berth for *Ark Royal* to go alongside, so she was anchored out in the harbour. Some of the guests attending the official reception in the evening were not feeling at their best after the rough trip out to the ship. The following day three inches of snow fell on the flight deck and some of the ship's company were left stranded ashore. One of those men was Ray Amphlett, who recalled: 'I went ashore in the afternoon, but the sea was too rough to get back aboard that night so I, along with other members of the ship's company, had to sleep rough. I found a space in the back of a truck and when I woke up in the morning four inches of snow had fallen. It was not until midday that the ship's boats could be launched to start ferrying those stranded members of the ship's company back.'

Ark Royal sailed from Genoa for two days of flying exercises, before entering Malta for a three-week self-maintenance period and Easter leave. *Ark Royal* sailed to begin a fortnight of work up on 8 April prior to two exercises which were held at the end of the month. Exercise Apex was to practise the art of screening the carrier group from submarine attack. Exercise Shotgun saw *Ark Royal* providing air support for amphibious landings on the south Sardinia coast.

A Sea Hawk takes the barrier in March 1958.
(Revd Mike Pennington via the author)

A Sea Hawk of 804 Squadron being hooked up to the catapult. (FAA Museum)

Having successfully completed the exercises, *Ark Royal* changed course for Naples. She arrived off the port on 28 April. Before *Ark Royal* could begin her visit to the harbour she embarked a number of VIPs for a demonstration of her capabilities. The bad weather which was encountered on her arrival made the visitors' embarkation difficult and therefore reduced the numbers who attended. On the other hand the First Lord of the Admiralty had no such problems because he was embarked by helicopter. After the demonstration *Ark Royal* returned to Naples but the strong winds prevented her from entering the port. However, the VIPs were spared the discomfort of disembarkation by MFV and instead they were helicoptered back to Naples. When the weather subsided *Ark Royal* entered Naples for the rest of her visit, the highlight of which was the disembarkation of 804 Squadron when they were launched in harbour on 8 May, thus providing quite a spectacle for the locals.

Before the ship sailed on 10 May a BBC film crew was embarked to film footage for the TV programme *Skylarks*. As part of the embarked contingent the actor Mr A.E. Mathews came on board to play the part of Vice Admiral Sir Godfrey Wiggin-Fanshawe KBE, DSO, DSC. As part of the filming, the embarked section of Royal Marines became extras when they were used for the scene in which Admiral Wiggin-Fanshawe inspects them. While the embarkation of the film crew was a novelty for the ship's company it provided the electrical department with some headaches, as Pennington recalled: 'The film crew rang us up in the electrical department and demanded something like 600 amps in the mess deck in half an hour. This was the sort of load which would have been required after significant battle damage. Therefore, expecting us to slot it into place to

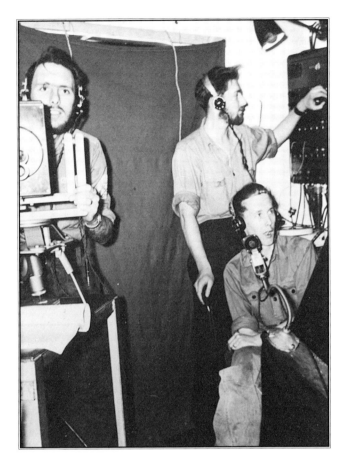

Behind the scenes of the ship's television station ARTV.
(Revd Mike Pennington via the author)

A Sea Venom of 893 Squadron
about to be launched. (Revd Mike
Pennington via the author)

cope with their lighting equipment that quickly was unrealistic. Normally it would take at least two to three hours because it would have required us to rig the damage control cables, as the normal ship's cables were not capable of supplying that amount of current. The damage control cables were cut to the length of the compartment that they were stowed in. Running through each bulkhead there were insulated terminals, so if the main cables of the ship were damaged you could run these emergency cables from bulkhead to bulkhead to restore power. This was the sort of job which was thrown at us by the BBC.'

The filming was brought to a premature end when the ship was sent to anchor off Malta on 15 May to embark Flag Officer Second in Command Mediterranean Fleet, Vice Admiral Sir Richard Durnford-Slater prior to sailing for Exercise Medflex a day early. When *Ark Royal* left the Malta area that evening she formed the centre of a task group consisting of eight destroyers and an under way replenishment group. The reason for the change of plan was that the Government wanted *Ark Royal* on standby in case she was needed off Lebanon. This requirement forced the plans for the exercise to be changed, because the exercise was originally due to move across the Mediterranean from west to east and culminate in a visit to Istanbul. But, because there was the real possibility that *Ark Royal* might be needed off Lebanon, the plans were changed to take the ships towards Lebanon so that if they were needed they could be quickly diverted from the exercise. The visit to Istanbul was also cancelled. The group of warships waited off Cyprus for further orders, until *Ark Royal* was eventually allowed to sail back to the UK, returning in June to host a shop window before entering Devonport on 5 July to pay off into refit. Two days later HM Queen Elizabeth the Queen Mother arrived on board by helicopter to begin a visit to the ship. Before she left, the Queen Mother presented the ship with a Drum Major's sash. Captain Hopkins left *Ark Royal* on 16 July and was relieved by the Commander, Cdr McIntosh DSO, MBE, DSC, who became the interim CO while the ship began a major refit.

Chapter Four

ICEBERGS AHEAD!

THIRD COMMISSION,

DECEMBER 1959–FEBRUARY 1961

As we have seen, the developments in carrier-borne aviation were moving at a rapid pace during the early postwar years. Therefore, after two years in service the Admiralty decided in the autumn of 1957 that *Ark Royal* was to undergo an extensive refit which would bring both the living conditions and the operation of aircraft up to date. Because *Ark Royal* was regarded by the Admiralty as the most important ship in the Royal Navy, they scheduled the refit to take priority over the four-year modernization of *Eagle*. Despite the priority given to *Ark Royal*, the Admiralty expected the work, which would have normally taken two years, to be finished within fifteen months. The refit schedule was disrupted by a serious fire which damaged part of the ship. This of course meant that the dockyard had to do the work they had completed again, as well as trying to finish the rest of the refit work on time. John Woollen, who served in *Ark Royal* at this time as a stoker described the aftermath of the fire: 'I was on the duty watch looking after the dockside "donkey" boilers and I remember the men who came off the ship said the most alarming thing was the smoke.'

Captain Peter Hill-Norton (now Admiral of the Fleet the Lord Hill-Norton GCB) assumed command of *Ark Royal* on 1 October 1959. He had previously served as Executive Officer (Commander) in *Eagle* during the final stages of her construction at Harland & Wolf and during her first commission. Hill-Norton explained the four major challenges that faced him before *Ark Royal* was recommissioned: 'Firstly, to set to work all the new machinery – catapults, after lift, virtually new auxiliary steam system, new turbo-generators. Secondly, run in new accommodation for nearly all the ship's company including mess decks, dining halls and bathrooms. Thirdly, to get rid of the mess and muddle of what amounted to a modernization, completed in fifteen months instead of about two years, so that extensive and complicated sea trials could begin immediately after recommissioning. Lastly, to ensure that no further fires were allowed to take hold. An average of about fifty sailors were employed day and night to supervise the dockyard mateys. One hundred and fifty-odd officers and men stood by the ship during the refit, which gradually built up around the time I took command to some five to six hundred men shortly before the main part of the commission arrived.'

Ark Royal's Supply Officer for the third commission was Cdr J. Harkness (now Rear Admiral Harkness CB). 'Before we commissioned, the key officers and ratings were busily planning how best to cope with the likely changes ahead. Of these the most important was the news that we, but not the embarked squadrons, would have to take a 10 per cent complement cut. As I had long held the view that our ships had become uncomfortably overcrowded I was in no position to argue, but had misgivings about the outcome, unless ways could be found for reducing the burden on people. However, Captain Hill-Norton said it was up to us to propose relaxations and for him to bear the responsibility if he approved them.'

Harkness described the benefits the refit brought to his department, as well as some of the challenges which he had to overcome before the ship recommissioned: 'The conversion of the galleys and dining hall to cafeteria messing allowed me, for the first time in my career, to offer a choice between six menus at all meals, a challenge to which everyone responded magnificently. No longer was the galley expected to provide 2,000 freshly fried eggs simultaneously. The Catering Officer, Sub Lt Eade, produced cards recording the quantities of ingredients, cooking instructions and so on for each dish, with space to record dates of use, and indications of popularity. The opportunity to offer choice also had the benign effect of pushing responsibility on to the less senior ratings in the galley. All in all, cafeteria messing represented progress at last. It contributed, however, to problems that exercised all the departmental heads for the whole commission. In the bad old days sailors slept, ate and relaxed in the same place, which it was their business to keep clean and tidy. It was one of the jobs of the cook of the mess, for example, to wash up, not only the plates and cutlery, but also the dishes in which the food had been collected from the galley. The washing up job was centralized and mechanized, but men were still needed to feed the machines. The dining halls added significantly to the spaces which had to be kept bright and shining. To do these chores and many others around the ship, all departments had to contribute to what we called the Communal Party which amounted to between two and three hundred men, most of whom, not unreasonably, would have preferred to do the more skilled work for which they had been trained. We considered, but rejected the idea of having a separate branch simply to do the chores. Even if such a notion, which had some fairly obvious drawbacks, were to be accepted it would do nothing for our time in the *Ark Royal*. All we could do was to ensure that no one stayed too long in the Communal Party.

'There were two other problems which bothered us. One was the working of the divisional system, in which the Divisional Officer had, by tradition, to be of the same branch as the men in his charge. This meant that in my department, for example, once the squadrons were embarked there were far too many cooks and stewards for any officer to pay each one the attention he deserved. The other problem was finding useful work for officer aircrew, likely to be airborne for not more than about twenty-five to thirty hours a month. The Commander (Air), Dicky Reynolds readily agreed to his officers helping out and as a consequence we were able to reduce the size of a division to about twenty men, a much more manageable number. Of course there was turbulence when squadrons changed or left, but this was far outweighed by the gains.'

As the ship was prepared for recommissioning many of the changes became visible, including the removal of the deck-edge lift. John Woollen said: 'The interesting thing about this was that it provided an opportunity to look at all the machinery needed to raise and lower the lift. You could normally see the chains but behind all of that there were huge hydraulic rams which were on the other end of the chains.' The lift well was converted into workshops for the air department and extra messes. Fly 1 was enlarged thanks to the removal of the starboard forward 4.5in battery. Both catapults were fitted with jet-blast deflectors, while the port catapult was fitted with wet accumulators and a rotor valve. The benefit of this was to increase the end speed of an aircraft launch by 4 to 6 knots. The deck landing mirrors gave way to the deck landing projector sight. An 'Alaskan Highway' was fitted to the starboard side of the island so that the flight deck transport could be parked there, and thus free up Fly 2 for condition one aircraft. Flyco was enlarged to provide improved visibility for Little F, Lieutenant Commander (Flying).

Comparing *Ark Royal* at the time of her recommissioning with her sister ship, Hill-Norton remarked: 'The two ships were in all important respects the same. *Ark*'s arrangements were, being newer, more convenient in every way, and more comfortable and easier to administer. By contrast the aircraft and everything to do with them were much more sophisticated and demanding. However, it should be understood that in 1959 because *Ark*

Royal was the most important ship in the Navy, all the officers, and many of the Chief Petty Officers and Petty Officers, were specially selected by their parent "schools", and were thus able to manage successfully much greater problems and demands than in lesser ships.'

Ark Royal was recommissioned on 1 December 1959, with the actual ceremony being held on the upper hangar deck on 28 December 1959. She sailed for sea trials on 8 January 1960 to complete calibrating gunnery and radio equipment as well as deck handling trials. One of the major challenges of the work up was to integrate fully a CAG of new aircraft types which were entering service with the FAA. The Sea Hawks and Sea Venoms of the previous commission had given way to a new generation of heavy aircraft, the Sea Vixen FAW1 and Scimitar F1, while the ASW role transferred from the fixed-wing Gannet AS4 to the Whirlwind helicopters. The Gannet had not disappeared from *Ark Royal*'s CAG, because it returned in its new incarnation as the Gannet AEW3 to replace the Skyraider AEW1. The only element of the CAG to remain unchanged was the Ship's Flight which still continued to operate the Whirlwind helicopter. Lt Cdr Bevans MBE, DSC was the Lt Cdr (Flying) for the third commission; about the new generation of aircraft, he said: 'When we completed the refit in Devonport we were the first RN carrier to operate a CAG comprised mainly of jet aircraft, with the AEW Gannets and the helicopters the only non-jet elements. As such *Ark Royal* was under close scrutiny to watch how the new aircraft performed.'

Lieutenant W.L.T. Peppe (now Commander Peppe OBE) served in *Ark Royal* during the third commission as a watchkeeping officer. Describing the work up period, he recalled, 'I was Assistant Cable Officer during the work up and we seemed to have endless cable deck problems. On one occasion when weighing from Cawsand Bay we lost steam to all cable holders and the capstan. So we rigged to weigh by deck tackle and actually started the evolution. The cable deck was very short for that sort of thing and the length of available pull, down 3 deck passageway on the port side, was also short, so it took for ever to heave in a fathom, let alone a shackle. Fortunately, we got steam back to complete the evolution.'

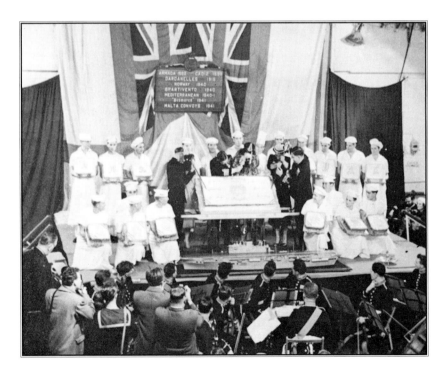

The commissioning ceremony. (Lieutenant Commander Bevans via the author)

A Gannet AEW3 from
849 Squadron A Flight.
(Lieutenant Commander Bevans
via the author)

As with any ship that has just emerged from an extensive refit it is necessary to continue the refinement of the ship's routines after commissioning. Harkness recalled: 'Shortly after we had commissioned, the Commander, Sam Brookes, asked me whether it would be possible to pay the sailors while they waited in the dining hall queue, instead of at the traditional pay parade, which took a sizeable chunk from working hours. I said I'd see what could be done, and asked my Cash Officer, Lt Cdr Len Truscott, for his ideas. We both knew that mustering men in the order in which their accounts were kept was the quickest way of doing the job, but we also knew that what saved time for the paymaster, in turn cost time for everyone else. After we had timed the speed of the dining hall queue at about eighteen men a minute, we had an idea of how quickly the ledger pages could be flicked over, and between us worked out how a new system of account numbering could allow us to pay at the same speed. The new system worked well, saving man hours in all departments including my own, so my willingness to cooperate was not quite as unselfish as it might have seemed.'

After five weeks of work up *Ark Royal* returned to Devonport late in February. On 3 March she slipped her moorings wearing the flag of FOAC, Rear Admiral Smeeton. Later in the day she embarked her new CAG for the first time, comprising 892 Squadron's Sea Vixen FAW1s, 800 Squadron and 807 Squadron both flying the Scimitar F1, 820 Squadron and 824 Squadron both flying the Whirlwind HAS7, 849 Squadron A Flight's Gannet AEW3 and finally the Ship's Flight of two Whirlwind HAS7s. The embarkation of the squadrons was a busy period for the flight deck crew which included stokers, as Woollen recalled: 'There was quite a large contingent of stokers on the flight deck because all steam machinery and hydraulics were attended by stokers, including the steam catapults, the arrester wires, the lifts and various pumps. It was a very exciting environment for a stoker.'

The Senior Pilot of 807 Squadron was Lt Cdr Freddie Hefford (now Captain F. Hefford OBE, DSC, AFC, RN). Describing both the good and bad characteristics of the Scimitar, he said: 'The Scimitar was a very powerful aircraft fitted with two 10,000lb thrust Rolls-Royce engines, which gave it a very high thrust to weight

A Scimitar of 807 Squadron is lined up on the catapult. (Alan Ellis via the author)

ratio when the aircraft was clean and carrying fuel only. The acceleration on take-off was very impressive, as was its rate of climb.

'My first flight in the aircraft was from RAE Bedford in July 1958. I had a couple of hours to study the pilots' notes, followed by a thirty-minute briefing, before getting airborne (there was no simulator at that time). The acceleration on take-off was a thrill to be remembered, it exceeded my expectations and although the undercarriage limiting speed was a generous 300 knots, one still felt that one had to be quick on the retraction button to avoid exceeding the limit. The rate of climb was excellent to 30,000 feet and was still impressive above that height. Although we were not allowed to go supersonic overland at that time, the aircraft easily reached near supersonic speed in level flight. However, I had been told that the rapid drag rise at high Mach number meant that a shallow dive was required to go supersonic. Manoeuvrability above 25,000 feet left something to be desired as the aircraft quickly got into the buffet zone. Below 25,000 feet it was a delight to fly and at high speed and low level well ahead of its contemporaries, although the aircraft was somewhat limited by having to carry all stores externally, which created extra drag.

'The aircraft lacked an intercept radar and an air-to-air missile. If it had been so fitted the poor high-altitude turning performance would have been less limiting. Of course without a radar, night operations were rather limited unless a friendly Sea Vixen, or an AEW Gannet could be persuaded to direct us onto our targets, a technique that we used several times. I recall attacking the Dutch cruiser *De Ruyter* and a USN destroyer during exercises, and *Hermes* twice off Malta.

'When landing on a carrier one feature that one had to keep in mind was the hook to eye distance, i.e. the height between the pilot's eye and the hook bill, which at 19 feet was greater than any other aircraft in service. Speed control on the carrier approach was not easy since the aircraft had a flat-bottomed drag curve in the approach configuration, i.e. very little change in drag with speed, allowing the speed to wander from one side to the other of the drag curve. To help the pilot, the aircraft was fitted with an airstream detection device (ADD) which enabled the pilot both to hear and see when he was on speed (at the correct angle of attack) for the landing approach. To improve the landing approach the aircraft was fitted with boundary layer control

(BLC), thus increasing the lift and decreasing the approach speed. The airbrakes could be used in the landing configuration to increase the drag, thus reducing the effect of the flat-bottomed drag curve.'

From Devonport, *Ark Royal* sailed to the Mediterranean to continue her work up, pausing at Gibraltar on the way. On 13 March the squadrons were disembarked to Hal Far so that *Ark Royal* could enter Grand Harbour for a ten-day self-maintenance period. During the SMP the divers discovered erosion on a rudder and a cracked propeller blade during a routine inspection below the waterline. This was to affect the programme as we will see.

When *Ark Royal* sailed from Malta it was the start of a troubled month. The new nylon crash barrier was used in anger for the first time when a Scimitar had to take it after suffering a hydraulic failure. Captain Hill-Norton also experienced his first problems with the main machinery, when the ship was reduced to two shafts for two days due to feed water problems. As he explained, he was dogged at various times throughout the commission by problems with the main machinery: 'The main machinery was unreliable and on many occasions we were reduced to three shafts, and on at least one occasion to only two. This was not only worrying but, if it coincided with insufficient wind, it made it impossible to operate aircraft.' The planned visit to Naples was cancelled because of the underwater faults found during the SMP in Malta. So after FOAC had declared he was satisfied with *Ark Royal*, half of the squadrons were disembarked to Hal Far on 24 April and she sailed for Gibraltar to spend two weeks in dry dock. As part of the work carried out during this unexpected docking two propellers were changed, and both rudders were repaired while the ship was painted. The engineers took this opportunity to catch up on some of their other maintenance jobs.

Ark Royal emerged from dry dock at the end of April to conduct further exercises in the Mediterranean, including an air defence exercise with the US Navy's Sixth Fleet prior to a four-day visit to Toulon. During the visit, preparations were made for the visit later in June of a squadron of Sea Venoms from the French Navy. The Sea Venom was built under licence for the French Navy and was known as the Aquilon. It was essentially the Sea Venom FAW 20 adapted for French Naval service.

After an air defence exercise with the French at Bizerta, and the American carrier *Saratoga* in the Mediterranean, *Ark Royal* hosted one hundred and thirty Spanish VIPs for a shop window exercise off Barcelona on 3 June, before anchoring off there for a five-day visit. From Barcelona, *Ark Royal* sailed back towards Toulon

Ark Royal fires a salute before entering Toulon for a four-day visit in May 1960. (Lieutenant Commander Bevans via the author)

Some of the French Navy Aquilons embarked during June 1960. (Lieutenant Commander Bevans via the author)

to disembark the Whirlwinds and embark the eight Aquilons for some training. The RN had agreed to embark the Aquilons in return for the French Navy hosting both of *Ark Royal*'s Whirlwind squadrons to gain anti-submarine experience with the French Navy. While the embarked period was successful for the French squadron it was marred by the loss of one aircraft and its pilot on the day of disembarkation. That night an appeal was launched on the ship's TV to donate to a fund for the dead pilot's wife which raised £376. The two Whirlwind squadrons were embarked and, after an air defence exercise with the US Navy, *Ark Royal* entered Gibraltar on 20 June for a fortnight's visit. On 4 July *Ark Royal* sailed from Gibraltar to begin a period of intensive flying. This was to be the first opportunity for Lt G. Wilcock, (now Cdr G. Wilcock) who had joined 892 Squadron as a newly trained observer, to be launched from an aircraft carrier. 'My pilot Mike Durrant and I were the first pipeline aircrew for the Sea Vixen (as distinct from those converted from flying earlier aircraft types). Our first catapult shot was very interesting to say the least. Mike had experienced one ashore, at RAE Bedford, but otherwise it was all new to us. It was very hot and we were on the flight deck with engines running for quite a long time so we had the cockpit temperature set on fully cold . . . The brief was for the pilot to rotate the plane off the end of the catapult to the correct slight climbing attitude by reference to the cockpit artificial horizon but, as we sped off down the deck, the cabin completely fogged out with cloud from the air conditioning – consternation in "the office" and some expletives from the left-hand seat. As the boss put it when we returned, "A bit slow rotating off the end" which, we gathered from the other professional spectators (who were always "goofing"), was something of an understatement. An hour later we were back, for our first ever deck approach. That "pass" produced a comment from the left-hand seat to the effect that this was not exactly easy. There cannot have been many pilots in 1960 who had been given such a large (14 ton) aeroplane for their first attempt at a deck landing. I asked Mike if he was game to have another go – to which he replied, "Well, we've got to" and of course we did. Three or four passes later came the order "Hook down" and we duly stopped on board, which was quite an experience from the coal-hole too – three-and-a-half seconds from 130 knots to stop without being able to see it coming. Yet within half a dozen sorties it seemed routine.'

This period of intensive flying once again highlighted a particular problem with the new types of aircraft, as Hill-Norton explained: 'A perennial, and frequently limiting, problem with the new types was the shortage of "on-board" spares. Aircraft were quite frequently grounded for their lack, but whether in the Med, the Northern Seas, or the Atlantic, I must pay tribute to the shore-side spares organization for meeting our cries for help as soon as they reasonably could.'

During this period of exercises, 849 Squadron A Flight encountered their first problems of the commission, when two of the Gannets had to take the barrier due to the collapse of their front oleo. After a visit to Athens, *Ark Royal* returned to Malta at the end of July. The day after her arrival, the newly commissioned light fleet carrier *Hermes* entered Malta. Like *Ark Royal* before her, *Hermes* had endured a prolonged period of building which had more than its fair share of suspended working periods. She was in the process of working up prior to participating in Exercise Swordthrust, which was to be held in the autumn and would be her first exercise. On 9 August *Ark Royal* sailed from Malta to conduct further flying exercises.

While the flying exercises provided vital training for the squadrons these periods also afforded the ideal opportunity to perfect a replenishment at sea, as Peppe explained: 'We were forever experimenting with better ways to carry out RAS. We pioneered using canvas slides down the forward lift well. These worked well, although one went in to the Sick Bay through a door designed to take flight deck casualties and the PMO, perhaps not unnaturally, hated the provisions going through his clean empire into the canteen flat. Less successful were canvas baffle chutes designed to get boxes and sacks vertically down a series of hatches. There was one such chute from deck 2 to 9E, at the bottom of which was a flour store. I remember being stuck down there with a working party while sacks descended in a never-ending and unstoppable stream. The baffle plates in the chute started coming adrift and the sacks descended faster and of course started to burst which was very character building. The pressure was always to get the stores clear of the flight deck so that we could start flying, but the below decks arrangements frequently weren't up to moving the stores on. So we ended up with enormous dumps in the most unlikely places which took many hours to clear. On one occasion we managed to continue night flying while doing a light jackstay RAS of potatoes, the point being just forward of the island. I was in charge of the jackstay and we operated it while launching and recovering Sea Vixens.'

After a brief visit to Palma *Ark Royal* changed course for home waters. When she arrived in the Channel she took the opportunity for a RAS with the newly commissioned RFA *Resurgent* which at that time had not been properly worked up, so the RAS was not as successful as it could have been. From the Channel *Ark Royal* headed north to Rosyth arriving there on 5 September for ten days of SMP. 'The Forth road bridge was being built and some of the sailors got into trouble for returning from Edinburgh by walking along the suspension cables,' Peppe recalled.

On 15 September *Ark Royal* left Rosyth to spend a week working up with *Hermes* prior to the start of the exercise. Sadly, during this time tragedy struck 892 Squadron when Lt Bond and Lt Marjoribanks were killed after their Sea Vixen landed short and broke its booms off before going into the sea. Despite the sad loss, the exercise itself was successfully completed. At the conclusion of Exercise Swordthrust the entire fixed-wing element of the CAG were disembarked as the ship sailed south to enter Devonport on 5 October for a leave period and SMP. When *Ark Royal* slipped her moorings on 26 October four hundred wives and children were embarked to watch the CAG embark, as Peppe commented: 'It was fairly remarkable that we operated aircraft with our families on board. There were no ear defenders, just "Keep your ears covered".' Once the squadrons had been embarked, *Ark Royal* anchored in Cawsand Bay so that the dockyard paddle tug *Pert* could come alongside for the families to be disembarked so that the ship could begin her voyage to the Mediterranean. When the squadrons were disembarked in October the ship said goodbye to 892 Squadron, which was bound for *Victorious*, while 820 Squadron was disembarking to be disbanded. When the new CAG was embarked it consisted of 800 Squadron and 807 Squadron both flying Scimitars, 824 Squadron's Whirlwinds, 849 Squadron A Flight's Gannet AEW3s and the Gannet ECM4s of 831 Squadron which were embarking for the first time.

On 5 November *Ark Royal* entered Malta for what was originally planned to be a weekend visit followed by ten days of trials with the Buccaneer. However, plans were changed because the Buccaneers encountered difficulties which had to be resolved before the trials could begin. Therefore, the planned visit to Toulon was cancelled and replaced with ten days of SMP. This change of plan presented the small problem that some of the aircraft which had been left on board for the original weekend visit were needed ashore for training when the weekend was extended. The solution was simple! Just take advantage of the powerful steam catapults and launch the aircraft while she was still at anchor in Bighi Bay and fly them round to Hal Far.

This was done on 7 November when two Scimitars of 807 Squadron were launched, as Hefford recalled: 'The squadron needed more aircraft ashore at Hal Far for training purposes and Cdr (Air), Cdr Reynolds agreed that 807 Squadron should calculate the conditions for launching these two aircraft whilst the ship remained at anchor. The calculations having been made and presented to Wings for checking, the Captain was asked for permission to launch in harbour. The ship was already pointed towards the harbour entrance and with a 10 knot wind from the port bow, both Scimitars were launched, the CO, Lt Cdr Jock Tofts first, followed by me. I had the satisfaction of seeing the CO do an immaculate launch, my own aircraft, launched very shortly after, dipped slightly off the bow. The launches, which were considered to be uneventful, must have made those in *Victorious*, which was anchored off *Ark Royal*'s bow, very envious as she had shorter stroke catapults than the *Ark Royal* and

One of the two Scimitars from 807 Squadron is launched and is about to be followed by a Gannet. (Lieutenant Commander Bevans via the author)

couldn't launch her aircraft under those conditions. Both aircraft landed safely at Hal Far and were soon engaged in the training programme.'

On 15 November the two Buccaneers from C Squadron, Boscombe Down, were ready to be embarked for their trials. The trials were not as successful as they could have been. Although thirty-six deck landings were completed in a week it became apparent that the Gyron Juniors were not giving the Buccaneer as much power as would have been desired. The engines were also suffering from reliability problems which brought the trials to an early conclusion.

At the end of the month *Ark Royal*'s CAG was complete once more when the newly formed 893 Squadron flying the Sea Vixen FAW1 was embarked. The Sea Vixens arrived just in time to participate in Exercise Royal Flush II which was an air defence exercise with the US Navy. The exercise saw a dominance of RN carrier power with both *Victorious* and *Hermes* also taking part in the one-day exercise. The rest of the month and the first part of December were taken up with exercises as *Ark Royal* participated in first, Exercise Pink Gin III, and then Exercise Decex. Despite the bad weather at the end of Exercise Decex which caused delays to the ship's programme and threatened the possible cancellation of FOAC's inspection, *Ark Royal* entered Gibraltar on

One of the two Buccaneers from C Squadron, Boscombe Down. (British Aerospace plc. (Brough Heritage Centre))

Captain Hill-Norton helps to stir the Christmas pudding. (Lieutenant Commander Bevans via the author)

Arctic RAS. Left to right: *Ark Royal*, *Tidesurge*, *Londonderry*. (Lieutenant Commander Bevans via the author)

15 December. Once alongside, the ship's company ensured that the ship was ready to be inspected by FOAC who carried out his inspection the following afternoon. When *Ark Royal* sailed on the morning of 18 December she had both the First Sea Lord, Admiral Sir Caspar John and FOAC embarked for a demonstration off Gibraltar of both *Victorious*'s and *Ark Royal*'s capabilities. The demonstration went well and both Admirals were disembarked to *Victorious* that evening so that *Ark Royal* could change course and head for Malta, arriving there on 19 December to spend Christmas at the island. The visit wasn't entirely for pleasure because during the visit ten days of SMP were completed. *Ark Royal* really got into the Christmas spirit by hosting a children's party for 2,000 Maltese children. 'Someone said that all children were happy if you gave them something to blow, so we gave each one a whistle as they came over the gangway. They then went into the hangar for stickies; the result was a noise dangerous area but the party was a great success,' Peppe recalled.

The New Year began early on 6 January 1961 when *Ark Royal* left Grand Harbour to begin a few days of flying exercises. This period was marred by the loss of the Sea Vixen of Lt Dudgeon and Lt Russell from 893 Squadron while members of the squadron were getting night deck qualified. On 14 January, with the flying exercises completed, *Ark Royal* paused off Malta to embark the Royal Marine contingent which had been left ashore when she sailed for the flying exercises. The ship was about to begin the voyage west, stopping at Lisbon, prior to crossing the wintry Atlantic to conduct cold weather trials off Greenland. This was the first time that a RN carrier had operated in this area. Discussing the objective of the trials, Hill-Norton recalled: 'The cold weather trials in the Davis Strait were designed by the Admiralty, who sent a strong team of uniformed and civilian observers and recorders. The object of all the separate trials was the same, simply to see how kit of all sorts, above and between decks, worked in very cold conditions. I was instructed to seek for and remain in temperatures between about 5 degrees and 15 degrees Fahrenheit, which is extremely cold. Although I cannot remember any specific trials of people, I do remember several reports on the effect of the cold on men's performance, particularly on the flight deck and in other exposed positions. It should be remembered that for launch and recovery of our heavy aircraft, a wind over the deck of at least 30 knots was required, and this produces a severe chill factor to go with the ambient temperatures. It was, for me, a nerve-racking period. There was very little wind, which meant very high speed for launch and recovery. There was very little sea room, and going 28 knots towards the thick ice with fifteen jet aircraft in the circuit, due to land at 30-second intervals, is character building. It only needed one to foul-up on deck to delay the recovery and I should have had to reverse course and put one or several aircraft in the sea. There were no diversion airfields, which is a carrier Captain's nightmare anywhere in the world.'

Peppe continued: 'Navigationally it was interesting as there were small bits of ice around everywhere and they didn't show on the radar. While the weather was generally excellent for the region, we had low winds and

Some members of the ship's company watching icebergs in the Davis Strait. (Commander Peppe)

therefore the ship was steaming at high speed so any chunk of ice could have made a nasty hole. To minimize the risk of hitting ice we plotted the positions of the ice during the day and then navigated around them on the local operational plot at night. The other major hazard was arctic sea smoke which boiled up in our wake as we thrashed around. Early in the day it was no problem, but as we went through the morning our wake trails gradually expanded until by lunch we were steaming around in fog of our own making. The compass platform might well still be above it and in 8/8ths blue sky but the flight deck, and therefore of course the centre line and projector sights, were in thick fog. During the trials I watched a Sea Vixen, piloted by Dick Slatter, with Tony Peebles as observer, take the barrier. The hook had stuck in the up position and because we were non-diversion flying the only option for recovery was to use the barrier.'

Woollen said of the arctic trials: 'They were cold, cold, and very cold. Two of the memorable things from being up on the flight deck were seeing icebergs for the first time, seeing just how big they really were, and the

A Sea Vixen from 893 Squadron is launched during the cold weather trials. Note the frozen flight deck. (Lieutenant Commander Bevans via the author)

Two Sea Vixens of 893 Squadron in Fly 1 during the cold weather trials. The effects of the steam from the catapults are exaggerated because of the cold. (Alan Ellis via the author)

constant sea smoke all the time. It was amazing to see the amount of ice that actually formed on the ship itself and how well the ship continued to operate in those conditions.' As Bevans continued: 'The Captain and Commander were concerned about the extra top weight of the ice forming on the ship, but that is a traditional hazard, operating any ships in freezing temperatures. To deal with this problem we used de-icing fluids and played steam jets over the flight deck to keep it clear.'

In addition to the problems posed by the operating environment of the Davis Strait the operation of *Ark Royal*'s aircraft was further hampered by external influences. 'We had to pay careful attention to local air traffic regulations because the Americans and Canadians were very sensitive about their Air Defense and Identification Zones which extend quite a long way out to sea,' explained Peter Bell, who as Lt Bell (now Cdr Bell OBE) was the tenth most senior Direction Officer in the third commission.

The trials were completed by 9 February much to the relief of the ship's company so that the ship could head for her next visit. Looking back at the results of the cold weather trials, Hill-Norton said: 'The trials were, I can only presume, of considerable significance to the RN, though I have no personal knowledge of this and therefore I cannot comment on the success of the trials. The combined reports were over 12in thick and must have weighed 20lb. Certainly we remained in the specified temperature zone. We flew twenty-four hours a day and never failed to launch and recover on time. Of course there were problems, that was the point of the trials, but there were none which actually prevented *Ark Royal* doing her job. They were the longest period of continuous Arctic operation by a carrier, or any other ship except perhaps *Endurance*, since the war.'

From the Davis Strait *Ark Royal* paid a short visit to New York before setting sail on 22 February for Devonport. The voyage home was a high-speed passage, so no flying was done and the squadrons were disembarked for the final time on 26 February. Describing the preparations prior to disembarkation Peppe recalled: 'I was OOW of the morning watch while the frantic preparation was going on. One Sea Vixen seemed to suffer every possible mishap. At one moment, supposedly being now serviceable, it came up on the forward lift only to start pouring fuel from a drop tank. So straight down again. Unfortunately, in the few minutes it had been at deck level, the radome had been extended. This was forgotten in the haste to strike it. So the nose wheel was lifted off the deck as the lift went down only to crash down as the fibreglass radome broke. The aircraft did get off, well strapped up with masking tape and engineers' prayers.'

Steam hoses are used to reduce the amount of ice on the flight deck during the cold weather trials. (Lieutenant Commander Bevans via the author)

Ark Royal leaves New York bound for refit in Devonport. (Lieutenant Commander Bevans via the author)

The ship's company. (Lieutenant Commander Bevans via the author)

Ark Royal arrived at Charlie buoy early on 28 February. Some of the families were embarked for the final passage of the commission up Plymouth Sound and into Devonport to pay off for refit. Hill-Norton recalled: 'On the final day, when we were due to make our passage from C buoy in the Sound to Devonport it was blowing Force 7 and Force 4 to 5 was the official limit for *Ark Royal* and *Eagle*. I was aware that there were 2,000 wives waiting on the jetty, with a corresponding eagerness to proceed. The QHM advised strongly against, so I asked for approval from the C-in-C who rather grudgingly gave it "at my sole discretion". This was meant to imply, and did, that if it went wrong I could expect a court martial. It is an extremely hazardous passage at the best of times for such a very big ship with so much windage. However, by this stage in the commission I reckoned I could pretty well write my name in the wake, so I decided to go, not without an anxious moment or two, particularly in the narrows off Mount Edgcumbe, and we made it without a scratch. A really enormous feeling of triumph, followed by the pain of ordering "Finished with main engines", for the last time in my life.'

Despite the short duration of the commission, *Ark Royal* had achieved a great deal in laying the foundations for the operation of the latest generation of heavy jet aircraft in the RN, with 4,931 fixed-wing sorties carried out in the commission. The helicopters had also achieved a lot by completing 3,701 sorties, including those of the Ship's Flight. Summing up the running of *Ark Royal* during his time in command, Hill-Norton said: 'As to the success of the whole organization, this was in effect, the resounding success in every respect of the whole commission. My own promotion to Flag rank, and the promotion of nearly all the Heads of Department and senior specialist officers, at or soon after, the end of the commission must make this clear.'

Chapter Five

A GLIMPSE INTO THE FUTURE?

FOURTH COMMISSION,

SEPTEMBER 1961–FEBRUARY 1964

While the ship was still in refit Captain Hill-Norton handed over command of *Ark Royal* to Captain D.C.E.F. Gibson DSC (now Vice Admiral Sir Donald Gibson KCB, DSC, JP). In his book *Haul Taut and Belay*,* Gibson wrote, 'I joined the ship on 14 August, arriving on board in Devonport, precisely at 9 a.m., wearing a sword and medals, the proper way for a Captain to join his new ship. I stayed in command of her for nearly two years, then, remaining on board as an Admiral, I was in her for three years altogether. During my time we served in the Home Fleet, in the Mediterranean Fleet and for some time in the Far Eastern Fleet, where we helped to maintain a naval presence during the time of the Indonesian confrontation.'

Gibson continued: 'Command of the *Ark Royal* was not much different from command of a destroyer except in the scale of the Captain's responsibility. From time to time we wore an Admiral's flag, normally the flag of the Flag Officer Aircraft Carriers, sometimes the flag of the Flag Officers second in command of various fleets; the custom had then begun of leaving Commanders-in-Chief ashore, with good communications, which allowed politicians to breathe down their necks. There are many good reasons for the above arrangement, but I am convinced that in war ships' companies rightly like to see their Admirals being shot at along with the rest. Nelson would not have been our immortal hero had he directed the battle of Trafalgar from a deep shelter in Northwood, even with Emma answering the direct telephone to Downing Street.'

The fourth commission officially started on 12 September 1961 at the Commissioning ceremony held on board in Devonport. Among the guests were FOAC, Rear Admiral R.M. Smeeton CB, MBE and *Ark Royal*'s Captain from the second commission who had by then become Rear Admiral F.H.E. Hopkins DSO, DSC, Flag Officer Flying Training. Three days after the ship's Commissioning ceremony in Devonport the Ship's Flight was formed at RNAS Culdrose. The Flight's CO was Sub Lt Robert Woodard (now Rear Admiral Sir Robert Woodard KCVO). Describing the early days of the Ship's Flight, Woodard recalled: 'The search and rescue Flight of *Ark Royal* consisted, *in toto* of two officers and fourteen ratings. The two pilots, myself and Sub Lt Bob Carnie (Senior Pilot) had come from 848 Naval Air Commando Squadron and had carried out an operational tour on the Whirlwind 7, mainly in the Far East.

The first thing to do was to find our aircraft and nobody seemed to have any idea where they might be. I took the Senior Pilot in tow and proceeded to do some SAR on two Whirlwind 7s. After numerous enquiries and

---

* Vice Admiral Sir Donald Gibson has kindly given me permission to use extracts from his book in addition to using his quotes from my interview with him.

much searching, one dark blue Whirlwind was discovered tucked away in the corner of a hangar; as no one wanted to claim it or have anything to do with it we decided it was ours! Not being able to find a second we decided it had not arrived and sure enough, after two days another dark blue Whirlwind arrived and was handed over to the Flight by the civilian ferry pilot. Our gratitude was such that he had to spend the night at Culdrose.

'The Ship's Flight was now at full complement and we began our work up in earnest. Culdrose were very good to us and helped in every way but appeared to feel no responsibility, as we belonged to *Ark Royal* and were not one of the recognized squadrons. Three weeks of hard flying followed, trying everything from night navigation exercises to all possible types of rescue and at the end of it we thought we were ready to go to sea.'

Ark Royal slipped her moorings for the first time after the refit, when she sailed from the dockyard on 7 October to tie up to Charlie buoy in Plymouth Sound. Gibson recalls from his book: 'The Admiralty had asked me to do a trial on a new nylon picking-up rope, and though the weather was good the splice pulled out at once. It is not funny for the Captain of a big ship or his buoy jumpers when the picking-up rope parts. Looking back, I realize that it was my fault, I should have told their Lordships where to put their nylon ropes.'

Once the post-refit inspection had been completed by C-in-C Plymouth, Vice Admiral Sir Charles Madden Bt, CB on 9 October, *Ark Royal* sailed to begin repair trials. Her Senior Engineer at this time was Lt Cdr Guy Crowden (now Captain G. Crowden OBE). He said: 'Prior to our deployment to the Far East we conducted high-speed trials close to Weymouth to find out how the ship would handle in the relatively shallow waters of the Persian Gulf. We found that in such conditions the stern dug in, as there was a lot of aeration around the propellers – the entrained air having a recognized effect on the normal buoyancy of the ship.'

Woodard said of the Ship's Flight's first days in *Ark Royal*: 'The first short period at sea was spent doing deck trials and the Flight was kept busy ferrying people and stores to and fro between the ship, Devonport and Portland as well as doing the routine job of plane guard. This was a foretaste of how we were going to spend the rest of the commission. Our first difficulty was to find somewhere to operate from; we had started by using the main briefing room, which had plenty of space when only a few of the front-line squadrons and their aircrew were embarked. When all the squadrons were embarked we no longer fitted. After much fuss and bother we were given a small room at the front of the island which was officially the embarked Flag Officer's typing office. Geographically, this office could hardly have been further from our aircraft when at readiness, as they were spotted aft by the round down. We were the first SAR flight to have crewmen trained as free divers; thus each crew consisted of a pilot, crewman and free diver and a lot of equipment to lug around! The divers had been included in the Flight as a direct result of a tragic incident, when Cdr Desmond Russell was killed in a deck landing accident whilst leading the embarkation of the first Scimitar squadron in *Victorious*; he was trapped in his aircraft when it went over the side.'

Once the full power trials had been successfully completed, on 17 October it was time to begin flying trials for ten days until the ship's return to Devonport for pre-foreign service leave. On 13 November *Ark Royal* sailed from Devonport bound for Gibraltar. On the same day she embarked her squadrons which included the Wessex HAS1s of 815 Squadron. The CO of 815 Squadron at this time was Lt Cdr A. Skinner (now Captain A. Skinner). Comparing the Wessex to its predecessor the Whirlwind, Skinner said: '815 was the RN's first front-line Wessex 1 anti-submarine squadron and thereby the first front-line all-weather anti-submarine helicopter squadron in the Fleet Air Arm. The move from the Whirlwind to the Wessex was a major step forward. The actual automatic equipment that brought the Wessex 1 to the hover a few feet off the sea was duplicated in some areas, but it was a far cry from the sophisticated triplicate systems in use today. Similarly, the flight stabilization system and rotor speed control in the Wessex, with its gas turbine engine, was a far cry from the unstabilized flight control, with no automatic rotor speed control of the piston-engined Whirlwind which preceded it.'

Skinner explained the background to 815 Squadron's mascot: '815 Squadron was traditionally based in Ireland and a liaison had been started with Guinness the brewers. The squadron badge was in fact a small Irish harp so when 815 Squadron was re-formed it was suggested that we should have a mascot and we thought we should have a full-blown harp. I put an advert in *The Times* in April 1961 which read, "Disused harp wanted as mascot. Playability or strings of no importance." I had many replies from people offering us harps, from real concert harps at fantastic prices through to someone who wrote, "For god's sake get rid of this harp for us. It has been cluttering up my house for years; it doesn't work." In the end we took one from a vicar in Norfolk who sent us the following letter, "We have a very large harp for the most part unstrung, but very handsome. It may be seen at the above address but it is not of the size or shape to be sent on approval." We collected the harp and had it spruced up for the Commissioning service held at RNAS Culdrose on 4 July 1961. When we embarked in *Ark Royal* for the first time on 13 November 1961, the harp was the first item of 815's equipment to land on the flight deck, slung underneath my helicopter. We had flown with a dummy underneath prior to embarkation to check that it would work, before using the harp itself. This same harp has been used by all subsequent 815 Squadrons.'

In addition to the Wessex HAS1s of 815 Squadron, *Ark Royal* also embarked the Sea Vixen FAW1s of 890 Squadron, the Scimitar F1s of 800 Squadron, the Gannet AEW3s of 849 Squadron C Flight and the two Whirlwinds of the Ship's Flight. The most noticeable difference in the composition of the squadrons between the third and fourth commissions was the emergence of big squadrons for both Scimitars and Sea Vixens. The carriers could not embark as many examples of the new larger types of aircraft as had been embarked in the days of the Sea Hawk. It was originally decided to maintain the number of squadrons but make them eight-plane squadrons. This would preserve the command structure so that in the event of war the squadron's allocation of aircraft could be increased and the command structure would already be in place to cope with it. However, this arrangement had not worked from the point of view of maintenance. If an aircraft was lost in a small squadron, you had effectively lost a higher percentage of your available aircraft than if you had lost one from a larger squadron. Therefore, prior to the beginning of the fourth commission it had been decided to create a smaller number of squadrons, but allocate a larger number of aircraft to each one.

As the ship headed south, 815 Squadron continued its learning process, as Skinner recalled: 'The operation of the Wessex HAS1 afloat posed few problems, with the necessary specialist technical test and repair equipment being set up in the ship's workshops. By the helicopter standards of the day, it was a pleasant aircraft to fly, and the first few days after embarkation were used to confirm the procedures for optimum take-off, approach and landing patterns that had been evolved during a twenty-four hour period of trials a few days before the squadron embarked. In general, the helicopters used a modified low level version of the fixed-wing approach, using the mirror for the final approach at night and in bad visibility.'

On 17 November *Ark Royal* entered Gibraltar at the start of a three-day visit before sailing to the Malta area for phase 1 of the work up period. During this work up the Ship's Flight had its first scramble on 27 November, as Woodard recalled: 'Ironically it was for the other Whirlwind which had collided with the mast of HMS *Croften*, whilst transferring a doctor to the night planeguard, in poor light with nil wind conditions, and onto the minesweeper's fo'c'sle. The poor doctor was halfway down on the winch wire when the tail hit the mast and lost most of the tail rotor. The machine managed to get back to the carrier and made a running landing at a speed seldom seen in a helicopter, and a dizzy doctor was relieved to be home! This resulted in the aircraft being landed by lighter at Malta and a replacement being flown out from Hal Far. The new aircraft was destined for an anti-submarine squadron and was thus in blue and yellow livery so for the rest of the commission we had one blue and one blue and yellow aircraft.'

At the end of the first phase of the work up *Ark Royal* entered Naples on 1 December for the start of a five-day visit before beginning the second phase of the work up. This was interrupted by a two-day visit to Malta between 8 and 10 December to disembark FOAC and 815 Squadron to *Victorious*. Skinner explained: 'Helicopter operations on the way out and in the Mediterranean revealed a serious technical problem in the rotorhead gearbox and the rotor brake. Sadly, on 28 November, only a fortnight after embarkation, the decision was taken that the squadron should leave *Ark Royal* in Malta, and return to the UK in *Victorious* for urgent modifications. On 9 December those aircraft of the squadron that were able to fly the few hundred metres across Valetta Harbour from *Ark Royal* to *Victorious* did so, my own aircraft arriving in *Victorious* amidst clouds of smoke coming from the rotor brake.' *Victorious* had stopped in Malta on her way home from the Far East.

The second phase of the work up was completed on 16 December when *Ark Royal* once more entered Malta, this time for a three-week self-maintenance period and to spend Christmas in Grand Harbour. The new year began in earnest for *Ark Royal* when she sailed from Malta on 5 January 1962 to begin the third and final phase of her work up which culminated in the fifty-two hour exercise Arkex 2. The CO of 890 Squadron at this time was Lt Cdr D. Monsell (now Cdr D. Monsell). He recalled: 'When we embarked I had seventeen aircraft and nineteen crews; by the end of the work up we had every pilot night qualified except for one and he was one deck landing short of being deck qualified. He hadn't qualified because he had had a cold and couldn't fly. We then had a whole squadron night qualified so the squadron was broken into two watches and we flew alternate nights. The amazing thing was that during my time we didn't lose a single crew from when we embarked in November 1961 through to July 1963.'

Once the exercise had been successfully completed *Ark Royal* set course for home on 9 January. On her way back *Ark Royal* paused at Gibraltar for a six-hour visit on 12 January before reaching Charlie buoy on 15 January. 'It was 16 January, and the tidal conditions would be right for our passage into Devonport at 13:00. I had anxieties about the weather, there were limits for moving *Ark Royal* through the Sound and into the dockyard, and on this occasion the weather was marginal, with the wind gusting to 28 knots. Following earlier bad weather there was a swell in the Sound which effectively increased my draft of 35 feet aft. In my opinion the weather conditions were not prohibitive, but called for thought,' Gibson explained in his book.

'I had several reasons for wanting to go alongside on that day. We were due to leave for the Far East on a date in February, before that, leave had to be given to two watches, the ship had to be stored and ammunitioned, and a large number of defects were to be made good in the dockyard. On only three days following were the tides high enough for the passage into Devonport, after which there would be a wait of ten more days. The weather forecast was worse for the next three days. If we stayed at the buoy complications would prohibit keeping to my important programme.

'The Navigating Officer, Lt Cdr E.M.C. Walker and I got into a helicopter during the forenoon and inspected the route; we landed ashore and had a consultation with the acting Queen's Harbourmaster (QHM) and Pilot, Mr Harry Nicholls, in the Long Room of the QHM's headquarters, which overlooked the Sound and was equipped with charts, pelorus and a good view.

'Plymouth was not, in my opinion, a good harbour for big ships. The passage for really big ships was tortuous, and there did not seem to be much positive cooperation between control of traffic in the Sound and the use of the buoyed channel up to Devonport; for instance, during our time at C buoy three or four merchant ships anchored unsupervised in the Sound, causing us some anxiety.

'Large ships entered the buoyed channel through the Smeaton Pass, just off the Royal Western Yacht Club. The course steered, or rather the track to be made good from C Buoy to Smeaton Pass was important, because the entrance involved turning left, like driving a car through a field gate; there was a marked shoal 300 feet south-east of this entrance, and there were other hazards in Jennycliff Bay on the approach. The position for putting the wheel over for the ship to enter the Pass was crucial and exact, as the entrance to the Pass was 700 feet wide, and the length of my ship was 800 feet. These considerations were by no means daunting, but they did call for careful thought and planning. At our conference we discussed these matters; we discussed the wind, 28 knots from the south-west, whether the ship would sail at a speed of 8 knots, the extra hazard of the swell, estimated at 6 feet, the provision of tugs, and other problems.

'We decided to proceed, but the responsibility for the decision was mine alone; the others were there to give me their expert advice, which I would be foolish to ignore. Had we known that the buoys marking the entrance to the Pass were 200 feet north-east of where they should have been we would have decided differently.

'The names of the buoys marking the entrance to the Smeaton Pass were North East Winter to port and Mallard to starboard. There was a shoal 300 feet to the south-east of Mallard buoy, which had a depth of 21 feet.

'The manner in which we did things was as follows: in confined water the Navigating Officer conned the ship, while I double-checked and gave the engine orders. The plan for approaching any port or anchorage was carefully worked out by the Navigator, and checked by me; this plan was always in great detail, with all the bearings on which the turns were commenced, all depths and reminders committed to the Navigator's note book, which he held in his hand as he stood at the pelorus conning the ship. The wheel and engine orders were passed to the steering position, which was situated under armour and out of sight.

'Mr Nicholls arrived on board, and we slipped from our mooring buoy at 12:59. We had two tugs, *Careful* and *Superman*. *Careful* was secured to the bow and led the way; the buoy was slipped, we turned the ship to the north, and steered for the entrance to the buoyed channel. Since those days I believe permanent leading marks have been erected on shore, but on this day we kept known, charted, shore objects in transit. Soundings were constantly taken and reported to us on the bridge. Below us in the operations room we had our blind navigation team checking us by radar. We had been worried by the position of one of the merchant ships anchored on our approach path, and at our request she had been moved.

'I was alarmed as we approached the entrance to the Pass, because North East Winter and Mallard buoys were in line, and there was no way of passing through them unless we shifted to the east. The Navigator was also worried, and we shifted a minimum amount, as from our transits we appeared to be on our proper track. We turned into the Pass with the North East Winter buoy very close to our port bow, about 300 feet from the bridge, and we entered the Pass safely, but when the Mallard buoy was about 35 feet abeam to starboard right aft shocks were felt, our rudders had touched ground. *Ark Royal* while under my command had touched ground *in the middle of the buoyed channel*, entering her home port.

'Fortunately the rudders, which had lifted on impact, dropped back onto their gudgeons and were serviceable, also we had two tugs to help us round corners, so we continued up into harbour, passing the thirty or so buoys marking the passage.

'When we were alongside Lt Cdr Walker and I discussed this horrible affair. We made a signal reporting the matter, wrote a full account, collated a lot of wheel orders, time of soundings, engine orders etc., and arranged for divers to inspect the hull.'

Captain Gibson went to see C-in-C Plymouth and told him he thought that the buoys were in the wrong place, so the Admiral ordered the survey ship *Shackleton* to investigate. '*Shackleton* made her survey and found the North East Winter buoy 005 degrees 110 feet, and the Mallard buoy 058 degrees 200 feet adrift from their charted positions,' Gibson recalled from his book.

As a result of the grounding Captain Gibson and the Navigator Lt Cdr Walker both faced a court martial. Captain Gibson was charged with four counts of negligence, while Lt Cdr Walker was charged with five counts

Captain Gibson gave this dish to Captain Griffin to thank him for defending him at his court martial. (Lady Griffin)

of negligence. Captain Robert White was appointed as the prosecutor for both trials. Lt Cdr Walker was defended by *Ark Royal*'s Commander, Cdr R.S. Forrest, and Captain Griffin (later Admiral Sir Anthony Griffin GCB, who was to become a future Captain of *Ark Royal*) was asked to defend Captain Gibson, as he recalled: 'Captain Gibson asked me to defend him at his court martial. Needless to say he was found guilty, but I was able to put together enough merit to show that it was quite unreasonable, even though a Captain of a ship is always regarded as ultimately responsible in the grounding of a ship, because there had been a serious gale at Plymouth and the effect of this gale was to drag quite a lot of the buoys hundreds of yards from their normal position. When the Admiralty Board saw the evidence from the court martial they cleared Gibson immediately. As a token of thanks he later sent me a small engraved dish with a Chang Kai Shek dollar in the middle of it.'

With the repairs to the damage caused by the grounding completed, *Ark Royal* was eased out of dry dock on 2 March. After a week alongside *Ark Royal* made her way to Charlie buoy on 9 March to embark the Ship's Flight and 815 Squadron which was making a welcome return to the ship after its rather unfortunate start to operational life. While at Charlie buoy the ship was searched by officers from the Dockyard Police and Plymouth Police Force because there was a rumour that a time bomb had been hidden in the engine room. Thankfully, nothing was found so the ship was able to set sail at the start of her historic voyage to the Far East on 10 March. *Ark Royal*'s Commander at the time was Cdr R.S. Forrest (now Rear Admiral Sir Ronald Forrest KCVO, DL). Explaining why this voyage was historic, he said, 'When *Ark Royal* passed through the Suez Canal at the end of March 1962, it was the first occasion that either *Eagle* or *Ark Royal* had been deployed to the Far East and transited the Suez Canal.' Gibson continued in his book: 'Such a large carrier had not before passed through

815 Squadron embarking in *Ark Royal* on 9 March 1962. (Captain Skinner via the author)

The rotor blades are spread on a Wessex as it comes up on the lift. (Commander Dawson-Taylor)

the Suez Canal, and, after careful study by my Navigator and me, we expressed certain reservations. My morale was much improved by the Fifth Sea Lord who said that if I found the prospect too alarming there were doubtless other Captains who would try.'

Later in the day *Ark Royal* embarked the rest of her CAG, as 800 Squadron, 890 Squadron, and 849 Squadron C Flight were embarked. In addition to these squadrons which had already formed part of *Ark Royal*'s CAG during her work up, she also embarked a flight of two Gannet ECM 6 aircraft from 831 Squadron A Flight. The Gannet ECM 6s were refurbished Gannet AS4s.

From Devonport, *Ark Royal* headed initially for the Malta area to conduct flying exercises prior to her passage through the Suez Canal. It was not to be a trouble-free period for 815 Squadron, as Skinner explained: 'We were involved in a CASEX, which was an anti-submarine exercise. We were about 10 miles away from *Ark Royal*, yet the visibility was good enough to be able to see the outline of the carrier in the distance. Suddenly an awesome noise came from the rotorhead. One's first reaction was to try and make it back to the ship. The problem was that I didn't want to be flying at high speed if the engine suddenly cut out, because we would hit the sea at high speed. However, having realized that we weren't going to make it back to the ship, I decided to get rid of the back-seat men but keep hold of the co-pilot. I reduced my speed and dropped to about 20ft and told them to jump out. The co-pilot and myself continued on back towards the ship with the rotor noise increasing to an erratic roar. Alas, several minutes after ditching the back-seat crew, rotor revs could not be maintained and we subsided into the sea. The Wessex sank fairly quickly and all four of us were safely picked up. Fortunately for the squadron, such information as the crew were able to give to the technicians on return to *Ark Royal* led them to believe that this incident was a one-off case, and was not a reappearance of the problems that had led us to disembark a few months before.'

Commenting on the rescue, Woodard said, 'We shared the rescue with an 815 Squadron Wessex, picking up two survivors each. The free divers proved to be a success and saved many lives; it takes a great deal of courage to leap out of a helicopter at 15 feet with full diving gear on, knowing that there is no guarantee of recovery.'

The following day *Ark Royal* set course to head for Port Said where she arrived on 22 March. On 23 March she made her way through the Suez Canal, as Gibson recalled: 'Mr Suddenam was the Chief Pilot of the Suez Canal. There is always a difficulty with an aircraft carrier because the bridge is on the side of the ship, so we used to rig a 20ft mast up forward so the pilot on the bridge could get a fore and aft line. At one stage I thought Mr Suddenham was letting her swing too much and I took over the ship from him. He stepped back and said, "Captain I am the Chief Pilot of the Suez Canal, but if you want to take her through the Suez Canal I will go down to the Wardroom and have some coffee." So I handed the ship back to him. We had a very sensitive instrument rigged on the bridge which showed you the slightest swing that the ship took. It was actually a mistake because it was too sensitive and one was inclined to get into a panic before it was necessary. We eventually had it removed because it was giving both myself and the Navigator kittens too often.'

Ark Royal passes through the Suez Canal on 23 March. (Alan Ellis via the author)

During her voyage through the canal *Ark Royal* came under close scrutiny by a MiG from the Egyptian Air Force. Once *Ark Royal* had safely completed her passage through the Suez Canal Captain Gibson sent a signal to the Admiralty simply saying, 'POP'.

On 27 March *Ark Royal* arrived off Aden to anchor about four and a half miles offshore. Also off Aden was the smaller carrier *Centaur*, which had been waiting for *Ark Royal* to make her way through the Suez Canal so that she could begin the long voyage for home. The following day *Ark Royal* weighed anchor to begin four days of flying exercises, using Khormaksar as the diversion airfield. The warmer climate of the Far East was to present new challenges in the operation of aircraft. The Cdr (Air) at this time was Cdr A.R. Rawbone (now Rear Admiral A.R. Rawbone CB, AFC), who said of the challenges of operating aircraft east of Suez, 'The normal maximum flying days at sea in the Far East during a month was twelve days. Much of this time was spent going from A to B, yet with essential tasks to be covered we tried to get as much as we could into every flying day. The aircraft fuel weight for deck landing was fairly critical and with few diversion airfields available and many first tour pilots in our squadrons this inevitably led to some tense moments, especially during night flying. In high temperatures the Scimitar was also adversely affected by the weight of fuel to weapon-load ratio at launch, which inevitably led to reduced range or the need for inflight refuelling.' The CO of 800 Squadron at this time, Lt Cdr A. Mancais (now Cdr A. Mancais OBE), continued: 'While the Scimitars had their own refuelling capability we very rarely used it. Instead we tended to use the Sea Vixens for refuelling. For practising the nuclear role we would launch, get up to altitude, take on fuel from a Sea Vixen, and then go on to perform the strike.' The problems were not confined to the fixed-wing squadrons. Lt David Dobson (now Vice Admiral Sir David Dobson KBE) served in 815 Squadron at this time. 'We realized that the Wessex, like the fast jets, did not operate so well in hot, humid and windless conditions,' he remarked.

With the completion of the flying exercises on 31 March, *Ark Royal* headed for Penang, arriving there on 9 April to conduct further flying exercises. One of the Sea Vixen pilots in 890 Squadron at this time was Lt Richard Burn (now Rear Admiral R. Burn CB, AFC). He described what the Sea Vixen was like to fly: 'It was my first operational front-line aircraft and in those days one came to the Sea Vixen via the Vampire, Sea Hawk, and Hunter. Therefore, the Sea Vixen was much bigger than any jet one would have previously flown. It

A Scimitar of 800 Squadron lands on board *Ark Royal*. (Commander Dawson-Taylor via the author)

was also one's first multi-jet aircraft. It was less responsive but big and powerful and I was particularly impressed by its rate of climb so you could get up to altitude quite quickly. It had a big wing and turned well at altitude. Supersonically it was unimpressive. You could get it supersonic in a steep dive, but this didn't serve a great deal of operational purpose unless you were pursuing another aircraft, or trying to get away from something.' Another of 890 Squadron's pilots at this time was Lt M. Layard (now Admiral Sir Michael Layard KCB, CBE). When he described the Sea Vixen he said, 'Those who flew the Sea Vixen came to love it but it had an unpleasant reputation for killing people, largely because all our carriers were designed to fly smaller and lighter aircraft. Therefore margins for error when catapult launching and deck landing were tight, and fuel margins low especially when flying in the heat and humidity of the Far East. It was quite a demanding aircraft to land on deck, particularly at night when visual references were few and deceptive. It was heavy and it was underflapped, thus speed control at low speeds was quite difficult. For its time, however, it was quite an advanced multi-role fighter.'

Before *Ark Royal* entered Singapore for the first time the squadrons were disembarked. Once again luck was not on the side of 815 Squadron. 'On our way down the Malacca Straits on 12 April 1962, we started to transfer the squadron to Sembawang using underslung loads in cargo nets. This was the first time the nets had ever been used in anger and the worst happened – the aircraft hook failed and masses of personal belongings ended up in the sea. Trailing for hundreds of yards behind us was this stream of suitcases, kitbags and other items bobbing along in the water – already there were small native boats pushing out from the shore intent on grabbing what loot they could. Needless to say none of it was ever seen again!' recalled Lt David Dawson-Taylor (now Cdr Dawson-Taylor) who was 815 Squadron's Air Electrical Officer at this time. After thirty-four days at sea *Ark Royal* finally docked on 12 April when she entered Singapore for a self-maintenance period. Gibson recalled from his book: 'When we arrived, Rear Admiral John Frewen was on the jetty waiting for us. We had been at sea for weeks, we had come across the Indian Ocean in the monsoon, but he was not satisfied with our appearance. I was therefore greeted on my arrival with the rudest signal from a Flag Officer I have ever read.' One of the high priorities was to ensure that *Ark Royal* looked shipshape again before she sailed. 'Painting the side of the ship using scrambling nets was a common practice, as it was the only way to get at the parts of the ship under the overhang of the flight deck, until later when we could get hold of a Simon's Platform which usually could reach from the dockside to touch up parts of the ship. Even then, it could only carry two men at the most in the box, so they could only do a small part of the ship at a time, whereas you could get quite a number of sailors into the netting if you had it in the right place,' Forrest explained. After twelve days of SMP *Ark Royal* slipped her moorings, wearing the flag of Rear Admiral Frewen, to participate in Exercise Fantail which involved the aircrews flying over the Malaysian jungle in support of 3 Commando.

From Exercise Fantail *Ark Royal* sailed to the South China Sea to participate in Exercise Sea Devil. Towards the end of the exercise, while operating off Manila on the night of 1 May, Lt Burn had an accident: 'We were doing a low-level CAP at night in a joint exercise with the Americans and Australians. We were being vectored by the ship to a target, and we were about to take control of the intercept when there was a great bang, followed by things getting darker, and the aircraft not responding to the controls as it should, although we weren't being thrown about. As we were at low level there wasn't much time to take any action so we made a quick decision to eject; and after some initial difficulty my observer Don Ross did and I followed him very quickly. Prior to pulling the handle I was full of trepidation, mixed with enthusiasm to get out of the aircraft very quickly. Once I had pulled the handle there was a bang, then I was hit by the airstream, which was followed by a jolt as the parachute opened. Briefly everything was peaceful, then the whole sky lit up with a huge bank of flame close by, but not close enough to barbecue me. The next thing I knew I was in the water. I didn't know what had happened but I thought we had had a mid-air collision with another aircraft. So after we had been picked up I reported that they should continue the search for survivors because I thought we had collided with another aircraft. They eventually called off the search when the other units operating aircraft in the area confirmed that all their aircraft were accounted for. The incident went unsolved for about a year, until someone in the MOD put together some records and found out that an American unit had in fact lost a Tracker on the same day, and in the same place, but it wasn't involved in the exercise and I am certain we collided with that.'

Once the exercise had been completed *Ark Royal* sailed for Manila Bay to spend three days at anchor along with ships from the other SEATO nations which had taken part in Sea Devil. From Manila Bay, *Ark Royal* headed for the US Navy base at Subic Bay, where she arrived on 5 May to begin preparations for cross-deck operations with the American carrier *Hancock*. The two ships sailed on 9 May to begin a work up programme which was to culminate in cross-deck operations between the two carriers. These plans was dramatically affected by world events, as Forrest explained: 'We were engaged in cross-deck operations with the *Hancock* when the Laos crisis flared up. The ships had immediate orders to return to their assigned action stations. For *Ark Royal* that meant sailing for Hong Kong, whereas we had been due to sail for Japan. The aircraft returned with some degree of excitement because both ships were on opposite courses and getting further apart.'

On 17 May *Ark Royal* made her first visit to the British colony of Hong Kong when she anchored off Green Island. During the visit the insufficient size of the anchors became apparent, as Gibson explained in his book, 'I was coming off from shore one night, and thought that the ship did not look quite in the right place. The Navigator and I found that we had dragged quite a bit, so we raised steam in about an hour and anchored her again in the right place with more cable. I remember going ahead very slowly, with the boats still on the booms, and the ladders down.'

A Wessex from 815 Squadron flies over Manila Bay with the American carrier *Bennington* and the Australian carrier *Melbourne* anchored. (Captain Skinner via the author)

Jenny's Side party attend to the mighty
Ark Royal in Hong Kong. (Alan Ellis
via the author)

The nine-day visit was far from a holiday for the ship's company because the visit was used as a SMP while the British Government watched the unfolding events in Laos. 815 Squadron also had work to do as Dobson recalled: 'After a bad harvest and famine in China there was a daily surge of refugees across the border into the New Territories. 815 Squadron was therefore tasked to patrol the border, with a police inspector embarked, to spot the infiltrators and direct foot patrols to round them up. I found it a sad experience, hunting down these unfortunate people, but at least they all received a good meal before being sent back across the border.' Eventually it was decided that *Ark Royal* would not be needed off Laos so she was able to resume a modified programme.

Intensive flying exercises were held in the five days after *Ark Royal* sailed from Hong Kong on 26 May. Describing the launching of a Sea Vixen, Layard said, 'Briefing would start an hour and half before take off. Punctuality was of the essence because the whole carrier cycle was based upon accurate timing. As you walked onto the flight deck the first impressions were of an amazing amount of activity with people in different coloured surcoats bustling everywhere. Often there would be a very strong wind over the deck, although if the carrier was not either launching or recovering aircraft, she would be heading down wind, so it would be

A Sea Vixen of 890 Squadron lands on board *Ark Royal*. (Rear Admiral Burn via the author)

relatively calm on deck. The fumes of the funnel had an uncanny ability to douse one in the most evil-smelling sulphurous smoke. You would walk down to the stern where your aircraft was parked, inspect it and get the Pilot's Mate to help you strap in and remove your ejector seat safety pins.

'You would start up your engines at the set time, hoping that you had no snags, and then wait for the signal to be marshalled out by the yellow coated director. At the appropriate time he would signal "It's your turn", and you would taxi out, lowering your wings and locking them. By this time the deck would probably be beginning to move about a bit as the ship turned into wind, so you could be taxiing out uphill one minute and downhill the next. Pinpoint accuracy was required when taxiing on deck and the director's commands were mandatory. The catapults were fitted with CALE gear which was self-aligning so that if you taxied up off line, it would line you up using a series of inward turning rollers. As you looked over the side there would be feverish activity as the "badgers" came in and you knew you were being hooked up to the hold-back and catapult shuttle. Eventually, you would see the Flight Deck Officer signal them away and you knew that your aircraft was tethered to the ship by two bits of wire. You would look for the signal from flyco: green, yellow and red lights. A flashing green light meant ready to launch. The Flight Deck Officer would look at you, and raise his green flag to signal you to bring your engines to half and eventually full power. Of course we couldn't do this too soon because there were men working below the aircraft, and some had occasionally been sucked into aircraft engines. Once at full power you would look round the cockpit and check all of your instruments and that you were getting fuel transferred from the two drop tanks. If you weren't it was critical, because if you were launched with one drop tank not transferring, you would have to land back on with one full tank. This not only gave asymmetric problems but reduced fuel reserves.

'Having completed the final checks you would signal that you were ready to launch with a raised hand. The Flight Deck Officer would nod acknowledgement, then look along the deck ahead of the ship, and if happy, would then drop his flag, by which time you would have put your head against the rest, held the stick firmly, and locked your hand on the two throttles. After two seconds, off you went with an amazing shove in the back as you travelled from 0 to 150 mph in the space of 150 feet. As you left the deck you would experience a slight feeling of sinking, although you were still accelerating. Once airborne, you would jink sideways to clear your jet wash from the next aircraft to launch, then join up with the rest of your division before setting off for your mission.'

Once airborne the aircrew would be practising one of the Sea Vixen's roles during the forthcoming flying exercise. Discussing the various roles of the Sea Vixen, Layard said, 'The primary role of the Sea Vixen was air defence but the Sea Vixen also had a number of other roles, including dropping tactical nuclear weapons, photo reconnaissance, and ground attack. For the nuclear role, there would be a nucleus of four aircrews who would be assigned to the role, and every so often they would be detailed to fly a sortie with a dummy bomb which would culminate in a lofting manoeuvre. On nuclear missions, the designated Sea Vixen would be given fighter cover for as long as it was considered safe to do so, then the aircraft would have to complete their missions flying very low to avoid radar contact. When weapon ranges were not available, training for the ground attack role would involve attacking the splash target towed astern of the ship, using rockets, guns, or bombs.'

When the sortie had been completed it was of course time to land back on board *Ark Royal*. Describing the recovery in a Sea Vixen, Layard recalled: 'About a quarter of an hour before "Charlie Time" the returning aircraft would come down to the "low wait" which was a circle off the port quarter of the ship when she was into wind. You would then orbit in groups of four. Eventually, it was time to run in and break into the "slot", aiming for a forty-five second interval between aircraft landing. When working well, the ship would be rolling out of the turn into wind just as the first aircraft was rolling out on finals to land. As one turned into finals and checked "four greens" (three wheels and hook locked down), the carrier looked the size of a postage stamp. On final approach to the deck, speed, line up and glide path angle were crucial, but sometimes complicated by the ship not only pitching and corkscrewing but also pushing out obscuring fumes from the funnel. A down-draught from a vortex generated by the flight deck angle, could also cause a sink over the round down. Add to all this, landing into a low sun with a salt-caked windscreen – all conspired to make deck landing a most challenging task and not one for the faint hearted.

'At night aircraft would invariably land using a carrier-controlled radar approach for recovery in conditions of low cloud and poor visibility. Launching and landing on a black night brought a new range of challenges and not a little fright factor. The target arrester wire was number three out of the four, and as the aircraft hit the deck and hopefully caught a wire with its hook, there was an immediate violent retardation which threw one hard against one's straps. Hook and flaps were selected up as one came to a halt and, with wings folding, a great burst of power from the engines got the aircraft clear of the landing area. Then, under the meticulous instructions of the flight deck director, one taxied gingerly up into the crowded parking area in the bows of the ship, as the next aircraft landed.'

On 1 June *Ark Royal* returned to Hong Kong for four days before sailing for Okinawa. Because her planned visit to Japan had been cancelled, thanks to the Laos crisis, she ended up spending most of June operating in the Okinawa area, including Exercise Rawfish. Prior to the exercise, 800 Squadron successfully completed Bullpup firings on Torishima range. Describing what the Scimitar was like to fly, Mancais remarked: 'It was a superb aircraft for handling. It had the best controls of an aircraft that I have flown, including a Hunter. It was nicely balanced and very good at reaching altitude quickly. It was originally built as a high altitude interceptor, but it was useless at high altitude because it had very thick wings, but at low level it came into its own as a fighter bomber. It was a very sturdy aircraft. The Americans couldn't believe that with 22,000lb of thrust we couldn't go supersonic straight and level.'

A Scimitar of 800 Squadron firing a Bullpup. (Lieutenant Commander Martins)

The various canvas chutes strung across the lift well during a RAS for getting the stores away from the flight deck as fast as possible so that flying could quickly resume. (Commander Dawson-Taylor)

Discussing the challenges of keeping the Scimitars airborne during a hectic exercise period, Wally Harwood, who was an Aircraft Artificer in 800 Squadron said, 'Invariably, at the aft end of the lower hangar there would be an aircraft on minor inspection and the components would have to be taken out for inspection so it would be robbed for parts to keep the other aircraft airworthy and, when the next one was due for inspection, you would "rob Peter to pay Paul" to get the first aircraft flying again, and the next one would become "the Hangar Queen" to keep the rest of the squadron flying until we had another RAS to pick up more spares.'

At the end of June *Ark Royal* arrived in Singapore for fourteen days of SMP. On 10 July Rear Admiral Hopkins hoisted his flag in *Ark Royal* for the first time as FOAC. Later that day *Ark Royal* sailed from Hong Kong for further flying exercises prior to Exercise Fotex 62, which was held between 24 and 26 July. The two-day exercise was conducted off the east coast of Malaya before the ship returned to Singapore for another SMP to prepare for the shop window Exercise Showboat.

The purpose of Showboat was to demonstrate to VIPs from both Malaya and Singapore the capabilities of the British warships of the RN's Far East Fleet. The day's demonstration was carried out in the South China Sea exercise area before the ship anchored overnight in Singapore Roads. The following morning the ship set sail for Australia. On 11 August light relief came in the form of the crossing the line ceremony, when King Neptune made his first visit to *Ark Royal*. To celebrate *Ark Royal*'s first voyage into the Southern Hemisphere Captain Gibson was awarded the Most Noble Order of the Flying Kipper, First Class!

As *Ark Royal* approached the Australian coast a small number of aircraft from 800 Squadron and 890 Squadron had to undertake some evaluation work, as Monsell recalled: 'Jock Mancais and myself each had to disembark

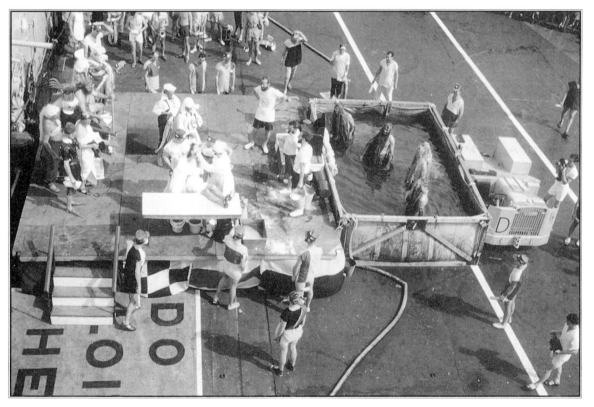

Crossing the line ceremony, 11 August 1962. (Commander Dawson-Taylor)

six aircraft because at that time there were some discussions of having a base in Western Australia. The objective of our disembarkation was to see if there were any problems operating from Western Australia. We got permission to perform a flypast when we arrived, and we asked if there were any sensitive areas not to fly over. We were told not to fly over two race courses because there were two different race meetings. The Australians didn't seemed worried about bothering people but they were worried about their race horses!'

On 19 August *Ark Royal* entered Freemantle to begin an eleven-day visit. While the passage up Plymouth Sound has always been regarded as a tortuous exercise by her Captains, the entry into Freemantle required just as much skill and care because she only had 2ft of water below her keel. During her visit, *Ark Royal* was opened to the public on a number of days, with 7,000 people visiting on one day alone. The hospitality of the Australians was so warm that thirty-three of the ship's company did not manage to get back on board in time before the ship sailed. Despite their momentary absent-mindedness they were not spared the voyage through the rough seas off Australia, as Harwood recalled: 'The sea off Freemantle has got a very long swell. If you were down below in *Ark Royal* you felt very little movement, yet if you went up on deck you could see the bow moving up and down, though it was a slow movement. The sailors who had failed to re-join *Ark Royal* before she sailed from Freemantle were subsequently rounded up and brought back to *Ark Royal* on a smaller RFA. We reckoned their punishment was the trip back to *Ark Royal* because the RFA was much smaller so they had had a very rough trip back and were as sick as dogs!'

On the passage from Freemantle to Singapore at the beginning of September 1962, Monsell remembered the heavy swell created a few problems for the aircrew: 'We had a terrific corkscrewing deck which was usable by day but, when we tried landing on at night, the process became exciting after a Gannet landed on the port mirror. We then had to land using the starboard mirror, which we hadn't used up until that time. It was only after that incident that we decided that we had better land using the starboard mirror one day a week, because it was a shock to have to land looking the other way, especially when the deck was moving the way it was, but we managed to recover everyone safely!'

After the encounter with rough seas on the voyage back from Freemantle *Ark Royal* finally docked for two weeks of SMP in Singapore on 14 September. During the period alongside, the first anniversary of the ship's recommissioning was marked by a service conducted on the flight deck by the Chaplain of the Fleet. On 28 September *Ark Royal* once more headed out to sea towards the exercise areas off Singapore to participate in the two-day Exercise Pintail. Following the successful conclusion of Pintail, *Ark Royal* set sail for a week's visit to Hong Kong between 5 and 12 October. During the voyage to Hong Kong, it looked at one stage as though the plans might have to be changed because of the effects of typhoon Dinah. In the end the only effect the typhoon had on the ship's programme was the cancellation of night flying on the night of 3 October due to the heavy seas which had been whipped up by the typhoon in the distance.

When *Ark Royal* left Hong Kong she conducted a number of flying exercises on her way back to Singapore. The Lt Cdr (Flying) at this time was Lt Cdr Peter Wreford. Describing his role Wreford explained: 'Little F is responsible to Wings (Cdr (Air)) for the operation of the aircraft within the close proximity of the ship. I would start the day by speaking to the met office to find out what the weather forecast was. The most important factor in planning the day's flying would be what the wind speed over the deck was going to be, because this determined the launch weight of the aircraft. Once I had seen the forecast I would work out what weight could be launched for that day. After breakfast I would go to flyco to check that the deck was as it should be, and talk to the men on the compass platform to discuss what wind speed I would need over the deck. Most of my day would be spent in flyco. When the conditions were right, i.e. when the ship was head into wind, I would launch the aircraft by putting on the green light. The Flight Deck Officer would then do the physical function of launching the aircraft. During this time I would be talking to the aircraft on the deck, but once they were clear of the ship they would talk to the flight direction department or the ops room. The launching would probably be organized into a leapfrog programme, which means that once the first batch of aircraft have been launched, the flight deck is then prepared for the next batch to be launched. At the same time anti-submarine operations took place. Between launches I might review the launching weight figures, because after the first launch I would know what the actual wind over deck was, rather than the original projected figures. In the event of an emergency landing, a message would come up from the ops room to flyco and I would signal to the Flight Deck Officer to clear the deck and prepare for an emergency landing.'

The amount of flying during this period was limited by the starboard catapult becoming unserviceable. The problems with the catapult were serious enough to need dockyard repair so the faulty steam pipe was disembarked to Singapore when the ship anchored off Singapore on her way to participate in her next exercise. On 17 and 18 October *Ark Royal* participated in Exercise Fantail Two which was an Army support exercise. The hot conditions of the Far East made living conditions for many of the ship's company very difficult, as Forrest remarked: 'There were sailors living on 6 deck, which was mostly bathrooms and the like, but there were one or two messes which were very hot in the tropics and the ventilation wasn't good. They must have been extremely uncomfortable for the people and I was very pleased with the way in which morale was kept up. This was partly because every effort was made to get people up on deck for fresh air during the dog watches and occasions like that.'

Despite the many challenges posed by the harsh operating conditions in the Far East, the ship's company still maintained the special spirit which had been built up during the previous commissions, as Forrest explained: 'The belief I had before joining *Ark Royal* certainly from the time I was first told of my appointment, which was about eight months previously, was that, for all the difficulties and problems inherent in a ship like that, the *Ark Royal* had a particularly good spirit which was what the Navy would call a happy ship; however, it doesn't mean that she didn't have accidents, problems or times of some stress, but this rather unknown quantity of a happy ship went a long way to overcome those things when they did happen. I heard the same thing said of her after I had left, as though nothing could come along which would break that feeling of a happy ship.'

Following the completion of the exercise, *Ark Royal* once more returned to Singapore on 19 October for a six-day stay which had been lengthened because of the decision to embark the men and equipment of the 11th Sphinx Battery of the 34th LAA Regiment Royal Artillery for the voyage to Aden. When the ship sailed from Singapore on 25 October she looked more like a commando carrier with her decks filled with various trucks and other equipment. Needless to say there was no fixed-wing flying during the voyage to Aden. The routine nature of the voyage to Aden was shattered on the morning of 30 October when the ship increased speed and the aircrews of 815 were summoned to a briefing. The reason for the change in pace was the receipt of a message from the French MV *Donai*. She was 75 miles from *Ark Royal* and reported that she had an engine room fire. The first Wessex was launched but later recalled when the *Donai* reported the fire was under control. Half an hour later the *Donai* reported that the fire had spread to the air intake of the engine, so two Wessexes were launched to deal with the fire. The fire was soon brought under control and *Ark Royal* was able to continue her voyage to Aden, arriving there on 1 November. The Army were quickly disembarked so that the ship could once more conduct fixed-wing flying, which she did between 5 and 9 November in the Aden area. On 13 November *Ark Royal* sailed to take part in Exercise Hollow Laugh and Exercise Longshot. The purpose of *Ark Royal*'s participation was to support amphibious landings made by the Royal Marines.

On completion of the exercises *Ark Royal* sailed for Mombasa, arriving there on 22 November to begin a four-day visit. From Mombasa *Ark Royal* began the long-awaited voyage back to Devonport. During the voyage to

Men and equipment from the 11th Sphinx Battery of 34 LAA Royal Artillery on board *Ark Royal* for the trip from Singapore to Aden at the end of October 1962. (Commander Dawson-Taylor)

Suez 815 Squadron made history when a Wessex, crewed by Lt Sirett, Lt Brown, Lt Palmer and Petty Officer Barker, performed the first night rescue by a RN helicopter embarked in a carrier. They rescued Lt Dobbie, the pilot of a ditched Sea Vixen from 890 Squadron. His observer was recovered by a sea boat from the frigate *Rothesay*. The Sea Vixen crashed in the Gulf of Aden because of a complete electrical and instrument failure. On 4 December *Ark Royal* was relieved by *Hermes* so she could finally pass through the Suez Canal and make for Plymouth, where she arrived at Charlie buoy on 15 December. However, due to bad weather the final passage up the Sound to secure alongside was delayed by three days. When *Ark Royal* did eventually sail into Devonport it was a historic occasion because she was accompanied by the commando carrier *Bulwark*, thus making it the first time that two major warships had entered Devonport on the same tide. Once alongside the ship's company were given a well-earned Christmas leave.

The new year brought an unexpected early change of command when Captain Gibson handed over command of *Ark Royal* to Captain M.P. Pollock MVO, DSC (now Admiral of the Fleet Sir Michael Pollock GCB, LVO, DSC) on 23 January 1963. Discussing the status of *Ark Royal* when he assumed command, Pollock said, 'The ship had been run very hard. She was supposed to be settling down to a home sea commission, which meant that she would return regularly to her home port of Plymouth where she would have had extensive dockyard help whenever in harbour and her operating cycle would have been a few NATO exercises and perhaps a trip to New York – a vastly reduced mileage compared with the first leg of the commission, and in weather conditions much less demanding on both men and machinery. But it was not to be. I took her over in January in one of the

A Wessex from 815 Squadron hovers over the
Donai. (Commander Dawson-Taylor
via the author)

coldest winters we had had for fifty years. I had originally been due to command the cruiser HMS *Lion*, and had in fact just finished my tactical course during which I had been given command of *Lion* and her supporting squadrons. However, the Deputy Chief of the Naval Staff had to be relieved at short notice due to illness, so Frank Hopkins became the new Deputy Chief of the Naval Staff, Donald Gibson relieved him as FOAC, and I became the new Captain of *Ark Royal*. It was a tremendous appointment to be given command of the largest and perhaps the most prestigious ship in the Royal Navy and a great personal challenge to me as a non-aviator.'

Explaining why a large number of the senior jobs in the Navy at that time were held by Gunnery Officers, Pollock said, 'The pre-war Navy was built around the big gun ship. The prestigious job as a young officer tended to be a Gunnery Officer because you were the man who ran the gun which was the reason for having the ship there. That meant that a large proportion of high-grade officers went into the Gunnery Branch. By the sixties and seventies those who had done so in the thirties and forties were, in the normal course of a successful career, coming up to the top levels of command in the Service. From 1968 to 1974 there were four First Sea Lords in succession who had been Gunnery specialists twenty or thirty years before. There was nothing sinister or preferential about this, and since then the other sub-specializations have predominated in their turn.'

On 4 February Captain Pollock took *Ark Royal* to sea for the first time as the ship performed the role of trials carrier for the next ten days. Before the first Buccaneer from C Squadron, Boscombe Down arrived on 5 February, a Sea Vixen from 899 Squadron and a Gannet from 849 Squadron embarked for wire-pulling trials. Two days later perhaps one of the most significant events in the course of the postwar FAA happened. On 7 February 1963 the Hawker P1127 VSTOL aircraft, piloted by Hawker's Chief Test Pilot Bill Bedford, made its first landing on an aircraft carrier. Explaining why *Ark Royal* was chosen as the first aircraft carrier to embark the P1127 for trials, Pollock said, '*Ark Royal* was chosen as the carrier for the P1127 trials because we happened to be the one running carrier in home waters. I had to take *Ark Royal* within the 10 fathom line, which isn't a thing you do lightly with a carrier which draws 6 fathoms if you have got to do any flying. Bill Bedford was going to fly from his home base, but then they found the experimental aircraft couldn't carry enough fuel to get from his home base to the ship, so they flew the P1127 down to Exeter and pulled me in as close as was sensible to make quite sure that Bill didn't run out of fuel before he got to us!'

A historic day! The first landing of a VSTOL aircraft at sea took place on 7 February 1963 when Bill Bedford brought the P1127 on board *Ark Royal*. (British Aerospace plc. (Dunsfold))

Describing the preparations for the P1127 trials, Rawbone recalled: 'We did what we were asked to do. A team of scientists were embarked and Bill Bedford wanted wind speed readings with an accuracy of less than 1 knot. Our instruments weren't that accurate, being nearer 2 knots accuracy. However, we were used to our operating criteria, and despite some initial scientist concern the whole trial ran smoothly to schedule. Although we had never operated the P1127 before, it was incredible to see a fixed-wing aircraft fly backwards down the flight deck and a gift from heaven to have an aircraft which hovered in and landed, as opposed to our normal embarked aircraft which came roaring in to catch a wire.'

Talking about the P1127 trials Forrest said, 'When the P1127 performed the first fixed-wing vertical landing and take-off from *Ark Royal* it was quite fascinating because none of us had ever seen it before. We knew the theory and had seen the helicopters come and go all the time, but to see this aircraft looking like one of the Buccaneers when it first appeared in sight and see it come closer to the ship then flying up the flight deck and stopping opposite the island and landing on the deck was quite wonderful.'

Despite the weather most of the trials were successfully completed and the aircraft were disembarked prior to *Ark Royal* entering Portsmouth on 15 February. This was to be a momentous visit for the ship's company because while the ship was alongside, the first news that *Ark Royal* was due to head out to the Far East again was announced, as Pollock explained: 'This trial period was a gentle run in for me, after which we were to embark the new Buccaneer squadron and the rest of the squadrons for a normal "Home Leg" year. In fact the ship was due to enter refit in November 1963. We came back from this first outing to find a signal from the Admiralty saying that one of the other carriers had been delayed, and we had to go to the Far East for a second leg to preserve the policy of two carriers east of Suez.

'When I say two carriers east of Suez, I mean two carriers east of Suez. The homeward-bound carrier was not allowed through the canal until the eastbound ship had transited south, thereby avoiding the risk that the Egyptian-controlled canal might suddenly be closed to foreign military traffic and the country be left with a gap in the presence of a vital strategic asset in the Cold War, which would have cast doubts on the Navy's fervent case being made for replacement carriers.

'This was a tremendous blow to the ship's company. They had been driven very hard in an old ship without air conditioning and even more, the machinery had been driven to the limit the whole time. The signal from the Admiralty was accompanied by other signals from FOAC saying, "Did I want him to come down and explain this to the ship's company? Could I manage?" I replied that as Captain of the ship this was my business, so I talked to the ship's company. I happened to be going down to the Wardroom that night because they had invited me down for a rare occasion when their wives could come on board. I was nearly torn in pieces by the wives! The Admiralty did what they could for us to soften the blow, but sent us out to Gibraltar because that was the only dock that could take us for a month's refit before we went out East. A month might sound a lot, but it isn't when you've got a ship over 50,000 tons, full of complicated gear which has got to be taken out before you can mend it. On top of this the Admiralty had to give each watch fourteen days leave during that period, which meant that we weren't able to do all the self-maintenance work we would normally have done. We landed the squadrons and I took my motor caravan on board into the empty hangars and we sailed out to Gibraltar. Gibraltar Dockyard did what they could for us, but it was much more in the nature of an assisted-maintenance period than anything like a refit. The ship's company flew back to the UK and my wife and I drove back across Spain in the motor caravan and had a week at home before flying back to join the ship.'

While the news that *Ark Royal* was going to the Far East was supposed to be secret until it was announced, it seemed as though the head Chinese laundryman had an insight into what was going to be in store. 'Now the odd thing was this. About 14:00 on the Monday there appeared the head Chinese laundryman and tailor who, with his teams, we of course had had to leave behind when we came home. "What on earth are you doing here, Lau?" I asked. Lau smiled enigmatically and said, "I just thought you might be needing me." I patiently explained that we were going to be west of Suez for the rest of the year and so we were not allowed to employ him. He persisted with his wish to see the Captain, but I persuaded him to make a start with the Commander; and of course on the Tuesday the Admiralty enabled us to engage Lau again. The mysterious thing is that he must have left Hong Kong before the Chequers weekend; so what access did he have to secret intelligence to persuade him to risk several hundred pounds of his own money on the air fare?', asked Richardson-Bunbury, who as Lt Cdr Michael Richardson-Bunbury was the Captain's secretary at this time.

Discussing the impact of the announcement, Richardson-Bunbury continued: 'Though Lau was happy, many of the ship's company were not. The thought of another nine months of incessant work in torrid heat, with very little fun, was depressing; and of course our wives were distinctly disenchanted at the thought of another nine months separation. Nearly three months after we had been told of the decision, Captain Pollock was holding Captain's Requestmen on the upper bridge as we transited the Suez Canal. Among the Requestmen were two Chief Petty Officers, for presentation with the Long Service and Good Conduct Medal. Captain Pollock liked to talk with Requestmen and when these two big, burly senior ratings appeared in front of him, he asked them how their wives felt about our returning east of Suez. The first Chief said that his wife was pretty choked, but accepted that it couldn't be helped. The Captain then turned to the second Chief who, great hunk of man though he was, replied simply, "I haven't dared tell her yet".'

Before *Ark Royal* sailed to Gibraltar for her refit, there was still a short work up to be completed, followed by Exercise Dawn Breeze. On the afternoon of Tuesday 19 February 1963 Buccaneers were embarked at sea for the first time in squadron service when the Buccaneer S1 of 801 Squadron CO, Lt Cdr E.R. Anson (now Vice Admiral Sir Edward Anson KCB) touched down on *Ark Royal*'s flight deck and was brought to an abrupt halt by an arrester wire. Talking about the Buccaneer, Anson said, 'Many people referred to the Buccaneer S1 as being underpowered, but if you flew a Sea Hawk with six 60lb rockets on board it accelerated slower than a Buccaneer. Therefore, the Buccaneer in that context did not feel underpowered. However, in between the Sea Hawk and the Buccaneer, the Sea Vixen and Scimitar with 20,000lb of thrust were introduced into service, so when you were launched off the catapult it felt very fast indeed. To then revert from the Scimitar to a Buccaneer, which was the same weight with only 12,000lb of thrust, the Buccaneer felt very slow. At sea level it went about as fast as a Scimitar and the visibility was very good. It had tremendous redundancy which meant if something failed there was a back-up unit.'

The Buccaneers were very distinctive on deck, thanks to the overall white colour scheme. Explaining why the Buccaneers were painted white, Anson remarked: 'The Buccaneers were painted white because of their nuclear

Three Buccaneer S1s from 801 Squadron in Fly 1. (British Aerospace plc. (Brough Heritage Centre))

capability. The boffins thought that if the aircraft were painted in a dark colour, the skin of the aircraft would overheat following the intense flash of a nuclear explosion. It was later decided that this would not be a problem, which was just as well because we did not like having white aircraft flying over the sea that could be seen from a long distance with the naked eye. The aircraft therefore reverted in due course to standard naval colours which could not be seen so easily.'

The Buccaneers' stay in *Ark Royal* was short-lived, because the aircraft had not at that point been cleared for weaponry and thus had to be replaced by the Scimitar squadron which had just returned from embarkation during the first leg of the commission. The Buccaneers' operations were also limited by the fact that there wasn't an arrester barrier capable of stopping a Buccaneer above its normal blown landing speed. This meant that they couldn't be flown when *Ark Royal* was out of range from a diversion airfield and this limited the Buccaneers' participation during Exercise Dawn Breeze held at the beginning of March. On completion of the exercise *Ark Royal* entered Devonport on 16 March. While alongside, the first leave party left the ship to begin their three weeks of leave, then on 19 March *Ark Royal* sailed from Devonport for Gibraltar to begin her short refit. Describing her docking on 22 March in No. 1 Dry Dock, Pollock said, 'There was so little clearance between the sides of the ship and the docksides, that the warping capstans could not haul her ahead into place and I had to force her in with the engines until she almost touched the head of the dock. Effectively our screws were pumping enough water out of the dock to make room for the huge hull to fit in! A hundred tons of mackerel came in with us and, in disposing of them, we ruined the local fish sales for a week!'

By 3 May the short refit had come to an end, as *Ark Royal* set sail from Gibraltar bound for the Far East. Shortly after her departure, a brief commemoration service was held over the site of the wreck of *Ark Royal III*. A Gannet flew overhead and dipped its wings in salute but no wreath was dropped. The squadrons were embarked the following day. Captain Pollock spent the next few days prior to the transit through the Suez Canal getting used to how *Ark Royal* handled, including an exercise with the new County class destroyer *Devonshire* which was working up in the Mediterranean following her commissioning. 'By the time we went through the

Workmen inspect *Ark Royal*'s rudders in dry dock. Note the large numbers of fish left in the dock after the shoal of mackerel came in with the ship. (Admiral of the Fleet Sir Michael Pollock via the author)

Ark Royal exercises with the newly commissioned *Devonshire* in the Mediterranean on 7 May 1963. (Admiral of the Fleet Sir Michael Pollock via the author)

Suez Canal I was satisfied that I had found out enough about her handling to do so safely – and indeed, in open water, she handled beautifully. Problems arose in the shallow water, in which we quite often had to operate, as her draught of 36 feet left little space between the keel and the bottom and there was nowhere for the water to escape when, for instance, coming alongside a jetty in Singapore; one of the many reasons why the Americans never at that time brought any of their, much bigger, carriers alongside. By the time that I had had her for a year and done a great deal of running, I really thought I understood her, but if I ever presumed upon this she would think up some new trick to tease me; it was very stimulating and a wonderful experience,' Pollock recalled.

Ark Royal anchored in Port Said Roads in the evening of 9 May prior to beginning her third passage through the Suez Canal the following day. Once she was through the canal *Ark Royal* once more relieved *Centaur* to take up station as the second carrier east of Suez. While there Captain Pollock was constantly walking the tightrope between meeting the operational requirements of ensuring *Ark Royal* was on station in the right place at the right time, and the need to maintain the number of flying hours required to keep the aircrews qualified to fly without a diversion airfield – few and far apart in the Indian Ocean. 'The idea was to keep one carrier off the East African coast and one off Indonesia but it never worked out like that. You always ended up wanting the carrier which had just gone through the Suez Canal in Indonesia, and then something flared up on the East African coast so what invariably happened was that the carrier that was supposed to be looking after Indonesia had to sail across the Indian Ocean, which is a long way! All this meant high-speed steaming, often with the wind in the wrong direction. So you couldn't get in your flying practice as you went across, which of course was very serious because one was struggling to get in the minimum number of flying hours which makes the pilot safe enough onto the deck and to remain night qualified. If you didn't get in those flying hours your flying was severely restricted and you couldn't do it out of range of a diversion airfield. Which in the middle of the Indian Ocean was extremely serious. So one was constantly trying to keep up flying hours, in spite of breakdowns in the ship and fast passages which meant that it was difficult to find the time for turning into wind for the launching or recovery of aircraft. All of this was very hard on the machinery and the men who looked after it,' Pollock explained.

On 2 June *Ark Royal* began her passage to Mombasa where she arrived on 7 June. 'We went into Mombasa for a short SMP. The trouble with self-maintenance out there, was that you were supposed to have a maintenance

The newly created 'Baron RAS' (Captain Pollock) discusses the finer
points of film-making with Commander Rawbone during the
crossing the line ceremony on 2 July 1963. (Admiral of the Fleet
Sir Michael Pollock via the author)

party join the ship so that you could give your own ship's company some relaxation. If we had been in home
waters we would have had a party of about fifty skilled ratings join the ship for the SMP. As we were running on
a diluted complement the whole maintenance problem of the ship became very serious without this help,'
Pollock recalled. During *Ark Royal*'s stay in Mombasa some of the more adventurous members of the ship's
company decided to attempt to scale Mount Kilimanjaro, while others settled for a safari. When *Ark Royal* sailed
from Mombasa she was bound for her Far East home port of Singapore. On 2 July King Neptune made his
second visit to *Ark Royal* for the traditional crossing the line ceremony. During the ceremony Captain Pollock
was created Baron RAS. Pollock explained the background of his special award bestowed upon him by the ship's
company: 'Operationally it is vital that you keep the period needed for a RAS down to a minimum, because you
can't fly while you are doing it and therefore under operational conditions you are useless. Therefore I used to
try and do it as quickly as we could, and I devised a method of coming up alongside, which brought us up fast,
and stopped us fairly quickly. It obviously impressed the ship's company enough so that when the crossing the
line ceremony was held they gave me a special award for my "flying RAS". They gave me my set of wings
because I wasn't an aviator and they thought I had better have them!'

With the festivities over, *Ark Royal* had one more task to complete when she faced an Operational Readiness
Inspection (ORI) on 6 July before entering the dockyard in Singapore on 11 July for a two-week visit. She then
sailed for Exercise Fotex 63 on 25 July. Describing the living conditions on board during *Ark Royal*'s second spell
of duty east of Suez, Pollock said, 'It was so hot on board we were fitted with a number of portable air-

conditioning units, but in the main these were used to keep cool those pieces of equipment which would not work if they were allowed to get too hot. To benefit from these, anyone who had access to one of these compartments went and lived there! The engine room temperature was routinely well over 100–110 degrees. The evaporator rooms, the auxiliary machinery rooms, the lower mess decks and the hangar decks had very high temperature and humidity and no air-conditioning. This was endured by people who had already served one spell of these conditions, and they were being asked to continue working beyond the call of duty without any amelioration. The ship wasn't designed for that sort of weather and in addition you couldn't have driven her any harder. She was being driven as many miles, with as many flying hours, as you would have achieved in wartime, which is what caused this running battle against a very high proportion of defects. It didn't cause the ship to cease to be an effective unit very often, but what it did do was to place an enormous burden on her ship's company.'

On 30 July 1963 the Minister for Defence announced that Britain was going to build a new aircraft carrier, CVA-01. The new 50,000 ton ship would enter service in the 1970s and operate the Hawker P1154 which was designed to replace both the RN's Sea Vixen and the RAF's Hunters. Significantly, she would replace both the *Victorious* which had emerged just five years previously from a complete eight-year reconstruction, and the *Ark Royal* which had only been in commission for eight years. The older *Eagle* was to be retained because she was about to emerge from an extensive four-year modernization in Devonport.

August 1963 was split between periods alongside in Singapore and exercising off Singapore. Grant Eustace joined *Ark Royal* as a Midshipman in Singapore on Saturday 17 August 1963. He recalled: 'By then the Gunroom had disappeared from *Ark Royal*, so the Midshipmen had the cabins right aft on the starboard side underneath the flight deck. We had a training programme which was a cross between education, and skills that included running boats, engineering, navigation, watchkeeping, and learning all the ins and outs of the aviation department. When we started our six weeks of engineering training on 26 August we were given a pep talk by the Cdr (E), Cdr J. Wigg who said, "You may think that this engineering training is for the purpose of teaching you nuts and bolts. Whatever you were told this is not so. You are with us to learn our limitations, our troubles and our working conditions so that in years to come you might not think quite so harshly of us when something goes wrong."'

On 29 August 815 Squadron repeated their success of the previous year when one of their Wessex helicopters piloted by the CO, Lt Cdr Kelly recovered both Lt Dunbar-Dempsey and Sub Lt Hart in darkness. The two had ejected from their Sea Vixen after both engines had failed. They had landed fifty yards apart and established a beach camp. By the time the Wessex arrived, they had already eaten their supper of sweets and water and had blown up their dinghies to use as mattresses for the night. 'There appeared to be some reluctance on their part to return with their rescuers to the hot and uncomfortable home base!' Pollock remarked.

On 2 September *Ark Royal* began her passage to Hong Kong. Describing the voyage, Pollock said, 'We had been driving her very hard since the Gibraltar maintenance period and we hadn't had any assisted maintenance since then. A lot of things were beginning to cause us trouble, particularly the distilling plants. Our passage up to Hong Kong, when we were supposed to have been flying intensively, was completely wasted, because we hadn't got enough distilled water to produce the steam to work the catapult, which for every launch expended 1 ton of the precious liquid in the form of steam.'

From Hong Kong, *Ark Royal* sailed for Singapore and participated in Exercise Dovetail between 17 and 19 September, before arriving in Singapore the following day. After three days alongside, she sailed for two days of flying exercises before beginning her voyage to the Gulf of Oman on 27 September. 'At lunchtime on Saturday 5 October 1963 *Ark Royal* anchored off Khor al Fakkan, which is a little village in Oman, for two days rest and relaxation. It was the Arabian equivalent of a one-horse town, with only a few dhows to its credit. It was somewhat of a problem for the Navigator because it was only the second time since the end of the Second World War that a British warship had been there, so information about the anchorage was scarce. The chief activity of those who went ashore was swimming. It was only marred by the necessity to keep the men in less than four feet of water for fear of meeting sharks or barracuda or other anti-social fish. To enforce this, boats were run along the five foot line and people were kept inside it to try and keep the unfriendly fish out,' Eustace recalled.

Ark Royal left the Gulf on 12 October 1963 bound for Mombasa, arriving there on 18 October. During her stopover in Mombasa the ship received an unusual request for help from the Tsavo Game Park who were trying to save the rare breed of antelope, the Hunter's Hartebeest, from extinction. Wreford recalled the background to Operation Antelope, and the operation itself: 'The request came to the ship from the British Consul. They had previously tried to move the antelopes by road but there was an unacceptably high mortality rate, so they had tried to move them by RAF Pioneer aircraft and that had not worked. The Captain eventually got clearance from the Admiralty to help during the SMP at Mombasa. The SMP was going to take some time and therefore we could be spared. I knew it would be necessary to visit the area and establish a helicopter operating site. The ship's AEO and myself volunteered for this task. We drove up there with the ship's photographer, having already had a meeting with the District Commissioner, a biologist who was looking at their feeding requirements, and a hunter who would round up the antelopes. While we were driving up there the Admiralty had already granted permission to strip out the ASW equipment of two of 815's Wessex helicopters. Air traffic control was provided by me with a portable radio.

Lieutenant Commander Wreford establishes air traffic control 'in the field' during Operation Antelope. (FAA Museum)

'It was agreed that the helicopters would not arrive until we had a load for them. To transport them wooden crates were made for each animal, and each Wessex could take three crates at a time. We set up a communications network to try and talk to the ship but, because of the distance and the nature of the land, we had great difficulty, so eventually, we set up a link via Nairobi to the ship. The hunter and his team would go out with the biologist to catch the antelopes using a truck and an instrument which was essentially a lasso on the end of a big stick, that they dropped over the neck of the antelope. Having caught the antelope they would wrestle with it until they got it onto the truck to bring it back to the camp. Once they were back at the camp the antelopes were placed in a pen.' Twenty antelopes were successfully moved from Bura to Voi National Park so that the Hunter's Hartebeest could become firmly established within the safety of the national park.

Ark Royal sailed from Mombasa on 1 November bound for Karachi arriving there on Saturday 9 November and anchoring some way off. There was a slight kerfuffle when *Ark Royal* arrived, because the American aircraft carrier USS *Essex* was anchored in *Ark Royal*'s allocated position, so *Ark Royal* returned the compliment by taking *Essex*'s position. The ships were gathering in preparation for a major CENTO exercise which also comprised ships from the Pakistan Navy and the Royal Iranian Navy. The ships sailed for the exercise areas on 14 November. 'During the afternoon aircraft from the *Essex* cross-operated with aircraft from *Ark Royal*. *Ark Royal* could only supply Wessex helicopters and Gannets, because the older hydraulic catapults on the *Essex* could not cope with either the heavy Sea Vixen or the Scimitar. The first American aircraft to arrive was the small but potent Skyhawk. Then came Sea Dragon helicopters. Later that evening one of these was involved in a tragic accident in which two people were lost and another three were rescued, but were seriously injured,' recalled Eustace.

The ships anchored off Karachi again on 16 November. 'I was one of a group of twelve Midshipmen to visit the *Essex* on 17 November. She had been converted into an anti-submarine carrier, which was a type of ship that we didn't have in the Royal Navy. Parts of her flight deck were still wooden and she had one long hangar deck. Of course the other major difference which I hadn't encountered before, was the fact that their ships were dry so there was nothing to drink when we stayed on board for lunch!' Eustace remarked. Pollock continued: 'The ships sailed for phase three of the exercises on 18 November and this gave our Air Group the chance to carry

Cross-decking with the USS *Essex* during November 1963. (Lieutenant Commander Martins via the author)

out a most successful pre-dawn raid on our Pakistan friends' airfield, at the same time carrying out a spirited defence of the carrier from their strikes: a sophisticated and quite marginal exercise which made a great finale to what turned out to be almost the last air sortie of the fourth commission, after which the entire force returned to Karachi on 22 November.'

Discussing the historic events which had unfolded further afield, Eustace commented: 'That evening *Ark Royal*'s flight deck was the scene of a huge smoking concert. The following morning the news of President Kennedy's assassination became common knowledge, which was particularly poignant because many of *Essex*'s ship's company had been on board for the previous night's concert.'

'We now had our programme changed again, with our nose turned for home which was very much needed. The technical officers were all busy preparing defect lists and essential repair lists, while the Admiralty were ordering modifications, alterations and additions. It was rapidly beginning to become apparent that if all of the repairs and defects which we were reporting, as well as all the "Alterations and Additions" which the Admiralty were feeding in were to be properly done, a great deal more time would be required than had been allocated in the *Ark*'s programme. For reasons explained earlier, this was extremely difficult for the Board to accept. I therefore wrote a long and detailed letter to the Admiralty explaining unequivocally why in my opinion the impossible was being attempted. Although my Secretary assured me that this would bring my career to an end, as he said a similar one had another carrier Captain's, I was heartened that my Administrative authority welcomed it and forwarded it with full support. Very soon after this the Director General (Ships), an old friend of mine from Bath days in an earlier appointment, arrived in Mombasa where the temperature was only in the high eighties. The next day we took him all round the ship (fifteen decks down and fifteen up again to get to some compartments), showed him the state of a lot of the machinery and convinced him of the strength and accuracy of our case. He returned home a very chastened man and, as a result of his visit, the whole carrier programme was recast and *Ark Royal* spent over a year in repair and conversion before sailing for her next commission under Tony Griffin. This was the price paid for the long period of hard driving of men and materials, during both legs of the fourth commission,' Pollock stated.

Ark Royal sailed from Karachi for Zanzibar, arriving there on 4 December 1963 to participate in the Independence Day on 9 December 1963, when the Duke of Edinburgh handed over the instruments of Independence. 'Rest and recreation was arranged on Prison Island which was one of four islands that formed a crescent, about three-quarters of a mile offshore. Apart from some giant tortoises Prison Island was uninhabited, but the former prison remained which provided makeshift accommodation for those who wanted to stay on the island,' Eustace recalled.

Ark Royal left Zanzibar on 10 December arriving at Mombasa on 11 December for the Kenyan independence ceremony. She left Mombasa on 14 December and then anchored off Aden for two hours on 18 December to disembark the advance parties for 890 Squadron and 849 Squadron. 815 Squadron disembarked at 11 p.m., remaining behind to re-embark in *Centaur* when she came through the canal.

The passage home was a classic example of the pressure under which the carrier squadrons were operating at the time. 'We had to drive on almost at any cost. The reason for that was there are only certain days on which you can get up the channel from Plymouth Sound to the dockyard with *Ark Royal*. With all of our defects, and the additional time that was needed, every day was vital to us. My engineers said that it would take six weeks for the equipment to be taken out, let alone mending it and putting it back on board. You couldn't do all this work within three months,' Pollock explained.

On 22 December *Ark Royal* anchored at Port Suez. The 23rd was spent at anchor because it was the anniversary of the British withdrawal after the Suez War. *Ark Royal* then made her fourth transit of the canal on

Christmas Eve. 'We ran into heavy weather in the Mediterranean and spent the whole of Christmas Day trying to do a RAS. We hadn't got one of our big tankers because they had all stayed east of Suez. The little tanker *Brown Ranger* was doing its best, but the ships were mismatched so that they drifted and pitched at different rates. We started the RAS at 08:00 and finished at 21:15. I didn't get to go round the mess decks on Christmas Day which was a grave deprivation!' Pollock remarked.

Ark Royal reached Charlie buoy in Plymouth Sound on 31 December but she was unable to proceed into Devonport, as Pollock explained: 'Because of the tides, we couldn't get up the harbour on 30 or 31 December or 1 or 2 January. We were going to move up the harbour on 3 January, but because it was blowing above the permitted limit for moving *Ark Royal*, which was 25 knots, the move was postponed until the 4th when we moved up the harbour at 08:00. Once alongside I ordered, "Ring off main engines" for the last time in my career.'

Richardson-Bunbury summed up *Ark Royal*'s second tour of duty in the Far East: 'We got through the nine months with morale maintained, for which great credit was due to the new Master-At-Arms who deservedly won a BEM for his wise handling of what in less skilful hands might have been an unhappy end to the commission. As it was the ship suffered more than morale did. *Ark Royal* was never designed for repeated high-speed steaming in the doldrums to work up enough wind speed over the deck for flying, and after two legs of the commission east of Suez she had almost shaken herself to bits. There were cracks in the hull plating; and much of the machinery was in such a dodgy condition that, as we made our way through the Mediterranean over Christmas, there was a real possibility that we might have to be towed the rest of the way home. Our engineers triumphed, but not before one of them had circulated a dialogue between an Engineer OOW going off watch and his successor. Having laughed my way through this catalogue of pieces of machinery deputizing in the most improbable way for their unserviceable counterparts, I remarked to the Senior Engineer that it was brilliant but obviously exaggerated. "On the contrary," he said, "it is almost verbatim from a watch handover last night."'

Looking back upon his time in command of *Ark Royal*, Pollock remarked, 'In spite of all the difficulties, and indeed dangers to ship and aircraft, these intensive months of operations had offered a huge challenge to everyone concerned and that it was achieved without disaster is a tremendous tribute to the dedicated and cheerful ship's company and squadron crews.'

Chapter Six

THE BATTLE OF BEIRA

FIFTH COMMISSION,

NOVEMBER 1964 – OCTOBER 1966

Shortly after *Ark Royal* began her refit in January 1964, Captain Pollock handed over command to Captain A.T.F.G. Griffin (later Admiral Sir Anthony Griffin GCB) on 24 January 1964. Prior to his time in command of *Ark Royal*, Captain Griffin had served as the senior Commander in HMS *Eagle*. He said of the differences between the two ships: '*Ark Royal* always had a better style about her, whereas *Eagle* was always more down to earth; which could perhaps best be summed up as: *Ark Royal* was the Cavalier while *Eagle* was the Roundhead.'

Because *Ark Royal* had been driven so hard during her two tours of duty in the Far East, the original three-month refit was extended to deal with all of the outstanding defects. Therefore, *Ark Royal* did not recommission again until 12 November 1964. During her time in refit the wording in the Commissioning warrant read on board in February 1964 had become dated. In the original warrant the words 'their Lords Commissioners of the Admiralty' had been used, whereas since April 1964 the separate ministries of the Armed Forces had become united under the present Ministry of Defence (MOD). Among the guests present at the Commissioning ceremony was the C-in-C Plymouth, Admiral Sir Nigel Henderson. In his speech Captain Griffin compared *Ark Royal* with *Eagle*, which was berthed astern, by describing *Eagle*'s recent modernization as 'putting on weight with advancing years while *Ark Royal* had retained her shape'.

In the fortnight that followed the Commissioning ceremony there were the usual inspections by senior naval officers, including Admiral Henderson's post-refit inspection on 20 November. Describing last-minute alterations prior to sailing John Reeve said, 'As an innocent and wholly unsuitable young electrical officer, with experience in only the Fleet Air Arm and one small ship, I was appointed to EEM's department at Devonport Dockyard, with responsibility for testing and tuning radar equipment. I found I had a splendid team of experienced diagnosticians who could commission any piece of electronics which came their way, and my boss's sage advice was to leave them to do the commissioning while I kept the ship's staff out of their hair.

'After two days in my new job my boss disappeared on three weeks leave and I was on my own. This was 1964 and Devonport Dockyard was in a turmoil, with no work being done on eight or nine smaller ships while our entire workforce was occupied trying to get *Ark Royal* back to sea after her refit. The great day came at last, *Ark Royal* throbbed with that going-to-sea expectancy, the tannoy chirped away incessantly, dockyardies left the ship in droves, and the last stores were loaded aboard. With a couple of hours to go before sailing, I was urgently summoned to one of the radar offices where my top experts were desperately attempting to get the main early warning radar to run without overheating and tripping off. Something serious had gone wrong. Without that radar *Ark Royal* could not go to sea.

'I arrived to find there was standing room only in the little radar office. Not only were four of my diagnosticians frantically trying to find the problem (with four ideas of what could be wrong), but standing behind them was the ship's chief radar tiffy, the Radar Officer, the Cdr (L) and Captain Griffin himself. As I appeared, the radar tripped off yet again and I watched as the equipment cooling fan slowed to a sickening stop and it went quiet. In the silence, the Radar Officer, to whom I had been introduced only the previous day, and who had invested in me a glass or two of duty-free, turned and saw me. "Ah!" he cried, "here's the expert." They all turned and made room; except that is for my four diagnosticians who had already decided the limitations of my technical worth in the brief time they had known me. I felt I had to say something, and the only thing I could think of was some advice given to me by an aged senior electrical officer while we were under training. "If in doubt, lad," he advised, "ask them – have you switched it on?" It's surprising how often that works, but clearly it wasn't going to work this time. I licked my dry lips and looked hopefully around the strange equipment for inspiration. As they all waited expectantly I cleared my throat. Suddenly, something odd I'd noticed as the radar tripped off came to my mind. The equipment was cooled by one of those centrifugal fans designed to rotate in a particular direction to achieve proper air flow. I'd noticed, as it stopped, that the shaft had been rotating the other way. "Why is the fan running backwards?" I asked. They all looked at my chief diagnostician. He shook his head in perplexity, and switched it on and off to check for himself. "I think you may have a wire crossed," I said with quiet satisfaction. He gave me a look of thunder. With the fan rewired correctly, the radar ran up happily and *Ark Royal* sailed only half an hour late. My reputation in Devonport Dockyard was assured for the time being, and they never did find out my true technical limitations.'

On 24 November *Ark Royal* sailed from Devonport to begin her first batch of sea trials and flying trials. After a couple of days at sea, the ship returned to Charlie buoy for trials of a new rocket-assisted ejector seat from

At the end of November 1964 trials were carried out of a new Martin Baker ejector seat for the Buccaneer S2. (Martin Baker Engineering Ltd)

Martin Baker for the Buccaneer. The two seats were mounted on top of a catapult dead-weight bogie which was fired off the catapult. As the dead-weight reached the end of the catapult, the two seats were fired off and the dummies were successfully ejected clear of the ship, to drift down to the sea on the parachutes. By the end of the month the trials had progressed far enough to begin the first flying trials, as a Gannet, piloted by the CO of 849 Squadron, on 30 November had the honour of becoming the first fixed-wing pilot to take a wire in this commission. The rest of the flying trials were completed by the end of the week, to enable *Ark Royal* to begin a four-day visit to Portsmouth. When she left on 8 December she completed a further six days of trials. Because the weather was forecast to deteriorate, it was decided to bring the ship back into port a day early on 14 December to begin Christmas leave.

The first six months of the new year were to be spent working up *Ark Royal* prior to her third deployment to the Far East which was planned to last a year. When *Ark Royal* sailed from Devonport on 14 January 1965 she embarked the Sea Vixen FAW1s of 890 Squadron and the Gannet AEW3s of 849 Squadron C Flight. C Flight's Gannets were known as 'The Zebras' on account of their black and white striped nose cones. Two days later, two new squadrons joined *Ark Royal*: 803 Squadron equipped with Scimitar F1s replaced 800 Squadron from the previous commission, because 800 Squadron had re-equipped with Buccaneers shortly after they had left *Ark Royal*. 819 Squadron, equipped with Wessex HAS1s, replaced 815 Squadron on board during the work up because 815 Squadron were still at Culdrose, having only just returned from a year in the Far East in *Centaur*.

The embarkation of the squadrons started a busy period for Lt B. Chilcott (now Lt Cdr B. Chilcott) who was the Guided Weapons Engineer Officer at this time. Explaining his role on board, Chilcott said, 'When the squadrons were embarked I had to provide them with the various weapons in a ready to fire state. The squadron would actually do the loading onto the aircraft themselves, except for the final arming of the nuclear weapons. I had to support Firestreak, Red Top, Sidewinder, Bullpup, Mark 30 torpedoes, and Mark 44 torpedoes. I was also responsible for the nuclear weapons, which I found quite a daunting prospect. *Ark Royal* carried the Red Beard 2,000lb free-fall nuclear weapon. It did not have any power, or guided systems, it was just a straightforward free-fall bomb, which would be carried by the Scimitars and Sea Vixens. They were stored in bits, in various compartments across the ship, and had been loaded in Devonport during a weekend and it was

Ark Royal prepares to start a RAS. Note the removal of the forward 4.5in gun turret from the aft pair of turrets on each side during her 1964 refit. (Captain Tofts via the author)

all done extremely secretively, except everyone knew about it. I was very nervous and unknowing of what it was all about, but you just had to get on with it and find out. But the problem was nobody really told you very much. Publicly, it was a case of "Nuclear weapons? What nuclear weapons?" To begin with it took about three hours to assemble the weapon, but with practice we got the process down to about an hour and a quarter. The interesting thing was that despite the illusion that the nuclear weapons were extremely powerful and secret weapons, the actual engineering and assembly of the weapon was very crude.'

From Devonport, *Ark Royal* spent nearly a fortnight working up in the Moray Firth, before sailing for the French naval port of Brest, where she arrived on 28 January. During this visit the French battleship *Richelieu*, which was moored ahead of *Ark Royal*, acted as host ship. Despite her reduction to reserve status after ten years as a static training ship, *Richelieu* was still an impressive sight. The atmosphere of the visit was dampened by the death of Sir Winston Churchill. A memorial service for Churchill was held on board on the morning of 31 January, which was attended by representatives from the French Navy and the city of Brest. On 2 February *Ark Royal* left Brest to continue her work up in Scottish waters, which took the rest of the month, culminating in the ORI by FOAC, Rear Admiral H.R.B. Janvrin CB, DSC on 2 March. With the ORI successfully completed, *Ark Royal* entered Rosyth for a two-day visit, before sailing on 5 March for Exercise Pilot Light. While at Rosyth *Ark Royal* acquired another Admiral, when the C-in-C Home Fleet, Admiral Sir Charles Madden GCB, embarked to direct the forthcoming exercise. Among the participating ships in the exercise was the former light fleet carrier *Venerable*, which was by then serving in the Dutch Navy as the *Karel Doorman*. In addition to the two Admirals who were embarked, six journalists were also on board, and as a result they produced two articles which highlighted the rather poor living conditions endured by some of the ship's company. While the articles were seen by some as an unwelcome intrusion into the RN's affairs, they did do some long-term good for future members of the ship's company, because it forced the planners of her major refit between 1967 and 1970 to make sure that the standard of accommodation was improved throughout the ship.

Describing the background to a souvenir which was given to visitors to *Ark Royal*, Griffin explained: 'I think what impresses one from the start is the size of both *Ark Royal* and *Eagle*. They were after all the largest that the RN has ever had or likely to have. Their size is matched by the numbers of their crew of 2,500 men, which led to enormous variety of life and the guarantee of a first-class crisis every day! Any visitor to the ship would be issued with a certificate to say that they had survived a day in *Ark Royal*. These certificates were covered in oil, blood and one corner was actually burnt off!'

At the end of the exercise *Ark Royal* sailed for Bergen, arriving there on 10 March to begin a five-day visit. During this period her two Admirals moved on, Admiral Madden transferring his flag to the cruiser *Lion* on 11 March, while FOAC returned to Southwick on the day of *Ark Royal*'s departure from Bergen on 15 March. From Bergen, *Ark Royal* sailed for Portsmouth, arriving there on 18 March for a four-day visit, having already disembarked the squadrons on 16 March. While she was alongside, a team of specialists were embarked from Boscombe Down in preparation for the trials of the Buccaneer S2. The aircraft was embarked on 23 March for eight days of clearance trials. The Buccaneer S2 was powered by two Rolls-Royce Spey engines, which were a vast improvement in terms of performance over the De Havilland Gyron Junior which had powered the Buccaneer S1. Due to the increased weight of the Buccaneer S2, *Ark Royal* became the first RN carrier to launch an aircraft with an all-up weight of 50,000lb. While the Buccaneer was conducting trials, Boscombe Down also seized the opportunity to embark a Sea Vixen FAW2 to conduct trials with the 37-tube 2in rocket launcher. During these trials the First Sea Lord, Admiral Sir David Luce GCB, DSO, OBE arrived on board, the 1,000th landing of the commission, so he was greeted by Captain Griffin with the traditional magnum of champagne. The trials concluded on 31 March when the Buccaneer was disembarked.

Trials of the Buccaneer S2 were carried out in March 1965 on board *Ark Royal*. (FAA Museum)

The Captain was the subject of a practical joke which caused him a few anxious moments prior to the arrival of the CENTO Military Committee on 1 April. 'I thought it would be a good idea to give the guests a short message of welcome in their respective languages of Urdu, Persian and Turkish. I wrote out a short speech and asked the schoolie to get it translated into the various relevant languages. About forty-eight hours before their arrival I asked the schoolie where the note was and he said, "I am terribly sorry, but I got through to the Naval Attachés in London and all I have are these tapes in Urdu, Turkish, etc., so there is nothing for it but to play these tapes and learn them all parrot fashion." I, of course had no idea what I was saying, but it sounded good. The committee arrived by helicopter and the Commander (Cdr Hugh Janion, later Rear Admiral Sir Hugh Janion KCVO) arrived on the bridge and told me that all was ready for my introductory talk. As we got into the hangar the Commander said to me, "I suppose you know what you are going to say to these people." I replied that I knew it in Urdu, Turkish, etc. and I knew it backwards. The Commander replied, "Well, in fact you don't, Sir, there is a deep-laid plot, and what you're going to say in their different languages is: I wish you shower would get off my ship!" I was of course nearly at the lectern to deliver my speech and it was about to be a moment of triumph or disaster, and images of the headlines, "Captain insults CENTO committee" flashed before my eyes, until I suddenly twigged that it was April Fools' Day. However, I managed to get my own back!'

The visit passed off successfully and *Ark Royal* entered Devonport the following day for Easter leave. After over a month alongside, *Ark Royal* sailed from Devonport on 17 May for exercises. She embarked the squadrons

A Scimitar of 803 Squadron is launched.
(Captain Rotheram via the author)

later in the day, with the exception of 819 Squadron, which had by that time departed to Ballykelly. 'Perhaps the most dramatic incident to occur during my time in command was with the Scimitar squadron in the North Sea. In May 1965 we had been fully worked up, and were allowed to have flying exercises outside the range of diversion airfields. On one occasion all eight Scimitars were airborne engaged in air exercises, when suddenly we were hit by a violent storm with high winds of about 60–70 knots and rough seas. We tried to recover the Scimitars but no one could stand up on deck, so the aircraft were ordered to return to high altitudes to conserve fuel while we thought of the best way to recover the aircraft. After a few moments it was decided to put the ship astern at 10 knots, so that the wind speed over the deck could be reduced by enough to enable people to stand up on deck. However, when the first pilot approached *Ark Royal* to land, he found that his canopy was getting caked in salt despite the use of his wipers. We therefore came up with the idea to fly them through a rain cloud to clear the canopies enough so that they could land. It did and we got all eight safely back on deck, although the last aircraft was running very low on fuel when it was recovered. It was a very interesting occasion to say the least,' recalled Griffin.

By the end of the month *Ark Royal* was back in Devonport for the start of Families Day on 26 May. Once the families had been embarked *Ark Royal* slipped her moorings at the start of an eventful day which included the launching of two cars from the catapult. By 3 pm it was all over, and she was secured alongside once more.

After appropriate leave had been given to the ship's company, *Ark Royal* set sail for the Far East for her third and final deployment to that station. She slipped her moorings at 7.45 a.m. on 17 June and the squadrons were embarked in the afternoon, just before the weather deteriorated. As part of the embarking CAG, 815 Squadron made a welcome return to *Ark Royal* to once more provide her with a resident Wessex squadron. Throughout the commission, the carrier on board delivery (COD) Gannet performed a vital yet largely unsung role in delivering various items to the ship whenever it was in range of an airfield, such as people and mail for the ship's company. The COD Gannet was a refurbished Gannet AS4 with all of the anti-submarine equipment removed, and had first joined *Ark Royal*'s CAG at the start of the fourth commission. One of the observers in 849 Squadron C Flight was Sub Lt Martin Rotheram (now Captain M. Rotheram). He explained how the COD Gannet fitted in with the other Gannets: 'The Flight consisted of four AEW Gannets and one COD Gannet.

There was always a COD Gannet pilot, who could fly the AEW Gannet but was assigned to the COD Gannet. The COD Flight had four ratings and the Flight operated on an independent basis from the AEW Gannets. The COD would fly ship's mail, stores, and people both on and off the ship.'

On the voyage to the Suez Canal *Ark Royal* made a brief two-day visit to Gibraltar between 22 and 24 June before conducting flying exercises off the historic island of Malta. *Ark Royal*'s arrival off Port Said on the evening of 28 June marked the onset of the heat that the ship's company would have to deal with for the next year. Chilcott recalled the living conditions in *Ark Royal* during her Far East deployment: 'It was tough, my cabin did not have air-conditioning. In the Red Sea the temperature rose as high as 120 degrees Fahrenheit. Some of the aircrew cabins were air-conditioned and occasionally they would allow us to sleep there. Sometimes, I used to

Ark Royal arrives off Port Said, 28 June 1965.
(Captain Rotheram via the author)

Ark Royal arrives at Singapore, 19 July 1965.
(Captain Tofts via the author)

sleep illegally in the workshops because they were also air-conditioned. The conditions down below for the men were very tough.' *Ark Royal* completed her fifth transit of the Suez Canal on 29 June, then steamed south to spend two days off Aden between 2 and 4 July. Having relieved *Victorious* on 8 July *Ark Royal* entered Singapore for the first time in this commission, for two weeks of SMP. While alongside, another former Captain of *Ark Royal* returned as an Admiral, when Flag Officer Second-in-Command Far Eastern Fleet (FO2 FEF), Rear Admiral P.J. Hill-Norton CB hoisted his flag in *Ark Royal* for nearly two weeks. He transferred his flag to the frigate *Falmouth* on 3 August to make way for FOAC, who made a three-day visit to the ship. *Ark Royal* sailed from Singapore for flying exercises on the day that Singapore declared itself independent on 4 August. When FOAC disembarked to return to the UK, the newly promoted FO2 FEF, by then Vice Admiral Hill-Norton CB, hoisted his flag once more in *Ark Royal*.

Between 23 and 25 August *Ark Royal* visited the American naval base at Subic Bay. Describing the encounter with the USS *Midway* after *Ark Royal* sailed from Subic Bay, Chilcott said, 'In the sea of Japan we met the USS *Midway* which had just completed her first deployment to Vietnam and had lost her first aircrew in combat. At the time she was obviously fully worked up and we took part in a war game against her. She beat us because she was on a true war footing and could launch more aircraft within a given time. Although we thought we could beat her, we were still at a leisurely peacetime pace compared to her vigorous war footing.'

Ark Royal returned to Singapore for the first half of September for a SMP. During this period alongside, Vice Admiral Hill-Norton transferred his flag to the County Class destroyer *Devonshire* on 14 September while his boss, the Commander FEF, Vice Admiral Sir Frank Twiss, visited the ship on the following day. *Ark Royal* sailed from Singapore bound for Hong Kong on 18 September. During the voyage *Ark Royal* had some unwelcome stowaways, as Griffin recalled: 'It was a perfectly quiet normal day when I noticed one of the telling signs of an impending typhoon when the entire horizon turned orange. We could see on the radar that our surroundings were closing in on us but we still had blue sky and calm sea, but then the sky suddenly darkened with locusts and birds. The air was so thick with locusts that you could hardly see. Unfortunately, we were steaming at the same speed as the typhoon. When we arrived at Hong Kong we were delayed by one day while the typhoon wreaked its havoc ashore, before we could dock in the harbour.'

The shape of things to come: a US Navy F4B performs an approach with the hook up. (Captain Rotheram via the author)

A US Navy C1A Trader COD aircraft visits *Ark Royal*. (Captain Rotheram via the author)

Ark Royal arrived at Hong Kong on 27 September at the start of a two-week visit. Leave had to be restricted on two occasions during the Hong Kong visit; firstly, on 1 October while the Chinese People's Republic celebrated their National Day; secondly, on 10 October when Nationalist China celebrated their National Day. By restricting leave it helped to avoid the potential for any of the ship's company to get caught inadvertently in the middle of any trouble which might have repercussions on a wider scale. As compensation for their restricted movement, a flight deck concert was held on both occasions which kept the ship's company entertained.

Ark Royal sailed from Hong Kong on 12 October bound for Singapore and another SMP, arriving there on 20 October. Nine days later Captain Griffin handed over command of *Ark Royal* to Captain M.F. Fell DSO, DSC* (later Vice Admiral Sir Michael Fell KCB, DSO, DSC*). Captain Fell's period in command did not get off to the best of starts, because two days later there was a serious fire in B boiler room in the early hours of Sunday 31 October. The Cdr (Air) at this time was Cdr W.A. Tofts (now Captain W.A. Tofts CBE, AFC). Describing the scene in the dockyard shortly after the fire broke out, Tofts recalled: 'I had been ashore that night, having dinner with a friend who was the CO of a Hastings squadron. I returned to the ship about midnight and I could hardly believe my eyes when I saw these fire engines alongside on the jetty. The fire brigades both local and dockyard were accustomed to having exercises with visiting warships, so my initial thoughts were that they had called this one a bit early. However, when I got back on board it quickly became clear what had happened.' After the damage caused by the fire had been inspected, it quickly became apparent that *Ark Royal* would not be able to participate in Exercise Warrior as had been planned. Instead she would remain alongside 8 Wharf for over a month while repairs were completed. As a result FO2 FEF transferred his flag to *Devonshire* and a detachment of two Wessex helicopters from 815 Squadron were embarked in RFA *Tidespring*. *Ark Royal*'s extended stay in Singapore caused problems for the ship's company of *Eagle* when she returned to Singapore in November. Because *Ark Royal* was still alongside 8 Wharf, *Eagle* had to remain moored to a buoy for her stay which meant

Captain Fell arrives on board *Ark Royal* to relieve Captain Griffin on 29 October 1965. (Captain Tofts via the author)

her libertymen had to make the trip ashore by boat. *Eagle*'s return also changed *Ark Royal*'s squadrons' routine because they had to move from Changi to Butterworth to make way for *Eagle*'s squadrons.

Having completed repairs to the boiler room, *Ark Royal* sailed from Singapore on 7 December for flying exercises. Sadly, this was not the end of *Ark Royal*'s troubles because four days later she had to return for a complete change of feed water, as frothing had appeared due to an errant detergent. Thankfully for the ship's company, the visit to Australia for Christmas was still possible, so it was with great expectation that *Ark Royal* sailed from Singapore on 17 December bound for Freemantle. The ship's arrival in Freemantle on 23 December was observed by the watchful eye of FO2 FEF from the deck of his flagship *Devonshire*. The following day he transferred his flag back to *Ark Royal*. With the festivities of Christmas over, *Ark Royal* sailed from Freemantle for flying exercises off the Cocos Islands before returning to Singapore on 8 January 1966 for another SMP.

Tofts recalled: '*Ark Royal* sailed from Singapore without an escort on 27 January for flying exercises. Plane guard and search and rescue duties by day and night thus became the task of the embarked helicopters. Helicopter aircrew in those days were considered almost as second-class citizens in some quarters of the Fleet Air Arm. It was decided, therefore, before reaching the operational area a night SAR exercise would be conducted. Fixed-wing aircrew were put over the side in boats and taken some distance from the ship. Then Wessex helicopters set about recovering them from the water, which they did successfully. Following the exercise the helicopter aircrew were held in higher regard because the fixed-wing aircrew realized that if anything went wrong it was the helicopter boys who would be bailing them out.'

On 1 February *Ark Royal* changed course for Mombasa, arriving there on 18 February. Discussing some of his additional jobs, Chilcott said, 'I was the ship's Mail Officer which is one of the major morale makers or breakers for a ship like *Ark Royal*. It was a tough but interesting job. For example, when we docked in Mombasa I had to go to a railway siding with a couple of sailors to recover one hundred and twenty sackloads of mail in tropical heat with no other help. The Mail Officer ran the small post office, was responsible for "Postie" himself and had to arrange for mail drops and pick-ups with the operations department. It was one of those jobs which was always allocated to a seaman officer, but in *Ark Royal* they tried to let some of us engineer officers get in on the act. One other job which was allocated to me was that of Confidential Book Officer. The CB Officer looked

Out in the Far East those who could took advantage of periods when there was no flying to sunbathe, and *Ark Royal*'s flight deck resembled that of a cruise ship. (Captain Tofts via the author)

after the confidential books and was responsible for accounting for every single page of each confidential book. It was the CB Officer's job to make all of the amendments and count the pages when the books were issued and when they were returned.'

Four days after *Ark Royal*'s arrival in Mombasa, the most significant decision made in the postwar era to affect the future of the RN's carrier force was announced on 22 February 1966. The Labour Defence Secretary, Denis Healey announced the cancellation of the new fixed-wing carrier CVA-01 in his Defence White Paper. The cancellation of CVA-01 and the rundown of the RN's existing carrier force in the early 1970s shattered the hopes of a whole generation of young Fleet Air Arm officers who could see their fast fixed-wing flying days coming to a premature end. The ironic thing about the timing of the announcement was that, just over a week after the announcement was made, *Ark Royal* departed Mombasa bound for the Mozambique Channel to enforce the Government's foreign policy over Rhodesia by undertaking the first Beira patrol. Because Rhodesia's Mr Smith had illegally declared independence, the British Government had enforced sanctions against Rhodesia. The Government was concerned that oil might be supplied to Rhodesia by pipeline from the Portuguese port of Beira, having been taken there by tanker. Therefore, the *Ark Royal*, supported by the frigates *Rhyl*, *Lowestoft* and later *Plymouth*, were there to ensure that the nationality of each tanker taking oil to Beira was checked. 'After the cancellation of CVA-01, several UK newspapers carried photos of the aircraft on patrol, with the caption "RAF Gannets fly Beira patrol". Evidently under political pressure not to admit the necessity of carriers so soon after cancelling CVA-01, when the RAF had no bases near Beira from which to operate!', Chilcott remarked.

Chilcott described the preparations for the Beira patrol: 'Because we thought we might be going to war we broke out the live weapons. The aircrew practised dropping VT fused bombs using the splash target towed astern, with the aircraft flying in a circuit. During one of these sessions we saw the Sea Vixen of Lt James Patrick and Lt Colin Lightfoot dive into the attack, and just as he released the bomb it went off and blew up the aircraft. As the smoke cleared and the bits came down, we then saw a parachute and thought, well, at least one of them had survived, but as the parachute drifted towards the ship it became clear that they hadn't. The ironic thing about the whole situation was that Lt Lightfoot was Rhodesian and had in essence died flying against his

A Sea Vixen FAW1 of 890 Squadron lands on *Ark Royal* with a Wessex HAS1 from 815 Squadron on the left. (Captain Tofts via the author)

A Scimitar of 803 Squadron takes the barrier on 7 March 1966 while *Ark Royal* was on the Beira Patrol. (Captain Tofts via the author)

own country. There is an atmosphere about a ship like that, when there is a crash. Although you could be in the depths of the ship, you can hear nothing and see nothing, but you know just by instinct that there had been an accident. For example, the ship's revolutions change or the ship shudders.'

The mid- to late 1960s were a difficult time for the FAA, because there were a high number of aircraft lost during routine carrier operations, as Rotheram reflected: 'During my first three months at sea I remember three men were killed and I thought it was perfectly normal that once a month we had to go to the quarterdeck to say goodbye to someone.'

Summing up the harsh reality of carrier operations, Chilcott remarked: 'You were there to do a job. If you got it wrong, you died; or someone else died, it is as simple as that! It's immediate, the effects are real, but on the other hand when you do your job well, the satisfaction is immense.'

Eagle relieves *Ark Royal* on the Beira Patrol, 15 March 1966. (Captain Tofts via the author)

Ark Royal leaves Singapore for the last time on 26 April 1966. (Captain Tofts via the author)

Between 5 and 14 March *Ark Royal* completed the first Beira patrol, yet it is the *Eagle* which will forever be associated with the patrol. This is because by the time she had docked after completing her long patrol between 15 March and 31 April 1966 she had remained at sea continuously for seventy-two days. 'There were a number of occasions when the jets could not be launched, so most of the flying during the Beira patrol was done by Gannets on four- and five-hour sorties,' said Rotheram.

After nine days on the Beira patrol *Ark Royal* was relieved by *Eagle* so that she could return to Singapore for another SMP. After a month alongside, *Ark Royal* slipped her moorings in Singapore for the very last time on 26 April. From Singapore, *Ark Royal* sailed to the Mozambique Channel to relieve the record-breaking *Eagle*. *Ark Royal* began her second Beira patrol on 5 May. Rotheram outlined the role of the Gannet AEW3 during the Beira patrol: 'At this time the Gannet essentially had two roles. Firstly, airborne early warning which was an air defence role. In general, we would be flying at between 2,000 and 5,000 feet on one engine. The radar was a pulse radar, so we had a lot of return from the sea and there was a balance between how much return you got from the sea and how much from aircraft. Secondly, the Gannets would perform a surface search for ships, which could be carried out in one of two ways. The objective of this role was to find tankers trying to break the blockade. One method would be to fly low level and visually identify the ships ourselves. Alternatively, we would use a probe aircraft to do the identification, while we flew between 10,000 and 20,000 feet directing the probes to each of the ships. The benefit of flying the Gannet at this height was that the surface horizon was increased to over 20 miles and thus we could see quite a long way. The probe aircraft were either a Sea Vixen or Scimitar.

The Gannet had two observers. The left-hand observer was the more experienced of the two, while the right-hand observer was usually on his first tour. The way in which the work was divided between the two observers depended entirely on the type of sortie. For example, on one sortie the junior observer would back up what the senior observer was doing, while on another sortie they might work independently and divide up the air space and look at a particular sector each.'

Rotheram recounted the story of his own ditching during the Beira patrol on 10 May 1966: 'We launched at 17:30 to perform a Beira search mission. The aircraft was XL475, the pilot was Lt Mike Jermy, and the other observer was Lt Miles Cullan. We either lost part of our nose wheel assembly on launch or it snapped off on landing. When we landed the nose went straight down and the hook went up, thus missing the wires. I remember banging off my door as we went over the front end of the angled flight deck. We went in slightly port wing down, hit the water, and turned through 180 degrees at 21:41. The aircraft floated for about a minute. I looked to my left and Miles Cullan was moving, so I jumped out, got into my life-raft, and floated away. Mike Jermy stood up in his seat, as the ship went past, before ending up in his life-raft. The Wessex was sent to recover us, but it was the early days of night SAR and they didn't have Doppler, so it was quite difficult

A Gannet AEW 3 of 849 Squadron C Flight about to land on *Ark Royal*. (Captain Tofts via the author)

Ark Royal during her second Beira Patrol in May 1966. (Captain Rotheram via the author)

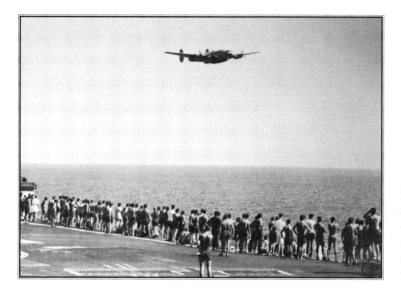

During the Beira Patrol the crew of this RAF Shackleton dropped a dummy mail canister which promptly sank. Unfortunately, mail was such an important factor in morale that no one on board saw the joke. (Captain Vincent via the author)

to find us. It was a calm moonlit night and fairly warm. They picked up Miles Cullan and made a number of attempts to pick me up, but they weren't getting close. A boat was then sent to recover both myself and Mike Jermy. When we got back to the ship the recovery of the boat went slightly wrong, and I remember thinking to myself how ironic it would have been if, having just survived a ditching, I was killed during the recovery of my rescue boat. However, we got back on board and were taken down to the sickbay to be checked out before going down to the Wardroom. That morning a Sea Vixen ditched and a man was killed. It was not uncommon for a Sea Vixen and a Gannet to ditch on the same day. (The Sea Vixen crash was the mission in which Alan Tarver won the George Medal for valiantly trying to save the life of his observer Lt John Stutchbury when his seat failed to eject. Alan Tarver very nearly lost his own life in the process.)'

While *Ark Royal* was still on patrol, a RAF Shackleton from Madagascar decided to play a practical joke on the ship's company, as Rotheram recalled: 'Mail was extremely important to the crew's morale, so when an RAF crew of a Shackleton dropped a spoof mail canister into the sea which sank, no one saw the joke.'

On 25 May *Ark Royal* began the voyage home to Devonport, stopping at Aden where she anchored on 31 May, before making her sixth and final transit through the Suez Canal on 4 June. After a three-day visit to Gibraltar *Ark Royal* finally arrived at Charlie buoy in Plymouth Sound on 13 June, prior to making the voyage up the Sound into Devonport the following day.

After a month and a half alongside, *Ark Royal* sailed from Devonport on 1 August to begin her final phase of the commission. From Devonport she sailed north to begin a work up prior to Exercise Straight Laced. Before the exercise started, Rear Admiral W.D. O'Brien, who had become FOAC earlier in the year, hoisted his flag on board. In addition to those officially participating in the exercise, there were a number of unofficial Soviet observers in the form of Bear, Badger and Bison aircraft, while a Kynda class cruiser and a couple of Elints

Ark Royal enters Portsmouth in time for Navy Days at the end of August 1966. (Captain Tofts via the author)

Queen Elizabeth the Queen Mother visited *Ark Royal* at sea on 20 September 1966. (Captain Vincent via the author)

The last catapult launch of the commission with the command being given in person by Captain Fell. (Captain Vincent via the author)

watched with interest from the distance. After the exercise finished on 19 August *Ark Royal* spent three days in Oslo before sailing for Portsmouth to play a starring role in the Bank Holiday Navy Days when 55,000 visitors took the opportunity to look round the great ship.

The highlight of September was when HM Queen Elizabeth the Queen Mother paid her traditional visit to *Ark Royal* while she was in the North Sea on 20 September. An uninvited guest also attended in the distance, when the 900 ton Russian tug *MB52* sailed alongside the carrier briefly. Captain Fell sent the following signal in Russian: 'You are in a dangerous position. My aircraft will be carrying out firing on my port side and astern of me. Keep outside the four-mile range from me.' The Russian tug, bristling with aerials, complied by dropping back into the distant haze, enabling the day to continue without any interruptions. Having toured the ship and watched an air display by the CAG, the Queen Mother left by helicopter at 3.30 p.m.

On 1 October the squadrons were disembarked for the last time in the commission. After *Ark Royal*, all of the squadrons faced the prospect of disbandment. 890 Squadron had been the last front-line squadron of Sea Vixen FAW1s, while 803 Squadron were the last front-line squadron of Scimitars. 815 Squadron and 849 Squadron C Flight were also disbanded shortly after they disembarked from *Ark Royal*. After the last aircraft had been launched, Captain Fell had the honour of giving the command for the last catapult launch from *Ark Royal* in the 1960s, when a toilet was fired off the port catapult, complete with paying-off pennant.

By the time *Ark Royal* was secured alongside in Devonport on 5 October 1966 she was in need of an extensive overhaul, as was clearly shown by the number of SMPs in Singapore which were necessary due to engineering problems. Over the next three years her equipment was overhauled and she was Phantomized, but not modernized to the same standard as *Eagle*.

Chapter Seven

THE WIND OF CHANGE

OCTOBER 1966 – FEBRUARY 1970

The £32 million Phantomization refit of 1967–70 was described at the time as a bigger undertaking than the building of the *QE2*, then under construction for Cunard at John Brown's shipyard on the Clyde. The Marine Engineer Officer, Cdr Guy Crowden gave an alternative description when he likened it to a three-year rugger match without extra time and no half-time. The challenge faced by those in charge of the refit was not helped by the severe limitations imposed by both money and time restrictions. Preparations for the refit began back in May 1966 before *Ark Royal* returned to Devonport to pay off. Once alongside, *Ark Royal* had to be fully destored before work could begin on the refit. About 45,000 different types of stores were removed, ranging from arrester wires, through to items of furniture held in thirty-two storerooms and various stowages, such as between hangar beams. Work formally began on *Ark Royal* on 27 February 1967. During this period Captain Fell left and was later replaced by Cdr R.J.S. MacPherson, who became the interim Commanding Officer until shortly before Captain Lygo was appointed to *Ark Royal* in 1969.

In July 1967 Cdr Guy Crowden (now Captain Guy Crowden OBE) joined *Ark Royal* as the Engineer Officer. Over the next two years he oversaw the complete overhaul of *Ark Royal*'s machinery. He described the scene that greeted him as he took up his appointment: 'She was dry docked and there were holes in the ship's hull where they had taken out generators and other items. A lot of machinery was removed for refit not only in Devonport Dockyard, but also in Portsmouth, and by the original manufacturers. For example, they had to dismantle Romeo 8 diesel generator and transport the bits to Lincoln for refurbishment, where I eventually went to see it on trials.'

As has already been mentioned there were severe time restrictions enforced for the refit, therefore any delays would be a major problem. Recalling possible risks which could have disrupted the refit, Crowden said, 'The major consideration was "Is the ship secure?" If there was a fire, could it be quickly extinguished before it became a major conflagration? Whenever there was a burning or welding operation, we always had a sentry from the ship's company standing by with a fire extinguisher. There were security rounds at the end of the day, an hour after all work by the dockyard had ceased, to see that there was nothing left that was smouldering, or areas left so that inadvertent access was possible. From time to time we had major exercises with the Plymouth Fire Brigade so that they knew the route through the dockyard and where the ship was located, how to get into the ship and how best to get to a boiler room if necessary. For this, they relied heavily on the knowledge of the ship's company. These routes had to be updated on a regular basis, because certain parts of the ship were excluded from access because they were stripping out the asbestos insulation. The removal of the asbestos was a major exercise undertaken by the dockyard, carried out by men wearing breathing apparatus and protective clothing.'

The first major landmark of the refit was the flashing up of the boilers in January 1969 in A boiler room. 'When steam became available on board it was well recognized among the engineers that the battle of the boiler

124

Ark Royal is eased out of dry dock. Her new silhouette is beginning to emerge but there is still much work to be done before her trials. Note *Eagle* still in commission in the background and the first hints that both ships will continue to differ significantly. (Captain Crowden via the author)

Ark Royal is gently brought alongside having been moved out of dry dock. From this view the new bow bridle catcher is very prominent. (Captain Crowden via the author)

rooms would be their first major encounter of the refit. However,' Crowden said, 'one of the most helpful factors in the refit was that the steam-driven equipment was getting shore-tested to full speed before it was fitted in the ship. This meant that over-speed and safety trips were assembled and checked and one therefore had complete confidence in the newly installed equipment. This was in stark contrast to some of my other jobs where the equipment had not been fully shore-tested and it invariably went "on the blink" at the wrong moment.'

When Cdr Crowden had a few 'spare' moments during the refit he decided to look at some pumps, which were referred to by some of the ship's company as the 'Ramillies Pumps'. He wanted to know whether this story was in fact true or if it was merely wishful thinking by some of the sailors. He explained his thoughts: 'The pumps in question were originally 15in gun-turret pumps that were used on board *Ark Royal* for the flight deck hydraulics, and were needed to raise and lower the radio masts. There was no identification on the pumps that they had come out of the battleship *Ramillies*, and in fact they could have come out of any British 15in armed battleship, or battlecruiser, of the period. However, it is interesting to think that there we were in the 1970s, flying the Mach 2 Phantom, and still using items of equipment in the ship which could have been in operation at the Battle of Jutland.'

While *Ark Royal* was still secured in Devonport, trials for the entry into service of the Phantom were getting under way. The flying trials for the Phantom were carried out in *Eagle* during 1969. One of the test pilots involved in these trials was the Commanding Officer of C Squadron from Boscombe Down, Cdr F. Hefford DSC, AFC (now Captain F. Hefford OBE, DSC, AFC). '*Eagle*'s jet-blast deflectors (JBDs), like all those fitted to British carriers, were solid metal, without cooling. The Phantom F4K had Rolls Royce Spey engines, which had to be installed at a slight downward angle, as compared to the US-engined versions. In addition, the nose wheel extension was increased to improve the catapult take-off and avoid the necessity for the pilot to put in a large tailplane angle change in order to rotate the aircraft as it left the bows. The resultant angle of jet efflux, combined with the very high temperature of the exhaust, would have caused serious damage to the deflectors. *Ark Royal* was therefore being fitted with water-cooled JBDs, but *Eagle* would not be fitted with them. However, a clever fix was being planned, which consisted of a half-inch thick steel plate, to be bolted to the deck just aft of the catapult. The JBDs would not be used. It was calculated that the plate would protect the flight deck from the heat. The plate would have to be cooled using the fire hoses after every launch, before aircraft tyres were allowed to pass over them. It was decided that, in the meantime, much useful data could be obtained from approaches and roller landings. Therefore, having gathered sufficient approach and landing data ashore, we flew to *Eagle* on 10 March. We used three Phantoms for the trials (XT865, XV567 and XT857). The weather was not good and many of the approaches were carrier-controlled approaches (CCA). Between 10 and 21 March, I did twelve CCAs and thirty-nine roller landings with the hook up,' Hefford recalled.

While *Eagle* was being fitted with the steel plate, development work continued as Hefford explained: 'We devised a stick restraining device for use during the catapult launch. The idea was to set a tailplane angle while holding the stick against a wire strap which was under tension, and retracted into the instrument panel when not needed. The tension was such that, should the pilot need more aft stick, he could overcome the restraining device. We completed tests at RAE Bedford before embarking and established that very consistent safe launchings were possible, whereas USN launches showed very large variations in the rate and angle of rotation off the catapult. We could not use the "hands free" launch which was designed into, and was so successful, in the Buccaneer, because the control system balance was such as to cause the stick to rotate aft during launch, but we felt that this was the next best thing. The disadvantage was that it had to be unclipped from the stick during the climb.'

Lt Cdr Peter Bell (now Cdr Peter Bell OBE) joined *Ark Royal* as the Direction Officer in May 1969. 'At the time I joined the ship she was due to begin her sea trials shortly. However, this deadline slipped and we did not go to sea until the December. The delays had in part been caused by the political uncertainty surrounding the future of *Ark Royal*. One factor which helped ensure the completion of the refit was the fact that *Ark Royal* was the dockyard's major project at the time, so if the government had cancelled the refit halfway through, not only would it have wasted the money spent up to that point, but it would also have meant that there would have been a large number of dockyard workers laid off because there was no other similar sized project for them to work on. One of the problems caused by the delay was what to do with the large number of ratings who had been assigned to *Ark Royal*. The ship was not yet ready to accommodate them and this presented a big problem because the barrack accommodation in Devonport was already over subscribed as it was. To solve the problem some of the old accommodation blocks at HMS *Drake* were reopened for the *Ark Royal* crew. These old wooden sheds were below the standard of the more modern barracks, yet the sailors seemed very happy. In my opinion they were happier in this boy scout style of accommodation than they were in the modern accommodation blocks.'

With the steel plate fitted, *Eagle* was ready for the second batch of Phantom trials between 2 and 13 June 1969, as Hefford recalled: 'For the second set of trials two Phantoms were used, XT865 and XT857. In all I did thirty day and four night arrested landings. Launches were tested at launch speeds from 15 knots above minimum launching speed to 10 knots below minimum launching speed. Trim settings for launch were varied from nominal, to both over and under trim, in combination with take-off weights up to 50,000lb with re-heat, to maximum take-off weight with full military power, i.e. without re-heat, the aim being to establish the limits for safe operation of the aircraft in service. Speeds below minimum launching speed caused the aircraft to sink after launch, under-trim caused a nose down pitch, and over-trim resulted in a pitch-up, and above minimum landing speed a steep climb. When the Phantom was launched, the plate glowed red until cooled by the firecrews. At night I'm told, since I never saw it, always being in the first aircraft to launch at night, it was white hot and rippling like water with an air hose played on it. The steel plate worked so well that *Eagle*'s Captain, Johnny Treacher, asked MOD if he could retain the plate on board, so that the ship could act as spare deck when so required.'

Ark Royal received her next Captain, when Captain R. Lygo (now Admiral Sir Raymond Lygo KCB) assumed command on 17 July 1969. Lygo recalled: 'The Admiralty did something which I believe had never been done either before or since, when I was appointed as in command of *Ark Royal* and also on the staff of Admiral Superintendent Devonport Dockyard. This meant that I was a Staff Officer so I could actually start telling the dockyard what to do, which came as a severe blow to their system. When I was told to go down to Devonport it was a politically worrying time because the refit was running late and there was every prospect that if the ship ran too late, and overran in cost, the Government would stop it, and the ship would not recommission, and that would be the end of aircraft carriers in the RN. It was therefore very important to get the ship out of dock on time, but it was a massive job. We had a completion date in the early part of December 1969 and I told the Commander that I wanted a notice placed on the gangway, showing the number of days left to go before we sailed. Gradually the dockyard began to realize that I meant to go. We had quite a tough time and it soon became a question of whether I would go with the ship incomplete.'

As the year progressed and the scaffolding began to be taken down, it revealed the many external changes to the ship. The refit provided *Ark Royal* with the biggest expanse of flight deck ever given to a British aircraft carrier. The flight deck was fully angled, from its previous 5½ degrees, to 8 degrees 24 minutes. Fly 1 was given a minor increase on the starboard side, while Fly 3 and Fly 4 were greatly increased by two new deck extensions. The starboard catapult was uprooted and replaced by a new 200ft BS4 waist catapult on the angled flight deck. While the port catapult was overhauled it remained both at its original length of 154ft, and in its original position. The performance of the catapults was enhanced by the decision to replace the old CALE gear roller mats and fit individual chocks for the Buccaneer and Phantom. This meant that the aircraft could be launched at the maximum stroke, which gave an effective gain of up to 9 feet, or 8 knots, more than the CALE gear. To cater for the Phantom, both catapults were fitted with water-cooled jet-blast deflectors. The need for these was clearly seen from the experience of the Phantom trials in *Eagle*. The Phantoms of 892 had also caused damage to the flight deck of the USS *Saratoga* during their period of training in October 1969. The front ends of both catapults were fitted with the Van Zelm bridle arresting gear, complete with the distinctive extensions beyond the edge of the flight deck. Although the American Navy had used bridle arresters for their carriers, the RN had not used them since the early 1950s, except for a brief period on *Victorious* in the 1960s. Four new

While the crews of 892 Squadron were waiting for *Ark Royal* to emerge from her refit, they were deployed to the USS *Saratoga* for a fortnight in October 1969 to gain useful experience of operating their new aircraft. (FAA Museum)

wires of the direct-action arresting gear (DA2) replaced the Mark 13 arresting gear. As part of the DA2, four tubes each 195ft long were fitted along each side of the upper hangar deckhead.

To enable Little F to observe all of the flight deck operations fully, flyco was completely rebuilt and enlarged. Although the island didn't receive the same attention as that given to *Eagle*, the amount of space was increased by building a two-deck extension over the Alaskan Highway, while aft of the island, a new structure was built to house the American precision Controlled Carrier Approach system AN-SPN 35, otherwise known as Spin 35, which provided full glide path information.

Down below she was essentially a new ship. Everything except the DC ring main was rewired, with an estimated 1,200 miles of cable used. An AC supply was fitted with a generating capacity equivalent to an AC Leander frigate. While the cable used sounds a lot, it is nothing compared to the work involved in connecting up the countless cable ends. The refit did improve one vital area, namely the accommodation throughout the ship, in particular the mess decks for the junior ratings. During the fifth commission the poor quality of accommodation on board *Ark Royal* was highlighted in the national press. The increase in the angled flight deck, the removal of the final pair of 4.5in guns, and changes to the aft end of the upper hangar, created more usable space to help create seven extra mess decks for junior ratings. In the Far East the heat down below had been oppressive. To counter this problem, air-conditioning was fitted throughout the ship. The days of hammocks had finally passed on board *Ark Royal*, as bunks were fitted throughout the ship, and the standard of accommodation was brought up to that of the Leander class frigates. The ship's TV system was extended so that every mess deck was provided with a TV.

Among the final set of trials to be completed before sailing, were the dead load firing trials, as Crowden recalled: 'A four wheel bogie was used which sat on the catapult, and there was a safety boat ahead of the ship and safety flags flying all over. You had to progressively increase the weight of the bogie being fired off the catapult, thus producing a big splash before it was recovered by the floating crane. This procedure was repeated over and over again. It could take anything up to half an hour between firings. Before the bogie could be fired again, you had to check that the rubber tyres were still intact. To increase the weight of the bogie, it was filled with water.'

Five hundred dockyard workers formed part of the ship's company during the preliminary sea trials. However, shortly before the start of the preliminary sea trials the number of dockyard workers entitled to Wardroom accommodation increased. 'To cater for this increase we accommodated many of these dockyard workers in the aircrew cabins, because obviously the squadrons would not be embarked for these trials. Accommodation problems were also eased by leaving behind all non-essential crew who were not required for the trials, which included most of the direction officers!', Bell remembered. 'For those dockyard workers not entitled to Wardroom accommodation, we had special cabins built in the hangars because they would not accept the living conditions of the ratings mess decks,' Lygo recalled.

'Before sailing,' Lygo said, 'I asked Captain Treacher, who was in command of *Eagle* at the time, if I could ride with him but it was impossible to do an entry or exit at that time. I also asked the Captain of *Hermes*, but he was not operating out of Devonport at that time, which was not surprising because she was a Portsmouth ship. I did, however, go to sea in both of them to get the feel of an aircraft carrier. The Navigator and I went down the Hamoaze in a tug so that we would get all the running marks and bearings. Before we left, I had all of the Engineer Officers in the boiler room go through all of the engine movements I was going to make, because there were a lot of engine movements needed to get her round the turns out of Devonport. As a result, they

Perhaps the first landing on board *Ark Royal* after her Phantomization as a Wessex tries out the new flight deck prior to sea trials. *Eagle* is berthed astern. (Commander Monsell via the author)

would know exactly where we were, and what was going on, which was crucial because inside she was essentially a new ship.

The first attempt to sail was cancelled at the last minute due to the low visibility, and the weather had not improved much the next day when Captain Lygo once more postponed her departure, this time due to high winds. On the third day Captain Lygo risked all, with only three out of the four boiler rooms in commission and the winds at Force 6–7, which was above the Force 4 to 5 limit for moving *Ark Royal* in and out of Plymouth. Lygo explained his reason for taking the risk on 15 December 1969: 'If anything had gone wrong I would have been blamed for hazarding the ship by taking it out before it was ready. But if I had waited for that ship to be completely ready it would have been a year late. By forcing her out and dragging everyone with me, I achieved the objective and we were able to commission the following spring, by which time the ship was in every respect ready.'

After the satisfactory completion of the four days of preliminary sea trials and *Ark Royal*'s return to Devonport on 19 December 1969, the next challenge to be dealt with was the completion of the remaining jobs prior to commissioning and the removal of 2,000 tons of gash. The recommissioning date was set for 24 February 1970 with a ceremony to be held on board which was to be attended by HM the Queen Mother. Therefore, the ship had to be at its very best for its royal visitor, and all of the ship's trophies had to be recovered from storage including the ship's bell, as Bell recalled: 'We suddenly remembered that we ought to go and get the ship's bell back on board. The only problem was that no one could recall where it was. Eventually, we managed to track it down to someone's office, where it had been placed when the ship was destored in 1966.'

The *Ark Royal* star and bars presented to HM the Queen Mother by Captain Lygo and Commander Crowden, the instigator of the *Ark Royal* bar and star. The bars denote six visits by the Queen Mother to 'her' ship. (Author)

As the refit was drawing to a close, Cdr Crowden came up with a novel way for those who had served in *Ark Royal* during the long refit to commemorate their service, by creating the *Ark Royal* star and bar. He explained this unique souvenir: 'The idea first started in the Marine Engineering Department and later found support throughout the ship. The bars would represent each year or part year served in *Ark Royal*. As any time served in *Eagle* provided equally valuable experience, it was decided that bars for *Eagle* as well as *Ark Royal* would be produced. Time in refit would count the same as sea time, because the work was probably just as hard and at times the conditions far more exacting! The design of the star was based on the 1939–45 War Star for simplicity, with the ship's badge of *Ark Royal* as the centre decoration. Messrs J.R. Gaunt Ltd of Soho, London, willingly accepted the order and produced special dies for the star and two bars. The stars and bars were struck in white metal, with a surface finish of electroplated nickel silver and suspended from the 1¼in plain crimson ribbon of the Victorian Army Long Service and Good Conduct Medal. This particular ribbon was withdrawn from use at the turn of the century, as it was getting confused with that of the Victoria Cross. The colour, however, was not far off the traditional colour for *Ark Royal* (and Marine Engineers), so the choice was perhaps appropriate. Just over one hundred stars were produced together with some two hundred and fifty *Ark Royal* and sixty *Eagle* bars.' The ship's patron HM the Queen Mother was not forgotten because she was presented with an *Ark Royal* star and bar, with five bars to commemorate each of her visits to the ship, by both Captain Lygo and Cdr Crowden at Clarence House on 11 March 1971.

Chapter Eight

THE KOTLIN INCIDENT

SIXTH COMMISSION, PART I,

FEBRUARY 1970–JULY 1973

Despite the Government spending £32 million on *Ark Royal*'s Phantomization refit, the future of the ship looked very uncertain at the time of her recommissioning ceremony on 24 February 1970 which was attended by the Queen Mother. Lygo explained: 'We had an enormous problem, because at that time the Fleet Air Arm was under sentence of death and I had to maintain the morale of the men. We were only going to have one more commission and then the ship was going to pay off. During the refit I had told the dockyard that they had to ensure that *Ark Royal* would be capable of remaining at sea for another ten years rather than one commission. At the time of her commissioning you weren't allowed to talk about aircraft carriers and I remember saying at the Commissioning ceremony, which was attended among others by David Owen who was Minister for the Navy, "Welcome to *Ark Royal*. For those of you who came up a covered gangway, you may not be aware that you actually have come aboard an aircraft carrier – there, I have actually said the words" and there was deathly silence. I then went on to talk about the merits of the aircraft carrier. I always sailed very close to the wind with such comments.' Over 4,000 people attended the ceremony, and after lunch the Queen Mother toured the ship to meet some of the ship's company.

With the festivities of the commissioning over, it was time for the ship's company to return to the long job of making *Ark Royal* fully operational again, by undertaking more trials. On 4 March *Ark Royal* left her moorings for heeling trials in Plymouth Sound, as Crowden explained: 'We were in Plymouth Sound and all machinery was running. We flooded various wing compartments to create a list of 10 to 15 degrees. This was to prove that the new machinery with lubricating oil sumps, as installed, wasn't going to lose suction through the permanent list for half an hour. We also had an inclining experiment in the ship's programme, which is when you have a dead ship, all the bilges are dry and all the tanks and watertight compartments are either topped right up or are dry. Weights are then moved across the ship from one side of the ship to the other. You have a plum bob on a long piece of piano wire down one of the after hatches, with the plum bob in an oil bath so that you can obtain an accurate measurement of the angle of heel with the ship listed to one side by the transfer of known weights. From this it is possible to calculate the ship's centre of gravity for stability purposes.' Having completed heeling trials in Plymouth Sound *Ark Royal* sailed for further performance trials in the Portland area. On 9 March the honours for the first fixed-wing recovery of the commission went to 809 Squadron when their Senior Observer and CO landed on board in a Buccaneer S2. Although *Ark Royal* had become the first aircraft carrier to embark the first operational squadron of Buccaneers when 801 Squadron embarked for a month in 1963, she had never operated Buccaneers on a regular basis until 1970. The following day, *Ark Royal* embarked her first RN Phantom for trials of the new jet-blast deflectors. It was during these trials in March that *Ark Royal* rendezvoused with

Inside one of *Ark Royal*'s boiler rooms.
(Captain Crowden via the author)

Ark Royal and *Eagle* meet for the last time at sea off the Moray Firth in March 1970.
(Commander Monsell via the author)

Eagle: it was the last time that these two great ships met at sea while in commission. *Eagle* was engaged in service release trials for the RAF Harrier GR1, to enable the Harrier to be operated at sea from RN carriers. 'We were very worried about the Harrier because they were taking off with only recovery fuel, which meant they should have landed straight back on deck,' Bell recalled. These trials were to lay the groundwork which eventually led to RAF Harrier GR3s being embarked in *Hermes* during the Falklands War, and the subsequent deployment of RAF Harrier GR5s to the Gulf in 1997/8. Once the flying trials with the Phantom and Buccaneer were completed, *Ark Royal* steamed north for two days of measured mile runs off the Isle of Arran before entering Devonport for post-trials rectification on 25 March. She remained there until 20 April when she slipped her moorings for further trials in the Plymouth and Portland areas, before setting sail for Rotterdam

Ark Royal on the Arran measured mile in
March 1970. (Captain Crowden via the
author)

and her first foreign port visit of the commission. While the ship was in Holland a new tulip was given the name
Ark Royal in honour of the ship.

After the three-day break it was time for yet more trials, as aircraft were once more embarked. Hefford
recalled the Phantom deck trials on *Ark Royal* on 30 April: 'Lt Cdr Richard Burn in XT865 and myself in XT857
flew to the ship off the south coast. After two roller landings we were told to land-on. I made my first attempt
with Air Commodore Browne, CO of Boscombe Down acting as observer but, to my dismay and his
consternation, I missed the wires and bolted. Richard was on first time and I, shortly after. The trials in *Ark
Royal* included: approaches using APCS and launches up to 56,000lb; launches and landings with asymmetric
stores; military power launches and all expected stores configurations. *Ark Royal*'s water-cooled jet-blast
deflectors worked well and proved to be reliable. Noise measurements were assessed and found to be no worse
than the Sea Vixen. Impact-at-touchdown measurements were taken to confirm that no damage would be done
to the deck at low wind speed over deck and at high aircraft weight (i.e. higher speeds at touchdown).' Flying
trials were continued at the beginning of May after a two-day visit to C buoy in Plymouth Sound for deadload
trials. The need for further deadload trials was caused by a flicker in the catapult instrumentation, but all was
found to be well. The subsequent trials were marred by the loss without trace of a Phantom from 892 Squadron
on 3 May. The situation was made worse for the families of the missing crew by certain parts of the press
circulating the idea that the Phantom had not been lost but in fact had defected to the USSR. Needless to say the
story was completely bogus and just caused unnecessary extra distress.

Lygo remembered other unusual items being fired off the catapult: 'Dudley Moore and Peter Cook came on
board to do some filming, on 4 and 5 May, for the programme *Not Only But Also*. The final scene was the piano
going off the catapult with Dudley Moore playing it. I was looking down from the bridge and I saw this piano.
I said, "I want a Fly Navy sticker on that piano", and so the message went down and the producer came back and
said, "No." When I was told this I said, "Well, the piano is not going." I am told that when the producer was told
"Captain says it's not to be launched", he turned to the sailor and asked, "Can he say that?", to which the sailor
replied, "That man can say whatever he likes!" Thus the piano had a Fly Navy sticker on it when it was launched.'
The ship also managed to get some personal advertising in a roadworks scene which was to form the opening

sketch. Part of the flight deck was made to look like a road, so that it only became obvious that they were in fact on board *Ark Royal* when the camera zoomed out. Letters 20ft high were painted, with water soluble paint, spelling out the title of the show while *Ark Royal* was written on the island.

After the completion of the flying trials, *Ark Royal* once more entered Devonport for rectification work on 15 May. While these trials established the effectiveness of the various departments of the ship, the supply department had to be fully operational. Lt Cdr O'Donnell (now Captain O'Donnell) was the Deputy Supply Officer at this time. 'I was responsible to the Supply Officer for the efficient running of one of the very largest departments of the ship which affected the morale of the entire ship's company as we paid them, fed them and clothed them. In addition, without us to provide all the spare parts for the entire floating city and squadrons, the ship would not remain operational,' O'Donnell remarked.

At the beginning of June 1970 the air group embarked for the first time. The new air group comprised 892 Squadron flying Phantom FGR1s, 809 Squadron flying Buccaneer S2s, 849 B Flight flying Gannet AEW3s and one Gannet COD4, 824 Squadron flying Sea King HAS1s, and the Ship's Flight consisting of two Wessex HAS1s. This line-up was to remain virtually unaltered until she paid off, except for two changes. Firstly, the replacement of the COD Gannet by an extra Sea King for 824 Squadron in 1972. Secondly, the updating of the Sea Kings to HAS2 standard in 1977. *Ark Royal*'s CAG included two aircraft types which were entirely new to the RN. For the Air Engineering department this meant the stowage of 16,000 stores items more for the Phantom than the Sea Vixen, and an extra 2,000 stores items more for the Sea King than the Wessex. The first embarkation of *Ark Royal*'s squadrons after her refit began a new safer era for the aircrew. Lt Gerry Kinch (now Cdr Gerry Kinch) served in 892 Squadron as an observer during this period. Previously, he had served as a Sea Vixen observer in 899 Squadron in *Eagle* during the Beira patrol. Describing some of the differences between the Fleet Air Arm of the mid- to late 1960s, which had suffered a number of tragic accidents, and the final phase of conventional fixed-wing flying in the RN after *Ark Royal*'s 1967–70 refit, he remarked: 'After we had

Sea King HAS1s of 824 Squadron frame their home. (Rowland Fleming via the author)

Buccaneer S2 of 809 Squadron lands on board *Ark Royal*. (Rowland Fleming via the author)

A Phantom of 892 Squadron coming in to land. (Rod Lampen via the author)

embarked for the first time in 1970, it took little time to appreciate the differences in the "heavy" element of the Air Group compared with the 1960s. Now geared to the Atlantic/Mediterranean NATO role, the composition and potential capabilities of each squadron had improved. The aircraft were more capable and reliable; the aircrew were more experienced overall and the threat was more clearly defined. In particular the accident rate tailed off dramatically. In the 1960s the mortality rate was unacceptably high, and this was reflected in the on board humour of the time which, looking back with the perspectives and attitudes of 1998, would be deemed totally unacceptable in the RN, let alone by the British public. I remember waking very early to the crash alarms sounding off, the ship going hard astern, then reaching the crewroom to find sodden aircrew making their way with or without help to the sickbay. On sadder occasions, nothing came back on board at all and an air of gloom pervaded the ship until at least evening bar opening, by which time a new commemorative verse to a popular FAA song had been written. Nobody considered that there was anything remotely macabre or sick in such goings on.' Lt Peter Hardy (now Lt Cdr Hardy) also served in 892 Squadron as an observer at this time. On the theme of improvements in safety in the 1970s on board *Ark Royal*, he said: 'Another safety improvement after the refit was the introduction of the Landing Safety Officer (LSO). The LSO actually sat on the mirror sight and told the pilot what he was doing, providing amplifying instructions where required, which, with the pilot making his own instinctive adjustments, provided a far safer, and controlled, deck landing environment.' It was also easier in the 1970s to draw dangerous situations to the attention of senior officers without having to worry about the repercussions, as Kinch explained: 'The *Anymouse* system is a system where anyone who comes across a set of circumstances which indicates a potential danger may report this anonymously but, as no one could spell anonymously, it was known as *Anymouse* with an appropriate little mouse logo. There was a special form which you did not have to sign and therefore preserved your anonymity. Once completed the form was posted in one of the boxes around the ship.'

In between work up periods, which were to continue until the end of July, *Ark Royal* made her first visit to Liverpool since she left Cammell Laird for acceptance trials in 1955. The visit, between 27 and 30 June, enabled the ship to rekindle its links with its birthplace as well as the city of Leeds, because Liverpool was the nearest port to Leeds capable of accommodating *Ark Royal*.

The date 31 July 1970 is one which will be remembered for a long time by many sailors because it saw the passing of an era. The Admiralty had decided to abolish the rum ration and 31 July was the last time it would be issued. To enable the ship's company to mark the passing of the tot in style *Ark Royal* tied up to C buoy in Plymouth Sound for the day. When the Admiralty made its decision Captain Lygo decided not to announce the decision over the ship's TV, instead he assembled the ship's company in the hangar deck and made the announcement personally, as Lygo explained: 'With the men fallen-in in front of me I could sense immediately

Ark Royal arrives in Liverpool on 27 June 1970, visiting her birthplace for the first time since she left in 1955 to begin her RN career. (Captain Crowden via the author)

The last rum tot sealed forever. (Author)

how the message was coming across, and I would know what they were thinking, whether it was going down well or going down badly. However, if I was in the TV studio I would be remote and could not see what was going on and that was why I never used the TV system for making those types of announcement during my time in command. On the day of the abolition of the rum tot we had a great ceremony, with a coffin draped with the last tot and marched it all round the ship.' Crowden recalled: 'I was invited to the engine room artificer's mess to serve the last tot in *Ark Royal*. Afterwards they said, "We want you to have the copper measure", which had been used in *Ark Royal* for dispensing rum to the senior rates, who could have their rum neat, as opposed to the junior rates who had to have it with water. One interesting point about the measure was that it was cut off in an uneven way so that the rum would not be quite the full measure. Therefore, everyone thought they were getting the full tot but there would be a small amount of rum accumulating at the bottom of the barrel which could be used for guests. Sometimes, in earlier days in the Wardroom, it was not unknown to solder a silver threepenny bit to do the same dodge – but only to bolster up a flagging wine account!'

Ark Royal spent the whole of August in Devonport for an assisted-maintenance period (AMP). During this period *Ark Royal* was the star of Navy Days in Devonport with 30,000 visitors coming on board for a look round the last of a dying breed. Following two days of flying exercises *Ark Royal* returned to C buoy to embark many of the ship's company's families on 5 September for an eventful Families Day, as Lygo recalled: 'We had about 2,000 families on board who were ferried out to *Ark Royal* by tugs, etc. and then I took *Ark Royal* out to sea with the decks covered in people. I was taking the ship out past the breakwater when the Commander, accompanied by this man and woman appeared on the bridge. The Commander said, "Captain, I would like you to meet Mr and Mrs Jackson." I was thinking to myself has this man gone mad? But it turned out that the couple had thought

Looking more like a cruise ship, *Ark Royal* is pictured here on Families Day, 5 September 1970. (Rod Lampen via the author)

they were catching the Torpoint ferry, instead they ended up having a day at sea in *Ark Royal*. They had travelled from Birmingham and were intending to see their son at HMS *Raleigh* when they caught the wrong ferry. When I was heading back into port I was very nearly committed to the entry, when there was suddenly this cry of "Man Overboard" so I turned the ship right round. A sailor who had been working in the boats had fallen out, so we picked him up and headed in. One way and another it had been an exciting day.' Lampen continued: 'My grandfather, who had served at the Battle of Jutland as a stoker, came out for the day and one of the things which he mentioned had improved since his day in the Navy, was the quality of the food which he thought was good. He was also amazed at how clean the ship was, which really isn't too much of a surprise when you remember that the ships he served in burned coal as opposed to *Ark Royal* which burned furnace fuel oil (FFO).'

With the congestion of Families Day on board over, *Ark Royal* sailed from Plymouth Sound on 7 September to begin ten days of flying exercises and work up in the Bristol Channel and Irish Sea. Between 8 and 9 September, *Ark Royal* stood by the burning wreck of the coaster MV *St Brandan* until the destroyer *Cavalier* took her in tow to Milford Haven to earn some salvage money. Describing the work up itself, Kinch recalled: 'The whole period was rife with difficulties for both the ship and her aircraft. The arrester wires were not sufficiently reliable to stay operational long enough to permit aircraft operations out of range from diversion airfields. One incident which typifies this was when I was part of a group of aircraft diverted to RAF Valley on 11 September 1970 at 22:45. We ended up at Valley with about five Phantoms, five Buccaneers and a couple of Gannets because the last arrester wire had broken. It was the fifth time that evening that the wire had broken.' The Phantom also experienced difficulties during its entry into FAA service, as Kinch explained: 'In the early days of the Phantom's service we had a number of problems with the Rolls Royce Spey engines, such as difficulties in starting them up. At one stage we were limited to no more than 1g and restricted to turning the aircraft at no more than 30 degrees for fear of an engine flame out, all of which enforced limitations upon our effectiveness in performing our role. But this was the price of fitting the Rolls Royce Spey engine and its sophisticated fuel systems into an airframe which had not been originally designed to take them. I don't remember these teething problems being dangerous, they were just irritating because everyone in the squadron wanted to use this

Ark Royal with the wartime destroyer *Cavalier* which at the time of writing is facing a very uncertain future. (Rowland Fleming via the author)

tremendous new weapon system.' Comparing the FAA's new aircraft which had replaced the proven Sea Vixen on board *Ark Royal*, Kinch said: 'The Sea Vixen was armed with the infra-red Red Top missiles which had a very limited head-on capability. Unless the target was coming towards you fast enough to generate enough infra-red for the head to detect it, you had to take the target from behind. The radar had a detection range of Sea Vixen to Sea Vixen of about 30 miles head-on and the aircraft could only achieve 0.95 Mach. But the Sea Vixen was very difficult to outperform at high altitude unless you were up against a Vulcan bomber which had better manoeuvrability at 50,000 feet. The Phantom had the Sparrow missile which was designed to be fired head-on and could be fired at about 13.5 miles. The Phantom also had a rear attack capability with either Sidewinder or Sparrow. The radar could detect small aircraft at up to 50 miles and larger aircraft, such as a Victor, at about 80 miles. When it came to fighting the Phantom, we incorporated a number of lessons which the Americans had learned from their experience in the Vietnam war. As a result we became much more effective in our overall role as defenders of the fleet, than we had been with the Sea Vixen.' Lt Douglas Macdonald (now Cdr Macdonald) served in 892 Squadron as an observer during this commission. Previously he had served in Sea Vixens as an observer. Explaining the differences between the Sea Vixen and the Phantom for the observers Macdonald said: 'The differences between the two aircraft as an observer were vast in that, as opposed to being shut down in a coal-hole with a great big radar set stuck in front of me, I was much more part of a crew. For example, when you were preparing to launch you could help the pilot with wing-tip clearances and lining up. In the Phantom we assisted in fighting the aircraft much more satisfactorily than we ever did as observers in the Sea Vixen and of course seeing out was a tremendous bonus. I remember my first flight in the back seat of a Phantom from Yeovilton and I thought to myself, what have I been doing for the last ten years stuck down in a coal-hole.'

At the end of September *Ark Royal* participated in her first major NATO exercise since her refit. Northern Wedding was held between 20 and 26 September. Any major exercise, by its very nature, tests the capabilities of all departments of the ship, and especially the Direction Officers. Bell described the role of the Direction Officer: 'The Direction Officers and the radar ratings received all the raw radar information and had to produce a picture for the command to appreciate the situation and take the appropriate action. In the air defence role on board an aircraft carrier, it was the Direction Officer who took the decision whether to attack a target or not, because events unfolded so quickly there was not the time to refer back to the command for a decision. However, the Direction Officer would keep the command informed of events. A major part of my job was to ensure the safe passage for recovery and launch of our aircraft through the protection zone formed by the escorting ships' weapons.' While the ship had been refurbished mechanically as part of the major refit, little had been done to her operations room, as Bell continued: 'Compared to *Eagle*, *Ark Royal*'s radar was still in the Stone Age. About the only advance was the addition of the two 965 Rs which had a moving target indicator (MTI) fitted. This meant we could set a gate at a certain speed, for example 60 knots. Thereafter anything which did not have a velocity of 60 knots was not shown on the screen and that cleaned up the picture no end. We were not able to operate both radars together, because I was told when I joined that it would have been too big an engineering/electrical job to have made the radars move round in phase. Therefore, only one radar was ever in use at a time, while the other one served as a back-up unit. Because of the way in which the aerials were mounted, if we had been able to use them together we would have had virtually gapless coverage, which while it still would not have been as good as *Eagle*'s radar, would have made a vast improvement to the effectiveness of *Ark Royal*'s radar fit.

On 28 September *Ark Royal* arrived at Oslo for the exercise debriefing which was held at the NATO HQ in Kolsas. When she left Oslo on 2 October the ship set course for Devonport to complete urgent repairs to the arrester gear and the catapults, which had been giving trouble during the exercise. Shortly after leaving, the ship ran into bad weather which continued to deteriorate through the night. On the following day some of the life-rafts were released by the heavy seas and the Ship's Flight were called upon to stand-by to recover them. However, one of the Sea Kings was later launched to go and sink the life-rafts by small arms fire so as to avoid sparking off a false alarm. Then, as the day progressed, *Ark Royal* received distress calls from two other ships close by. One of the two ships ended up requiring assistance, so 824 Squadron launched a Sea King to rescue three members of the German coaster *Leda*'s crew. *Leda* was already listing by the time the Sea King arrived and actually sank as the last man was winched off. On 4 October the ship entered Devonport for six days of work. Having completed four days of trials of the catapults and arrester gear, *Ark Royal* set course for the Mediterranean.

Prior to entering Malta for a self-maintenance period, Captain Lygo decided to allow the ship's company to take advantage of the good weather. 'I had called hands to bathe and about 1,500 men were in the water. The shadowing Russian Kotlin destroyer was amazed by this performance as he lay off watching this about a cable or so away. He then made a signal to us saying, "They go Malta". My chaps said, "The Russians say good morning, so what do you want to say?" I said, "Nothing, don't answer them." I would find that these youngsters would look at me and I would ask, "You want to know why I am not answering them? Because they don't have our sense of humour and whatever I say can be misconstrued, so I am not saying anything to them", and I never did', Lygo explained. *Ark Royal* then entered Malta for ten days of maintenance on 19 October. While *Ark Royal* was in Malta, Captain Lygo learned of the decision to extend *Ark Royal*'s service. 'I was having dinner with Flag Officer Malta and the Navy Minister had flown out to Malta. After dinner the Minister asked if he could take me to one side and have a word, so we went out onto the balcony overlooking Dockyard Creek and he said, "You have won." "How do you mean I have won?" I asked. "We are going to extend *Ark Royal*, well done Ray, you have won." "What about *Eagle*?" "No, I am talking about *Ark Royal*." "I know you are talking *Ark Royal*, you could not have avoided extending *Ark Royal* but what about *Eagle*?" "No, no, not *Eagle*." "Well, the point is you should be extending *Eagle* as well!"' Lygo recalled. At the end of October 1970, *Eagle*'s fate was confirmed in the White Paper on Defence, which attributed the decision to manpower shortages and the potential cost. The £5 million needed to enable *Eagle* to operate Phantoms on a permanent basis would have been a relatively small price to pay compared to the £32 million which had already been spent on the less capable *Ark Royal*. Had this money been spent she could possibly have continued to operate into the 1980s, because she was always regarded, mechanically, as much more reliable than her younger sister ship.

When *Ark Royal* left Malta bound for Exercise Lime Jug there was a greater feeling of confidence on board in the ship's ability to perform to her potential. It seemed as though the earlier faults with the catapults and arrester gear, which had plagued the ship since she recommissioned, had been solved. However, the events of the night of 9 November were to ensure that the exercise was remembered for very different reasons, when *Ark Royal* collided with a Russian Kotlin class destroyer which had been previously shadowing her. At the time it was the height of the Cold War, and the Russians were always looking to see just how far they could push the Captains of Western warships before they would give way, as Lygo explained: 'The Russians would arrange to get themselves into position where they would force you to give way by putting you under the Rule of the Road as a giving way vessel. Then even if you had the right of way, they would come straight at you and alter course at the last moment which was OK for the smaller Russian ships but it was not so easy for the bigger Western ships such as *Ark Royal*. The Americans had decided that this was so dangerous that they would have a separate signal between the two sides. I said no, we weren't going to do that because there were international rules for the prevention of collision at sea and they were perfectly adequate. I was not going to have any special signals because that would be a concession. The destroyers which were sent to shadow us would change over at night, so your shadowing destroyer would disappear off the screen astern and then it would reappear. It was not until the next morning that you would see that it was a different destroyer.'

Describing the events of 9 November, Crowden recalled: 'From first light it had been a normal flying day for the fixed-wing operation of Phantoms, Buccaneers and Gannets, and regular flights for the Sea King helicopters. At one period when not required for SAR duties, the Wessex helicopter had done a "milk run" with fresh bread rolls, mail and papers to the frigate in company. This frigate would be the plane guard for the evening's night-flying. A spectator to the day's activities had been the SAM Kotlin, the uninvited but ever present Russian observer.' Lygo continued: 'We had a change of shadowing destroyer and I think he was "the new boy on the block". He started doing his shadowing and we then began night-flying. We were about 200 miles south of

The Russian SAM Kotlin 365 destroyer passes very close to *Ark Royal* during the day prior to their collision. (Rod Lampen via the author)

A Gannet AEW3 of 849 Squadron B Flight. (Mick Smith)

A Ship's Flight Wessex HAS1. (Mick Smith)

Crete. I was having my supper just behind the bridge in the Captain's night cabin. The Officer of the Watch asked, "Permission to come to flying course". I replied, "Yes, if it is clear to do so and where is the Russian?" He answered, "He will be well clear when we come round", so I told him to come round and I finished what I was eating before going out on the bridge. The ship was still turning and we came on to the flying course. The Officer of the Watch then said to me, "The Russian is on a steady bearing." I told him to keep an eye on him and make sure that all the flying lights were burning brightly. These lights signal that you are operating aircraft and have right of way over everything else. The officer confirmed that the lights were burning brightly, so I ordered him to start flashing the signal "Uniform" at him which means, in the International Code of Signals, "You are standing into danger". We launched the first Phantom which at night is quite a fireworks display, but still the Russian approached us, so I ordered the officer to signal "Uniform" on the 20in lamp, which illuminated the Kotlin as it continued to approach. By this time the second Phantom was warming up prior to launch but as the Kotlin continued to approach I ordered the launch to stop and I sat there to see what would happen. The International Rules are quite clear on this point, because they state that the ship which has right of way should maintain its course and speed until collision becomes unavoidable. I waited until the Kotlin disappeared under the flare of the bow. I then ordered full astern and she came up all-standing because we were only doing about 10–12 knots. The Kotlin came shooting out the other side having struck *Ark Royal*'s starboard anchor. This had rolled the Kotlin over and the propeller guard clipped *Ark Royal*'s stem.'

The observer in the Phantom that was just about to be launched prior to the collision with the Kotlin was Lt Kinch. 'I was due to fly with the CO of 892, Nick Kerr. We were sitting on the catapult and were in communication with flyco on channel 1, and in visual communication with the Flight Deck Officer (FDO). At this stage the adrenaline was beginning to flow and the FDO brought up his green wand which winds you up into afterburner. Not surprisingly, you get a residual glow through the rear view mirrors from the afterburners. We seemed to stay in afterburner for ages and we asked each other, "Can you see anything? Is there anything wrong? There's nobody ducking down below the aircraft?" We spoke to flyco and they replied, "Stand-by", which was not the kind of thing you wanted to hear because you mentally ask yourself, "Is there something wrong? Am I about to get a reduced power catapult shot? (a cold shot)." Then up came the red wand which cancelled the launch. We were taken off the catapult and taxied into Fly 1 still wondering what was happening, because everything appeared to be working. At that stage I looked down to port and there was this warship almost broached to. How did it get there without going almost under us?'

Describing the scene below decks immediately after the collision, and the damage inflicted by the collision, Crowden recalled: 'The effects of the impact were quickly established by the damage control teams and reported to Damage Control Headquarters – HQ1. HQ1 in turn would pass the damage reports to the Captain on the bridge. The first task of the damage control parties was to achieve the highest state of watertight integrity by closing doors and hatches, and isolating ventilation systems where they penetrated decks and bulkheads below the waterline. Simultaneously a check of every man on board was started to determine if anyone was missing or had become a casualty. The ship had been holed in the boatswain's store and there was a 3ft by 4ft hole in the ⅛in steel stem contour plate. Fortunately, the hole was about 4ft above the waterline and very little water had entered the ship. The Shipwright Officer inspected the damage and assessed the repairs required for restoring watertightness and hull strength. Clearly the hole would require some hours of outside work in daylight. The immediate action was therefore to seal off the damage to the stem as quickly as possible. This would enable the ship to get under way again without risk of flooding from the bow wave. The position of the hole made the construction of a cement box possible and in addition a small cofferdam or watertight bulkhead would be built.

'Unknown to the Mate of the 'tween Decks, the newly painted ship's company heads made an admirable mixing area. Tins of fast-setting damage control cement were piled in one alcove and two or three hardboard mixing pads were elsewhere. Each mix was stirred and prodded professionally by a stoker with a shovel. (Yes we still had a use for shovels!) Granulated cork was added to the mix to give it body and in the cement box extra reinforcement was given by adding short lengths of angle iron. This was to be no normal cement box since it would have to take the pressure of the ship thrusting its way through the water when operating aircraft, and in a month's time it would have to withstand the stresses of a full power trial, which was to be followed shortly afterwards by a winter passage through the Bay of Biscay. About six hours after the collision the cofferdam plate was welded in position and a temporary plate had been secured over the hole used for filling the cement box. The ship was then ready to get under way again at speeds up to 12 knots.'

Lygo described the aftermath of the collision: 'The trouble with a ship like *Ark Royal* is you can't stay stopped for long because the pressure builds up in the boilers, and the temperature rises, and sooner or later you need to start turning the engines to get rid of the heat. We sat there for a bit and I had the Engineer Officer on the phone fairly quickly to tell me the temperatures were rising. In the Wardroom that evening the officers were having their evening meal but when we went full astern everything went flying off the tables. We then learned that the Kotlin had lost seven men. I launched the helicopters and lowered the ship's boats. The Russian contribution was one boat under oars, with three men on one side and two on the other with the result that they went round in circles. While the helicopters sounded good, I soon realized that the best way of finding those lost men was in silence and to listen for their cries, so I quickly recovered the helicopters. We then began to recover some of the crew and returned them to their ship. I was given a message that we had found a Russian but he wouldn't get in the boat, so he swam back to the Kotlin with our boat escorting him.' O'Donnell described *Ark Royal*'s unexpected visitor: 'We recovered one crewman, who was taken to the sickbay for observation. One of my Midshipmen spoke a smattering of Russian and he was asked to accompany the crewman back to the Russian ship. We had dressed the Russian sailor in a new pair of shoes and action working-dress trousers and shirt. On arrival at the Russian ship, our Midshipman was not allowed any further than the top of the gangway, where he witnessed the poor Russian sailor stripped of his smart new clothes and shoes before being led away in his underwear. The clothes and shoes vanished, presumably to the Captain's cabin.'

Lygo explained one of the possible consequences if he had acted differently: 'Five crew from the Kotlin were recovered but two were missing and there were no casualties in *Ark Royal*. If I had not gone astern when I did, the Kotlin would have gone into the side of the ship and into a PO's mess which was full of men at the time.' While the collision with the Kotlin destroyer was a very serious event with possible international implications, there were a few light-hearted moments surrounding the incident as O'Donnell recalled: 'I was playing bridge at the time, down in the Wardroom with three of my fellow officers, when the alarm sounded. We dropped everything and ran like hell to get to our emergency stations, as the ship was rapidly shut down to achieve maximum watertight integrity. By about 01:00 I went back down to the Wardroom to make sure that everything had been secured after the emergency was over. Behind the bar was one of my stewards who asked politely if I would like to finish my bridge hand. I looked at him enquiringly, and from behind the bar he carefully produced all our cards and tricks that he had meticulously preserved when we ran to our emergency stations – I was greatly amused and very impressed at his concern for my well-being.'

Once the search had been called off *Ark Royal* completed a day of maintenance at sea on 11 November before rejoining the rest of the exercise on the following day. With the exercise over, *Ark Royal* set course for Malta on 14 November. 'A Board of Inquiry was to be convened in Malta on arrival. Captain David Scott who was the Captain of HMS *Fife* was appointed as the President of the Board. I wanted to do a boiler clean before I arrived in Malta and so I shut down two boilers so that I could do the clean at sea. David had a group of ships and I had an oiler so he asked permission to fuel and I replied "For you, Mr President, anything!" After refuelling he continued towards Malta. After dusk I had a message from *Fife* "I am on fire" and stating the position; by then he was about 45 miles ahead of us. With two boilers shut down I could not make more than 22 knots. I asked David what he wanted and he requested foam, which was ferried by both of the Wessex helicopters. As I closed in he was within one degree of having to launch his Sea Slugs because the temperature in the magazine was rising. So he told me to keep clear in case he had to start firing missiles. With a tremendous sense of humour, as we appeared David said, "Good evening, Mr President!" because he knew he would also be facing a Board of Inquiry,' Lygo recalled.

While *Ark Royal* was undergoing repairs in Malta, a new trophy was created as O'Donnell recalled: 'In the process of repairing the damaged area of the bow the torn steel was cut away and a piece shaped like a breaking comber was burnished like silver and mounted on a piece of polished teak. When the Board of Inquiry finally sat, there as a centrepiece on the table was this superb sculpture, with a small silver plate on it titled "Creation" by Sam Kotlin.'

The Board of Inquiry lasted one day with the result that Captain Lygo was cleared of any blame and allowed to continue his job as the Captain of *Ark Royal*. 'The real clincher was the track charts from our escorting frigate which proved beyond doubt what I had said. A few weeks after the collision Ted Anson, who was the Naval and Air Attaché in Tokyo, was at a cocktail party and he asked the Russian Naval Attaché Gorschov what really

'Creation by Sam Kotlin' – a piece of the damaged stem was mounted on polished teak and formed the centrepiece of the table at the Board of Inquiry. (Author)

A hot air balloon piloted by Lieutenant Terry Adams of 849 Squadron B Flight about to be launched early on the morning of 29 November 1970. (Rod Lampen via the author)

happened during that episode in the Mediterranean.' Anson reported: 'In the course of the conversation we were talking about what Gorschov planned to do when he retired and I asked him if he would get another sea job; "No" he replied, so I asked him would the man driving the Kotlin get another job at sea. He replied, "He was a foolish man, he got it wrong, he made a stupid mistake, and there is no way he will ever go to sea again." I wrote all this down and sent it back through the normal channels to London. The report was the first concrete evidence that the Russians admitted it was their fault and not the *Ark Royal*'s.'

Once the repairs had been completed *Ark Royal* left Malta on 26 November to conduct four days of flying exercises off the island. On 29 November before the day's flying got under way *Ark Royal* had one rather unusual airborne launch to complete, as Lygo recalled: 'I was told by Cdr (Air), Derek Monsell, that Lt Terry Adams from the Gannet squadron was a hot-air balloonist and that he had brought his balloon on board. I asked Cdr Monsell what he wanted to do with it, to which he replied, "He wants to fly it here." The day came and we had a gimmick that it was going to be the first delivery of mail to Malta by balloon. The trick was to get zero wind over the deck. This meant steaming downwind but we had to launch him upwind of Malta. We turned towards Malta and they started blowing up the balloon. I was steaming towards the cliffs of Malta and I kept asking if he was ready yet. The response was "No, not yet". The Navigating Officer was getting more and more worried and he finally said to me, "We are going to have to turn now, Sir, we can't hold on much longer." The poor old Navigator was getting paler and paler, and then suddenly there was this great cry of "He's off!" and I ordered 35 degrees to port and round we went. We stood there and watched him as he disappeared towards Malta, when suddenly there was a wind shift. I thought oh no, he's going to miss Malta and I will have to go round and try to get under him to recover the balloon.' Despite the Captain's concern, the *Bristol Belle*'s flight lasted for twenty-five minutes and ended with Lt Adams landing at Qrendi because the change in wind direction ruled out his intended destination of Ta' Qali. To commemorate the occasion a special First Day Cover was issued by the ship. The instigator of these First Day Covers was Lt Howard 'Stamps' Draper, who also produced covers to commemorate the commissioning and first embarkation of the squadrons, as well as the last day of the tot. In addition to providing a nice souvenir for the ship's company and their families, the covers were a useful source of money for the Welfare Fund.

With the flying exercises completed, *Ark Royal*'s first year back in commission was drawing to a close. On 3 December she entered Naples at the start of a five-day visit. While the use of illegal drugs has always been strongly dealt with in the Royal Navy, Lygo described an amusing incident during the ship's visit to Naples: 'The Commander came to see me and told me that 2,000 men had been ashore the night before and there had been no problems, to which I replied, "Oh good." "There is one problem," the Commander said, "they are selling drugs at the side of the dockyard gates, but don't worry Sir, they are in fact cigarettes full of donkey droppings." "Fine," I said, "don't tell them!"' With the visit to Naples successfully concluded, all that remained to be completed before *Ark Royal*'s return to Devonport for Christmas leave was two days of flying exercises off Sardinia and a two-day visit to Gibraltar, followed by her passage up Plymouth Sound on 18 December.

As the new year dawned, *Ark Royal* underwent nearly four months of docking and essential defects (DED). The major event of this time was the change of command when Captain Lygo handed over to his successor, Captain J.O. Roberts (now Rear Admiral Roberts CB), on 9 March 1971. As with his predecessors before him, one of the early hurdles to be negotiated during his time in command was the passage from the dockyard through Plymouth Sound and out to sea, as Roberts explained: 'Plymouth Sound is a fairly twisting entrance and in certain parts of the approach it's not only narrow but there is only about six feet of water under the keel. While she was in dry dock I went to see the bottom of the ship and it seemed to stretch out forever. I suddenly thought of this thing like a flat iron moving along with less than my height between it and the bottom of the channel and it was frightening to think just how close the margins really were sometimes. The first time I took her to sea, it was pretty frightening because I had never done anything like it before. From the time I assumed command to when I first took her to sea, I lost some sleep at night thinking about how I was going to get her out of Devonport. Much to my pleasant surprise my first trip down Plymouth Sound in command of *Ark Royal* went very smoothly and as we passed the last breakwater I breathed a sigh of relief.' Lampen, who served in *Ark Royal* as a Petty Officer, said about the change of command: 'On a big ship like *Ark Royal* you didn't really notice the change of Captain, whereas on a small ship or a submarine, the change was very noticeable because you came into contact with the Captain on a daily basis.'

Having successfully negotiated the tortuous passage down Plymouth Sound it was time for *Ark Royal* to begin the period of trials and work up which always follows any prolonged period alongside. Hardy recalled the wire-pulling trials in the middle of April 1971: 'Tim Gedge was my pilot when we embarked early for wire-pulling trials. The purpose of the trials was to check that the arrester wires were working properly, so you would do a normal approach to the carrier and land on correctly. The aircraft were embarked at this stage solely to check the wires, so if there was a problem we would not launch again until the wire had been fixed. Once the trials were successfully completed the rest of the CAG would then embark. During the trials, which typically lasted half a day, there would be an aircraft of each type as there were different settings for each aircraft type.' Describing what it was like to land on board *Ark Royal* in a Phantom, Macdonald recalled: 'One moment you're in controlled approach flight at about 135 knots, depending on the weight of aircraft. The weight of the aircraft would determine the perfect landing speed. Then from slamming onto the deck at 135 knots, to being stopped within 200 feet of pull out, it was like hitting a brick wall. You were flung forward in your seat with your straps holding you into the ejection seat. It was then heads up, looking out of the cockpit for the marshals; we had a number of calls we had to give, such as up with the hook and flaps up, we were then moved from the arrester wires as quickly as possible, while the wire was reset and the next plane would be about half a mile astern ready to land on. We aimed to complete the recovery within forty seconds.'

Due to the RAF Harrier trials in May, the work up and post-DED trials were condensed into a fortnight in the Moray Firth. On 4 May, two Harrier GR1s from No. 1 Squadron RAF were embarked for ten days of trials

RAF Harrier GR1 from 1 Squadron conducting trials during May 1971. (British Aerospace plc. (Dunsfold))

to assess the Harrier's capability to be fully integrated into the air group of an aircraft carrier. During the period of the trials, *Ark Royal* hosted three hundred visitors, including representatives from the navies of America, Argentina, India, and West Germany, to watch the Harrier in action at sea. These trials were a follow-up to those carried out in *Eagle* during the previous March. By way of thanking the ship's company for its part in helping Hawker Siddeley in its attempts to export the Harrier, they presented every member of the ship's company with a free can of beer.

Having completed a fortnight of self-maintenance, it was time for *Ark Royal* to depart Devonport bound for her first visit to America for ten years. During the passage across the Atlantic, Captain Roberts made an interesting discovery. 'When we were halfway across the Atlantic, having decided that there were no other ships about, I took a walk and went down to the hangar. I came across this corner where there were three huge oil drums full of earth. I thought, this is funny, I had been in carriers for twenty years so I knew that fire was a danger, as was a fuel spill, and that there were usually buckets of sand all over the place. So I thought, this is a big ship, perhaps they have a big 50-gallon drum of earth instead. Perhaps sand was getting expensive or something but it had set my mind wondering why there were 150 gallons of earth in the hangar. I called a sailor over and asked, "What's this? I have never seen this in the hangar of a ship before. Is this a new thing which

A five-ship RAS. (Rod Lampen via the author)

I haven't been told about?" "I don't know, Sir. Petty Officer X will know more about it, Sir." I told him to ask the petty officer to come over. "Oh yes. Sir I'm glad this has come up and I am very sorry but I have been so busy since we left Devonport that I haven't been able to come and tell you about it. One more thing, Sir, you see those boxes over there?" "Yes," I replied, "are those aircraft spares?" "No Sir, they are flower pots." "Flower pots! What is all this?" "When we get to Fort Lauderdale we shall be opening for visitors and about five to ten thousand Americans will come on board." "Yes, that's the idea and maybe more." "Well, we have the earth here and we have five thousand flower pots there. On the day the ship is open, I am going to have a whole lot of trestle tables on the flight deck and each of these pots will be filled with earth and the notice at the back will say this soil comes from the area by the steps in Plymouth from where the Pilgrim Fathers sailed, price $5. Half the money will go to ship's funds and the other half will cover expenses." "Fine, let me know how it goes." By 16:00 on the day the ship was open, this Petty Officer knocked on my door and gave me $12,500 for the ship's fund, which I thought was a brilliant bit of initiative,' Roberts recalled.

Ark Royal made her visit to Fort Lauderdale between 22 and 29 June 1971. As Roberts explained, he had a visit from the Harbour Master shortly after she was secured alongside. 'He casually said, "I presume you have the facilities within the ship to take care of all your garbage and toilet waste." Getting a little worried I asked, "What do you mean?" He replied, "It is not permitted to discard any sewage into a harbour in the USA." I thought this means we can't use a single toilet on board or have a shower because everything was discharged over the side. There were no storage tanks for that sort of thing on board *Ark Royal*. It certainly wasn't something I had thought of!' The visit went very well and it was the beginning of a close relationship between the people of Fort Lauderdale and the ship's company of *Ark Royal* which lasted until the ship was decommissioned.

After the pleasures of Fort Lauderdale and a week's self-maintenance period in Mayport, *Ark Royal* sailed to the Atlantic Fleet Weapon Ranges for flying exercises and the hot weather trials of the Phantom between 11 and 18 July 1971. Hardy recalled: 'We had three test pilots from Boscombe Down, Lt Cdr Burn, Lt Cdr Tristrum and Lt Cdr Tarver. When the pilots were sent out, a request had been made for two front-line observers to be earmarked for the trials. I was selected along with Leo Gallager for the trials, which concentrated on the launch and recovery aspects of the aircraft. My first flight during these trials was with Lt Cdr Burn. Shortly after take-off we checked in with air traffic control. Our call sign was 01, but we were told that 01 had crashed so we replied, "Check call sign. We are 01, and to the best of our knowledge we have not crashed." It turned out they had got the numbers the wrong way round and it was 10 which had crashed after getting into a spin. The crew ejected safely and we circled over them for about an hour while they were in a dinghy which had been dropped by a P3 Orion. They were eventually picked up by a SAR helicopter.' Explaining one of the weaknesses of the Phantom which led to the crash of 10, Macdonald recalled: 'The Phantom was a pig in high angles of attack and was prone to what was called "departing". A wing would suddenly drop and the plane would go into a spin which was sometimes not recoverable.'

Following the successful trials of the Phantom, and two days anchored at St Thomas, *Ark Royal* sailed for Devonport. About three hundred miles south-west of Land's End, on 28 July *Ark Royal* rendezvoused with Chay Blyth's yacht *British Steel*. Chay Blyth was returning to the UK from his single-handed voyage around the world against the westerlies. Having made use of this excellent opportunity for good publicity, *Ark Royal* continued her voyage back to Plymouth in preparation for her next dose of publicity. While secured to C buoy in Plymouth Sound, a BBC film crew was embarked in *Ark Royal* ready for a live broadcast during Exercise Lymelight. Exercise Lymelight was in fact the name given to this operation which was intended to demonstrate *Ark Royal*'s capabilities. The exercise was the result of months of joint planning between the BBC and the Royal Navy. Describing the challenges posed by this operation Roberts recalled: 'The thing that required attention was the fact that if we went more than twelve miles away from the point on shore where the BBC received the transmission signals from the cameras on board *Ark Royal*, the viewers would not see what was going on. This meant that we had to condense our operations, being careful that we didn't go too far out to sea, yet equally that we didn't run aground heading towards the coast. The challenge which faced us at that time of year was the fact the wind tends to die in the evening. Which meant that we had to steam that much faster to get enough wind speed over the deck, hence with the distances needed to turn the ship and get up to full speed, we had to do a dumb-bell circuit to keep within the transmission area and complete the flying.' The programme lasted for fifty minutes and included twenty-seven events, such as film of the various aspects of operating aircraft, film taken on board the accompanying submarine *Otus* as it dived, and a RAS. The exercise was the biggest outside broadcast since the Coronation and the most technically challenging ever undertaken up to that time by the BBC. With the filming completed *Ark Royal* returned to C buoy ready to embark a thousand families for the passage up into Devonport. When *Ark Royal* sailed from Devonport on 14 September it marked the beginning of three months of exercises. First on the list was Exercise Royal Knight, held between 27 September and 4 October, followed by Magic Sword IV in the North Sea on 7 and 8 October. November led to a change of direction when *Ark Royal* was deployed to the Mediterranean and a four-day visit to Naples, starting on 5 November. From Palma, *Ark Royal* sailed to the Ionian Sea for Exercise Med Passex with the American aircraft carrier *Independence*. The exercise included cross-deck operations with the Americans, swapping four of their F4Bs for four 892 Squadron F4Ks. Macdonald described his impressions of cross-operating with the *Independence*: 'While the flight deck of an American carrier was bigger than *Ark Royal*'s, the actual landing area was much the same size with a slightly bigger wingtip clearance area. There was probably less room to manoeuvre on deck because the American carriers had so many more aircraft than *Ark Royal*.'

The rest of November was spent engaged in flying exercises in the Mediterranean. Despite the Kotlin incident of the previous year *Ark Royal* was still subjected to close scrutiny by the Russians. Describing some of the antics they got up to in *Ark Royal* to keep the Russians guessing Roberts said: 'We had an old radar dish on board which didn't work and was going to be landed at the first available opportunity, so I said put it on one of the Ship's Flight Wessex helicopters on some sort of mounting and put some sort of transmitter inside it so if the Russians have a listening device it will make noises. I then told them to have it hovering by the bridge of this Russian ship and when about four or five Russians are coming to have a look, open the door for about ten seconds and then shut it again. They of course saw this great radar dish mounted inside a helicopter, which they had never heard of and would wonder what this apparition was doing, whether we had been "milking" their tapes or whatever. We did this two or three times and on each occasion more and more Russians went to have a look at this helicopter.'

On 2 December *Ark Royal* entered Gibraltar at the start of a two-day visit on her way back to Devonport for Christmas leave and another assisted-maintenance period which was to last until 20 January 1972. During this period the ship acquired a new Navigating Officer, when Lt Cdr Tim Lee (now Captain Lee) joined the ship at Devonport in January. Lee described the duties of the Navigating Officer: 'I was responsible for getting the ship in and out of harbour without running it aground. This was quite a daunting task for someone who had only up till then navigated frigates or submarines. *Ark Royal* was the largest ship in the RN, carrying a lot of windage in spite of her 36ft draught, and with four propellers to control separately when in pilotage waters. Another significant difference from normal ships was that the bridge was over the starboard side instead of on the centre line. This was a particular problem for pilots in some ports we visited, who invariably did everything by eye rather than by precise pilotage. The best advice I had on joining, from the navigator of *Eagle* (who had run aground entering Devonport about a year previously), was "Don't pay too much attention to pilots." At sea my life revolved around training officers of the watch and ensuring that the ship was in the right place at the right time for aircraft launch or recovery. For this an accuracy of two miles was generally sufficient rather than ten yards or so when entering or leaving harbour, so life was more relaxed.'

When the ship sailed on 20 January it was bound for the Virginia Capes area, yet circumstances were to dictate otherwise as Roberts explained: 'We were on our way west from Plymouth and were just about to complete a RAS with RFAs *Olmeda* and *Regent* when on 26 January the signal "Proceed with all dispatch" arrived.' British Honduras was under threat of invasion by neighbouring Guatemala and the Captain had been ordered by MOD to launch Buccaneers to overfly Belize. As soon as the RAS was completed *Ark Royal* altered course and increased speed to 26 knots. On the 27th, five Buccaneers were launched to check out AAR pods, while a Gannet was flown to Bermuda to collect documents relating to British Honduras. The following day *Ark Royal* was within range to launch two Buccaneers on a 2,600 mile round trip which was to last six hours as they fulfilled the mission to fly over Belize. They were supported by two tankers which refuelled them on the way out, and a further two Buccaneer tankers met them on the way back. Despite the length of their mission they only had ten minutes air time over Belize, but it was enough for the Guatemalans to get the message that if they invaded British Honduras they risked incurring the wrath of *Ark Royal*'s powerful air group. Therefore, the intended second mission which had been planned for the following day was postponed. This mission was yet another example of just how effective a true fixed-wing aircraft carrier is in the support of Britain's foreign policy. A lesson which the Government was not prepared to take fully on board.

While the ship waited to hear if it was going to be necessary to launch a second mission, flying exercises were quickly arranged in the Key West area. MOD decided on 1 February that it no longer required *Ark Royal* to cover the British Honduras situation, which freed the ship to make its intended week-long visit to New York. The visit did not get off to the most relaxing of starts, as Lee recalled: 'In the days of the *Queen Mary* and *Queen Elizabeth*, *Ark Royal* used to berth at the Cunard Pier, where there was sufficient water. Since the *QE2*'s draught was only 32 feet, the berth had silted up, and the New York authorities were unwilling to dredge out the berth

A Buccaneer of 809 Squadron overflying Belize City on 28 January 1972. (FAA Museum)

just for our visit. Eventually the US Navy decided to provide head and stern buoys in the Hudson River a short distance upstream from the QE2 pier. The moorings were stated to be capable of a 10,000 ton pull which, in spite of the rather odd terminology, sounded as if they should be good enough. We arrived off the Ambrose Light early in the morning after a very rough passage north. Two pilots came aboard and we proceeded up the main channel, most of whose marker buoys had shifted in the gales the night before to such an extent that we passed the wrong side of two of them (much to the consternation of the pilots!). Arriving at the buoys two hours later we secured two bridles to the forward buoy in about eight minutes – an incredibly fast time in the freezing force 5 wind – and while doing this we found that the after buoy was forward of the quarterdeck – in other words the buoys were at least two hundred feet closer to each other than requested. Nevertheless we started to secure a picking-up rope to it, and while this was in progress I noticed that the ship was quite definitely moving downstream over the ground. We established that we were still connected to the forward buoy so there was only one explanation – it was dragging or the mooring had broken. We cleared all hands off the quarterdeck and went astern to get into the middle of the river, accepting the need to part the picking-up rope. It appeared to do so at the end secured to the buoy and whiplashed inboard at phenomenal speed, and it was only later that we found out that the ring on the buoy had snapped rather than the nylon rope. The tugs (all ten of them, controlled separately at each end by the two pilots, who could not talk to each other!) then turned the ship round and we steamed all the way down the Hudson River past the Statue of Liberty to the Quarantine Anchorage at Staten Island, still with the forward buoy attached. The senior pilot then anchored us while going

153

Ark Royal passing the familiar skyline of
New York on 4 February 1972. (Rod Lampen
via the author)

down tide, and we only just managed to stop the ship before running out of cable. However, that was not the
end of it because a Coastguard officer came on board, took some bearings, and calculated that we had been
anchored in the main channel – we therefore had to move. Two attempts later, and about twelve hours after we
had arrived at the Ambrose Light, we were finally anchored in an acceptable berth. Needless to say the last
anchorage was performed without the advice of the pilot! We soon sent divers down who discovered that the
mooring cable below the buoy had parted – not surprisingly since the cable was just half the size of our own
anchor cable, and quite incapable of taking our weight. Had the cable parted later when the tide turned and we
had no steam on the turbines, we could have ended up as a permanent feature of the New York waterfront, with
seven hundred cocktail party guests on board watching the fun!'

Ark Royal's arrival in New York brought good news for the Captain. 'Once we were finally secure, the mail
was delivered to the ship and I received an official-looking envelope from C-in-C Fleet saying "Dear John, I am
very pleased to be able to tell you that at the meeting of the Admiralty board a couple of days ago they decided
to promote you to Rear Admiral",' Roberts recalled.

Ark Royal sailed on 11 February for more flying exercises, this time in the Puerto Rico areas. For
809 Squadron this period was marred by the loss of one of their aircraft, 031 (XT269), early on the morning of
15 February. The flight deck at the time was listing and slippery. The aircraft broke its lashings and it rolled over
the side. Fortunately, the brake number had just climbed out of the aircraft otherwise he would have had an early
morning dunking. The aircraft was lost in very deep water so it was never recovered. 'I was called at about 02:00
and the chap said, "Excuse me, Sir, there has been an incident. A Buccaneer has just fallen over the side!",'
Roberts remembered. 'The Officer of the Watch for the middle watch was Harry O'Grady who, coming aft after
being relieved of his watch, met the CO of the fourteen embarked Buccaneers of 809 Squadron, Lt Cdr Carl
Davies who was rubbing his eyes and wondering why he had been called to see the Captain on the bridge. Harry
said to him, "What's it like to be the CO of the only thirteen aircraft squadron in the RN?",' Lawrance recalled.

After two days break at Virgin Gorda, *Ark Royal* took part in Exercise Lantreadex which was an air defence
exercise for the benefit of the Americans. In addition to the American ships, a number of other NATO ships had
been invited to participate, including the RN County class destroyers *Glamorgan* and *London*. *Ark Royal* joined the

exercise in its third and final phase, operating with the American aircraft carrier *Franklin D. Roosevelt*. The highlight of the exercise was on 25 February when the Americans kindly offered the RN first go at the target ship. The attack on the former destroyer escort USS *Connolly* provided the Buccaneers of 809 Squadron with their first live target since the *Torrey Canyon* affair of 1968. 809 Squadron dropped eight 1,000lb bombs close enough to the ship to leave it in a sinking condition, while 892 Squadron took the honours for finishing the job and having the satisfaction of watching their target sink. The exercise was brought to an early close on 27 February to enable some of the participating American ships more time to redeploy to the Mediterranean because bad weather was expected in the Atlantic.

Ark Royal's programme was also cut short by a week because of the need to get back quickly, as Roberts explained: 'We encountered very rough weather during the voyage from Roosevelt Roads back to Plymouth. The tug personnel in Devonport were threatening a strike and we needed a tug to get back into Devonport. This was coupled with the fact that there were only about three days out of every fourteen when we could get into Plymouth, because of the tides. So we had to get back by 9 March, thus we had to keep up a high speed and we ended up doing a lot of damage to the ship. I remember discussing this with the Navigator because we had to balance between steering for Plymouth, as if we didn't get there in time we would have to anchor out and no work could be done, or altering course slightly to reduce the thumping into the sea. The Chief Shipwright kept coming to see me every hour on the hour to ask couldn't I slow down a bit but I felt we had to make Plymouth in time.' Wally Harwood who served in *Ark Royal* at this time as an Aircraft Artificer on 892 Squadron recalled: 'The waves kept hitting the port side aft and kept banging and banging against the side of the ship. As the waves hit the side of the ship, they were being diverted up towards one of the port side boat decks. The continual banging of the waves eventually shifted the boat deck up and damaged the boats on the deck. Where the boat deck was attached to the side of the hull was actually split for about thirty feet on 4 deck but because it was above the waterline all that happened was that the watertight doors either side of the split were closed and access to the deck was prohibited. The water simply flowed in and out of the compartment but caused no other damage. You don't actually realize the power of the sea until something like this happens.' Other damage caused by the rough weather included the loss of forty-five life-rafts, a smashed motor cutter and undercarriage oleo collapses on seven Buccaneers. Despite incurring quite a lot of damage, Captain Roberts achieved his objective of reaching Plymouth by 9 March and the ship started her DED on time.

Ark Royal emerged from her DED on 6 June, sailing for post-DED trials in the Plymouth and Portland areas. When the CAG embarked prior to beginning of flying exercises it included one type of aircraft for the last time. 849 Squadron B Flight were about to shortly lose their Gannet COD4 which was to be replaced by an extra Sea King for 824 Squadron. The Gannet COD4 had not been embarked when the CAG came in January but it was included this time for a final swansong. Most of June and July was taken up with flying exercises broken up by *Ark Royal* entering Portsmouth on 30 June for an eleven-day visit and SMP. *Ark Royal* was subjected to her operational readiness inspection (ORI) on 17 July before entering Devonport the next day for an AMP which was to last until 31 August. When *Ark Royal* made her passage up through Plymouth Sound on 18 August she passed the sad sight of the destored *Eagle* for the first time. The week before, *Eagle* had arrived in Plymouth having been towed from Portsmouth where she had been stripped of much of the easily reusable equipment since her arrival there on 26 January 1972. Over the next six years, *Eagle* was continually raided for spares to keep *Ark Royal* and other ships operational. It was also a glimpse of what was going to happen to *Ark Royal* herself after she was decommissioned.

The major event of the AMP was the change of command when Captain J.O. Roberts handed over to Captain A.D. Cassidi (now Admiral Sir Desmond Cassidi GCB). Cassidi described some of his preparations prior to taking command: 'I attended the tactical course to refresh my memory of the latest tactics and then visited the air stations where the squadrons were disembarked and met the squadrons ashore before joining the ship.' He recalled some of the highlights from his time in command: 'There is a great thrill in watching these great aircraft taking off and landing in a ship like *Ark Royal* and particularly so when you are night-flying. When you are night-flying there is a considerable nervous tension about whether it is going to be OK or not. Taking a big ship like that in and out of Devonport is a highlight because it is always a nerve-racking experience due to the lack of room for error for those passages. Visits to the various east coast ports of the USA, such as Fort Lauderdale and Mayport, are also highlights of any deployment. On a personal note I was made an ADC which was a great personal honour. The Commander explained in ship's Daily Orders that I had just been made an ADC and that I would be available to wait on Her Majesty whenever it was required. As quick as a flash a cartoon appeared with Her Majesty at the end of a long table and a drawing of me with a napkin over my arm saying "More figgie duff, Ma'am?"'

Ark Royal sailed from Devonport on 31 August for seven days of flying exercises, prior to taking part in Exercise Strong Express between 14 and 28 September which was the largest NATO exercise held for some years, with 300 ships and over 1,000 aircraft involved. The role of *Ark Royal* was to provide close air support for the amphibious landings on the north Norwegian coast. October was taken up with a flying exercise in the Moray Firth followed by a five-day visit to Oslo between 12 and 17 October and an eighteen-day visit to Portsmouth for a SMP until 7 November. After a week of flying exercises in the south-west approaches *Ark Royal* made a five-day visit to Barcelona. The Direction Officer at this time was Lt Cdr Colin Lawrance (now Captain Lawrance). While *Ark Royal* was anchored in Barcelona Harbour she lost one of the tractors, as Lawrance recalled: 'It was about 18:15 and we were all standing around in the Wardroom as one does at that time, having the first drink of the evening when we suddenly heard this large thump. It turned out that a naval airman, who wasn't a qualified tractor driver, but wanted to be one, had driven this tractor over the side. The bump we heard was it hitting the side on the way down. The naval airman had by this time jumped clear. They dropped the dan buoy almost immediately but no one could ever find any trace of this tractor which obviously due to its great weight had sunk into the depths of the mud at the bottom of the harbour.'

Ark Royal sailed from Barcelona on 22 November for Exercise Corsica 1972. Once again *Ark Royal*'s role was to provide close air support for amphibious landings. The landings were carried out on the west coast of Corsica, using the commando carrier *Bulwark* and the amphibious assault ships *Fearless* and *Intrepid*. At the end of the month *Ark Royal* conducted two days of cross-deck operations with the American aircraft carrier *Forrestal*, before entering Gibraltar on 6 December for a two-day visit while on her way back to Devonport for over a month of AMP and the giving of Christmas leave.

The spring deployment was made up of three major exercises, namely Sunny Seas held off Portugal, Sardex held in the Sardinia area and Exercise Ruler held in the western Mediterranean. These exercises were broken up by a visit to Gibraltar between 9 and 12 February and a visit to Malta between 23 February and 6 March. Prior to *Ark Royal*'s entry into Malta she had been cross-decking with the *Forrestal* again, but this time one of the US Phantoms became unserviceable and had to remain on board during the visit to Malta. The guest Phantom was banished to the lower hangar deck not to surface again until the ship left Malta. When the aircraft emerged from the bowels of the ship it sported a very stylish 892 omega insignia. Whether the US Marines appreciated this is unclear. On 5 March *Ark Royal* received a very distinguished visitor, as Cassidi recalled: 'Lord Mountbatten was very particular about meeting people who had served with him, so a notice went up around the ship to ask those people who knew Lord Mountbatten to make themselves known. One of the sailors who came forward had served in the Blues and Royals prior to his naval service, and had been Mountbatten's groom when he had to get

An integrated amphibious force comprising the assault ships *Fearless* and *Intrepid* and the Commando carrier *Bulwark* backed up by fixed-wing air support provided by *Ark Royal*. (Rowland Fleming via the author)

Ark Royal cross-operating with *Forrestal*. A number of Phantoms and Buccaneers can be seen on the deck of the American carrier. (Rowland Fleming via the author)

dressed up for the Queen's Birthday Parade on Horse Guards Parade. We positioned the sailor cleaning something on the flight deck. When the party arrived where this sailor was working, I said to Lord Mountbatten "I believe you know this sailor", and they spent the next ten minutes discussing various horses, which was quite incredible.' With the completion of the third and final exercise *Ark Royal* set sail for Devonport and two weeks of AMP.

When *Ark Royal* left Devonport on 30 April it was at the start of her last deployment of this part of the commission. Having completed five days of flying exercises in the Plymouth area *Ark Royal* began her passage to the West Indies. During the voyage across the Atlantic *Ark Royal* spent two days of exercises with the task group of the French aircraft carrier *Foch*. *Ark Royal* also met up with a much smaller Atlantic voyager on 7 May, as Lee recalled: 'We were sailing across the Atlantic and saw this tiny white speck and found this little boat of about

Cross-decking operations, with *Forrestal* in the background. (Captain Lee)

fifteen feet with a broken mast. The First Lieutenant, Lt Cdr Martin and some men went across in the motor whaler to find out if they could provide any assistance. Mr Moore was en route to Barbados, and his boat had capsized in a gale the night before. He was grateful for some spars to make a jury repair to his mast, and a few provisions. He didn't want us to contact anyone at home since he "didn't think anyone would be interested". Almost as an afterthought, he asked us for the correct time since he had lost his watch overboard. I believe that he made it to Barbados – against all the odds.'

Once *Ark Royal* arrived at Roosevelt Roads, the ship was given a local area and range procedure briefing before beginning nine days on the Atlantic Fleet Weapon Ranges. This was in turn followed by a weekend banyan at St Thomas, to ensure the crew were suitably refreshed for Exercise Landtreadex with the *Franklin D. Roosevelt* once again. This time when it came to the Sinkex, the Americans had learned their lesson of the previous year and reserved first go at the target ship for themselves. By the time the Buccaneers of 809 Squadron had arrived all that was to be seen was a collection of bubbles and a patch of clear water where the target had been earlier in the day. Talking about the results of an exercise such as Lantreadex, Cassidi said: 'A lot of the analysis does not come out until long after the exercise because you don't get the submarine reports back and they're usually analysed by an analysis team ashore who go through all the exercises in considerable detail and you try and learn lessons from their reports.'

The rest of June was spent principally between the visit to Fort Lauderdale between 8 and 14 June and the SMP in Mayport between 19 and 30 June. When *Ark Royal* visited ports such as Fort Lauderdale she was always a tourist attraction. Cassidi explained some of the factors which needed to be considered when opening *Ark Royal* to the public: 'To enable as many people as possible to visit the ship, you need to have an alongside berth. Obviously, opening the ship to the public presents a potential security problem, so you have got to work out a route, and post sentries around the ship so that people don't wander off down below. Generally, when she was open people would be led through to the hangar deck and one of the lifts would be going up and down to the flight deck. People would then be led out the ship via another route.'

Ark Royal set sail from Mayport on 30 June, bound for the UK. The passage across the Atlantic began to underline the fact that *Ark Royal* was in need of the refit she was due to begin at the end of July in Devonport. At this time the ship was plagued by shaft and evaporator problems. July was spent preparing for Exercise Sally Forth which was a demonstration to the NATO council and NATO Military Committee. By the 24th it was over and *Ark Royal* made her way back to Plymouth for her final commitment prior to entering refit, namely Families Day on 26 July when 1,600 families were embarked. Cassidi recalled the programme: 'We sailed out of Plymouth Sound to a point far enough away to be able to stage a limited flying programme, with a few catapult launches and landings to demonstrate the fixed-wing flying, followed by a display with the ASW and SAR helicopters. Safety during a Families Day had to be watched very carefully and we had age-limit rules for children which caused some controversy at the time. On the whole these days were a great success and very popular. It was always a real eye opener for the families to see what the living conditions were like at sea.' At the end of the Families Day *Ark Royal* entered Devonport to begin the preparations for the refit.

The refit did not have the most promising of starts as Rowland Fleming, who served in *Ark Royal* as an Able Seaman, recalled: 'On our way into dry dock the ship came very close to being swept down to St Budeaux. The wind got up and the tugs were unable to control the *Ark*. It was only after more tugs arrived that we were taken under control and a very embarrassing incident was avoided.' Describing the changes in routine once the ship entered refit Fleming continued: 'Being in refit turned the ship into a noisy place during the day but if you were

The Freedom of the City of Leeds was given to *Ark Royal* at a ceremony held in the city on 25 October and attended by the Queen Mother and Captain Cassidi. (Captain Lawrance via the author)

The document granting the Freedom of the City of Leeds to *Ark Royal*.
(Captain Lawrance via the author)

on board at night, fire party, etc., it was like a ghost ship – cold and spooky. Most of my time during the day was spent stripping paint off and putting paint on. We used to go into the bilge tanks through a small opening, to strip paint using a chipping hammer or scabbler and repaint again, this was warm, noisy and very claustrophobic. I also had to go into scrambling nets over the side of the ship, again chipping and painting. This I found rather hair-raising as the bottom of the dry dock seemed a long way down. There were electric cables and rubber hoses for evermore coming on board, all the wooden decks were covered in hardboard and I used to wonder if it would ever get back to normal in time to return to sea.'

While the ship was being refitted in Devonport *Ark Royal* was granted the freedom of the city of Leeds at a ceremony held in the city on 25 October 1973, which was attended by HM Queen Elizabeth the Queen Mother, Captain Cassidi and members of the ship's company. The granting of this honour was the culmination of the close relationship which had been built up between the city and the ship by the various Commanding Officers of *Ark Royal* and the various Mayors of Leeds since before the ship was completed. Lt Cdr Lawrance was chosen as the liaison officer between the city of Leeds and *Ark Royal*. 'We trained up a Royal Guard and I had three hundred and fifty sailors up at Strensal camp near York for three weeks prior to the event. The ceremony involved the presentation of a scroll which was given to Lt Ted Hackett, who then led the march past through the streets of the city of Leeds,' Lawrance recalled.

Cassidi remembered a light-hearted moment during the day at Leeds: 'About a dozen of the ship's company who were from Leeds were gathered in the foyer of the City Hall to be introduced to the Queen Mother. As she got halfway down the line of sailors she asked one sailor what his name was. He replied in a very croaky voice. The Queen Mother sympathetically said, "Oh my poor chap, you do have a terrible cold." She then searched her handbag and presented the sailor with a cough sweet saying, "Try one of these I find they are frightfully good!"'

Chapter Nine

FAME AT LAST

S I X T H   C O M M I S S I O N ,   P A R T   I I ,

J U N E   1 9 7 4 – N O V E M B E R   1 9 7 6

While the ship was deep in refit, Captain Cassidi handed over command of *Ark Royal* to Captain J.R.S. Gerard-Pearse (now Rear Admiral Gerard-Pearse CB) in November 1973. Gerard-Pearse summed up his time in command: 'My lasting memories are of a happy, exhilarating and busy commission. The propulsion was getting fairly old and the technical officers and ratings did an excellent job in keeping the ship running. Having never served in an aircraft carrier, I was surprised how the whole ship's company pulled together as a team, and how much the squadrons were missed when they were disembarked during the ship's time in Devonport.' Captain Cassidi's promotion to Rear Admiral was not to be the end of his association with *Ark Royal*, because he was to fly his flag in *Ark Royal*, in his new role as Flag Officer Carriers and Amphibious Ships (FOCAS), when the ship emerged from refit. Lt Cdr Graham Wilcock (now Cdr Wilcock) was the Operations Officer in *Ark Royal* at this time and, as part of his job, he was responsible for planning the long-term programme for the ship. 'When Captain Cassidi was about to become FOCAS he told me that he wished to consider the ship visiting the Far East in 1975. I registered reservations because of certain logistic problems associated with such a deployment and suggested that, if we were permitted to go outside the NATO area, consideration could be given to South America and perhaps Rio for Easter. The idea was developed – and a programme subsequently agreed for that.'

As the ship settled into refit it became apparent that the selected date posed an interesting challenge – it would be Good Friday (which effectively meant the following Tuesday). Wilcock explained how he avoided incurring delays which would have affected the ship's programme as she emerged from refit: 'My anxiety as Operations Officer was that there would be tremendous pressure to get the ship operational out of refit and properly worked up in time for the major autumn exercises. It was already questionable how much time there would be for summer leave and I was anxious to make sure that we weren't going to be handicapped by Easter, or indeed any other grounds for slippage. I went to see the Engineer Captain in the dockyard to ask if we could complete a day early, on Maundy Thursday. The carrot for the dockyard workers would be that, if we could sail that day, many of them would have to come with us over Easter – and they would get extra pay. The incentive appeared to work and we put to sea on the Thursday. As a result, by Easter Sunday, we had succeeded in identifying a host of main propulsion machinery snags, we were down to one shaft and two boilers, and we were at anchor in Plymouth Sound putting things right. At the same time, we brought forward anything we could from later in the trials programme, including "pre-wetting" I recall. The following Thursday, just one week out of refit, we completed a successful 80 per cent full power trial in the Channel during which we embarked two aircraft from each squadron towards getting the "main armament" working.'

On 1 May *Ark Royal* entered Devonport for just over a month, to rectify the faults highlighted by the first set

Ark Royal at speed. (FAA Museum)

A Buccaneer of 809 Squadron prior to launching with the plane guard Wessex in position in the background. (Captain Lawrance)

Having completed her first batch of post-refit trials, *Ark Royal* returned to Devonport. She was overflown by the RN Historic Flight from Yeovilton. (FAA Museum)

of post-refit trials. On 4 June *Ark Royal* sailed to begin her second work up but, due to boiler problems, she was forced to return to Devonport for further rectification. On the evening tide of 4 July *Ark Royal* sailed once more from Devonport to begin her work up in preparation for her ORI. Events further afield were to lead to the postponement of the ORI until the autumn. In July 1974 the Cypriot President, Archbishop Makarios was deposed by the Greek-led Cypriot National Guard. In place of the Archbishop, who was flown into exile by the RAF, the Greek Cypriot extremist Nikos Sampson became President. Soon after, Turkey invaded Cyprus, so the C-in-C Fleet took the precautionary measure of dispatching *Ark Royal* to a waiting zone off Gibraltar to await further instructions. 'Because we received no warning of the Cyprus situation I only had limited tropical kit on board, some rather ancient. When I walked into the Wardroom wearing my shorts which were actually rather long, one of the young pilots said to me, "Good morning Sir. I am glad to see the Empire is not dead yet",' recalled Cudmore, who as Lt Cdr Mike Cudmore (now Cdr Cudmore OBE), served in *Ark Royal* at this time as the Air Engineer Officer of 892 Squadron.

During this period the ship's flying programme was limited, due to the failure of one of the ship's evaporators and a steam leak. This resulted in the shutting down of one of the ship's boilers, thereby limiting the ship's speed and the amount of available steam, which in turn reduced the ship to one catapult. The UN managed to organize a ceasefire which appeared to be holding, and thus stabilized the situation in Cyprus enough to enable *Ark Royal* to be stood down on 24 July. She then began her voyage back to Devonport for summer leave.

The office of Little F. Lieutenant Commander R. Edward (seated, holding his pipe) was the Little F at the start of this part of the sixth commission. (Lieutenant Commander Edward via the author)

Ark Royal had been due to sail on 3 September but her sailing was delayed by twenty-four hours due to feedwater contamination in one unit. She eventually sailed with high winds and rain at 7 p.m. the following evening with both the Ship's Flight and 824 Squadron already embarked. On 7 September, while *Ark Royal* was in the Portland exercise area, she received a mayday message from the 420 ton coaster *Greta C* which was sinking fifteen miles to the south-west of Portland in a force 8–9 gale. Wessex 047 of the Ship's Flight was launched to rescue the crew. As the Wessex was moving away from the hover the engine surged and the pilot managed to crash-land the Wessex on the round down at the front of the angled flight deck. 'I was on watch in the compressor compartment on 8 deck and I felt the ship shake followed by the announcement, "Crash on deck, crash on deck." The pilot jumped out quickly because he thought the Wessex was about to fall off the edge of the deck and he damaged his back as a result,' recalled Salter, who served in *Ark Royal* at this time as a stoker. The Wessex was left in a somewhat precarious position as it was perched on the round down with the remains of the tail between the port bridle catcher and the decked sponson that once housed two 4.5in gun turrets. With the drama over on board *Ark Royal*, the *Greta C* still needed assistance, so two Sea Kings from 824 Squadron were launched at 7.10 a.m. On board one of the Sea Kings was the SAR diver, Leading Seaman Higginson, who had survived the Wessex crash and insisted on participating in the rescue. The two Sea Kings managed to recover four members of the crew who had already abandoned the *Greta C* and were found alive in an inflatable life raft. Sadly, the coaster's master was not so lucky and his body was subsequently recovered by a Sea King.

Ark Royal then sailed for the Moray Firth work up areas. On 12 September the stripped airframe of the crashed Wessex from the Ship's Flight suffered the indignity of being airlifted from *Ark Royal*, slung underneath a Sea King from 824 Squadron. The Ship's Flight had taken delivery of their replacement Wessex the day before. Between 16 and 27 September *Ark Royal* participated in Exercise Northern Merger. The exercise saw the return of the ship's previous Captain, when FOCAS, Rear Admiral Cassidi, embarked with his staff for the duration of the exercise. Cassidi recalled the experience of returning to *Ark Royal* as a Flag Officer: 'One of the things you have to be very careful about when returning to "one's own ship" as a Flag Officer is that you are not there to tell the Captain how he should do his job. Of course you do know a lot about how the ship operates, so you

Wessex 047 of the Ship's Flight crashed back on board *Ark Royal* after suffering an engine surge. (FAA Museum)

know where to look if there is going to be a problem. But it is not really a problem because you are there to do your own job.' The programme for the exercise was disrupted by heavy seas and high winds. The weather was to be in marked contrast to *Ark Royal*'s next destination, which was the warmer climate of the Mediterranean, and the island of Malta, arriving there on 5 October for a ten-day visit.

During the passage to Malta AB Fleming was to learn at first-hand about some of the dangers involved during a RAS. 'I had a very scary moment while working for the Bosun's Party on our way to Malta. My job was to prepare the forward fuelling pocket for refuelling, making sure that the winch was working, all block and tackles were in position and basically anything else to do with the seamanship side. I had to connect the jackstay to the side of the ship to allow the refuelling hoses to be pulled over from the RFA to supply furnace fuel oil (FFO) and aviation fuel (AVCAT). The hoses had been winched over and secured just before pumping had begun. The ropes used to pull the hoses over on the jackstay had been coiled down, when the jackstay winch, which was self-tensioning on the RFA *Olna*, jammed, causing the hoses to part spewing AVCAT and FFO out, and the ropes to fly back outboard very fast. There were screams and shouts, a large bang and a flash. I felt something hit my ear which turned out to be shrapnel from a piece of metal; I was knocked to the floor and slid towards the side. Luckily I managed to hook my arm around a stanchion before I went overboard. Luckily everyone else was uninjured, but I lost a piece of my ear. The incident changed me forever and, as a result of the trauma, I was medically discharged from the service some five years later.'

The good weather which had greeted *Ark Royal* on her arrival on 5 October was not to last because, when the ship left Malta on 15 October, she was once more setting off in bleak weather. The strong winds across the mouth of the harbour delayed the ship's sailing from 9 a.m. to 4 p.m., which meant the squadrons could not be embarked until the following day. With the aircraft re-embarked *Ark Royal* began six days of flying exercises in the Malta area.

On 20 October *Ark Royal* received her second mayday message in just over a month. This time the mayday came from the Italian coaster *Giovanni Assenso*. Once again, two Sea Kings from 824 Squadron were scrambled to provide assistance. They were joined by one of 849 Squadron B flight's Gannets which was diverted from its planned sortie to help. One of the pilots in 849 Squadron's B Flight at this time was Lt David Hobbs (now Cdr Hobbs MBE). Hobbs recalled what the Gannet was like: 'Flying a Gannet has been compared to driving a double-decker bus from the top, with the pedals going all the way down to the bottom. It was a bit heavy, you couldn't throw it about much, but then you weren't meant to. It had a lot in common with other contemporary aircraft. For example, it had similar instruments and controls to the Hawker Hunter. It was a stable aircraft and everything fitted together well.' Having located the coaster, six survivors were winched to safety and flown to Malta, via RFA *Resource* where the Sea Kings stopped to refuel on board before continuing their flight. Having become a hazard to shipping following the evacuation of its crew, the *Giovanni Assenso* was kept under close observation by the Gannets of 849 B Flight, until it subsequently rolled over and sank at noon on the following day.

Normally cross-deck operations were concentrated on the fixed-wing squadrons exchanging aircraft with their American counterparts but when *Ark Royal* rendezvoused for three days of exercises off Sardinia with a small group of Italian warships it was the turn of the Sea Kings from 824 Squadron to experience pastures new. They performed a number of operations from the Italian Navy's two helicopter cruisers, *Andrea Doria*, and *Caio Duilio*. The Sea King crews, who completed night cross-deck operations on the two Italian ships, thought it was easier to operate from them than it was from Fly 3 on board *Ark Royal*, which might sound surprising when you compare the relative sizes of the flight decks. The three days of exercises did not pass entirely without their drama as the CO of 892 Squadron, Lt Cdr W.L.T. Peppe (now Cdr Peppe OBE) found out while flying his Phantom: 'We were operating off Sardinia using the Italian-controlled NATO base Decimomannu as the diversion airfield. I had volunteered myself to do the 540lb VT fused bomb QAAT (Quality Assurance Air Test). This was partly because I wished to, and being the boss must have some perks, but partly because there had been

A Sea King is brought in to land.
(Commander Wilcock via the author)

a cloud over VT fuses in the RN since the fatal accident during the Beira patrol with one of *Ark Royal*'s Sea Vixens. As an AWI, I was sure that the problem had been solved and that the fuses were quite safe but there were those who were less certain. The test involved loading the aircraft with a full load of thirteen live bombs, getting airborne and dropping the lot in one go where all could see. No great problem, except that on the first pass none came off. There followed much consternation, reading of checklists and discussion with AEOs over the radio. At the end of all this and by contorting the aircraft I managed to get rid of two or three but was left with an embarrassing ten or so. SOPs said, "Don't land back aboard with live hang-ups, particularly ones that just might be in a sensitive condition, so divert to Decimomannu." On my way then, but Decimomannu were not at all keen, indeed the ship was told in no uncertain terms that my landing there would create a major diplomatic incident and probably result in NATO being denied the use of the base. So back to *Ark Royal* and the prospect of one pass, very overweight, with a doubtful load of bombs. Of course, my observer and I told ourselves, we know these bombs to be perfectly safe in this condition, don't we? But the only other option was to eject and that didn't seem attractive at all. There was no problem of course but I was told that all non-essential personnel were cleared to below 4 deck for the landing.'

After a brief stopover in Gibraltar on the voyage home, *Ark Royal* entered Devonport on 5 November for DED and Christmas leave. *Ark Royal*'s spring deployment began early in the new year when she sailed from Devonport on 7 January 1975 in cold foggy weather bound for the warmer climate of the Caribbean. After two days at Roosevelt Roads, *Ark Royal* sailed on 20 January for exercises in the Atlantic Fleet Weapon Ranges (AFWR). On the 24th, *Ark Royal* received a call for assistance from the MV *Sherman*. One of the members of its crew had suffered two heart attacks and required urgent attention from a doctor. 824 Squadron flew one of its Sea Kings over to RFA *Resource*, which then steamed towards the *Sherman* until it was within the range of the Sea King. In the meantime *Ark Royal* launched a Buccaneer and Gannet to search for *Sherman*, to provide the Sea King with an accurate position so that the helicopter could make the most of its limited air time. Unfortunately, although the aircraft managed to locate the *Sherman* they could not hold the Sea King on radar and thus provide the helicopter with a relative position to update their navigation. Therefore, when the Sea King arrived at the search datum it did not find the *Sherman* on radar, and thus had to spend valuable air time searching for her. Just as it looked as though the Sea King would have to turn back to *Resource* without having found the *Sherman*, they located the ship and were able to lower the doctor down to her before heading back swiftly to *Resource* to take on fuel. To make the situation worse the *Resource* had updated her position, which meant that the Sea King had an extra forty miles added to the return flight. Luckily, the crewman's condition was not as serious as had been thought, so once the Sea King had completed its fuel stop, it returned to the *Sherman* to retrieve the doctor and return to *Ark Royal* via a further fuel stop on *Resource*. Thus completing another successful long-range rescue mission.

With the *Sherman* situation over, *Ark Royal* continued flying exercises in the AFWR which went smoothly until 29 January. 'While we were flying from the ship we had a hydraulic failure which in theory shouldn't have happened. We went through emergency procedures and found that we couldn't get the wheels down. We could get the starboard side main wheel down and locked, but there were red lights for the port wheel and nose wheel, which was not a very comfortable situation, so we went ashore to Roosevelt Roads. In theory, having gone through all the drills and not being able to get the gear down, we should have ejected because it was one of the configurations in which you couldn't land the aircraft but we thought it was worth a shot. We put it down very gently; not surprisingly shortly after landing the port wheel collapsed, and the nose wheel collapsed, and we hurtled off the runway, and ground looped, at which point Mike Bickley, who was the observer and CO of 809 Squadron, ejected. I didn't and eventually the aircraft came to a slithering halt and all was well. Mike damaged his back for a few months so I became the acting CO of 809 Squadron for the rest of the deployment,' said Morton, who as Lt Cdr A. Morton (now Captain A. Morton DSC) served in *Ark Royal* as the Senior Pilot of 809 Squadron, prior to becoming the CO of 809 Squadron at this time.

The rest of January and the first half of February followed the same pattern of five days of exercises, followed by a weekend banyan, followed by a further five days of flying exercises. Lt David Hobbs (now Cdr D. Hobbs MBE) was one of the pilots in 849 Squadron B Flight at this time. He described a typical sortie from preparation through to recovery: 'An hour before the sortie you would attend a briefing of about fifteen minutes in the main briefing room, which was 809's in the island. From this you would get the met, details of the launch, ship's call sign, and you would be briefed for an instrument recovery in case the ship found itself in bad weather or fog, although you were expected to do a visual recovery. Next you would attend the squadron brief in 849's briefing room, which was a small room just across the flat from 809's. It was in the extension built during the 1967–70 refit over what had been the Alaskan Highway. The room was not big enough to accommodate the entire Flight. The squadron brief covered the details of the sortie and, if it was just your Gannet that was to be launched, the briefing consisted of the pilot being briefed by his observer.

'Typically there was about half an hour to go before the sortie, and next stop would be the 700 office at the aft end of the island. You would make your way through the different sections of the 700 aircraft log looking for acceptable deferred defects. An acceptable deferred defect would be when the aircraft was serviceable to fly, but there were minor things wrong with it, such as a faulty cockpit light. Once the checks through the 700 were complete you would make your way out to the flight deck.

'The Gannet was usually pre-loaded on the catapult and thus the first aircraft launch. The Gannet required the lowest steam pressure because it was the lightest of *Ark Royal*'s aircraft. If the Gannet was not on the catapult it was usually parked aft of the island and you would start up there and taxi to the catapult. The Gannet was a pain to taxi because it didn't have nose wheel steering. To get round this a steering arm would be attached and two handlers would move the arm to manoeuvre you. The handlers didn't like this because they were only a few feet from the propellers.

Ark Royal at speed, about to launch one of 809 Squadron's Buccaneers. (Commander Wilcock via the author)

'Before climbing aboard the Gannet you would complete as many of your pilot checks as possible, bearing in mind that with the wings folded, you couldn't physically touch everything. About twenty minutes before take off flyco piped, "aircrew man aircraft". You would climb aboard and strap in, bone-dome on, plug in, and on with the battery master switch. At this point the intercom would come live so that you could talk to the observers and make sure you could hear them. While the pilot was doing his pilot checks, the observers had their own set of checks to complete in order to fire up the radar, although they would not transmit while the aircraft was on the deck. The Gannet cockpit was quite spacious and it had an underwater seat for the pilot. It was so designed that if the aircraft went over the side and sank, that at a set water pressure, which equated to ten feet below the water, the two panels behind the cockpit fell in, the cockpit filled with water, and a certain hydrostatic valve would mate, blow the canopy off, and then blow the seat clear of the aircraft with compressed air. You were connected by a personal equipment connector on the right-hand side which would inflate your life jacket. The downside was that you would arrive on the surface with your oxygen mask on, with the bottom of its tube on the right knee, underwater. To counter this problem an anti-drown valve was fitted, which stopped water coming up the pipe. The downside was that if water didn't come up the pipe, nor did air, which created a vacuum, so if you weren't conscious potentially you could suffocate. However, if you were conscious enough to flip off your mask you were all right.

'The maintainers would hook up the palouste to the wheel well to start one engine, before going off to start the other aircraft down the range. The second engine was started by putting the first engine to full power and unfeathering the propeller on the second engine, which would windmill up to speed in the slipstream of the first engine. When the propeller of the second engine reached the appropriate rpm, you would press the relight button, bring the lever up, and start the engine.

'When the final checks were completed you would give the thumbs up to the maintainer, by which time the ship would be increasing her speed and turning into wind. You would then be given the signal to unfold the wings. Once the wings were successfully in position, you would close the canopy and bring the Gannet up to full power, check all the Ts and Ps were good, then give the FDO a white glove against the canopy, and you would get a nod back from the FDO. The FDO during my time in *Ark Royal* always gave us a nice smile. His line in the bar was it might be the last thing you see on this earth and he wanted it to be a nice experience. The FDO would hide the red flag behind his back and produce the green flag. He would check back with flyco that he had a green light forward and aft. He would circle the flag, you would check full power, then down with the green flag, followed by a pause of two seconds, and then you were off down the catapult. As soon as you were off the end of the catapult, your hand was right forward on the throttle, finger forward, pressing the up button, and the landing gear would come up, then flaps up. The observers would put the radar on load and change frequencies on to the Directors' frequency.

'Contrary to popular belief, the Gannet AEW3 did not operate very high and normally flew between five and ten thousand feet. The AEW3 could not be operated above 20,000 feet because of fears that the differential pressure would fire the underwater seat. Normally, we would fly out to our operating zone quite quickly and then shut down one engine. Before the engine was shut down, you would close one of the oil coolers so that the oil in that engine was warmed right up, so that you did not encounter problems because the oil was too cold. Once on station you would alternate the engines to be shut down, with one hour on, and one hour off. One of the things you could have checked in the 700 was if one engine needed to be favoured over the other, and this could determine which engine you shut down.

'Typically, the sortie would last about three hours and it was not unknown for observers to be still controlling other aircraft while the Gannet was in the slot to break into the circuit for recovery. You would head back to the Gannet wait position, which was 1,000 feet on the starboard side of the ship. While you were in the wait you would keep an eye on what was happening back on deck to see if there were any problems. You would aim to let down to 400 feet on the starboard side and break left into the circuit fifteen seconds after passing the island. You were given a Charlie time and you were expected to hit the deck plus or minus fifteen seconds of the Charlie time. The reason for this was simple, the objective during the recovery of aircraft was to get all of the aircraft back on deck as quickly as possible. While the ship was steaming in a straight line, it was vulnerable to torpedo attack because the course of the ship was predictable. The LSO would be sitting on the landing sight and if you had a good approach he would only say, "Roger, Roger", and not much else. If you had a bad approach he would be issuing correction instructions. Following the thump on deck and the aircraft coming to a stop, the wire would pull you back, and then fall off the hook, but if it didn't there would be two handlers who would pull it off. While this was happening you were given the fold sign and then you would taxi forward into Fly 1 to be parked as close to the next aircraft as possible.

'Once in position, the lashing chains were fitted, and the engines were cut, and you climbed down from the aircraft. While you were walking back to the 849 briefing room for a debrief you might give a thumbs up or down, to indicate if the aircraft was serviceable or unserviceable, to the senior 849 line supervisor. This would dictate whether the aircraft needed to be struck down to the hangar for maintenance, or if it could be left on deck to be refuelled for the next sortie. If the aircraft was unserviceable, you would probably have told the Direction Officer before landing. During the debrief the LSO would stick his head round the door to give the pilot his comments about the recovery.'

On 19 February *Ark Royal* entered Mayport, Florida, in true American style, escorted by tugs spraying hoses, while *Ark Royal* exchanged gun salutes with the Naval Station. The purpose of the two-week visit was for the ship's company to complete a self-maintenance period. This visit was not all hard work because it provided many of the ship's company with the opportunity to visit most of the internationally renowned places of interest, such as the Kennedy Space Centre, and Disney World.

With the two-week break over, it was time to get down to work and participate in the biggest exercise of the deployment, Exercise Lantreadex. *Ark Royal* joined the start of the exercise off the Florida coast and, over the next fortnight, the fleet of over twenty ships worked their way towards the AFWR. The ships were grouped

One of 849 Squadron B Flight's Gannet AEW 3s lands on board *Ark Royal*. (Commander Wilcock via the author)

around the *Ark Royal* and the American aircraft carrier *Independence*. Prior to the start of the exercise the embarked squadrons spent a day cross-operating because each carrier would act as a spare deck for the other ship during the exercise. At 2.16 a.m. on 19 March 1975 Sea King 051 of 824 Squadron ditched following an engine failure in the hover. The crew stayed with the helicopter until 5.15 a.m. They had hoped to attempt a single-engine water take-off at dawn. While they were waiting equipment services were gradually lost, until it was decided to shut down and abandon the aircraft. At 5.35 a.m. the aircraft capsized but remained above the water. *Ark Royal* left the exercise to recover the Sea King, as Fleming recalled: 'We were unable to send divers down to make a recovery as there was a general purpose machine-gun (GPMG) with its belt-feed ammo still attached and they were worried that it might fire off due to the current. My Petty Officer (GI) Harry Burles and I went to assist. He was asked to shoot one of the flotation bags with one of the SLR rifles so that one side of the helicopter would sink and the other with the GPMG would come to the surface. This worked and a full recovery was made.'

'The one thing I remember about watching the Sea King in the water was the incredible bubbling noise it made. I was standing on the flight deck and you could hear it fizzing like an Alka Seltzer,' recalled Kinch who as Lt Cdr G. Kinch (now Cdr G. Kinch) was the Senior Observer of 892 Squadron at this time. The aircrew refreshment bar (ACRB) was a much valued facility by the aircrew especially during a hectic exercise as Kinch explained: 'The ACRB was located just below the island and provided non-stop coffee, hamburgers, bacon butties and the like when the ship was at flying stations. It was most important in the aircrew's lifestyle to have this facility which provided food to suit aircrew schedules, unlike the more rigid meal times of the Wardroom.

Sea King 051 of 824 Squadron is recovered on 19 March 1975, having ditched earlier in the day after suffering engine failure. (FAA Museum)

The aircrew refreshment bar. (Steve Riley)

However, while the ACRB did provide a few cans of beer for aircrew after night-flying – if it hadn't all been drunk while you were debriefing – we preferred to use the Wardroom bar if it was still open. The Commander allowed us this concession in flying overalls provided we did not touch or sit on anything or use it as an excuse for not shifting into the correct rig. This was a great improvement over cramming in the Wardroom flat with the stewards who were waiting to clean up.'

After the completion of Exercise Lantreadex it was time to give the ship's company and the squadrons a well-earned break over Easter, so the ship sailed for Barbados for a four-day visit, anchoring off the island on 27 March. Perhaps the most noticeable event was the changeover of command on Good Friday, when Captain Gerard-Pearse handed over to Captain W.J. Graham (now Rear Admiral Graham CB). On 31 March *Ark Royal* left the sunny beaches of Barbados as she set course for Norfolk, Virginia, to begin an assisted-maintenance period. Despite arriving off Norfolk on 3 April, it was a further three days before *Ark Royal* could enter the American port, because the authorities refused entry until the combination of wind and tides was right to enable the ship to berth. 'While we were disembarked at NAS Norfolk during April 1975 one of the American squadrons, RVW120, which was the E2 training squadron, painted the tails of the Gannets in distinctive yellow and black stripes. The design was refined over the next three years,' said Lt Cdr Rotheram (now Captain M. Rotheram) who was the Senior Observer of 849 Squadron B Flight at this time.

While *Ark Royal* was alongside, the ship was joined by new sailors including Colin Brazendale (now Lt Cdr C. Brazendale MBE) who was a maintainer in 892 Squadron. He described his first few days trying to find his way round the ship, and how the departure of the ship from Norfolk on 21 April only led to further complications: 'I lived in 5 Golf 7 mess which was deep within the bowels of the ship. When coming in and out of harbour the ship closed down to its watertight state in case of accidents. Our normal route to the showers was across the weather deck on the starboard side. So when it was all shut down you had to find a "camel route" through the ship, firstly down to the 809 Squadron messes through some stores departments and, because I was new to the ship, I got lost at this point and ended up using the showers for other people who I didn't know. It later turned out that the other sailors in my mess thought I didn't wash because they never saw me in the showers!'

Once *Ark Royal* had slipped her moorings she set course for the most eagerly awaited trip of the deployment, namely her visit to Rio. While on passage to Rio it was decided to hold both the celebrations for the twenty-fifth anniversary of the ship's launching and the crossing the line ceremony on 3 May. It was the first time the ship had crossed the line since her days in the Far East in the mid-1960s. However, the voyage to Rio was far from a luxury cruise for those working in the hangar decks to keep the aircraft operational, as Brazendale recalled: 'The Phantoms were on the upper hangar deck, with the Gannets behind us. Through the forward lift you could see the two Wessex helicopters from the Ship's Flight at the front of the hangar deck. In a quiet moment at night we would make paper aeroplanes and try to get them across the lift well over to the Wessex. The temperature on the hangar deck was beyond belief when we went to Rio. We had a large double-skinned tea urn with a tap

This view clearly shows *Ark Royal*'s two hangar decks. (FAA Museum)

which was topped up with what we called "limers". This was made up of a crystallized powder which was mixed with water and topped up with ice, because the squadrons were given extra ice rations in the hangar. One of the worst jobs as a Phantom "greenie" (electrician) was the removal of the rear circuit-breaker panels. This required squashing into the rear cockpit which was 20 degrees higher than the hangar temperature. We would be in tropical rig, which in the hangar consisted solely of your shorts and rigging boots; it wasn't long before the shorts and socks required changing!'

Ark Royal anchored off Rio on 7 May to begin a week's visit, which coincided with that of a task group headed by the Flag Officer First Flotilla, Vice Admiral Henry Leach (now Admiral of the Fleet Sir Henry Leach GCB, DL). Leach remembered the visit: 'I took a Task Group of the cruiser *Blake* (my flagship), the nuclear submarine *Dreadnought* and four frigates to Rio de Janeiro for a final bright lights visit, before returning to the UK following a nine-month deployment to the Far East. Our visit coincided with that of *Ark Royal* wearing the flag of Rear Admiral Desmond Cassidi, Flag Officer Aircraft Carriers and Amphibious Ships. It had been mutually agreed that he would do all the official stuff and I would take a low-key break.' It was the last time that Rear Admiral Cassidi flew his flag in *Ark Royal* as FOCAS, because at the end of the visit to Rio he flew back to the UK to haul down his flag and hand over to his successor Rear Admiral Eberle.

'One day, dressed in an open-necked shirt and slacks, I visited the famous Monte Christe Statue which dominates the harbour. Going up in the cable car I spotted a small group of *Ark Royal*'s sailors, went across and chatted them up. After quite a lot of questions and answers had been exchanged one of their number rounded on me and said, "You're asking a lot of questions – who are you?" I told them my name and that I was Flag Officer First Flotilla; they immediately shut up like clams!' Leach recalled.

Summing up the trip, Kinch said: 'Rio was the reintroduction into one's aviation career of "this is what we joined for". Looking back, one might be accused of not being grateful for the Mediterranean and Far East ports which were our repair and logistic support stops of the 1960s. However, of all the western Atlantic seaboard ports, Rio was the exotic visit of the commission which hardly anyone had visited before.'

All too soon the visit was over as *Ark Royal* weighed anchor on 14 May to participate in an exercise with the Brazilian Navy and the ships from Vice Admiral Leach's Task Group. 'Soon after sailing from Rio, as previously

Ark Royal fires a salute prior to anchoring off Rio on 7 May 1975. (Lieutenant Commander Brazendale via the author)

A stunning shot of a Buccaneer seconds before it is fired off down the catapult. (Commander Wilcock via the author)

arranged I helicoptered across to *Ark Royal* to experience being catapulted from the deck in a Buccaneer of 809 Squadron. The previous year I had flown a sortie in a RAF Buccaneer from 237 OCU, Honington and the amount of "g" pulled while carrying out lay-down and medium-toss bombing runs over Tain range had seriously upset my insides. So it was with some apprehension about making a fool of myself that I approached the latest venture. Lt Duggie Hamilton was my pilot; a short, stocky, charming young man – tough as a nut and an experienced Buccaneer pilot. Once clear of the deck he climbed to height and took me through shallow and steep dive-bombing, lay-down and medium-toss, and intercept procedures, ending up by flashing past the bridge of my flagship at upper deck level. Observers in *Blake* later remarked that they thought they discerned a distinct aura of green around the rear cockpit during the manoeuvre! We landed on and parked in Fly 1; when the canopy was raised I was suddenly overwhelmed by nausea (reaction) and only just managed to climb out without disgracing myself. I had asked for "the works" and I had got them,' Leach commented.

To make room for three SH-3D Sea Kings from HS-1, which was normally embarked in the Brazilian aircraft carrier *Minas Gerais*, two of 824 Squadron's Sea Kings were disembarked to RFA *Olwen*. The generosity of the Brazilian aircrew caught the fixed-wing squadrons off guard as Hobbs recalled: 'We were told that they were going to make a presentation in the Wardroom. We naturally assumed that they were going to make the presentation to the Sea King squadron but they got up and said, "We would like to make this presentation to all of the squadrons on board". This was followed by a stampede by the three fixed-wing squadrons to find something we could give back.'

With the joint exercise successfully completed the Brazilian warships headed south while Vice Admiral Leach's Task Group headed north. *Ark Royal* remained off Salvador for a further two days of flying exercises. Morton described what the Buccaneer was like to fly: 'It was designed to be good at low level/high speed which it excelled at. In these conditions it was very stable and went through turbulence very smoothly, while at high altitude it was a bit of a dog. As a weapons platform it was good but it never had a good weapons avionics package. It was designed to drop nuclear weapons from high level into roughly the right place, yet over the years we tried to use it effectively for precision bombing, which it was never designed for, and thus it was always quite a challenge to achieve good results. If we had had a better weapons system it would have been a formidable aircraft. The Buccaneer at low speed, particularly in the approach configuration, was rather wallowy and needed

A bombed-up Buccaneer.
(Captain Morton via the author)

setting up from some distance out. Once it had been set up, providing you didn't do anything dramatic, it flew very well, but it wasn't an aircraft you could take liberties with once you had set it up. Although the S2 had got the more powerful engines, it was not as nimble as the S1 in the carrier circuit and approach configuration, because of its extra weight.'

On the second day of the flying exercises the Ship's Flight lost its second Wessex of the commission when Wessex 046 suffered an engine failure. It was about to take up its plane guard position, thus leaving the pilot with no other option than to ditch alongside the ship. All three crewmen were recovered by the standby SAR Wessex. The remains of Wessex 046 were subsequently recovered, minus the rotor blades and tail cone.

Ark Royal once more rendezvoused with Vice Admiral Leach's Task Group off Madeira for Exercise Last Chance. *Ark Royal* failed to participate in most of the exercise because of evaporator problems, before entering Gibraltar on 5 June at the start of a two-day visit. When *Ark Royal* left Gibraltar the Under Secretary for Defence and Portsmouth MP, Mr Frank Judd MP, was embarked for a two-day visit to experience fixed-wing carrier operations for himself. On 11 June *Ark Royal* anchored in Mount's Bay and 824 Squadron was disembarked. *Ark Royal* returned to C buoy in preparation for Families Day on 12 June. After a packed programme for Families Day *Ark Royal* entered Devonport to begin her DED.

The ship sailed for its post-DED work up on 15 September. The first week's flying was restricted to embarking the Ship's Flight but, during a machine-gun sortie, the flight once more lost a Wessex when an engine fire forced the pilots to ditch the Wessex 3 miles from the ship. Once again luck was on the side of the aircrew when they were recovered by the second Wessex from the Ship's Flight. The following week, a RAF Harrier GR3 was embarked from No. 1 Squadron to conduct trials to complete a certificate of airworthiness and sea performance trials. Describing some of the difficulties encountered by the RAF ground crew due to the change of operating environment, Hobbs recalled: 'The Harriers had a great deal of difficulty aligning their navigation heading and attitude reference system. I remember a disgruntled Sergeant complaining it didn't work and he couldn't figure out why. It transpired that they were setting the thing on zero when it was in the hangar and it hadn't dawned on

Ark Royal passes the deteriorating hulk of *Eagle*, waiting for her final voyage to Cairnryan for scrapping. (FAA Museum)

them that the hangar was doing 20 knots heading east or whatever. In the end they had to go back to Ferranti for modification.' Once the flying trials had been completed *Ark Royal* returned to Devonport.

Ark Royal sailed for her autumn round of exercises on 3 October, sailing first for the work up areas off the Moray Firth. Brazendale described everyday life on board for the junior sailors: 'I lived in a mess with about forty other sailors who slept in bunks three tiers high. Being a junior sailor I got the bottom bunk and, as the tour progressed, you moved up the bunks, but never to that elusive top bunk. There was no privacy and you had little tin lockers for your gear. We had about half a dozen Leading Hands (killicks) with a Leading Hand of the mess. They were real authoritarian figures and they all occupied top bunks. We had a daily ice ration for the mess, so I or whoever was given the duty would take the gash bags down to the evaporator rooms where they would make ice. I would see the watchkeeping "clanky" as we called them and we would lift a 4 foot by 3 foot block of ice out of the tanks which had cooling elements running through them and place the ice on the metal deck before smashing it with a wooden hammer and placing the large chunks in a gash bag for transfer back to the mess. Water rationing was a part of normal life in *Ark Royal*. Because of the catapults, the evaporators couldn't cope with the requirements for fresh water, so the first thing to be introduced was water rationing for the sailors.'

Between 6 and 13 October, *Ark Royal* conducted flying exercises to work up the squadrons prior to the major forthcoming exercises. On 14 October *Ark Royal* received a visit from HM Queen Elizabeth the Queen Mother. The Fleet Master-at-Arms at this time was FMAA Wilkinson BEM (now Mr Wilkinson MBE, BEM) He remembered the Queen Mother's visit: 'The ship's Land Rover had been polished so that it gleamed. The Land Rover had been parked so that it was offset from where the lift came down into the hangar deck. Ben Brettle was standing by the Land Rover ready to drive the Queen Mother round the hangar deck. Either side of the hangar deck various displays had been put up representing every department of the ship. For example, the bakery had fancy loaves baked and the seamen had got wire-splicing. The Queen Mother descended from the flight deck on the lift. When she arrived at the hangar deck she asked, "What is this, Captain Graham?" "These are some displays for you Ma'am, if you get into the Land Rover we can drive past them," he replied. "Oh no," she responded, "if they have taken the trouble to put this on for me, the least I can do is see it all, so I will walk." The look on Ben's face was a picture when she said that she would walk round the hangar deck. It wasn't funny really because he had put a lot of work into getting the Land Rover into shape but the Queen Mother did talk to him before she left.

'In the hangar deck there were ring bolts everywhere to chain down the aircraft while the ship was at sea. Of course you're not allowed to touch a royal person but I had to keep advising Her Majesty about the ring bolts. After a couple of mentions about ring bolts she turned to me and said, "Oh, you are looking after me", to which I replied, "Well, we have to, otherwise what would your daughter say." She thought that was very amusing.'

By the end of the month *Ark Royal* sailed south with a brief pause off Newcastle to embark Jimmy Savile OBE by helicopter. The visit was a great success as Salter recalled: 'He stayed up for twenty-four hours and he went round the ship everywhere and even did a radio show. He was very interesting because he told us what had happened to people in the pop business and was very down to earth about it all, it seemed like a documentary but on the radio. When he was stirring the Christmas pudding, the paddle broke. He thought he had broken it but the chippies had got to it first.'

Ark Royal entered Portsmouth for a week's visit on 27 October. Before sailing, FOCAS, Rear Admiral Eberle, embarked for Exercise Ocean Safari which was held between 8 and 20 November. During the exercise a large number of Russian ships were seen by *Ark Royal* as Wilkinson recalled: 'One of the things that was noticeable from our side was that the ship's husbandry left a lot to be desired. We encountered rough weather during the exercise and in bad weather the rise and fall of the bow could be up to about 130 feet. I had a chap up forward in the cells and I went up there to see how he was. I found him with a bucket and the sentry with another; they

At the end of October 1975 Jimmy Savile visited *Ark Royal*, managing to stay up for 24 hours visiting sailors all round the ship. He is seen here trying to stir the Christmas pudding, although someone got to the paddle before him! (Lieutenant Commander Brazendale via the author)

were both seasick. When she went down into a trough you were almost weightless while you felt much heavier as the bow rose again, it was a very strange feeling. And when you went forward below the waterline when we were operating in colder waters it was quite cold.' In addition to the various Russian surface ships, which included two Kresta II guided missile cruisers and six AGIs, numerous Bear and Badger aircraft were sighted in the area. *Ark Royal* also came under close scrutiny from the Russians, as Brazendale recalled: 'This Russian Hormone helicopter came alongside very close and then, suddenly, the door on the side of the helicopter burst open and out popped this camera with a telephoto lens on a tripod, which initially looked like a machine-gun, taking photographs of the ship.'

After the post-exercise debriefing at Rosyth, *Ark Royal* sailed for Devonport, arriving there on 27 November to begin her DED and Christmas leave. While the ship was alongside, white blocks were painted on the edge of the angled flight deck markings to improve visual recognition during night recovery. When *Ark Royal* left Devonport on 5 February 1976, to begin her spring deployment to the east coast of America, she had four extra people embarked who were going to be on board for the six-month deployment, to film footage for the BBC documentary *Sailor*. It was this series which helped secure *Ark Royal*'s place in the hearts of the British public and generate the climate for serious consideration to be given to her preservation when she was finally decommissioned.

John Purdie was the producer for the BBC TV series *Sailor*. He described the background to the series: 'I was working in the BBC documentaries department at the time and I had just made a film called *Ambassador* which was a portrait of the American Ambassador in London. It was the start of a new style of documentary, covering behind the scenes. Prior to that documentary everything was set up and it was almost prescripted. You told everyone what you were trying to do and they re-enacted their lifestyles. However, this was the start of a new era when you tried to do it first take for real. You asked people to ignore the camera. We were moving more towards important institutions and important jobs, trying to capture them in a documentary format. The *Ambassador* film had involved spending a fair amount of time with the American Embassy in Grosvenor Square, following the Ambassador around, seeing his daily ritual. In the course of doing this I got to know the First Secretary and Press Officer in the American Embassy and he invited me to a NATO briefing in Naples to see how defence correspondents are briefed because I might find another story there for a future documentary.

'I attended the briefing given by an American Admiral and then went on to a NATO exercise in the Mediterranean with the US Navy Sixth Fleet. I was hosted on board the American aircraft carrier USS *Forrestal* which was the flagship for the exercise. I was introduced to some senior US Navy officers who in the course of conversation mentioned their colleagues, the British, who were just over the horizon, telling me about a carrier called *Bulwark* which they were going to visit later in the day and perhaps I might like to go along with them. I went off and visited the *Bulwark*. It was the first time that I got an inkling of Navy humour and Navy grace and style. During the helicopter trip across to the *Bulwark*, one of the US Navy officers turned to me and said we love visiting the Royal Navy, so I asked, "Are they impressive?" to which he replied, "They're great guys but the Royal Navy is wet, the US Navy is dry."

'Having completed three months of filming in the American Embassy, and the world of diplomacy, the one thing which immediately impressed me about the British officers was how incredibly outspoken they were. I told the *Bulwark*'s Commander that I had just completed the filming of the *Ambassador*. He said, "You've got to make a film about how the Navy really is." "It is my first time on a British carrier," I replied. "The 'Rusty B' is a miracle. If the guys back at Whitehall knew how we kept this going, we would all get medals." After lunch he took me on a guided tour of the ship and it gradually began to sink in that this is a major job to keep one of these things going. It had been impressed upon me that it was a way of life and that each of these carriers was a small town.

'After I had flown home I thought more and more about it. I really liked the guys I had met out there and I loved their honesty and frankness. I wrote to the MOD explaining I had been on this trip and thought *Bulwark* was perfect. I knew their routines, the way of life, the social life with things like concerts and I knew what the Americans thought of them. Up to that point all service documentaries were incredibly old-fashioned, they were scripted, etc. MOD invited me to discuss my ideas. I told them I loved the honesty of the guys and that everyone had a secret sneaking affection for the Navy. I thought it was a great story which had never been told before. It had only previously been covered by the old Noel Coward style of documentary but it wasn't like that, there was another layer of humour and wit. But I made the mistake of saying that if you went on board the "Rusty B" the guys had to make do and the man in the Ministry said, "I'm not sure we want everyone to know that, but we like your enthusiasm and its a good idea."

'They came back to me and said, "Forget about the *Bulwark*, we don't feel the *Bulwark* is good enough. Everyone knows it's a terrible ship and we think you should go on board the *Hermes*. The *Hermes* is going on a NATO exercise off Norway and you will see us with our NATO allies, etc." I went down to see *Hermes* but everything I had seen in the Mediterranean on board the *Bulwark* had vaporized. Everyone was being very proper and terribly polite, etc. After my return I told them I didn't feel it was going to work with *Hermes*, not least from the practical point of view because, if she was going to Norway in March, the days would be very short and, with the snow, sleet, etc., it wouldn't look very good. However, I was also now interested in a carrier that actually launched jets, so I was told about *Ark Royal*. The *Iron Village* film had just been made and I knew the cameraman but the one thing which I felt was missing from that film, and I wanted to bring out in mine, was the people. Eventually, the MOD came back and said, "We will compromise. You wanted *Bulwark* and we wanted *Hermes*. We take your point about *Ark Royal*, and yes, you can do it", so I went down to Devonport to see the ship.'

Lygo recalled: 'I was the Vice Chief of the Naval Staff and Keith Lepard came to see me. He said, "We have got the opportunity to do a programme, but the RAF were approached to do a programme called *Squadron* and they turned it down." I therefore asked, "Why?" He replied, "Because they couldn't script it themselves." I gave the go-ahead although Lepard reminded me that we would not have any control over the programme. I asked, "What have we got to fear? If there is something wrong with the Navy I want to know what it is."

Purdie talked about his discussions with Captain Graham about the guidelines for the series during his first visit to the ship: 'I said to the Captain I can't ask every single person on this ship for their permission to film, but by the same token we can't expect everyone on the ship to be ordered to take part in it. I can talk to them on the ship's TV, but the ground rules should be this: we are a part of the ship and we should be able to film everything within reason, because I want to push the boundaries as far as the bounds of taste. I want to be able to film first and discuss later, and it must be stressed at every level that because we film something it doesn't mean it will go on air. If for whatever reason and it sounds fair, because obviously film costs money so the reasons couldn't be whimsical, if someone says, "I know you filmed me doing so and so, but I'd rather you didn't use it", then I won't use it. It has to be an act of faith. You have to take my word which is a personal thing, because I couldn't let the BBC know I was doing this, but this is how I operate. When we put the programme together we could then have a factual approval session, which wasn't editorial approval but it would allow selected people from MOD or *Ark Royal* to check that we haven't distorted the facts. Wid Graham said, "That sounds OK to me, but you need to speak to my Commander", who, he said, "was a top rate Commander who was in line to become a Captain." He then said, "You know the difference between a Captain and the Commander on a ship like this. He runs the day to day routine below decks. Everything you see is his responsibility, so if there are any warts it will be David's warts." I spent a long morning with David in his cabin.

He said, "I don't like it. What you're asking is unprecedented. You're asking to be able to film on board whatever you fancy." We had a break and then he asked to see me again.'

As part of his assessment of the situation Cdr Cowling sent for Fleet Master-at-Arms Wilkinson. 'I was sent for by the Commander. The Commander asked me what I thought about it. I asked, "Is it going to be warts and all?" "Yes," he replied. I said to John Purdie, "If you want to make it work you have got to become a sailor. You must include the sailors and earn their trust. If you don't you can forget it and put your camera away and go."' Purdie continued: 'Eventually David said, "I want you always to tell me if you can, what you are doing", which I said I thought would be difficult, but I would do my best and at the start of the day I would touch base with him to tell him what I was planning to do that day, and would tell him at the end of each day what we had done, to which he replied, "I will know".'

Having gained the necessary clearances to begin work on the series, the actual filming itself presented a few technical challenges, as Purdie recalled: 'There were some very dark corners where you were filming literally by the light of a 40 watt bulb. We soon learnt our way round the ship and discovered ideal places to shoot, and which times of the day the sun got into certain parts of the ship. The heat which built up on some of the decks was a problem, because with heat came a build-up of condensation which was a nightmare for the cameraman. Every night the assistant cameraman had chores with a hairdryer to dry out the camera. The size of the ship also presented a challenge to know what was going on the whole time. While I like to believe the series was fairly representative of life on board, it was in fact one particular portrait of what was going on because you can't film everything. If I had placed five film crews on board I would have ended up with five different versions of life on board, so I had to make editorial decisions about where to go and what was representative. I had to look at the different groups and where the stories for each of these groups would come from, as well as looking at the ages involved, so that you had old hands as well as young sailors.'

When the series was eventually screened, one of the stars of the series turned out to be John Pooley and his puppet 'Little Wilf' which regularly appeared on the ship's TV. Graham remarked about the puppet: 'He was a great chap! While the act sailed very close to the wind, it was very funny. I found it very useful because it did give me a clue, up to a point, what the ship's company was thinking at any given time.' Wilkinson recalled the impact of the puppet: 'When I joined the ship the "Little Wilf" puppet was already an established part of the ship's TV and a lot of people didn't like it. It came close to contempt to a lot of people, mainly junior officers

'Little Wilf' on tour. He is seen here meeting Colin Brazendale. (Lieutenant Commander Brazendale via the author)

and a few senior rates. The morale of the ship's company was sky high and the puppet was their champion. To them it was a person who voiced any criticisms on their behalf.' FMAA Wilkinson sent for John Pooley to discuss the guidelines for the puppet show to avoid unnecessary problems: 'I said, the thing is, what you have got to realize is, who you are having a go at. Make sure you have got your facts right, whatever they are, but don't put yourself in such a position that someone who can't take a joke could turn round and say, that is contemptuous behaviour or language or whatever and formulate a charge against you, because if they have a case against you it comes into my realm and I have got to do something about it. So don't embarrass me or yourself and more importantly don't appear before me because of a prat who can't take a joke. Yes, do it, but do it nicely, don't do it with any malice, do it respectfully, and Pooley did a very good job only upsetting a few people.'

After two weeks of exercises *Ark Royal* prepared to mark the twenty-first anniversary of her first commissioning. The ship received numerous messages that morning, but one was to create the circumstances for the most dramatic footage of the *Sailor* series. The ship received a message on 22 February from the American nuclear-powered attack submarine *Bergall* asking for assistance because a crew member was suffering from acute appendicitis and was in need of hospital treatment. 'It was very fortunate that when the signal came through saying this chap was in trouble, John Purdie just happened to be there as well, so I turned to him and said, here's something that will interest you, so he went off and got hold of the cameraman and sound man and

The 21st anniversary of the ship's commissioning was marked by the dramatic rescue of a sailor from the
US Navy submarine *Bergall*. (FAA Museum)

got them into one of the two Sea Kings that were launched,' Graham recalled. The two Sea Kings had to fly three hundred miles from *Ark Royal* to Lajes in the Azores, where they would refuel and establish the position of the submarine for the transfer. Originally the transfer was to have been carried out at night, but the patient's condition was reported to have improved so the transfer could wait until the following morning. The crews of both helicopters therefore stayed the night at Lajes before launching the following morning. 'The four of us went and we split into two. I sent the cameraman and sound recordist in the principal helicopter and the assistant cameraman and myself went in the second Sea King. When I was editing I could have cut a lot between the two cameras, but it would have looked like it was faked for a feature film. However, there were two problems. Firstly, the submarine wasn't where it was supposed to be, and secondly no one was supposed to know where it was. It obviously came up in an emergency, so the last thing the Americans would have wanted was a TV crew on board, and they didn't know about it until afterwards. When we landed in the Azores there were Americans on shore who wanted the film, but the bunch from *Ark Royal* closed ranks and told us to get back on the Sea King and we got off the Azores and back to the ship. Once back on board I sent the film back to London because I got worried about the tape getting seized because everyone told us the Americans didn't know about it. We got away with it because it was decided that as no one would know where the submarine was by the time the programme was transmitted it wouldn't pose a problem. One of the things which I have been asked over the years was "Did we fix it in the editing that this film would appear on the ship's birthday?" When we got up that morning, all that had been arranged for that day was that Wid Graham was going to cut a cake and read out a message from the Queen Mother, but it did all happen that day and there was nothing fixed about it,' Purdie recalled. Thanks to the actions of the helicopter crews, the American sailor made it to hospital in time and later made a full recovery.

After a brief stopover at Roosevelt Roads, *Ark Royal* sailed on 3 March to participate in Exercise Safe Pass. The weather steadily deteriorated as the ships headed north. On 13 March the cry that no sailor wants to hear was made, when the man overboard alarm was sounded. Thankfully, it was a false alarm and within thirty minutes every man had been accounted for. After a brief improvement in the weather which enabled the squadrons to complete some sorties, the weather closed in once more and flying was suspended. 'On the quarterdeck the swell was so great that when the bows went down, the stern rose out of the water allowing full view of the screws, and when the bows lifted you were looking at the wave crest some thirty to forty feet above you. I was Acting Leading Seaman at the time and was checking the rating on the stern who was there in case anyone fell overboard. (Someone kept a twenty-four hour watch all the time we were at sea),' recalled Fleming.

The conditions provided John Purdie with the idea for some real 'action shots' but he and the sound recordist nearly paid a very high price, as Purdie explained: 'One of the junior officers told me there were waves coming into the quarterdeck so I asked the Captain if I could see this. He told me that the quarterdeck was in fact out of bounds, but if I wanted to see it he would get someone to take me down there. I went down there to have a look, and lo and behold the waves were coming into the quarterdeck, smashing around and billowing over the side, great shot, I thought! So back I went to the Captain and I asked could we film it and he asked how would we do it. I said the waves are coming in and breaking over the deck, and I would really like the cameraman to go down there because the worst that would happen is that he would get caught by a wave up to waist height. We could see a corner where he might get his ankles wet. The Captain said, "It is dangerous. Do be careful because, if he goes overboard, we can't get him back. We certainly can't launch a helicopter but if you lash him to a bulkhead, and I want a couple of seamen to go with him, you can do it." I said I wouldn't go down there, it would be just the cameraman. The sound recordist and myself would stand at the top of the Queen's Steps, because we could get the wind noise from anywhere.

After we had recorded about five minutes of wind noise, we were standing there talking about how extraordinary it all was, when this wave crashed in and the next thing I knew I was under water. The Queen's Steps were swept clear and the same wave had covered the cameraman and the two sailors. The sound recordist and I fell off the steps into the water on the deck and were lying in the middle of the quarterdeck. We knew there would be more waves coming, and the next one could wash us towards the edge and possibly over the side. We both got up and ran towards the two sailors who were reaching out for us, and pulled us in before the next wave hit, which once again crashed in and swept things out. Had we remained where we were, we would have been swept over the side. We ended up as the lead story on the ship's TV as "prats of the day". "Who were the prats of the day? – they were two guys from the BBC who were warned it was dangerous and were nearly swept overboard."'

'Meanwhile at the other end of the ship the cabledeck was out of bounds for two days, secured off and watertight doors closed. When the weather subsided and we did manage to get in there, the fairleads, which is where the headropes pass through to secure the bows in harbour and is normally covered by two gates secured by two 9in circumference bolts so that no one can fall overboard at sea, were open to the full force of the sea on the starboard side. The force of the sea had sheared the bolts, swung the gates upwards on the hinges and fused them to the bulkhead. It required the shipwright and his cutting gear to release them,' recalled Fleming.

Because the weather showed no signs of improvement *Ark Royal* was ordered to break off from the exercise on 17 March and head south together with her escorting group. It was possible to resume flying once the ship had entered better weather off the Virginia Capes area. Two days later *Ark Royal* entered Mayport for a combination of leave and maintenance over nearly three weeks. Brazendale remembered the incident of an upwardly mobile chef on board *Ark Royal*: 'While we were in Mayport there was a young chef who had been ashore the night before and met up with some young ladies. He had obviously told them that he flew Phantoms from *Ark Royal*, so the next day these ladies turned up on the gangway and a ship's broadcast was made, "Would the chef who flies Phantoms please come to the starboard gangway."'

While the work was under way it was discovered that the shuttle guides and covers of the catapults had suffered excessive wear, and there were doubts over their effectiveness despite temporary repairs. Although there were still lingering doubts about the effectiveness of the catapults, the ship sailed as planned. The first day at sea proved to be a challenge for some of the new aircrew, as Hobbs recalled: 'We took a new batch of RAF aircrew and the CO of 809 Squadron decided that you could not fly from *Ark Royal* unless you had completed a carrier medical, so he got the ship's doctor in on the prank. The RAF aircrew spent their first day trying to find the doctor, who managed to avoid them. They kept on saying, "Can't we fly and sort it out later?" "No," they were told, they had to do the carrier medical. Up a flight of steps from the main Wardroom was Wardroom 2, which had the war role of being convertible into an operating theatre. These men were finally cornered and taken in there, stripped naked and stood on scales, before going through a semi-medical which got them a tick in the box for practising the wartime role of Wardroom 2. The Chief Sick Berth Attendant then gave them each a towel and said if they went down the flight of steps and waited in the next room he would come in and see them. When they went down the flight of steps and opened the door, they found the Wardroom full of people having their dinner. Some of them thought it was very amusing and dined in their towels, while two of them stormed out saying it was an outrage and that they had never been so humiliated in all their lives.

'Keith Somerville-Jones wanted all of his squadron to know something about the ship. He sent one of the new RAF pilots down to the boiler room for an hour's watchkeeping and the pilot concerned really didn't want to do it, saying he was there to fly etc., etc. Somerville-Jones said you are going to do it or you're off my squadron. So this officer turned up in white overalls with black feet drawn all over them, with a placard round

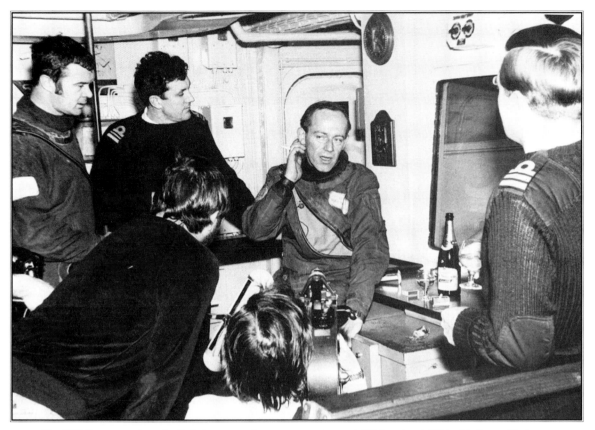

The BBC film crew making the 'Sailor' series conducting an interview with 809 Squadron's CO Lt Cdr Somerville-Jones.
(FAA Museum)

his neck saying, "Weep for me, I've got to spend an hour in the boiler room." When he got down there the Chief of the boiler room said, "Ho ho, very funny, Sir" and gave him a dustpan and brush, and opened up the grid in the plates which they stood on, so he ended up in the bilges in three feet of rusty oily water with a dustpan and brush, with instructions to clean it out. About three-quarters of an hour later this officer was nearly reduced to tears, when the Chief said, "OK, up you come. Do you want a cup of tea before you go off?" The Chief continued, "It's all very funny you coming down here dressed up like a prisoner, we have to spend four hours down here." "Yes," the officer gulped. "See up on the boiler face there's a big red light?" "Yes." "When we are flying that light comes on. If we are flying, even if it destroys the boiler, we will still keep steam to the turbines to keep the ship moving because, if the ship slows down, it could end up killing you, do you understand." "Yes." This chap came back up saying, "I didn't know." He was a completely changed man,' Hobbs remarked.

Sadly, the doubts about the catapults proved to be well founded, so it was decided to enter the Naval Base at Norfolk, Virginia on 19 April for an assisted-maintenance period to rectify the catapults. This unexpected second spell alongside was not all bad news, because it enabled some of the other departments on board to catch up on maintenance, while the ship received a visit from the daughter of a rather important American, as Hobbs recalled: 'The Midshipman, who was due to introduce the Azalea Queen who was President Ford's daughter said, "Captain, can I introduce you to Miss ——, Miss ——", at which point one of the Secret Service Agents leant forward and whispered, "She is the daughter of the President of the United States of America", and he

The Navy's biggest alongside the world's largest carrier: the *Ark Royal* spent three weeks in April/May 1976 moored alongside USS *Nimitz*. (FAA Museum)

said, "Yes, yes", and he still couldn't remember her name. It nearly caused a diplomatic incident, until Captain Graham said, "Miss Ford, hello, how do you do?"' Across the pier to which she was moored, *Ark Royal* was alongside the American nuclear-powered aircraft carrier *Nimitz*, which at the time was the world's largest aircraft carrier and dwarfed Britain's largest ever carrier. The repairs were completed by the end of the first week in May, so that *Ark Royal* was able to re-embark the CAG and begin an intensive period of flying exercises held both during the day and at night.

Hobbs described night-flying in the Gannet: 'The drawback with flying Gannets was that you were always the last to land on. You flew duskers, the sun had gone down, it wasn't quite daylight and it wasn't quite dark. The Phantoms and Buccaneers dusked first, so by the time the Gannet dusked it was good and black and I was peering out wondering where's the ship? I had to do three nights of duskers into a fairly dark trap. At the end of the third I thought that's it, I can think of a million reasons why I don't want to do this, I will be lantern-jawed and brave, and walk right up to the boss, look him in the eye and say, "I am too young to do this, I don't want to play the night game any more." When I got down to the crewroom and threw down my helmet, the boss shoved a drink in my hand and said, "Welcome to the club, any fool can land by day, it's only the men who can land by night". Yeah well, why not? I thought.'

Salter remembered the living conditions in his mess during flying exercises: 'It was very noisy in our mess. They used to do ground runs with a Phantom chained to the deck above us, with a false ceiling of about four to five feet, the vibration was terrible. There used to be a 4.5in gun in place of our mess, and if you looked out of

A Phantom at the moment of take-off. Note the strop falling clear. (Commander Wilcock via the author)

Captain Graham and Rear Admiral Eberle (FOCAS) join in an evening of onboard entertainment with the ship's company. (Lieutenant Commander Brazendale via the author)

the scuttle you could just see the waist catapult bridle catcher. One night they piped, "Close all scuttles and deadlights to darken ship". One of the men in our mess climbed up to take the clips off to drop the deadlight, and a Buccaneer was launched off the catapult and blew the scuttle open, filling the mess with aircraft fumes.'

FMAA Wilkinson highlighted the plight of sailors like Ben Salter living in the messes which were located in reclaimed parts of the ship, such as the former gun mountings. 'We had a group of four officers from the Ship Planning Department at Bath. They asked about heat and I said, "I will show you heat", to which the Commander said, "Yes, show them some of our good spots." I took them to one of the mess decks which had been built in the space once occupied by one of the 4.5in gun turrets. I said, "You expect us to house fourteen men in this mess deck, so I have to accommodate fourteen men or else we are short of fourteen bunks, but you have the two extremes in here. When we are steaming in bitterly cold waters, you can just imagine a sailor down here trying to keep warm, yet in the hot weather the temperatures are over 100 degrees Fahrenheit, so why do you do it?" "Point taken, Mr Wilkinson," replied one of the officers, "you have certainly given us something to chew on when we get back."'

After three weeks of successful flying exercises *Ark Royal* left the AFWR to head for Norfolk and nearly two weeks of AMP. The ship set sail again on 14 June and the two main events of the second half of the month were the ORI held between 16 and 17 June and Operation 200 held between 21 and 25 June, which culminated in cross-deck operations with the American carrier *John F Kennedy*. With the month drawing to a close, it was time for *Ark Royal* to alter course to head for Fort Lauderdale and the bicentenary celebrations. Before *Ark Royal* could play her part in helping to celebrate the bicentenary anniversary of American independence from the UK, the ship's company worked hard, with sailors devoting many hours to polishing below deck, while the flight deck was repainted. In keeping with the occasion, the ship entered Fort Lauderdale in procedure Alpha, and an extra 650 sailors were formed up to spell out 1776–1976 on the flight deck. Four Sea Kings from 824 Squadron flew along the sea front each flying an appropriate flag. *Ark Royal* held a ball on board on the night of 3 July which was attended by Fort Lauderdale's local dignitaries. 'An American submarine fired a smoke candle and it landed on our flight deck. *Ark Royal* signalled the submarine "The war is over you don't need to open fire on us!" 892 Squadron marked the occasion by spraying the white numbers 976–1976 on the side of their aircraft, and when the Americans were suckered into asking "What does that mean?", the reply was, "A thousand years since King Alfred formed the Royal Navy",' Hobbs recalled.

Like all good things the bicentenary celebrations had to end, and on 6 July *Ark Royal* slipped her moorings to head for home. Captain Graham only had ten days to complete the voyage, so he had to steam at a steady 17 knots. 'At night when we were at sea on passage I would quite often go down to the engine room and visit the watchkeepers, because I felt they thought that they were forgotten and I felt that it was important that they should know that I knew they were there,' Graham recalled. 'I thought the Captain's surprise visits were good because I, as a junior sailor, knew who the Captain was by sight, yet when I served in the fifth *Ark Royal* as a ship's officer I knew that there were some men who didn't know who the Captain was,' Brazendale remarked.

A Phantom of 892 Squadron cross-decking on a US carrier. (Lieutenant Commander Brazendale via the author)

US Navy aircraft on board *Ark Royal* during a cross-decking exercise with an American carrier. (Lieutenant Commander Brazendale via the author)

Early on the morning of 16 July *Ark Royal* once more entered her home port of Devonport at the end of a successful deployment which had been recorded for posterity by John Purdie and his team. While the ship went into a DED, John Purdie had the unenviable task of deciding what to include and what to leave out so that the series was ready for transmission in August.

'When we came back from the deployment and started editing the material, I had to take out more than the average number of expletives, as you would imagine, because that is the way they talk in the services and it is naive to think that they don't. For the sake of the BBC, who didn't at that time allow any expletives on the screen, I had to remove them, although I did argue very strongly in favour of keeping some in to give a realistic flavour of life on board. Wilf the puppet was the rudest of them all, singing the most outrageous songs which had everyone falling about, and out in the middle of the Atlantic it was entertaining. However, I did include something which was most extraordinary. I asked the Church of England Padre, Revd Bernard Marshall, "How do you spread God's message in a place like this? You're terribly middle class and educated, yet you are dealing with people who are about as rough and direct are you can get. Wherever you go there is someone saying fuck this, fuck that, etc., so how do you cope with that?" He replied in the interview, "If I walk into a mess and someone says 'Quiet lads, here comes the fucking padre', I don't bat an eyelid; it doesn't bother me in the slightest, this is the way these guys speak. I don't try to correct them because I would never get a dialogue going if I spent most of the time picking them up on their language. If they blaspheme and take the Lord's name in vain I tell them up front I am not having that, but if they are using good old Anglo-Saxon four-letter words, then so what? What's it got to do with decency and morality? So it doesn't bother me." I argued very strongly within the BBC to keep it in the series, because I said this man is making a profound statement. This is what gets people into church when he says, "I am the same as you but I am a man of God, and I want you to be a man of God and this is his mission". The BBC conceded and allowed it to stay, so the only swearing within the whole series came from the Padre. I had other people say "The Padre, did he swear?"; they didn't hear the swearing, they heard the man,' Purdie remarked.

While the ship was still alongside, the first episode of *Sailor* was transmitted at the beginning of August. Purdie recounted the reaction to the series: 'The MOD was not happy when they saw the first episode of the series because it featured drunken sailors, strip joints, etc. My boss told them, "Before you make any judgement, see at least four episodes, because you have to see the episode in which an NCO risks his life by going into the water to save an American sailor who had been swept off a submarine during a helicopter transfer, because it says so much for the Royal Navy in operation." But for that to work you have to have the rest of the story, and after the episode with the helicopter rescue the MOD began to relax.'

The most immediate effect of the series was that at the Navy Days held in Devonport that year *Ark Royal* was unquestionably the star attraction.

Chapter Ten

THE FINAL CURTAIN

S I X T H   C O M M I S S I O N ,   P A R T   I I I ,

S E P T E M B E R   1 9 7 6 – D E C E M B E R   1 9 7 8

Thanks to the success of the *Sailor* series *Ark Royal* was now a national star as she entered her final two years in commission. After playing a key role at the Navy Days, held in Devonport, *Ark Royal* sailed on 2 September for her round of autumn exercises. From Devonport, she headed north for a work up in the Moray Firth. During this period *Ark Royal* played host to a large number of guests, including her former Captain from the third commission, by then Admiral of the Fleet Sir Peter Hill-Norton GCB, who was just about to retire from his last active post as Chairman of the NATO Military Committee. He had come back purely for nostalgic reasons, to spend three days on board, which he thoroughly enjoyed. Having completed the short work up, *Ark Royal* sailed for the NATO exercise, Teamwork 76, in which *Ark Royal* provided air support for amphibious landings on the Norwegian and Danish coasts. As ever, the Russians were keeping an eye on the exercises, with Bears and Badgers providing the Phantoms of 892 Squadron with additional jobs, while a couple of Kresta II Russian cruisers watched from a distance. At the end of the exercise *Ark Royal* headed south, stopping briefly on 25 September to collect Captain Anson, who was shortly to replace Captain Graham in command.

Anson spoke of his preparations prior to taking command of *Ark Royal*: 'I flew out to *Ark Royal* off Faslane by helicopter. During the voyage to Lisbon, prior to my taking command, I read the Navigation Data Book and Ship's Book for both *Eagle* and *Ark Royal*. Since *Eagle*'s withdrawal from service her Navigation Data Book and Ship's Book had been kept on board *Ark Royal* because they were sister ships and handled in much the same way. The Ship's Book tells you what there is, where it is, and how it works. The Navigation Data Book should tell you the recommended way of coming alongside, approaching a buoy, dropping an anchor, and so on.'

On 28 September *Ark Royal* anchored in the River Tagus to begin a four-day visit to Lisbon. The major event was on the day of arrival when Captain Anson (now Vice Admiral Sir Edward Anson KCB) relieved Captain Graham as *Ark Royal*'s Captain. 'The day I took command was a non-event in a sense because I was already on board so there was no great ceremony of handover. My predecessor slipped quietly ashore to catch his aeroplane back home,' Anson recalled.

There was to be no gentle run-in period for Captain Anson because, when she left Lisbon on 4 October, *Ark Royal* sailed for Exercise Display Determination in the Mediterranean. An impressive armada of about a hundred warships from five nations gathered for the exercise, including the two American aircraft carriers *Nimitz* and *America*, as well as the French aircraft carrier *Clemenceau*. Towards the end of the exercise *Ark Royal* cross-operated with the American carrier *America*. Among the aircraft embarked from *America* was the US Navy's newest fighter, the F14 Tomcat, which operated from *Ark Royal* for the first time. At the end of the visit *Ark Royal* entered Toulon on 13 October for a five-day visit. To ensure that the refit work could proceed as soon as the ship docked in Devonport, a team from the dockyard embarked in Toulon to begin planning the schedule for the refit and establishing what work had to be completed. When the ship sailed from Toulon on 18 October the fixed-wing squadrons disembarked later in the day to head for home.

To speed up the process of destoring prior to the start of the refit, *Ark Royal* conducted a back RAS of ammunition, fuel and stores to her accompanying RFAs. *Ark Royal*'s Supply Officer for the final part of the sixth commission was Cdr O'Donnell (now Captain O'Donnell). He explained how *Ark Royal* was kept fully provisioned and some of the hazards of a RAS: 'When operating at sea, keeping the ship provisioned and fuelled was one of the major evolutions that occurred with monotonous regularity – every ten to fourteen days for provisions and stores; fuelling could be more frequent depending on how much flying we were doing – flying always required high-speed steaming to get sufficient wind over the deck to launch our relatively heavy aircraft. To provision and store the ship, with storerooms spread throughout the ship forward to aft at all deck levels, required imagination and a high degree of organization.

'We achieved this by splitting the stores parties into football divisions. The First Division handled the flight deck, Second Division the routes below decks, and Third Division manned the storerooms. All departments were required to provide certain levels of manpower to produce the football teams. Each team was overseen and supervised by one of the professional stores staff. Flight deck lifts were lowered to different levels and a variety of special canvas chutes criss-crossed the space, going to different levels where access had been cut to passageways leading to various storerooms. In an emergency, the retaining lines for the chutes could be quickly cut and the lifts brought to flight deck level. In one instance, where an Inglefield clip fractured on a messenger line under tension, and part of the clip flew across the flight deck and struck a bystander in the face, it was quicker to bring the lift to the flight deck and then lower the individual down to the sickbay, than to get a medical team up to the flight deck to tend to his very serious injury. Luckily the clip struck the man just on the eyebrow, fracturing it, but the eye was undamaged and the young man made a full recovery.

'Another hazard accompanying a RAS was the danger of falling overboard. In one instance the forward beer party was in the port forward flight deck catwalk (about forty feet above the water) loading beer cartons into a special access to the NAAFI beer stowage, when a rogue wave enhanced by the venturi effect between the *Ark Royal* and its accompanying RFA, just washed them right out of the catwalk and dumped them down between the two ships. Luckily they were not sucked into the prop wash of either vessel, and were soon recovered by the SAR chopper, very wet and not much worse for wear.'

Ark Royal continued her voyage home, following a two-day stopover in Gibraltar on 20 and 21 October, securing alongside in Devonport at 7 a.m. on 25 October. Although this was the last commission, the ship still managed to notch up a number of 'firsts', including this passage up Plymouth Sound, which was completed in darkness.

While it is always important for a ship to complete its refit on time, there was a special motivating factor to ensure that *Ark Royal* completed this refit on schedule, as Anson explained: 'Because we were due to attend the 1977 Spithead Fleet Review, there was a clear target to get the ship looking better than it had ever looked before, both externally and internally. The hard work put in by the ship's company paid off, because many people at the review, who had previously served in *Ark Royal*, said to me that they had never seen *Ark Royal* looking so polished and buffed.'

While *Ark Royal* was undergoing her refit in Devonport, Captain Anson spent part of the time completing a helicopter conversion course at RNAS Culdrose in Cornwall. Back at Devonport, Captain Anson went to see the Principle Stores Transport Officer Navy (PSTON) in the dockyard. 'In *Ark Royal* we had bridle catchers for the catapults. In *Eagle* we didn't. So every time we launched an aircraft from *Eagle* we lost the bridle. This was not a problem with Buccaneer bridles because they were not very expensive. However, the Phantom bridles were expensive because they had special forged metal eyes, so that the same bridle could be used twenty times. If I did not have to use the bridle catchers I could use the same type of bridle as used for the Buccaneer, which could only be used once on the Phantom anyway, and thus save time by not having to recover the bridle from the end of the catapult. So I said to the officer that when *Ark Royal* returned to Devonport never to go to sea again, I did not want to have five thousand of these bridles left on board, when we could have been launching aircraft with a very short interval, made possible by not using the bridle catchers. Obviously, if after we came back in, there was an emergency which led to *Ark Royal* being sent back to sea again, we would need to have a small supply of bridles left over to use while new bridles were manufactured. He agreed to ensure that I would be cleared to fire these bridles off during each launch,' Anson recalled.

The optimistic rumours that had been circulating about *Ark Royal* remaining in service until *Invincible* commissioned in 1980 were finally dismissed when the Government announced on 21 February 1977 that she would be withdrawn from service at the end of 1978. While this news confirmed the end was near for *Ark Royal*, it did eventually lead to the recommissioning of *Bulwark* to bridge the gap between the departure of *Ark Royal* and the commissioning of *Invincible*. *Bulwark* had been placed in a type of reserve known as 'Preservation by Operation' in May 1976 at Portsmouth. She was reactivated and recommissioned on 23 February 1979, just nine days after *Ark Royal* was finally decommissioned in Devonport.

During the refit the *Ark Royal* benefited from an unexpected windfall as Anson recalled: 'Our Achilles heel was fresh water. Thanks to all the steam leaks we were losing about 5 tons of fresh water a day. This refit was supposed to fix this problem by curing the steam leaks and by having all the evaporators reconditioned. The dockyard refused to refit more than five evaporators due to cost and the time needed to complete the work. While I was trying to reverse this decision, the Engineer Officer came to see me and showed me a crate which had just arrived on board. "You see that crate there?" he said. "Yes," I replied. "That crate has got in it a cylinder head for a diesel generator." "Yes." "But when you open it up, it has two new evaporator combined pumps inside it and no one knows about it." The two extra combined pumps proved to be very useful.'

The ship's company moved back on board *Ark Royal* on 13 April, thus beginning the final leg of the refit towards the completion date of 1 June 1977. Having passed the Flag Officer Plymouth's inspection on 1 June, *Ark Royal* went for a fast cruise with a difference on 8 June. The only thing was, that *Ark Royal* did not actually leave the quayside. The object of this exercise was to test the ship's machinery as well as the ship's company, before leaving Devonport for post-refit acceptance trials on 9 June. These trials continued until 19 June when the dockyard civilians were disembarked at Charlie buoy and the ship set course for Portsmouth for the Fleet Review.

Prior to taking up her position off Spithead, *Ark Royal* paid her last visit to Portsmouth on 20 June to embark the staff of the C-in-C Fleet, Admiral Sir Henry Leach KCB (now Admiral of the Fleet Sir Henry Leach GCB, DL). Leach spoke about the Fleet Review: 'Earlier that year I had taken over as C-in-C Fleet and for this occasion I flew my flag in *Ark Royal*. The review took place on Tuesday 28 June. I helicoptered in to *Ark Royal* a few days before, to receive and return the calls of the visiting Flag and Commanding Officers from other Navies, check on the final arrangements and carry out an inspection/rehearsal the day before.' When *Ark Royal* sailed out of Portsmouth on 23 June Captain Anson was joined by *Ark Royal*'s first Captain, by then Rear Admiral Cambell CB, DSC (retired).

Leach continued: 'Calls started at 10:00 and went on all day with a short break for lunch. They were staggered at thirty minute intervals, but my Flag Lieutenant was instructed to report clearly that so and so's barge was alongside after fifteen minutes had elapsed; this gave time for me to encourage the visitor to finish his coffee and cognac, sign my book, present him with his mementos and lead him unhurriedly back to the quarterdeck, exchange farewells and pipe him over the side. For obvious reasons of endurance I did not drink brandy, but was presented on each visit with a balloon glass of matching-coloured cold tea. All went well until the motor whaler of a certain NATO Commander missed the gangway, had to go round again, missed it again and only just made it at the third attempt – which took time. So long, in fact, that the barge of the next in the queue was already lying off. The best I could do was to limit the latecomer to inspecting the front rank only of the guard, handing over his presents on the quarterdeck and hustling him back into his boat.'

He described the dress rehearsal for the Fleet Review: 'The assembled ships were required to man ship and give three cheers as I passed along the line in the helicopter training ship *Engadine*, following the route which the Queen would take in *Britannia* the next day. The USS *California* wearing the flag of Rear Admiral Dixon looked very smart and had lined her decks impeccably but remained dead silent as we passed. On my return to *Ark Royal* I sent across a note mentioning this and giving him the option of adhering to his navy's (silent) drill – alone in the entire fleet – or departing from USN tradition and cheering ship like the rest. He chose the latter, so I did not have to warn the Queen. At the far end of the line was the Shell training tanker *Opalia*, immaculately painted and manned by smart cadets. But astern of her was the BP supertanker *British Respect*; her hull and upperworks were streaked with rust, a rope end was trailing over the side, she had not manned ship at all and several crew members dressed in singlets were lounging on the guard rails. On my return I drafted a carefully worded note: "As a token of British respect, when the Queen passes tomorrow I hope you will man ship and give Her Majesty three cheers." Merchant ships came under my command for berthing and navigational safety but not otherwise. Next evening I enquired of the Queen what had happened and thankfully the errors had been corrected.'

On the evening of the Fleet Review the Queen attended the banquet, held on board *Ark Royal* in the upper hangar, as guest of honour. 'That night we dined two hundred and fifty-strong in *Ark Royal*'s hangar. (Three decks up and a considerable distance away from the galleys, with a huge team of cooks and stewards to make up in part for it.) The full Admiralty Board and every Flag and Commanding Officer in the fleet except those on patrol were present. When the Queen arrived, it fell to me to present the Flag Officers and Minister; simple enough but the further up the line one went, the longer became the ranks and titles – and, conversely, the better the Queen knew them and the faster she moved. Then aft to the cuddy for a pre-dinner drink. I had been at pains to find out from the palace precisely what HM and Prince Philip would have and there sure enough was a specially selected smart young steward holding a silver salver on which was a dry martini. I indicated this to the Queen who rather sharply asked, "What on earth is that?" "A dry martini, Ma'am, which I understood to be your preference!" "It doesn't look like it to me!" (Impasse.) "Well would you care to try it, Ma'am, and if it's not to your taste we will try to do better." Very gingerly, as if handling a snake, the Queen picked up the glass and took a sip, albeit with a look of considerable uncertainty. Then her whole face lit up and with a smile of immense relief she turned back to me. "You're quite right – it is!" Similarly with Prince Philip: smart steward, salver, pink gin. "Oh, do you think I could have a gin and tonic?" Of course he could, but it wasn't the prescribed thing, and it wasn't actually to hand. You can't always win,' Leach remarked.

He continued: 'I led the Queen into the packed hangar and round the professional ranks until we eventually came to our places, where I endeavoured to persuade HM to be seated. But she was disinclined to do so and asked, "Do we have Grace or something now?" It is the practice in HM ships and naval messes to say Grace seated but this was not the moment to say so. Because everyone was standing I could not see the Chaplain (Ray Roberts) nor did I know at which table he was; seizing the gavel I gave it a resounding, if optimistic, thump and to my great relief the voice of the man of God responded. I sat with the Queen on my right and Jim Callaghan

Ark Royal on the day of the Fleet Review, moments after the Queen had passed by in HMY *Britannia*. (Mike Lennon)

(Prime Minister) on my left. In the course of dinner at one point I was enthusing on the qualities of *Ark Royal* versus *Eagle*; how the latter, though characteristically smarter-looking externally, had a less good flying record and had never developed the same human spirit that *Ark Royal*'s ship's companies had; and how the Queen Mother still lunched with her Captain once a year. At which point the Queen remarked "Steady on Admiral, you remember who launched *Eagle*" (I had forgotten it was she), adding wistfully, "Yes, Mummy has green fingers and everything she touches grows." Wasn't that a nice way of putting it?'

Before the ships dispersed after the Fleet Review there was still one task to undertake, as Leach recalled: 'Next morning we put to sea and *Ark Royal* led the fleet to steam past the destroyer *Birmingham* by way of saying goodbye to Admiral of the Fleet Sir Edward Ashmore who was on board on the eve of his retirement as Acting Chief of the Defence Staff.'

With the festivities of the Fleet Review over *Ark Royal* headed west to continue with her post-refit trials, pausing at Charlie buoy to collect the flight deck trials team, before sailing into the Channel to embark a mini CAG of three Phantoms, three Buccaneers and two Gannets for a week of wire-pulling trials. On completion of these trials *Ark Royal* returned to Devonport on 12 July for post-sea trials rectification and summer leave. The highlight of this period was her final appearance at Devonport Navy Days over the August Bank Holiday when a record 31,648 visitors took advantage of this last opportunity to look round the ship in her home port.

When the ship sailed from Devonport on 1 September to head north for the Moray Firth area the Ship's Flight and 824 Squadron were already embarked as had become normal practice during her final years in service. Among the new members of the squadron who were embarking in *Ark Royal* for the first time was 824 Squadron's Senior Pilot, Lt Cdr Peter Fish (now Commodore P.A. Fish CBE) who had joined the squadron after the Fleet Review. He explained his role: 'As Senior Pilot I was responsible for looking after the day to day flying programme of the squadron, determining who took off, when, and for how long, while the Senior Observer (Lt Cdr Jim Milne) was responsible for the exercise and long-term programme dealing with what the squadron would be doing over the coming weeks and months.'

When the fixed-wing squadrons embarked on 5 October they also had a few new faces. One of them was Flight Lt Steve Riley. He was one of the many RAF pilots to serve in 892 Squadron during the 1970s. He had previously flown Lightnings from RAF Wattisham. Describing how he ended up in 892 Squadron flying the Phantom, and the training he completed before embarking, he recalled: 'The RN had not been training its own fixed-wing aviators for about six years; this left a void which was eagerly filled by suitable applicants from the RAF looking for an extra challenge. My own background in the Lightning was appropriate for 892 Squadron's primary role of air defence so I asked my desk officer for a posting to 892 Squadron and two weeks later it was all sorted. The RAF found me a space on the Phantom OCU at Coningsby; it was a four-month course squeezed into four weeks. The Navy's own course on the Phantom Training Flight (PTF) at Leuchars was the perfect antidote. PTF was a curious amalgam; an integrated RAF/RN unit, it was commanded by light blue and the planes belonged to the RAF, but the instructors and maintainers were unequivocally RN and together they gave us five weeks of brilliant flying. In addition to a custom-built tactical flying schedule, we also trained for the discipline of deck landings. A mirror landing sight was installed alongside dummy deck markings on the runway and we practised several approaches at the end of each tactical training mission. At Bedford we climbed the Phantom onto the static steam catapult (like a small railway platform but with a big kick) and got boosted into the sky like cannon shells until our heads spun.

'A few weeks later when I rolled my Phantom out on *Ark Royal*'s own deck landing datum for the first time, I felt surprisingly comfortable. My main concern though, was all around me. The sea. The landing area seemed so short and so well hidden behind the Phantom's long nose, that if I flew a little too high then I might sail over the ship and land in the water. Lowering the nose for a peek at the deck would only exacerbate the situation.

When the RN stopped training its own fixed-wing aircrew their places were gradually filled by RAF pilots and navigators; by the time *Ark Royal* was paid off they made up nearly half of the aircrew of the fixed-wing squadrons. This is the RAF aircrew for the three fixed-wing squadrons on board *Ark Royal* during her final commission. (Steve Riley via the author)

This sequence of photographs shows the launch of a Phantom. (Steve Riley)

A few more anxieties flitted through my mind and suddenly it was over. The Phantom hit the deck and with the stick in my stomach and the throttles wide open we rose back into the air. "One more like that 014 and you can try it with the hook down."'

As the work up progressed, Colonel P.F. Baillon came on board to look at one of his sections, namely the 55 Carrier Borne Ground Liaison Section (CBGLS). During the last part of this commission this section was commanded by Major A.S. Hughes, Royal Welch Fusiliers. Hughes explained about the section and its role: 'Our headquarters was HQ CBGL Group at Plymouth. There were originally sections in the other carriers, such as *Eagle* and *Hermes*, as well as a section at RNAS Lossiemouth. For large-scale NATO exercises, our Colonel and a Major from HQ CBGL Group would embark so that we could maintain a twenty-four hour watch.

'The CBGLS was always commanded by a Major. The rest of the team consisted of an (Army) Captain who was our naval gunfire support expert, a Sergeant Chief Clerk, Corporal Clerk and a driver. Both officers, known as CBALS (from Carrier Borne Army Liaison Section) had completed courses in photographic interpretation and recognition training. Both CBALS complemented each other and the NCOs assisted as required. We had a Land Rover, which was embarked as required, and necessary stores and UHF radio to enable the team to conduct forward air controlling as required. The Land Rover was entirely for our use. I made a point on overseas visits to offer day-long trips to the squadrons and departments. We also organized "expeds" of up to a week's duration such as the trip to the Great Smoky Mountains in America during July 1978.'

Operationally the tasks of the CBGLS were briefing and debriefing aircrews on overland missions; keeping the Captain and embarked Admiral informed on the land battle situation; manning the operations desk as required; sending and receiving necessary aircraft tasking signals; receiving inflight reports from Buccaneer missions; assisting the photographic interpreters, and participating as members of the ship's Strike Planning

Ark Royal's last CBALS officer Major Hughes, pictured conducting splash target exercises. (Major Hughes via the author)

Team. In the training role, the CBGLS would perform all this as well as organizing and conducting close air support training for 809 and 892 Squadrons, and carrying out safety scoring for the ship's towed splash target.

In addition to their operational and training roles the CBGLS also performed a number of other duties, as Hughes explained: 'We had to assist the Gunnery Officer to train the ship's landing and boarding parties in weapon training and internal security training; assist in aircrew survival training; we were responsible for the provision of all overland maps worldwide for which role we carried approximately 1½ million maps; assist in recognition training for aircrew; maintain the Intelligence Library; inter-service liaison and any ship's duties as required. For example, during my first tour in *Ark Royal*, I was the Mail Officer.'

The first phase of the work up ended with five days moored to No. 1 buoy in the Firth of Forth about six miles from Leith. *Ark Royal* headed back to the Moray Firth work up area on 20 September to begin phase two of the work up. From a VIP point of view the busiest day was 21 September, when the ship was visited at different times by both the First Sea Lord, Admiral Sir Terence Lewin, and HRH Prince of Wales. The First Sea Lord embarked by helicopter, while HRH arrived in a more spectacular manner in the back seat of a Buccaneer, piloted by the CO of 809 Squadron, Lt Cdr A. Morton (now Captain A. Morton DSC). 'When we took off from Yeovilton there was a problem with the intercom so we couldn't communicate for a while which was irritating. We did a couple of rollers in the Moray Firth and then landed on board at 11:45,' Morton recalled. Having landed on board, the Prince then visited various parts of the ship.

'Later in the visit the Prince of Wales was invited to join selected officers in the Wardroom dining hall. Undesirables were banished to the Wardroom bar. HRH seemed to sense this and asked, "Who is in there? I'd rather like a Coca Cola." He stepped into the bar and immediately recognized some familiar faces. He impressed us all with his ability to put names to people he had not seen for some considerable time,' said Riley.

'The briefing prior to HRH's departure made a big deal about the establishment of purple (royal) airspace: around the ship, down the departure corridor and around Lossiemouth, the destination. Great detail was provided about the dimensions and the duration of the special airspace to the obvious (we thought) embarrassment of our guest. The briefing sailed on and eventually the Prince turned to the flight crew lurking at the back and said, "I'm sorry to be such a nuisance, chaps", at which point Wings stepped in and called a halt,' Riley recalled.

The purpose of the Prince's visit was to experience a catapult launch, thus making him the only member of the royal family to do so. Amid much attention from the embarked press photographers the Prince climbed into the Buccaneer to be launched at 3.45 p.m. 'The Prince of Wales wanted to fly past *Ark Royal* at deck level. He had already had quite a battle with the Prime Minister Jim Callaghan to be able to fly in a Buccaneer at all. Tony Morton asked could he do the low fly-by and I said no, because the press were still hanging about. However, I had said to Wings that if we could get the press out of the way then the Prince could have his low flypast. A few moments later Wings said that the press had watched the launch and having now lost interest they were down in the bar. With the press out of the way I gave the go-ahead, because I did not want Jim Callaghan to find out about the fly-past unless it came direct from Prince Charles,' Anson explained.

Having completed the second phase of the work up at the end of September, *Ark Royal* paid a week's visit to Hamburg for the first time. The 70 mile inland voyage up the Elbe did not pass without its dramas, as Anson recalled: 'We had to take three lots of pilots separately. Firstly, from the North Sea through to Brunsbüttel to take us through the channel past the sandbanks. When we got to Brunsbüttel with the RFA *Lyness* in company it was blowing force 7 to 8. We had sent a signal saying *Ark Royal* has flared overhangs and therefore it is essential that when we get to Brunsbüttel and the pilots come alongside they must be in a boat that can retract its masts or have a low mast. The Germans took no notice of this and the pilots arrived in a boat which could not come alongside, so we had to lower a cutter and take the pilots off their pilot boat. While this was going on we were

Prince Charles shortly before his catapult launch in a Buccaneer flown by the CO of 809 Squadron, Lieutenant Commander Morton. (Captain Morton via the author)

stopped with the high winds on the beam. At this stage the *Lyness* signalled that she had to go ahead otherwise they would go aground. Normally, due to protocol this would not have happened but in the circumstances there wasn't an option. We drew more than the *Lyness* so the speed by which we drifted sideways was much slower. With the pilots on board we continued up the Elbe with the tide by now behind us, so that we were doing 14 knots over the ground. As we came round a corner this great big dredger came into view and I turned to the pilot and said, "What's that?" "He shouldn't be there," the pilot said. "Well, he is there, tell him to move," I replied. The pilot told the dredger to move but he was secured to the ground by cables and anchors. The channel looked very wide between the marking buoys but if you draw 36 feet it isn't. In order not to go aground I had to go very close to the dredger. I took the ship myself, because I thought if we prang the ship it might as well be me that does it. We slipped past without touching, except for my outer starboard propeller which was chipped. I complained about this incident to the Naval Attaché who complained to the Germans. The propeller was not changed because the chip was very small; but it gave us a distinctive underwater noise signature thereafter.'

All too soon it was time to return to the Moray Firth and begin the third and final stage of the work up prior to the ORI. On 10 October FOCAS, Rear Admiral Staveley embarked prior to conducting the ORI. The other new arrival was Cdr Mike Layard (now Admiral Sir Michael Layard KCB, CBE) who became the new Cdr (Air). He had been the CO of 899 Squadron embarked in *Eagle* when *Ark Royal*'s Captain Anson had been the Cdr (Air). Describing the role of Wings, Layard explained: 'If the Commander and the Wings got on well then the ship ticked, because none of the departments or squadrons would try to play one Commander off against the other. On a typical day one of my operations officers would have drafted a flying programme the day before,

Close encounters as Captain Anson carefully negotiates his way past a moored dredger during his passage up the Elbe. At the time this photograph was taken Ark Royal was steaming at 14 knots over the ground! (via the author)

having negotiated with the various squadrons about how much flying they were going to do and what they were trying to achieve. On a good day we would achieve over a hundred training sorties day and night, which included the ASW Sea King squadron, who tended to "ripple" throughout the twenty-four hours. This would in part depend upon what ranges were available and what the air space situation was, because this could change daily. I would then OK the programme, having added my input in the light of what we were trying to achieve in, say, a three-month period in terms of the FOCAS Training Directive. There was always a need to check that the aviation part was dovetailing in with the overall operational capability of the ship. Once I had had a few hours sleep after night flying I would be up at dawn for the day's flying. I would always be at every major briefing, with the first one starting at 05:00. The first aircraft launch would be at 06:30 so that we could make full use of daylight hours. I would be in flyco for the launches and landings and then in the operations room to monitor what the aircraft were doing.'

Having successfully completed the ORI, *Ark Royal* participated in the major NATO exercise Ocean Safari between 17 and 28 October 1977. Fish described a typical routine of a Sea King in an exercise environment: 'The role of the Sea King was active dipping with the sonar, so we would seek to maintain a screen in advance of the ships. We would probably have two Sea Kings on task continuously, up threat of the task force. This required a busy flying programme with three airborne at any time; with one Sea King on dip, one on the way to take up station, and the third returning to the ship. Once we had got into the rhythm that cycle would continue twenty-four hours a day for as long as was necessary. An hour before the sortie there would be a briefing, firstly a sortie brief, followed by a crew brief. About twenty minutes before the sortie you would walk out to the aircraft, complete your checks, and then take off at your allocated time. We mainly operated from Fly 3 because it did not interfere with the fixed-wing landings and take-offs. The sortie would typically last about four hours. If you were working with another Sea King, once a contact had been made, one Sea King would keep contact, while the other helicopter would break dip and jump to a new position and make sonar contact. Eventually, you would get to the position where you were confident about what the intentions of the submarine were and what threat it posed. From there you would move into the attack phase. One Sea King would maintain sonar contact and

Prior to the start of this commission 824 Squadron received the uprated Sea King HAS2, which are instantly distinguishable from the original Sea King HAS1s by the barn door in front of the engines. (Admiral Sir Michael Layard via the author)

control the other helicopter by radar into a drop position so that the homing torpedo would enter the water, search and then acquire and attack the submarine. Unlike the fixed-wing aircraft *Ark Royal* did not have to turn into wind for recovery of the Sea Kings. If the ship was sailing downwind and there was still too much wind coming down the deck the helicopters would land facing aft.'

During the exercise the Sea Kings were also required to perform night flying, as Fish continued: 'The difference between day and night flying for the Sea King crews was not as marked as it was for the fixed-wing aircrews, therefore it did not present major problems. In some ways it was easier at night when the fixed-wing aircraft had finished flying, because we had the flight deck to ourselves and therefore we had more space. Because of the benefits of extra deck space at night you would often find that some check flights for Sea Kings, after major maintenance, were carried out at night.'

The exercise was completed on 28 October. Having disembarked FOCAS to Portland the ship headed south to spend November in the Mediterranean via a twenty-four hour stop at Gibraltar over 1 and 2 November. From Gibraltar, *Ark Royal* sailed to Malta for a week's visit, which provided the ship's company with a golden opportunity to catch up on maintenance as well as some well-earned leave. By the time *Ark Royal* left Malta on 12 November she was looking shipshape again, ready for her visit to Toulon. The weather was to dictate otherwise because during *Ark Royal*'s voyage north, the mistral wind was increasing in strength, thus preventing the intended visit prior to Exercise *Isle D'or*, which as the name suggests was organized by the French. The exercise was principally an ASW exercise, which initially ignored the AEW role because the French thought that the Gannets of 849 Squadron B Flight were the old obsolete torpedo-carrying AS version rather than the AEW version. The scope of the exercise was dictated by the weather because the seas, which had been whipped up by

A Phantom refuelling from a Buccaneer. (Steve Riley)

Ark Royal was not immune from the effects of the sea: some of the CAG are lashed firmly to the deck as she takes on the Mistral in November 1977. (Commander Cudmore via the author)

the mistral, forced flying to be cancelled on a number of occasions and eventually led to the premature conclusion of the exercise.

From the Toulon area *Ark Royal* sailed for Naples and into better weather when she arrived there on 28 November for a week's visit. After the bad weather of the previous couple of weeks the ship's company took the opportunity to visit many of the historic surrounding sights such as the Roman city of Pompeii. The weather was not to last because when *Ark Royal* left Naples on 5 December the cold weather of winter had returned. The *Ark Royal* was now homeward-bound with only a two-day visit to Gibraltar between 8 and 10 December, before she entered Devonport on 16 December to begin her AMP and the ship's company to take Christmas leave. Despite the best intentions, not everyone got their Christmas leave because some of the ship's company were deprived of it when they had to man Green Goddess fire engines to cover for the firemen who were on strike.

On 26 January 1978 Cdr James Weatherall (now Vice Admiral Sir James Weatherall KCB) joined *Ark Royal* as her last Commander. When he joined the ship, the debate about what should happen to her when she decommissioned had already begun in earnest. 'In the months before we sailed for the last deployment I had to show people around *Ark Royal* who were trying to preserve her. While showing them round the ship I tried to explain to them that preserving *Ark Royal* was going to be a very expensive operation. To back this up I took these people to parts of the ship that they would never see and said, here is your problem, the ship will speak for itself, I am not going to persuade you one way or the other,' Weatherall recalled.

Weatherall discussed the challenge that faced him when he was appointed as the Commander: 'There was a lot of emotion surrounding *Ark Royal* so, with a ship's company of 2,700, it was a quite a large man management and morale challenge. The morale challenge being to make sure that you made the ship work right up to its dying day, because if you didn't do that you would go into the rundown period and people would lose enthusiasm and it would get out of hand. One of the ways in which I managed to maintain the ship's company's morale was to insist on keeping the ship clean because I thought it was firstly a very good advert for the Royal Navy, because everyone wanted to visit *Ark Royal* in her final days; secondly, it made everyone take pride in the ship and allowed nobody to relax in the business of maintaining the ship.'

On 21 February *Ark Royal* sailed for post-AMP trials having left some of her ship's company behind. The very cold winter which had brought large amounts of snow had led to some of the ship's company being unable to reach Devonport in time because they were snowed in. Those men who had been left behind were airlifted out to *Ark Royal* from Portland the next day as the ship passed the Dorset coast. The bad weather also affected the embarkation of the Buccaneers so that 809 Squadron embarked a day late due to fog at RAF Honnington. Bad weather continued to plague the ship throughout its work up as the ship headed north off the east coast of the UK. Having passed the Sea Inspection Day under the watchful eye of FOCAS on 4 March *Ark Royal* once more headed south, having disembarked most of the fixed-wing squadrons except the few aircraft needed for the flying display to be held during the Families Day. *Ark Royal* returned to Charlie buoy on 8 March to spend the night there prior to the invasion of families for the ship's last ever Families Day on Thursday 9 March 1978.

'We were preparing to enter Devonport in the late afternoon, at which time the visibility was about a mile and a half, so I spoke to the Queen's Harbour Master and asked if he was happy for us to come in, and he said yes, you're clear to come in. If we hadn't come in then we would have had to moor up to Charlie buoy and disembark the families from there which was a much longer exercise. Once you have passed Charlie buoy you are committed to entering Devonport and there is no turning back. We went through the Smeaton Pass and turned to run along the Hoe. As we did this the fog suddenly came down and I could not see the jackstaff. No one had ever taken *Ark Royal* into Devonport in the fog. After we had run along the Hoe, we had to make a 180 degree turn with the assistance of a tug at the bow. As part of this manoeuvre the tug was in the narrows while *Ark Royal* was completing the turn. When the tug was in the narrows he called up and said, "Request instructions, I cannot see the shore." I replied and said, "Keep going and do what you are doing, because we can't see the shore either and we can't see you." When you have gone through the narrows, you are pointing straight at the Admiral's house and the Flag Officer Plymouth used to come out and take the salute, as we piped him going out and coming in. The last time we had gone out of Devonport we had received a signal from the Admiral because he had seen a face at a scuttle. Apparently you aren't supposed to have people looking out of the scuttles when you are either leaving or entering port. On this occasion the Admiral wasn't there because it was foggy, but we still piped him so that he could hear us, in case he sent a signal asking us why we had not piped him. The Commodore of the Barracks was on the shore and could only just see us as we passed the narrows. As we got into the harbour the fog suddenly lifted to about a mile visibility and thus we came alongside without any problems. As soon as the shore telephone lines had been connected I had a telephone call from the Admiral, who said, "I see you're in, Ted." "Yes, Sir." "Bit foggy?" "Yes Sir, you didn't see any faces at scuttles did you?" The Admiral was lost for words,' Anson recalled.

Ark Royal remained alongside for the rest of March, as members of the ship's company took their last leave before the hectic nine-month deployment which was in front of them. For the three fixed-wing squadrons it was time to mark their imminent demise, because when they next embarked in *Ark Royal* they would be leaving their home bases for the last time. On 29 March 849 Squadron made their presence felt over Morayshire by staging a farewell flypast of nine Gannets which was the largest number of Gannets airborne at the same time since the squadron moved from RAF Brawdy in 1970. For 892 Squadron they officially marked the end of their six years lodging at RAF Leuchars by marching past FONAC, Vice Admiral Cassidi on 31 March. Unofficially, a series of pranks marked their passing, when the White Ensign on the 892 hangar was complemented by the White Ensign flying briefly over the airbase, while in the local press the station's ceremonial goat was offered at stud. On the embarkation day, the station commander and his officers paraded behind a pipe band to present a giant haggis as the RAF's farewell gift to its naval guests. After embarkation in *Ark Royal* the squadron discovered that the haggis was in fact made from rotten meat and old socks!

The beginning of the end arrived when on the afternoon of 5 April 1978 *Ark Royal* slipped her moorings in Devonport, for the last time under her own power as the pride of the Royal Navy. To mark the occasion *Fearless* made the following signal, 'Farewell big sister, you will be sorely missed, very best wishes for your final deployment.' As *Ark Royal* made her way out to sea she passed the silent hulk of *Eagle* for the last time. By the time *Ark Royal* returned at the end of the year *Eagle* had been towed away to Cairnryan to be broken up for scrap. For the men on board *Ark Royal* her departure was not a day of sorrow, instead there was an air of anticipation of the months to come as she headed west towards Roosevelt Roads. Shortly after passing the Azores, *Ark Royal* received an SOS from the Liberian-registered 39,000 ton tanker *Tarseus III* which was on fire and had suffered a number of casualties. Two Sea Kings were launched with a medical team. By the time they had flown the

Ark Royal at sea during her final years. (FAA Museum)

180 miles to the tanker the fire had been extinguished, but there were three crewmen suffering from severe burns who were air-lifted back to *Ark Royal* for attention.

With the *Tarseus III* drama over, *Ark Royal* continued with her voyage west, arriving at Roosevelt Roads for a three-day visit on 17 April. The fixed-wing squadrons needed to disembark so that they could continue with their flying to get night qualified. However, 824 Squadron did not suffer the same constraints when deciding whether to disembark, as Fish explained: '824 Squadron did not have the routine of disembarking the Sea Kings in the same way as the fixed-wing squadrons. The decision on whether to disembark would depend upon how the long the ship would be in port and what the ship's requirements were. For example, during the ship's six-week visit to Mayport we disembarked to Naval Air Station Jacksonville, because work was going to be done to the flight deck and the hangars so we could neither maintain nor fly our helicopters from the ship. However, if we went to a port such as Roosevelt Roads, we would operate from the ship while it was alongside, practise some exercises and recover back on board the ship.'

While *Ark Royal* was alongside in Roosevelt Roads Major Hughes took a little outing, as he recalled: 'I arranged to take Cdr Layard for a Land Rover outing up the El Yunque mountain forest reserve. This is reputed to be the oldest jungle in the world. On our way up the mountain we stopped to cut bamboo to take back to the ship to decorate our cabins! While we were returning down the mountain, we were stopped by the Forest Rangers, who wanted to arrest us. Apparently it was against the law to cut down anything in the reserve. They settled for us to put down our cuttings in the jungle edge.'

Between 20 April and 8 May both *Ark Royal* and her squadrons worked up using the excellent facilities of the AFWR. At the end of April FOCAS visited *Ark Royal* for a nine-day visit which included Admiral's Divisions on

Flyco at flying stations. (Steve Riley)

30 April, when the roar of launching aircraft and the thud of aircraft landing on the flight deck gave way to columns of smartly turned out members of the ship's company in their best white uniforms.

Between 9 and 15 May *Ark Royal* anchored off Charlotte Amalie, which is the main town of St Thomas. For many of the ship's company the visit was all too short, with the banyans on Magens Bay beach among the highlights of the visit. However, it was soon back to work when the ship weighed anchor on the morning of 15 May to head for the Jacksonville area. While crossing the infamous Bermuda Triangle, King Neptune made his final visit to *Ark Royal* on 17 May to preside over his henchmen as they performed the ceremony of initiation into the Bermudan Triangle Crossing Society for selected members. Among those selected were Captain Anson and the Fleet Master-at-Arms. As the afternoon progressed a flight deck fair was held. There were a number of stalls, which helped raise £585 for charity, including 849 Squadron B Flight's contribution, which was to photograph people in the cockpit of a Gannet and sell them the photographs.

The following day *Ark Royal* arrived off the Florida coast in the Jacksonville sea areas for further flying exercises. While operating in this area 824 Squadron was able to fulfil another of their roles, as Fish explained: 'The Sea King sometimes operated in the helicopter delivery service (HDS) role. For example, if we were operating in the Mayport or Florida exercise areas about sixty miles offshore we would send Sea Kings ashore to collect mail, stores and people. The Sea Kings would not only collect for *Ark Royal* but also for the other ships in the task group. Once the Sea Kings had returned they would fly a round robin, transferring stores, mail and people between the ships. These operations were handled by *Ark Airways*, which had a PO handler whose sole

The Chinese tailors hard at work in the depths of the ship. (Steve Riley)

Helicopter vertrep: the two Wessex helicopters of the Ship's Flight conducting vertical replenishment during a RAS. (Lieutenant Commander Brazendale via the author)

role was to look after the movement of passengers and cargo. The equipment fit of the Sea King at this time was fairly light, so it did not have to be stripped out to perform this role. Another important role which the Sea Kings performed in conjunction with the Wessex from the Ship's Flight was helicopter vertrep (vertical replenishment). We would pick up underslung loads from the accompanying RFA and drop them on board *Ark Royal*. It was great fun and very competitive because you would try to catch up the other helicopter and pretend that you were being held up by the other helicopter. The Sea King would be used for the heavier loads because they could lift up to 6,000lb compared to the 4,000lb limit of the Wessex.'

On 23 and 24 May *Ark Royal* made a guest appearance in the US Navy Exercise Solid Shield, to strike the American carrier *John F Kennedy*, thus providing some intensive flying for *Ark Royal*'s squadrons. But not all of *Ark Royal*'s time at sea was hard work as Weatherall recounted: 'On the few days at sea without flying, we went partying on the flight deck. One of the activities we organized was horse-racing evenings. One of the lifts would be marked out as a racecourse in chalk and lowered slightly so that the spectators could see clearly what was going on. There would be broomstick horses' heads and various people, mainly young pilots, would volunteer to be jockeys. Various syndicates would club together to buy a horse, and if the horse won they would get winner's earnings as well as what they had backed on the horse. The profits would usually go towards a large party for the ship's company.' Other activities were organized for the ship's company on 25 May, as Anson remembered: 'We organized a kite-flying competition between the mess decks and the Wardroom. One of the entries was made using broom handles and thus it didn't fly very well. Nevertheless, events like this helped to maintain morale when we were at sea for long periods.'

On 30 May *Ark Royal* entered Fort Lauderdale for a busy two-week visit. Since *Ark Royal*'s first visit to Fort Lauderdale, the locals had taken the ship to their hearts so it was tinged with great sadness when *Ark Royal* left her 'second home' for the last time on the afternoon of 13 June. However, when she left, fifty-two of her ship's company were absent because they had been lucky enough to be selected for the five ship's boats which were travelling on the Inter-Coastal Inland Waterway to Mayport to rejoin *Ark Royal* when she docked there later in the month. Between 14 and 23 June *Ark Royal* operated in the Jacksonville sea areas. Once again the evaporators were having problems and water rationing was introduced again on several occasions. From the engineers' point of view the biggest achievement of the period was the full power trial of 18 May, when she reached a top speed of 29 knots. On 23 June *Ark Royal* entered Mayport wearing the flag of Rear Admiral Staveley for the last time as FOCAS. The ship was about to start a six-week AMP which provided most of the ship's company with an opportunity for leave, with many of them flying their families out to join them for a holiday. While the ship was alongside, the squadrons were disembarked ashore to continue with their training.

On 8 August *Ark Royal* departed Mayport to head north and conduct a few days of flying exercises, wind and evaporators permitting, before entering the world's largest Naval Base on 14 August to secure alongside the world's largest aircraft carrier *Nimitz*. While *Ark Royal* was berthed opposite *Nimitz*, Cdr Weatherall visited his opposite number in the American carrier, as he recalled: 'The American Cdr asked me how many men did we leave behind when we sailed? So I thought back for a moment and answered, "Well, on a bad day, three." "What!" replied the Cdr. So I asked him how many men did they leave behind. "Never fewer than 100," the Cdr remarked.'

When *Ark Royal* slipped her moorings on 21 August she was given a tremendous send-off by the Americans. Members of one American squadron expressed their feelings about *Ark Royal*'s imminent demise by displaying a

The forward lift is slightly lowered for an evening's horse racing. (Commander Wilcock via the author)

While *Ark Royal* was alongside in Norfolk, Virginia, 892 Squadron deployed to NAS Oceana. As can be seen, one of their aircraft has received attention from the US Navy squadron VF171. (Steve Riley)

banner saying, 'HSL-32 SAYS KEEP THE ARK AFLOAT THE RAIN MAY BE COMING'. Her departure was far from quiet, with both the ship's Royal Marine band and the band of the C-in-C US Atlantic Fleet playing as she made her way out to sea.

From Norfolk, *Ark Royal* sailed for Exercise Common Effort which was designed to practise the reinforcement of US Forces. It was a useful preparation for the major autumn NATO exercise Northern Wedding held between 4 and 19 September. Over two hundred warships from nine different nations assembled to participate in Exercise Northern Wedding, which was held in both the Norwegian and North Seas. As ever, the Russians sent along their own unofficial contingent of observers to get in the way and watch the proceedings. For a number of days *Ark Royal* was shadowed by a Kresta II cruiser and a modified Kashin destroyer. Describing his interception of a Russian Bear on 5 September, Riley said: 'My observer was Peter Budd and he picked up a contact on the radar which he didn't like the look of. It was big, it was low and it was moving too fast to be a surface contact. We called it in to the fighter director and we were told to haul off, as it was friendly, exercise traffic; one of us, allegedly. We were a good few hundred miles north of Lossiemouth and we had just been overflown by an Interceptor Alert Force package of Bear, Victor and RAF Phantoms, way up above us in contrails, so we knew that there was Soviet activity nearby. Pointing at our contact we inevitably drew closer and after a few minutes we were close enough to get a "visual" on the Bear, by now about fifteen miles away. Northern Wedding, like most exercises of its type, was being conducted using minimal communications. This was intended to confound the intelligence-gathering task of the Warsaw Pact observers,

Watching you watching us! A Phantom escorts
a Russian Bear. (Captain Rotheram
via the author)

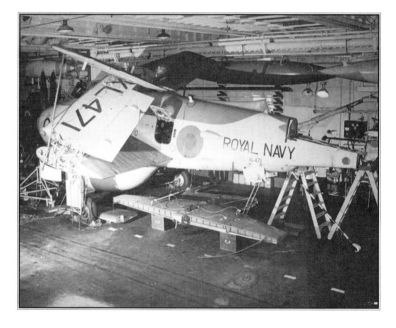

A Gannet AEW3 undergoing extensive
maintenance on *Ark Royal*'s hangar deck.
(Commander Cudmore via the author)

while improving the skills of the NATO participants. The effectiveness of these endeavours soon became clear to us. After Peter had photographed the Bear to his satisfaction, we waved goodbye and accelerated away towards the fleet. Letting down through the cloud we confidently expected to see *Ark Royal* turning into wind for the next launch. When we broke through all we could see were the escorts, and after a few minutes rushing from one horizon to the other we still had not located the Ark. We climbed up to the cloud-tops and started working rather more methodically and while doing so we reintercepted our Bear. As he flew across our nose he started a gentle turn away leaving us in trail behind him, almost back in formation again. As we closed on his wing he started a descent towards the ocean and after a few minutes he flew over *Ark Royal* at low altitude and waggled us off with his wing.'

On 14 September the last Gannet AEW3 to be overhauled by Westland came to a premature end, as Rotheram recalled: 'I was up in flyco when Lt Slade was making a night to dawn landing. He was a bit off-centre and his wing-tip clipped the Jumbo mobile crane and the canopy of a Buccaneer.' While the damage looked initially minor the ship's AEO, Cdr M. Cudmore was ordered to write off the aircraft and strip any reusable equipment from the airframe before disposing of it. It had been decided that in light of the fact that the Gannets were due to be disposed of at the end of the year, it wasn't worth spending the money on flying out the relevant parts to repair XL494.

As ever, the weather dictated the scope of flying which could be achieved in the exercise. On the 16th and 17th the ship encountered the remnants of Hurricane Flossie. Flying was cancelled during this encounter as the hatches were battened down and only the few aircraft which couldn't be accommodated on the hangar deck were left on the flight deck, as Cudmore explained: 'The safest place for the aircraft on deck during a rough storm would be in the middle of the deck with extra storm lashings to hold the aircraft in place.'

The ship itself sustained damage, as Weatherall recalled: 'I was having a bath, when the ship came down on the after sponson and the whole ship shook. It was a most extraordinary feeling. All of my lights shattered, so I was not sure how much glass there was in my bath, or on the deck. I thought I would be cut to ribbons but I managed to get out without any problems. As soon as I had dressed, I quickly went to see what other damage had been done. We had suffered the most appalling damage. The Queen Mother's steps had been lost, as had the wooden tabernacle for the ship's bell and all the covers for the bollards, not to mention all the other damage that had been incurred around the ship, such as damaged guard rails and ship's boats. The bell itself managed to survive unscathed because it was clamped in position in a special stowage on the quarterdeck.' Explaining why the *Ark Royal* had incurred so much damage, Anson said: 'Because we were so long, the swell was of such a length that when we went into it, the bow pitched up, causing the stern to sit down, and water came flooding in through the openings on the quarterdeck, thus creating the damage to items on the quarterdeck.'

The exercise finished on 19 September, giving the ship's company most of the day to prepare the ship for HM Queen Elizabeth the Queen Mother's last visit to 'her' ship the following day. The original programme which had been put together for the Queen Mother had to be changed because it was regarded as tame, and in fact she wanted to see as much of the ship as possible. Before leaving she went to the upper hangar to address 1,000 members of the ship's company. In her speech she made the following observation, 'It might seem strange to some people that a man-made floating construction of steel and weaponry should evoke the intensity of feeling and indeed emotion which I am sure you are experiencing today. So many memories, so much achieved, difficulties overcome, friendship, danger, relaxation, high comedy and occasional tragedy but above all the sense of belonging to a community.'

Riley remembered: 'I was sitting in my Phantom close to the after lift. The lift had been lowered so that the Queen Mother could come up to the flight deck in the ship's VIP Land Rover. I was looking down the lift well at the time and I wasn't prepared for seeing the Queen Mother. While I was looking down she suddenly came into view and looked up from the darkness of the hangar straight at my aircraft. I instinctively waved at the Queen Mother and she responded with a wave back. As soon as I had waved at her I thought to myself, now should I have done that?' The Queen Mother left in the afternoon and soon it was time to embark the next group of visitors and stores before setting sail for her next port of call, as *Ark Royal* started her final stage of the deployment, which was to be a visit to Gibraltar followed by a tour of the Mediterranean.

Ark Royal moored up for the first time in five weeks when she entered Gibraltar on 25 September to begin a week's visit. Two days later members of 849 Squadron B Flight gathered on deck to bid farewell to the carcass of XL494. The officers wore No. 5 uniform with wing collars specially for the occasion, as the Gannet was

Captain Anson bids farewell to the Queen Mother at the end of her last visit to 'her' ship on 20 September 1978. (Captain Rotheram via the author)

lowered over the side onto the waiting lighter to the sound of the Last Post from the Royal Marine bugler. The airframe was to be used by the RAF at Gibraltar to practise fire exercises. When *Ark Royal* slipped her moorings on 2 October she flew her 450ft paying off pennant for the first time. Because the pennant was so long an orange met balloon was attached to make sure it flew, rather than drooped along the flight deck.

Once in the Mediterranean, *Ark Royal* entered Exercise Display Determination on 4 October. The exercise had started in September and included the American carriers *Forrestal* and *John F Kennedy*. During the exercise C-in-C Fleet, Admiral Sir Henry Leach GCB paid a final two-day visit to the ship which had served him so well as his flagship during the previous year's Fleet Review. Leach said about the background to his last visit to *Ark Royal*: 'I did not want to join the crowd of family and well-wishers standing on the jetty in Devonport watching with tears trickling down their cheeks as this fine ship berthed for the last time. Instead, I planned to go out to the Mediterranean and spend a couple of days in the ship while she was still fully operational; I also wanted to fly a sortie with each of the embarked squadrons. My Flag Lieutenant was given dates and told to set it up. In due course a draft programme for me was produced; it contained little flying (no fixed-wing) and was pedestrian in the extreme: not what I wanted at all. Flags was summoned and admitted the ship seemed fairly reluctant to catapult me off in a Phantom (my particular request) because I had not been put through the wet parachute drill at Yeovilton. Irritated, I gave instructions to fix a date for me to do the drill at Yeovilton and get back to the ship to re-cast the programme completely and maximize flying time including a Phantom sortie.

'The day for Yeovilton came. I am one of the world's worst swimmers and was not much looking forward to it but, if that was a pre-requisite to flying a Phantom from the deck, so be it. The drill consists of standing in full flying clothing on the high diving board facing away from the big pool. To your parachute harness is secured a heaving line held by a PTI at the other end of the pool. After you have signalled that you are ready, you take a deep breath and the PTI pulls you over backwards into the water. On hitting the water you spread your arms and legs wide, plane up to the surface, remove the split pins from your parachute harness and then push up and pull down on the release clips of the harness. Up to that point you are being dragged along by the line but you are then clear to swim to the side of the pool and get out. "Keep your arms and legs well spread and your head back and you won't have a problem, Sir," they said, "you'll just plane along on the surface!" Trying to hide my considerable trepidation I mounted the high board and signalled ready. It all happened exactly as predicted – a piece of cake – and feeling frightfully pleased with myself I paddled to the side of the pool. "Well done, Sir," they sycophanted, "told you it was no problem. Now you have to do it again but this time you've lost an arm from banging out of the aircraft; which arm have you lost, Sir?" Being right-handed I selected left, and the helpful PTI whispered in my ear "I'll only give you a very gentle pull, Sir!" Again I mounted the high board. It had all been so quick and simple that I didn't bother about too deep a breath. And of course it was a point of honour not to cheat. Back down I went. Arms and legs out, head back, but I did not plane to the surface. That damned PTI's gentle pull was set fair to drown me. I stayed down lungs bursting and now wrestling with both hands to release the harness. It appeared to be stuck and I swallowed a great deal of water. It is true that in such moments you relive your life in kaleidoscope – I did. Then they put a diver in to get me out, just before I passed out, and I lay like a stranded fish by the side of the pool. But I got a clearance chit and *Ark Royal* could now be told to get on with it.

'I flew in an HS125 to Greece and, on 10 October, helicoptered out from Arraxos to *Ark Royal* in a Sea King of 824 Squadron. Although he bravely let me fly and land it, the captain of the aircraft was Dick Ormshaw who had only just shipped a stripe from being a Midshipman – an interesting relationship for a full Admiral because he was the professional in charge and I was the amateur subordinate. It is a unique relationship and very good for de-pomping senior officers.

'The next forenoon after a medical and briefing, including ejection seat drill, I climbed into the back seat of a Phantom. Checks completed, we engaged the catapult and wound up to full power for launch. But at the last second the launch was aborted due to a small oil leak and we unmanned and took off our gear. For me it was a rare experience to undergo all the excitement and tension before the launch, followed a second later by all the flatness and frustration of abortion. No doubt the professionals get hardened to it, but never completely I think. For the remainder of my time I visited night and day most parts of the ship and flew several sorties with helicopters of 824 Squadron and the SAR Flight, finally disembarking to Sigonilla on 12 October.'

Leach looked back at *Ark Royal* as a flagship: '*Ark Royal* was frequently somebody's flagship – usually FOCAS's and, rarely, C-in-C's. She was thus fully familiar with the finer points of being a flagship and the ship's company were prompt to a man, and went out of their way to be friendly, helpful and efficient. In *Ark Royal* people concentrated on the things that mattered, starting with flying – *raison d'être*. Externally as often as not she was quite weather-worn; internally she was spotless. Above all she maintained, commission after commission, a splendid rapport and spirit. She was a happy ship and she was efficient. You only needed a few hours on board and you somehow felt this – as you do in a good ship.'

Ark Royal's part in Exercise Display Determination drew to a close on 11 October. For the next few days the squadrons continued with a series of private flying exercises before the ship headed for the Straits of Messina and Naples for a five-day visit. Before the ship sailed on 21 October, she was joined by Admiral of the Fleet Sir Michael Pollock GCB, MVO, DSC, who of course had commanded the ship for the second half of her fourth commission. He had embarked to take passage to Athens, as he recalled: 'It was quite extraordinary. There was this great ship going out of service at the end of this trip and they were still flying as if there was no tomorrow. They were still cramming in every hour they could get for pilot training.'

A Sea King during the final commission. (FAA Museum)

Cudmore described the preparations prior to the start of *Ark Royal*'s five-day visit to Athens: 'On each side of the tail of all fourteen Buccaneers of 809 Squadron was painted an enormous squadron crest. Regrettably this was also the sign of the previous national coup by the four Colonels, so in the interests of diplomacy these had to be painted out: actually we covered the tails in paper and sprayed them grey. The CO's cabin door by the quarterdeck had to be sprayed before the cocktail party for the same reason.' *Ark Royal* dropped anchor in Phaleron Bay on 27 October at the start of her visit.

From Athens *Ark Royal* sailed for the island of Malta, arriving there on 6 November to begin a ten-day visit, as Anson recalled: 'We had no sooner got into Malta and secured to two buoys in Kalkara Creek than the British Government decided to choose that moment to complain to the European Commission that Malta had exceeded

A Wessex HAS1 of the Ship's Flight. (Steve Riley)

The launching of a Buccaneer. (Steve Riley)

its quota of sweaters. A general strike was called immediately and thus there were no tugs available. Rear Admiral Cecil, who was the port Admiral at Malta, asked if I would take *Ark Royal* out of Malta without any tugs to provide assistance. I said no, because as soon as the Maltese know I am going to do that, if they are on general strike and being awkward, they will moor a ship stern-on at Bighi Bay and I won't be able to get past without the assistance of a tug. Later on I went with the Admiral to see the Maltese Prime Minister Mr Mintoff and we talked about everything except tugs. We were sailing the next day and needed four tugs, but when the time came to set sail six tugs arrived. The British High Commission could not have organized this because they were hardly on speaking terms with the Maltese. As we went out of Grand Harbour, the Admiral's picket boat accompanied us and, next to the Admiral, was this gentleman who bore an incredible likeness to Mr Mintoff!'

Over 10,000 Maltese and British people turned out to watch from every available vantage point as *Ark Royal* slipped out of Grand Harbour for the last time. *Ark Royal*'s final voyage from Malta saw the beginning of a twenty-four hour visit by the First Sea Lord, Admiral Sir Terence Lewin GCB, MVO, DSC. During this visit he told Captain Anson that he wanted him to become the next Flag Officer Naval Air Command in June 1979 and that he would be made a Rear Admiral. The Maltese departure also saw the start of the five-day visit of the famous wildlife painter David Shepherd who had been commissioned by the Fleet Air Arm Museum at Yeovilton to paint the *Ark Royal*. The finished painting now hangs on public display in the museum. Shepherd described the challenge posed by this commission: 'One of my ambitions had, for years, been to go onto a great aircraft carrier at sea, and we only had one left anyway, I thought that this was at long last my chance – my last chance – to play with the *Ark Royal*. The principal challenge when painting any aircraft carrier for the Royal Navy or aircraft for the Royal Air Force is to meet their demands for accuracy; the aircraft or the ship has to be the right shape. The Navy are perhaps the most demanding of the three services, and I had to have the painting of the *Ark Royal* scrutinized by the Captain before it went to print. It was inevitable that I had made a few mistakes. For example, I had painted the jet-pipe intake covers on the Buccaneers on the after end of the flight deck as little touches of red, but as I was told that their engines would be running I had to paint these out. There was also another problem. I suspect that, because of her age the *Ark* had some difficulty in reaching maximum speed; but

David Shepherd in action in the Ship's Flight Wessex making sketches for his painting 'The Ark, turning into wind' for the FAA Museum. (David Shepherd, via the author)

I had to see what a bow wave looked like when the prow of a great fleet aircraft carrier is cutting through the sea. This was impossible with the *Ark*, so, after my return home, I was given HMS *Bulwark* to play with.' From his trip in *Bulwark* David Shepherd used photographs and sketches of her bow wave to create the right effect for his *Ark Royal* painting.

Despite their continued interest in *Ark Royal* throughout her time in service, the Russians declined David Shepherd's invitation to join him, as he explained: 'When the arrangements were being made for my visit to the *Ark Royal* I asked if we could have the Russian spy ship in attendance. The world knows that wherever the *Ark Royal* used to go, a Russian trawler, ostensibly fishing but in fact bristling with antennae and aerials of every possible description, was always hanging around in case it could glean any military secrets. With typical British aplomb and diplomacy, an official signal was sent from Yeovilton to the Captain of *Ark Royal* stating, "Artist requests Russian guests to be in attendance." In fact, the Russians didn't turn up. I can only assume that at this stage in her long career, the Russians knew everything about the *Ark*'s technology anyway.'

Shepherd said of his impressions of the activity on the flight deck: 'To someone like me, the flight deck of an operational aircraft carrier at sea was so full of excitement that I could hardly think straight. Gannet aircraft seemed to be coming from around every corner, and every few seconds it seemed a Buccaneer or a Phantom was either being catapulted off the deck or was storming in and landing on the arrester wires. Everywhere aircraft seemed to be moving around, folding and unfolding their wings, and coming up from the inner depths of the ship on the lifts.' During his time in *Ark Royal* most of each day was spent in the Ship's Flight Wessex but

A Gannet AEW3 taxies up to the bow catapult. (Steve Riley)

he did not have the best of starts to each day, as he recalled: 'I enjoyed the most wonderful hospitality on the *Ark Royal* but the only thing that I didn't like was the early morning tea. I have never served in the Navy but I suppose if you do, over a lifetime you get used to it. I can drink almost any type of tea in any place, but the stuff that was poured out of a bucket into a tin mug at 5 o'clock in the morning was indescribable.'

He continued: 'If I have an inflated ego, I believe that it was this experience on the *Ark Royal* that is responsible. I have never worn a uniform in my life, so it was all the more of a thrill, as a mere civilian, to ask the Captain of the 50,000 ton carrier to steer in a different direction, and then watch while he did it. I had noticed, for instance, that the shadow cast by the overhang of the flight deck on the hull was creating some fascinating shapes, and it occurred to me that if the carrier swung a few degrees to starboard, this might inspire some further ideas for the painting. In radio contact with the Captain via the helicopter pilot, I asked therefore if he could turn just for me, and minutes later the great ship started to swing round. I got carried away with this and, by the end of five days, when the Captain and I were on Christian name terms, I was well and truly playing with the *Ark Royal*. On being flown off in the helicopter at the end of my stay as his guest, to fly home from Italy, I apologized for all of the trouble I had caused. "Don't worry, David, it gave the Navigator something to do, going home in a zigzag instead of a straight line!" The Navy are super people.'

During the two days after *Ark Royal*'s departure from Malta the fixed-wing squadrons completed their last sorties. The last fixed-wing landing on *Ark Royal* took place on 18 November when Gannet 044 with the CO of 849 Squadron B Flight, Lt Cdr Martin Rotheram, Lt Hugh Slade and Lt Cass landed. A Buccaneer of 809 Squadron had vied for the distinction but dwindling fuel forced him to land and allow the Gannet to take the honour. Once the Gannet had come to a stop, a crash on deck exercise was held and the aircrew were taken down to the sickbay and that was the end of fixed-wing flying in the RN. No great ceremonies were held because the objective was to play the whole thing down and let it pass quietly into history.

Later in the day, in keeping with true *Ark Royal* end-of-commission antics, it was decided to follow the example of *Eagle*, during her final voyage to Portsmouth to pay off, by firing the Wardroom piano off the catapult. 'The piano had been obtained from RAF Honnington when we went to sea at the start of the last stage

A Gannet AEW3 of 849 Squadron B Flight coming in to land. (Captain Rotheram via the author)

of the commission. It wouldn't fit down into the Wardroom through the hatches, so it had to be taken to bits to get it down to the Wardroom. It was crudely reassembled so it was never going to be a great piano. Having got the piano down to the Wardroom, we were left with the decision of what to do with it at the end of the commission because it wasn't going to survive being taken apart for a second time, so it was decided to launch it,' said Morton. While the launch was a source of amusement to those who participated in it, it was a cause of anger to one member of the public, as Anson recalled: 'I had a letter from a lady saying how unfeeling and awful it was that we should do such a thing, when she had been scrimping and saving to buy her daughter a piano to learn on.'

Two days later *Ark Royal* entered Palma for her final visit to a foreign port. Once again Major Hughes organized one of his outings, as he recalled: 'I arranged to take the Commanders for an outing in the Land Rover. All of the Commanders came except Cdr O'Donnell. Having stopped for lunch we continued through some high mountains. On one mountain a "golf ball" radar was mounted. It was suggested that we drive up there to see the view. We came to a fork in the road and just past it was a barrier across the road with a Spanish Air Force sentry. We explained by pointing to the mountain where we wanted to go. He lifted the barrier and I started to move. Immediately I heard the sound of a rifle bolt. I looked round to see the sentry aiming at me. We were taken back to a barracks nearby and kept for an hour or so. The Commanders were beside themselves as the whole hierarchy of *Ark Royal* was arrested! Eventually they let us go. Further on we met the Gunnery Officer in one of the ship's Land Rovers, so we stopped for a chat. He asked where was a good place to go so I explained that the view from the mountain top with the golf ball was marvellous. I never did discover how he got on.'

While David Shepherd had been busy recording the last days of *Ark Royal* as an active aircraft carrier, the newly promoted Captain Guy O'Donnell was planning the final days of *Ark Royal* during the voyage back to Devonport from Palma. 'I had been tasked with overseeing the rundown and decommissioning of the ship – an enormous task that required a very professional team of extremely competent officers to focus their skills on a complex and ever-varying programme. Not only did we not have the time after we returned to the UK to destore and de-ammunition, we also would not have the manpower, as the drafting Commodore at HMS *Centurion* could hardly wait to get his hands on this enormous pool of manpower that he saw as surplus, the moment the ship arrived in the UK in December. We overcame much of this by de-ammunitioning at sea under way – a hazardous and time-consuming operation which the weapons department carried out with enormous skill, ably abetted by the teams aboard RFA *Regent* which was tasked with taking back all our munitions. We also managed to offload a fair amount of general stores, and allowed our provisions and fuel to run down to safe minimums. When the squadrons were disembarked for the final time only skeleton crews were left behind to offload the final bits and pieces after our return.'

For the fixed-wing squadrons, their eight-year association with *Ark Royal* came to an end on the ship's final disembarkation day on 27 November 1978. The weather conditions were far from favourable as the ship battled against the rough seas whipped up by the mistral. Throughout the day the aircraft were launched to head for home, although the departure of a few aircraft was delayed by last-minute faults. The honour for the last catapult launch in the Royal Navy appropriately went to a joint RN/RAF crew, comprising Flt Lt M. Macleod and Lt D. McCallum in Phantom 012. They were launched at 3.11 p.m. down the waist catapult. The Gannets were to head north for RAF Lossiemouth, from where the aircraft would be flown to their final resting places, while both the Phantoms and Buccaneers were flown to RAF St Athan, as Morton recalled: 'I thought the way it all ended was very sad, because we flew the Buccaneers to RAF St Athan, took off all our flying gear, handed the aircraft over to the RAF, and then got into another aircraft bound for RAF Honnington to pick up our things and disperse to our new jobs.' For the RAF aircrews the end of the deployment meant a return to RAF flying. Looking back upon his naval interlude, Riley remarked: 'You couldn't follow that type of flying. Anything else just seemed like a disappointment in comparison.'

With the squadrons finally gone, the process of back RAS got under way in earnest. Meanwhile, preparations were under way by some members of the ship's company to ensure that naval charities cashed in on the public interest in *Ark Royal* which had been generated over the previous few years. Ashore, a number of companies had increased production of typical souvenirs such as T-shirts and mugs, etc. One businessman from the Midlands had invested £16,000 in wall plaques which also provided some income for naval charities. On board, members of the ship's company were ordered to search the ship for redundant copper, brass and easily removable woodwork which was to be remodelled into traditional naval rum jugs and other souvenirs which were to be sold to raise funds for the naval charities.

As *Ark Royal* approached the UK coast, and with only three days left to go at sea, the Government announced that the name *Ark Royal* would not fade from the ranks of the Royal Navy. The third ship of the Invincible class was originally to have been given the name *Indomitable*. However, due to the public outcry over the demise of *Ark Royal IV* it was decided to make the change and keep the name alive.

So the end came on the morning of 4 December as the ship's company manned the ship's side for Procedure Alpha for the very last time. As she slipped past Plymouth breakwater her 450ft paying off pennant was flying

Ark Royal returns home for the very last time early on the morning of 4 December 1978. (FAA Museum)

from her after lattice mast, gently fluttering in the breeze. As she made her way up the notorious passage into Devonport, thousands turned out to welcome her home despite the early hour. Describing the passage into Devonport, Anson recalled: 'It was the first time that we were exactly on track all the way through, with every fix bang on. It was very early in the morning and the sun was only just rising, so the initial part of the approach was made when it was quite dark.' Once *Ark Royal* was securely alongside Captain Anson ordered the engines to ring off at 8.50 a.m., thus bringing to an end his own career as a Captain as well as finishing *Ark Royal*'s seagoing days.

After the *Ark Royal* had arrived in Devonport there was a Wardroom ball for present and former officers of the ship, which was arranged by a team headed by Cdr Cudmore. The organization for the event started months beforehand, and even at a late stage the unexpected occurred, as Cudmore explained: 'To stop ladies' long dresses getting dirty, we painted the hangar deck. A local MP got to hear about this and we heard that there was the possibility of a parliamentary question being asked on the cost of the paint. I went to see Captain Anson and asked him how we should handle this. He replied, "The cost was £100 but it was written-off paint." We never heard anything else about it.'

'We paid for the ball out of the ship's funds and we kept the receipts because, needless to say, an MP asked who was paying for all of this and we were able to turn round and say, "We are and here are the receipts", which was a very satisfying moment! The ratings had been offered the opportunity to hold their dance on board, but they wanted their event ashore which surprised me,' remarked Weatherall. Prior to the start of the ball Captain Anson hosted a dinner for the former Captains of *Ark Royal* in the Admiral's cabin, while Cdr Weatherall held a dinner for the former Commanders of *Ark Royal* in his cabin.

Lt Cdr Fish had previously served with 826 Squadron during the final year of *Eagle*'s service. He recalled the differences between the demise of the two ships: 'The demise of *Ark Royal* was more poignant because she was the last of the fixed-wing carriers. For when *Eagle* paid off the *Ark Royal* was still in commission and therefore there was still a limited period of fixed-wing flying left for the Royal Navy. While the paying off of *Ark Royal* meant a major change of life for many of the naval aviators on board, it was very much business as usual for the aircrews of 824 which was the only squadron to keep its aircraft in naval service. We disembarked for Culdrose in Mount's Bay and then watched the arrival of *Ark Royal* in Devonport on the television the following morning.'

Lt C. Waite (now Captain C. Waite) was a pilot with 849 Squadron B Flight. He was also a former member of 826 Squadron embarked in *Eagle* when she was paid off and recalled: 'The main difference between the demise of the ships was the expectation of a future for carrier aviation after *Ark Royal* had gone. *Eagle* was in a better material state when she paid off, particularly between decks, than *Ark Royal*. We thought we were scrapping the wrong carrier but there was a determination to keep the ship smart and fully operational right up to the end. When *Ark Royal* paid off she was not at anything like the same level of material state. It was very hard work for the marine engineers to keep that ship running. The job they did was brilliant, they worked their hearts out to keep her going. However, the same principle applied to keep the ship fully operational right up to the end. In a way it was slightly easier to see the point of *Ark Royal*'s paying off because she would have to have completed another extensive refit to have kept her going. The other difference between the ending of both ships was that when *Ark Royal* paid off we knew that there was going to be a limited fixed-wing capability in the form of the Sea Harrier embarked in the Invincible class whereas, when *Eagle* went, it looked as though fixed-wing flying in the RN would end with *Ark Royal* whose future looked extremely uncertain.'

Chapter Eleven

A STAY OF EXECUTION?

DESTORING, POSSIBLE PRESERVATION AND

SCRAPPING, DECEMBER 1978–1984

Ark Royal's days under the White Ensign were coming to an end. Her operational service was over and all that remained was to complete the task of destoring and removing any equipment which could be reused on other ships. The man appointed to oversee this sad assignment was Captain Guy O'Donnell. He recalled the day he took command of *Ark Royal* on 15 December 1978, and some of the reactions to his appointment: 'I donned my Captain's uniform and formally relieved Captain Anson as Commanding Officer. This was a unique situation, for while the ship was technically non-operational she was still fully in commission (in fact I received command pay and entertainment allowances) and here I was – a Pusser – commanding the last fixed-wing fleet carrier. There had been some concern among the diehard traditionalists, that a seaman officer should have been given the task, but when I called on the First Sea Lord, Admiral Sir Terence Lewin, he advised me that he had sanctioned my appointment for the job and felt I was ideally suited to the task ahead. By the time I got to command *Ark Royal* all the glitter and glory was over. All the VIPs who wanted to be seen supporting Britain's last great fixed-wing carrier had been and gone, and to be honest we were thankful to be left alone to get on with the job in hand. The attitude of the bona fide seaman Commanding Officers to my appointment was interesting. I was invited to attend FOCAS Carrier Captains' meeting in *Hermes* in Portsmouth in January 1979 – as was my right, as I was commanding a carrier in commission. FOCAS very kindly sent his personal staff car to bring me to the ship but, on arrival at the ship, the *Hermes* did not accord me the courtesy of piping me on board – because her Captain felt that I was not a seaman officer and thus I was not entitled. The "white mafia" in me came to the fore, and I murmured in the ear of the Admiral's secretary at luncheon, who murmured with the Captain and Commander of *Hermes*, and when I departed I received the full honours to which I was entitled. I am not bitter in any way, quite the reverse, I am just amused and slightly saddened that these fellow officers of mine should feel so threatened by a simple Pusser like me.'

Before Christmas, with her engines now silent forever, she was dragged into No. 5 basin in Devonport Dockyard, with only inches to spare at the entrance to the basin, ready for the process of being stripped of any reusable equipment.

O'Donnell continued: 'To speed up the enormous task of destoring the millions of items held in the ship, we enlisted the help of the Sappers who built a huge temporary ramp from the dock up to the flight deck level so we could drive lorries straight on board, lower them on the lifts into the hangars, load them up and then drive them out again. The whole operation went incredibly smoothly, with only one incident when a loaded fork-lift truck ran amok down the ramp and ploughed into a dockyard Portakabin at the bottom. Several dockyard civilians were surprised when the end wall of their office suddenly descended upon them, but no one was hurt, and thereafter we placed a sturdy barrier at the foot of the ramp in case we had more incidents.'

As he explained, keeping up the morale of the ship's company was just as important in these final days as it had been when she was in her prime: 'As the numbers of the ship's company dwindled, and more and more of the compartments were sealed, it became vitally important that the morale of the remaining ship's company be maintained as well as possible. The First Lieutenant was tireless in this respect and was constantly coming up with events to test the imagination and stamina of the crew. We even had a silly sports day at which I failed dismally when it came to "tossing the welly", only succeeding in gaining considerable altitude with the recalcitrant boot rather than distance.'

While the destoring was under way the Sappers decided to indulge in a little advertising. O'Donnell recalled: 'We used to have a huge sign we displayed on *Ark Royal* which said Fly Navy and we put this up whenever the ship was open to visitors and other occasions. When we were finally closing down we put the sign on the side of the ramp which could be clearly seen from the Wardroom windows of HMS *Drake*. I was phoned by the Commodore Drake one day, who was having a sense of humour failure because the Sappers had removed our sign and put in place another which said Sail Army. We on board *Ark Royal* thought this was a huge joke and left it there as long as we could before the Commodore got too apoplectic!'

Ark Royal was decommissioned on 14 February 1979 when her White Ensign was lowered for the last time, twenty-four years to the day since her first ship's company moved on board while she was still alongside at

Captain O'Donnell returns the *Ark Royal*'s engineering plate to Tony Smith, Chairman of Cammell Laird. The quarterdeck tread plate was also presented and is in the foreground. (Captain O'Donnell via the author)

Cammell Laird's yard. How times had changed! In 1955 her ship's company was looking forward to taking her to sea at the start of an exciting commission while twenty-four years later the remnants of her ship's company were busy preparing her for one last voyage, as yet destination unknown (officially anyway!). As the job of destoring continued it was time to ensure that some parts of the ship found new homes. The ship's bell went on public display at the Fleet Air Arm Museum at Yeovilton to await the completion of *Ark Royal V*. At the time of writing the ship's bell has once more returned to the museum where it is on public display, following the paying off of *Ark Royal V* into reserve while she awaits her extensive refit at Rosyth. The museum also has a second bell from *Ark Royal* on display which was the bell issued by the Admiralty specifically for *Ark Royal IV*, whereas the bell normally referred to as the ship's bell will pass from *Ark Royal* to *Ark Royal*. On 4 May 1979 Captain O'Donnell presented Cammell Laird's Chairman with *Ark Royal*'s engineering number plate and one of her deck tread-plates at a ceremony held in Birkenhead which was attended by one hundred and fifty men who had helped build her.

As *Ark Royal* was emptied of all the bits which could be reused by the Navy, various groups continued to try and produce credible proposals for her preservation. Captain O'Donnell appeared on TV and radio several times to defend the board's decision to scrap her, which he believed was right at that time. 'The last thing I felt that should happen was to have a huge semi-rusting hulk somewhere, which would quickly fall out of fashion as the public memory is very short,' O'Donnell remarked.

On 31 May 1979 the job was finished. All of the equipment and stores that were going to be removed had gone. It was now time for Captain O'Donnell to hand over the keys to Cdr G.C. Chapman of the Fleet Maintenance Base at Devonport Dockyard. O'Donnell said about the moment he left *Ark Royal* for the last time: 'The final day came when the last padlock was secured and the remaining few officers posed on the gangway for a photograph before leaving for ever. We held a last supper, courtesy of a well-known Devonport whisky distributor and it was all over – well not quite as *Ark Royal* sat around for a while before her final voyage to Cairnryan.'

Although Captain O'Donnell's official duties came to an end he still had one last job to do which would ensure that more than just the ship's bell would make the transition from *Ark Royal* IV to her successor. When he moved on to his next posting Captain O'Donnell took with him the Captain's table as he recalled: 'I knew that if it got into dockyard hands it would disappear, so I took it upon myself to take it to Portsmouth to my new residence in the dockyard, and subsequently to the Naval College in 1981. As I was finishing my tenure there the new *Ark Royal* was almost ready to go – I had attended her launch – and I arranged for the table to return to its proper place in the new ship. It was gratifying to lunch on board the new *Ark Royal* some years later as the guest of Captain Jim Weatherall and sit at the same table where I had previously wined and dined my own guests, albeit for a few months.'

The handing over of *Ark Royal* to the Fleet Maintenance Unit meant a return to his old ship for CPO Brian Ahern, who had previously served in *Ark Royal* between 1969 and 1972 as a stoker PO: 'I was coming up to the end of my time in the RN when I was granted an extension of service for another five years. I was drafted to the Fleet Maintenance Unit. When I got there they asked how would I like to go to *Ark Royal*. I thought it was a joke because I never thought I would end up back on board *Ark Royal* and be responsible for her during her final days. When Captain O'Donnell and his men walked off, we walked on.'

The week after Captain O'Donnell left for the last time, *Ark Royal* was moved from No. 5 basin in the dockyard to spend her final days on the same moorings previously used by *Eagle* while she awaited her final voyage to be scrapped at Cairnryan in Scotland. The move took two hours to complete, at the end of which she became what the RN terms a 'dead ship'. For fifteen months the deserted silent *Ark Royal* deteriorated and even grass began to grow on the flight deck which had become reddened with rust. Like the *Eagle* before her, *Ark Royal* provided a new landmark for the boats operating day trips around Devonport. Describing his job looking after *Ark Royal* during her final days Ahern recalled: 'I had to check *Ark Royal* every day. Six of us went out in a boat to *Ark Royal* comprising a Chief Stoker (me), an Artificer, two Stokers and two Seamen. We started at the bow from 1 deck and went right the way through the ship. The ship was completely dead at that stage so if we needed power on board we had to take out a power barge.'

One of the proposals for *Ark Royal*'s preservation was announced on 14 March 1980 by the *Ark Royal* Preservation Trust. The Trust was headed by Vice Admiral Sir Richard Smeeton who had flown his flag in *Ark Royal* as Flag Officer Aircraft Carriers during the third and fourth commissions. Their plan was to moor *Ark Royal* at Greenwich as a museum and a centre of education and nautical research. To get *Ark Royal* to Greenwich would have involved towing her stern first through the Thames Barrier. While some were proposing *Ark Royal*'s preservation, the process of obtaining bids from scrapyards continued which resulted in some of the scrap merchants visiting *Ark Royal* for themselves, as Ahern recalled: 'Everyone who was intending to make a serious bid was entitled to come out and look round the ship. We had to search them before we took them out to *Ark Royal* to make sure that they didn't have any magnets so that they could check which metals were ferrous and which were non-ferrous.'

On 29 March 1980 the speculation about the *Ark Royal*'s future was brought to an end by the Ministry of Defence's announcement that *Ark Royal* was to be sold for scrap. The announcement came as a bitter blow to those who had been trying to secure *Ark Royal*'s future. Over the following months these groups continued to try and reverse the MOD's decision without success. When the decision was announced the First Sea Lord was Admiral Sir Henry Leach GCB. Leach remarked: 'The fate of *Ark Royal* was a straightforward Navy Department matter and without difficulty. It was decided that the various bids were all equally inappropriate, and should therefore be rejected, and the old lady given the ship's equivalent of a decent human burial: scrap.'

The day finally arrived, on 22 September 1980, for *Ark Royal* to leave her home port of Plymouth for the very last time. The final decision on whether to go or not was made just under two hours before she slipped her

Ark Royal is eased out of her home port for the last time. To give the old ship some dignity CPO Ahern set off some smoke charges in the funnel so that she did not look completely lifeless. (Mike Lennon)

In with the new and out with the old: a Sea Harrier from 800 Squadron to be based on board *Invincible* flies over the silent
Ark Royal as she is towed to Scotland. (FAA Museum)

moorings at 4.11 p.m. It had originally been planned to move *Ark Royal* during the previous week but strong
winds had forced the plans to be postponed. As she was prepared for the voyage ahead she was still very much a
'dead ship', devoid of all power, steering, and operational navigation equipment. Despite the short notice,
thousands turned out to witness her final departure which contrasted so sharply with her exit of April 1978
when her ship's company lined the decks as she made her way down Plymouth Sound. Two years on, the decks
were deserted except for a few members of her skeleton crew dotted around the vast expanse of her empty
flight deck. There were no flags flying or Royal Marines band playing, but CPO Ahern was determined that she
wasn't going to leave Plymouth without some sign of life, as he recalled: 'We stuck about twenty-six smoke
flares in the funnel because I was determined that she wasn't going to go without at least something. So when
we came round the corner to run past the Hoe I set off these flares. On my return I was detailed off to see the
Flag Officer Plymouth because I had exceeded my authority. When he saw me he said, "I hope you feel suitably
chastised and regretful." "Yes Sir, I do." He then said, "Off the record, well done Chief."'

By 6.10 p.m. *Ark Royal* had passed the breakwater at the start of a six-day voyage, bound for the Scottish
scrapyard at Cairnryan. She had been purchased by Mountstar Metal Corporation which had leased the port
from Shipbreaking Queensborough Ltd (SQL). The actual work of demolishing the hull was subcontracted to
Kitson Vickers. *Ark Royal* entered Loch Ryan on 28 September watched by thousands who had lined the banks to
catch a glimpse of their newest landmark as it made its way up the loch to be secured for the last time. Over the
course of her demolition Kitson Vickers was replaced by Northern Shipbreaking, who in turn were replaced by

Ark Royal enters the picturesque Loch Ryan at the end of her final voyage. (Donnie Nelson)

SQL when they purchased the 9,500 ton hulk from Mountstar in 1982. By this time the cut-down hulk had been beached as the ship-breaking entered its final stages. Not all of *Ark Royal* was destined to be melted down or burnt. The Admiral's cabin was dismantled and reassembled in the Knocknassie Hotel, where Barry Vickers who was a Director of Kitson Vickers had stayed. He had become friendly with the hotel's owner Mr Nabb who had fought off very strong interest from around the world. As with many of *Ark Royal*'s fittings, her portholes were sold off and occasionally you will find them in the most unlikely places, such as the main bar of the Ferry public house in Salcombe.

In 1983 Tom Wilkinson visited Cairnryan to watch the final stages of *Ark Royal*'s demise, as he recalled: 'By that time I had left the Navy and I was working for the BBC. They asked me to go to Cairnryan as part of the filming for the programme *Seven Years On*. They didn't tell me that the *Ark* was where the cars stopped, they just

By February 1981 the scrapmen at Cairnryan had really got their teeth into this once-mighty warship but it was a long job which took another three years to complete. (FAA Museum)

One of the anchors was taken back to Yeovilton to stand outside the entrance to the FAA Museum opposite an anchor from *Eagle*. (Author)

said she's over there. They apologized for it afterwards but the Producer, Patrick Thurley, wanted to get my reaction. They certainly got it because it broke my heart to see the remains of the old lady. What they didn't show was there was just this skeleton left, and among all the mud and snow on the jetty were the beautiful mahogany ladders with the chrome fittings just laying there. Straight away in my mind I drifted back to 1977 and I could see we had just had a refit. We were putting things right prior to sailing to Spithead for the Fleet Review. I could see those lads on their hands and knees polishing those ladders with beeswax.'

By the time the commando carrier *Bulwark* arrived the following year, very little remained, as the last loads of scrap were being prepared for their journey to a Spanish smelter. Now that *Ark Royal* has gone, the closest that many of us will ever get to sampling what it was like to be in *Ark Royal* will be the Carrier display in the Fleet Air Arm Museum at Yeovilton, which is a one-third slice out of the centre of an angled flight deck carrier which includes the island. When the Trustees of the Museum decided to give the go-ahead to the project the aim was to recreate the feel of the flight deck of a 1970s RN carrier (*Ark Royal* by any other description). While it is impossible to recreate exactly the spectacle of the flight deck of an operational fixed-wing carrier within the confines of a hangar, the display does give a good impression of what it would have been like. Certainly, when you look down from the goofers position on the recreated island the view is pretty realistic. Within the island, you will see a number of displays which recreate many of the parts of the ship which have been covered in this book, such as flyco, the operations room, and the aircrew refreshment bar. While most of the equipment in the displays has come from decommissioned Leander class frigates, such as *Cleopatra* and *Hermione*, it does include a few items from *Ark Royal*.

Chapter Twelve

THE *ARK'S* AIRCRAFT

FIXED-WING AIRCRAFT

Hawker Sea Hawk FGA6
Role: fighter, fighter bomber, ground attack
Squadrons embarked: 800 Sqn, 802 Sqn, 804 Sqn, 898 Sqn
Crew: pilot
Engine: 1 × 5,200lb Rolls-Royce Nene 103
Max speed: 520 knots
Max weight: 16,200lb
Span: 39ft
Length: 39ft 10in

The Sea Hawk was a popular aircraft among the pilots who flew it and it was regarded a joy to fly. The Sea Hawk formed the largest part of *Ark Royal*'s CAG for the first two commissions before it was superseded by the next generation of aircraft.

Sea Hawks of 898 Squadron overflying *Ark Royal* (FAA Museum)

Fairey Gannet AS1 and AS4
Role: anti-submarine search and strike
Squadrons embarked: 824 Sqn, 815 Sqn
Crew: pilot, observer and aircrewman
Engine: 1 × 2,750shp Armstrong Siddeley Double Mamba
    101 Unit
Max speed: 360 knots
Max weight: 23,700lb
Span: 54ft 4in
Length: 43ft

The AS1 Gannet embarked with 824 Squadron in 1955. 824 Squadron was the only squadron from *Ark Royal*'s first commission to be embarked during her last commission. The AS Gannets service was cut short prematurely by the development of the Whirlwind in the anti-submarine role and therefore they only formed part of *Ark Royal*'s air group during her first two commissions.

A Gannet AS4 of 815 Squadron banking over *Ark Royal*. (FAA Museum)

Douglas Skyraider AEW1

Role: airborne early warning

Squadrons embarked: 849 Sqn B Flight

Crew: pilot and two observers

Engine: 1 × 2,700hp Wright Cyclone R-3350-26WA

Max speed: 305 knots

Max weight: 24,000lb

Span: 50ft

Length: 38ft 10in

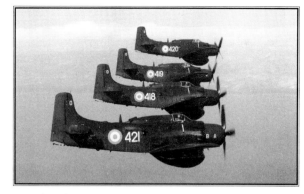

Skyraider AEW1s of 849 Squadron B Flight in formation.
(FAA Museum)

The Skyraider AEW1 was the FAA's first AEW aircraft and was embarked in *Ark Royal* during her first two commissions before being replaced by the Gannet AEW3.

De Havilland Sea Venom FAW21

Role: night and all-weather fighter

Squadrons embarked: 891 Sqn, 893 Sqn

Crew: pilot and observer

Engine: 1 × 4,950lb thrust Ghost 104

Span: 42ft 11in

Length: 36ft 7in

A Sea Venom FAW21 of 809 Squadron. (FAA Museum)

The Sea Venom was developed from the RAF's Venom night fighter. Initially the Sea Venoms were not fitted with ejection seats until the early production aircraft were retrofitted with them in 1957.

Westland Wyvern S4

Role: torpedo strike fighter

Squadrons embarked: 831 Sqn

Crew: pilot

Engine: 1 × 4,110hp Armstrong Siddeley Python ASP3
    turboprop

Max speed: 330 knots

Max weight: 24,500lb

Span: 44ft

Length: 42ft 3in

A Wyvern S4 of 831 Squadron with everything down.
(Lieutenant Commander Farquhar via the author)

Although the Wyvern was a superb weapons platform, its period of service was brief and notorious due to the high number of deck landing accidents. The Wyvern was only embarked in *Ark Royal* for the second commission.

Fairey Gannet AEW3

Role: airborne early warning

Squadrons embarked: 849 Sqn A Flight, 849 Sqn B Flight,
    849 Sqn C Flight

Crew: pilot and two observers

Engine: 1 × 3,875shp Armstrong Siddeley Double Mamba
    112 (D8)

Max speed: 280 knots

Max weight: 26,000lb

Span: 54ft 4in

Length: 44ft

A Gannet AEW3 of 849 Squadron B Flight. (Captain
Rotheram via the author)

The Gannet was able to – and occasionally did – carry a
1,000lb bomb on each pylon.

De Havilland Sea Vixen FAW1

Role: night and all-weather fighter

Squadrons embarked: 890 Sqn, 892 Sqn, 893 Sqn

Crew: pilot and observer

Engine: 2 × 11,250lb thrust Rolls-Royce Avon 208

Span: 50ft

Length: 53ft 6½in

The Sea Vixen was the last De Havilland fighter and the first
FAA aircraft to have an all-missile armament. 892 Squadron
became the FAA first front-line Sea Vixen squadron when it was
formed in July 1959. The squadron embarked in *Ark Royal* in
March 1960 until transferring to *Victorious* later in the year. 893
Squadron replaced 892 in October 1960 for the rest of the third
commission. 890 Squadron embarked in *Ark Royal* at the beginning of the fourth commission and remained as her Sea Vixen
squadron until the end of the fifth commission, by which time it
had become the last front-line squadron of Sea Vixen FAW1s.

Sea Vixen FAW1s of 890 Squadron being prepared for
launch. (Captain Rotheram via the author)

Supermarine Scimitar F1

Role: fighter, reconnaissance and strike

Squadrons embarked: 800 Sqn, 803 Sqn, 807 Sqn

Crew: pilot

Engine 2 × 11,250lb thrust Rolls-Royce Avon 202 turbojets

Max speed: 625 knots

Max weight: 40,000lb

Span: 37ft 2in

Length: 55ft 4in

A pair of Scimitar F1s engaged in in-flight refuelling.
(Captain Tofts via the author)

The Scimitar was the last Supermarine fighter and it could
trace its development back to the immortal Spitfire. It was
certainly one of the most elegant postwar FAA aircraft. The Scimitar was the first of the FAA's second generation jet fighters but it was
soon eclipsed by Blackburn's Buccaneer in the strike role. However, the Scimitar managed to survive *Ark Royal*. When *Ark Royal* returned
in October 1966 to pay off for her Phantomization, 803 Sqn disbanded as the last front-line Scimitar squadron.

Fairey Gannet COD 4

Role: carrier on board delivery of mail stores and passengers

Squadrons embarked: 849 Sqn B Flight, 849 Sqn C Flight

Crew: pilot, and up to two passengers

Engine: 1 × 2,750shp Armstrong Siddeley Double Mamba
101 Unit

Max speed: 360 knots

Span: 54ft 4in

Length: 43ft

The COD Gannets were former Gannet AS4s with their anti-submarine equipment removed.

A Gannet COD4 at the moment of launch. Below the tail code letter R (indicating that the Gannet is from *Ark Royal*), are initials indicating that the aircraft is being used as the transport for Flag Officer Aircraft Carriers. (Captain Rotheram via the author)

Buccaneer S1

Role: low-level strike

Squadrons embarked: 801 Sqn

Crew: pilot and observer

Engine: 2 × 7,100lb thrust DH Gyron Junior DGJ1

Span: 44ft

Length: 63ft 5in

Ark Royal had the distinction of operating the first front-line squadron of Buccaneer S1s when 801 Squadron embarked in *Ark Royal* for a month between February and March 1963.

A Buccaneer S1 of 801 Squadron coming into land. (Rolls-Royce)

Blackburn Buccaneer S2

Role: low-level strike

Squadrons embarked: 809 Sqn

Crew: pilot and observer

Engine: 2 × 11,100lb thrust Rolls-Royce Spey 101 turbojets

Max speed: Mach 0.85

Max weight: 62,000lb

Span: 44ft

Length: 63ft 5in

Ark Royal had the distinction of operating the last front-line squadron of FAA Buccaneers, from 809 Squadron, between 1970 and 1978.

A Buccaneer S2 of 809 Squadron. (Admiral Sir Michael Layard via the author)

McDonnell Douglas F4K Phantom
(known in the RN as the FGR1)
Role: interceptor and ground attack fighter
Squadrons embarked: 892 Sqn
Crew: pilot and observer
Engine: 2 × 12,250lb thrust reheated Rolls-Royce RB 168 Spey
    Mk 201 turbofans
Max speed: Mach 2.2
Max weight: 56,000lb
Span: 38ft 4in
Length: 57ft 7in

Phantom FGR1s of 892 Squadron. (Admiral Sir Michael
Layard via the author)

Ark Royal embarked the only FAA front-line squadron of
Phantoms. The Phantom F4K was the first variant of the Phantom
to be produced for a customer outside the US. It was essentially
the same as the US Navy's F4J with some modifications for RN
service. The principal differences included Rolls Royce Spey
engines, nose gear extendable by 40in, folding radome and radar
antenna to enable the Phantoms to use *Ark Royal*'s smaller lifts. In
Jane's Fighting Aircraft it was stated that the RN Phantoms were
cleared for minelaying which the squadron never actually
practised. The Omega insignia on the tail was chosen because
Omega is the last letter in the Greek alphabet and 892 Squadron
was destined to be the last conventional fixed-wing fighter
squadron in the RN.

HELICOPTERS

Westland Dragonfly HR3
Role: search and rescue
Squadrons embarked: Ship's Flight
Crew: pilot and aircrewman
Engine: 1 × 550hp Alvis Leonides 50
Max speed: 90 knots
Max weight: 5,870lb
Rotor diameter: 49ft
Length: 57ft 6½in

The Dragonfly was developed by Westland from the Sikorsky
S51. A Dragonfly piloted by Captain Cambell had the distinction
of being the first aircraft to land on board.

This is the first ever landing on board *Ark Royal*, carried
out appropriately enough by Captain Cambell flying this
Dragonfly HR3. (Rear Admiral Cambell via the author)

Westland Whirlwind HAR3 and HAS7

Role: anti-submarine search or strike, search and rescue

Squadrons embarked: 820 Sqn, 824 Sqn, Ship's Flight

Crew: one or two pilots, observer in HAS version

Engine: (HAR3) 1 × 700hp Wright R-1300-3 Cyclone

Engine: (HAS7) 1 × 750hp Alvis Leonides Major

Max speed: (HAS7) 90 knots

Max weight: (HAS7) 7,800lb

Rotor diameter: 53ft

Length: 41ft 8½in

Whirlwind HAR3 of the Ship's Flight. (FAA Museum)

The Whirlwind was developed by Westland from the Sikorsky S55. *Ark Royal* embarked her first Whirlwinds in the first commission when two Whirlwind HAR3s operated in conjunction with a pair of Dragonflys operated by the Ship's Flight. The Whirlwind HAS7 only served in the third commission in the anti-submarine role when HAS7s from both 824 Squadron and 820 Squadron were embarked. Despite suffering from serious engine problems during its early years in service the HAS7 continued to form part of *Ark Royal*'s air group until she paid off for Phantomization in October 1966. By then *Ark Royal*'s Whirlwind HAS7s were the last to be used by a carrier's Ship's Flight.

Whirlwind HAS7 of the Ship's Flight. (Admiral of the Fleet Sir Michael Pollock)

Westland Wessex HAS1

Role: anti-submarine search and strike, search and rescue

Squadrons embarked: 815 Sqn, 819 Sqn, Ship's Flight

Crew: one or two pilots, observer in ASW role

Engine: 1 x 1,430shp Napier Gazelle 161 turbine engine

Max speed: 115 knots

Max weight: 12,600lb including 4,000lb underslung load

Rotor diameter: 56ft

Length: 65ft 9in

Length with tail rotor folded: 38ft 2in

Wessex HAS1 of the Ship's Flight. (Steve Riley)

The Wessex was developed by Westland from the Sikorsky S58. *Ark Royal* had the distinction of operating the FAA's first front-line squadron of Wessex helicopters when 815 Squadron embarked in November 1961. 815 Squadron remained part of *Ark Royal*'s air group for both the fourth and fifth commissions. *Ark Royal* didn't operate the HAS3 because when she emerged from her Phantomization refit in 1970, the Sea King HAS1 had replaced the Wessex in the ASW role on board. However, the Wessex remained an important part of the air group until the end of *Ark Royal*'s service with the operation of two Wessex HAS1s by the Ship's Flight for search and rescue.

Anti-submarine version of the Wessex HAS1 of 815 Squadron. (Captain Skinner via the author)

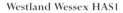

Westland Sea King HAS1 and HAS2

Role: anti-submarine search and strike

Squadrons embarked: 824 Sqn

Crew: two pilots, observer and sonar operator

Engine: (HAS1) 2 × 1,500shp Gnome H1400

Engine: (HAS2) 2 × 1,660shp Gnome H1400-1

Max speed: 120 knots

Max weight: 21,500lb

Rotor diameter: 62ft

Length: 72ft 8in

824 Squadron became the FAA's first front-line squadron of Sea Kings when they embarked in *Ark Royal* in June 1970. From March 1977 *Ark Royal* 824 Squadron's Sea Kings were progressively updated from the original Mk1 standard to the Mk2 standard which included the fitting of improved engines. The obvious external difference was the fitting of the barn door in front of the main engines.

Sea King HAS1s of 824 Squadron. (Lieutenant Commander Brazendale via the author)

PROTOTYPES/TRIALS AIRCRAFT

This section covers the various prototype aircraft and aircraft embarked in *Ark Royal* for trials during her twenty-three years of service.

De Havilland DH110

Role: prototype

Crew: pilot and observer

Engine: 2 × 11,250lb thrust Rolls-Royce Avon 208

Max weight: 35,000lb

Span: 50ft

Length 52ft 1½in

Sea King HAS2 of 824 Squadron. (Admiral Sir Michael Layard)

Trials were conducted on board *Ark Royal* during April 1956 using the third DH110 prototype XF828 which was completed as a semi-navalized pre-production aircraft. While XF828 was the first DH110 with an arrester hook, it did not have folding wings, or undercarriage built to withstand the same level of stress as the production Sea Vixens. Having completed its test programme it was delivered in November 1960 to the School of Aircraft Handling at RNAS Culdrose where it was used until January 1968 when it was retired. Despite some interest in its preservation it was used for fire-fighting practice in June 1970. After further development, the DH110 entered FAA service as the Sea Vixen FAW1. *Ark Royal* also hosted the trials of the first production Sea Vixen FAW1 in July 1957.

A DH110 moments after landing. Note the arrester wire below the twin booms of the aircraft. (British Aerospace plc. (Farnborough))

Supermarine N113D

Role: prototype

Crew: pilot

Engine: 2 × 11,250lb thrust Rolls-Royce Avon 202 turbojets

Max speed: Mach 1 (in a shallow dive)

Span: 37ft 2in

Length: 55ft 4in

The first prototype Scimitar embarked in *Ark Royal* for trials in April 1956. The third prototype Scimitar was embarked in January 1957 for a second batch of trials which were limited due to bad weather.

Supermarine N113. (FAA Museum)

Blackburn N39

Role: prototype

Crew: pilot and observer

Engine: 2 × 7,100lb thrust DH Gyron Junior

Span: 44ft

Length: 63ft 5in

In addition to the flying trials of the N39 *Ark Royal* also conducted trials for the Buccaneer S2 in March 1965.

Blackburn N39. (British Aerospace plc. (Brough Heritage Centre))

Hawker P1127

Role: prototype

Crew: pilot

Engine: 1 × 11,000lb Pegasus 2

Max weight: 15,500lb

Span: 24ft 4in

Length: 41ft 2in (excluding probe)

The landing of the P1127 on *Ark Royal* on 7 February was the start of *Ark Royal*'s long association with VSTOL aircraft which was to continue after her Phantomization.

P1127 about to make the first landing of a VSTOL aircraft at sea. In the background the Ship's Flight Whirlwind is standing by in case of an emergency. (British Aerospace plc. (Dunsfold))

Sea Vixen FAW 2
Role: night and all-weather fighter
Crew: pilot and observer
Engine: 2 × 11,250lb thrust Rolls-Royce Avon 208
Max speed: 610 knots
Max weight: 46,750lb
Span: 50ft
Length: 53ft 6½in

While the Sea Vixen FAW2 was never embarked in *Ark Royal* as part of her air group, *Ark Royal* did play host to Sea Vixen FAW2s on a few occasions. At the end of March 1965 a Sea Vixen FAW2 was embarked in *Ark Royal* from Boscombe Down for minimum speed launching trials while carrying the 37 tube 2in rocket launcher. The last time Sea Vixen FAW2s embarked in *Ark Royal* was during her work up in May 1970 when two Sea Vixen FAW2s from 899 Squadron, normally embarked in *Eagle*, spent two days for calibration of *Ark Royal*'s catapults. The purpose of the trials was to enable *Ark Royal* to operate Sea Vixen FAW2s should the need ever occur.

A Sea Vixen FAW2. (Captain Rotheram via the author)

Hawker Harrier GR1 and GR3
Squadrons embarked: 1 Sqn (RAF)
Crew: pilot
Engine: (GR1) 1 × 19,200lb Pegasus 6 Mk 101
         (GR3) 1 × 21,500lb Pegasus 11 Mk 103
Max speed: 737mph at sea level
Max weight: 25,000lb
Span: 25ft 3in
Length: 45ft 8in

The first Harrier GR1 landed on *Ark Royal* during March 1970 when two Harriers were conducting service release trials for deck operations of RAF Harriers on board HMS *Eagle*. One of the Harriers landed on *Ark Royal* while both ships were sailing alongside each other. The next occasion when Harriers returned to *Ark Royal* was in May 1971 when two RAF Harriers from 1 Squadron embarked for trials to evaluate the viability of operating Harriers at sea. The last set of Harrier trials was completed in October 1975 when two RAF Harrier GR3s from 1 Squadron were embarked for trials.

A Harrier GR1 of 1 Squadron (RAF) with a Buccaneer of 809 Squadron in the background. (British Aerospace plc. (Dunsfold))

Chapter Thirteen

ARK ROYAL — THE DETAILS

BATTLE HONOURS

Armada	1588	Spartivento	1940
Cadiz	1596	Mediterranean	1940–41
Dardanelles	1915	*Bismarck*	1941
Norway	1940	Malta Convoys	1941

COMMANDING OFFICERS

Dates in Command

Captain D.R.F. Cambell DSC, RN	25/2/55 – 16/7/56
Commander J.C.Y. Roxburgh DSO, DSC*, RN	16/7/56 – 25/7/56
Commander I.S. McIntosh DSO, MBE, DSC, RN	25/7/56 – 1/11/56
Captain F.H.E. Hopkins DSO, DSC, RN	1/11/56 – 16/7/58
Commander I.S. McIntosh DSO, MBE, DSC, RN	16/7/58 – 3/9/58
Lieutenant Commander C.S. Moseley RN	3/9/58 – 5/11/58
Commander S.S. Brooks DSC, RN	5/11/58 – 1/10/59
Captain P.J. Hill-Norton RN	1/10/59 – 14/8/61
Captain D.C.E.F. Gibson DSC, RN	14/8/61 – 23/1/63
Captain M.P. Pollock MVO, DSC, RN	23/1/63 – 24/1/64
Captain A.T.F.G. Griffin RN	24/1/64 – 29/10/65
Captain M.F. Fell DSO, DSC*, RN	29/10/65 – 17/10/66
Commander G.I. Pritchard RN	17/10/66 – 20/12/66
Commander R.J.G. Macpherson DSC*, RN	20/12/66 – 31/3/69
Commander N.I.S. Hunt MVO, RN	1/4/69 – 17/7/69
Captain R.D. Lygo RN	17/7/69 – 9/3/71
Captain J.O. Roberts RN	9/3/71 – 21/8/72
Captain A.D. Cassidi RN	22/8/72 – 26/11/73
Captain J.R.S. Gerard-Pearse RN	27/11/73 – 27/3/75
Captain W.J. Graham RN	28/3/75 – 28/9/76
Captain E.R. Anson RN	28/9/76 – 14/12/78
Captain J.G.H. O'Donnell RN	15/12/78 – 31/5/79

Author's Note: To complete the historical record of who commanded *Ark Royal* I have listed from the Ship's Book all of those Royal Navy officers who commanded *Ark Royal* during her time in the Royal Navy. Those Captains highlighted in Bold were the Captains who actually commanded *Ark Royal* at sea. In addition to the Royal Navy officers who commanded *Ark Royal* in naval service, Captain Lentaigne (retired) was employed by Cammell Laird for contractor's sea trials in June and September 1954.

DISTANCE RUN PER COMMISSION

First commission	23,773 nautical miles
Second commission	68,163.2 nautical miles
Third commission	77,395.5 nautical miles
Fourth commission	138,755.56 nautical miles
Fifth commission	108,151.3 nautical miles
Sixth commission, Part I	179,923.4 nautical miles
Sixth commission, Part II	139,895.12 nautical miles
Sixth commission, Part III	76,381.3 nautical miles
Total distance steamed	812,438.38 nautical miles
Pennant number	R09
Deck recognition letter:	O 1955–1957
	R 1958–1978
Launched weight excluding cradle	24,800 tons

DETAILS ON COMPLETION 1955

Full load displacement	46,000 tons
Standard displacement	36,800 tons
Length overall	808¼ft
Length between perpendiculars	720ft
Beam waterline	112¾ft
Draught maximum	36ft
Complement	2,345 including front-line squadrons
Angle of angled flight deck	5½ degrees
Machinery	Parsons single reduction geared turbines, four shafts producing a total of 152,000shp
Boilers	8 × Admiralty three-drum type, 400lb psi pressure 600 degrees Fahrenheit
Maximum speed	31.5 knots
Gunnery	8 × twin 4.5in
	5 × sextuple 40mm Bofors
	2 × twin 40mm Bofors
	7 × single 40mm Bofors
	4 × single 3 pdr

CHANGES TO DETAILS, POST-1958–59 REFIT

Full load displacement	53,340 tons
Standard displacement	43,340 tons
Beam overall	160⅓ft
Gunnery	4 × twin 4.5in
	4 × sextuple 40mm Bofors
	4 × twin 40mm Bofors
	4 × 3 pdr

CHANGES TO DETAILS, POST-1964 REFIT

Gunnery	2 × twin 4.5in
	2 × quadruple 40mm Bofors
	3 × twin 40mm Bofors
	2 × 2 pdr

CHANGES TO DETAILS, POST-1967–70 REFIT

Full load displacement	50,786 tons
Standard displacement	43,060 tons
Length overall	845ft
Beam (hull)	112.8ft
Beam overall	166ft
Angle of angled flight deck	8½ degrees
Draught forward at full load displacement	35ft 1in
Draught aft at full load displacement	36ft
Draught after destoring in 1979	31ft 6in
Complement	260 Officers (as flagship)
	2,380 ratings (with air staff)
Armament	Fitted for 4 × quadruple Seacat
Search radars	two sets of Type 965, Type 993
Aircraft direction radars	Type 982, Type 983
Carrier-controlled approach radar	AN-SPN 35

COSTS

Construction	£21,428,000
1964 refit	£3,750,000
1967–1970 refit	£32,500,000

Chapter Fourteen

THE *ARK ROYAL* LEGEND

From the Spanish Armada to the hunt for the *Bismarck*, ships of the RN serving as *Ark Royal* have answered the call of duty from their country. When you are faced with a legend as enduring as that of the *Ark Royal* it is difficult to pinpoint where it started and why that special spirit has passed from ship to ship. Although the first two *Ark Royals* both played an important role in naval engagements of their time it was the short-lived, yet illustrious, career of *Ark Royal III* which first saw that special *Ark Royal* spirit. Since her sinking in 1941 two further *Ark Royals* have served in the RN and the *Ark Royal* spirit has continued to grow despite some difficult times. Four of the five ships named *Ark Royal* have been known at one time by a different name, but it is as *Ark Royal* that all five will always be remembered.

ARK ROYAL I (1587–1636)

Sir Walter Raleigh commissioned the Deptford shipbuilder R. Chapman to build the first *Ark Royal* in 1586 as the *Ark Raleigh*. It was common in Tudor times for privately financed armed ships to be named after their owner.

Ark Royal I. (Cammell Laird Archives)

The following year, while she was still under construction, she was purchased by Elizabeth I for £5,000 and promptly renamed *Ark Royal*. The Queen bought the 692 ton vessel because she was concerned by the small number of ships that were available to counter the growing threat posed by Spain. The purchase was later endorsed by the Lord High Admiral of England, Lord Howard of Effingham, in a letter he wrote to the Queen's secretary when he said, 'I pray you tell Her Majesty from me that her money was well given for the *Ark Raleigh*, for I think her the odd ship in the world for all conditions; and truly I think there can be no great ship make me change and go out of her.' Lord Howard flew his flag in *Ark Royal* in 1588 during the battles against the Spanish Armada, and again eight years later during the joint navy/army operation against Cadiz in 1596. Later that year she was used by Sir Walter Raleigh as a flagship when Spain once more tried to dispatch another armada. In the event the Spanish fleet was hit by bad weather before it reached the English Channel and the surviving vessels limped back to Spain before entering the English Channel. It was appropriate that she should have been the flagship of Sir Walter Raleigh as he was after all the instigator of her chequered career. When she completed an extensive refit at Woolwich in 1608 she was renamed by James I *Anne Royal* in honour of his wife. Her last major deployment was as the flagship of Lord Wimbledon who led an unsuccessful expedition against Cadiz in 1625. On her return out of a total crew of 425 men, 130 were dead, while a further 160 were unable to do anything. She sank in April 1636 when she was moved from the Medway to be used as Sir John Pennington's flagship. She was lost as a result of stoving in her timbers on her own anchors. Despite her subsequent salvage, which cost more than her original building cost, she was found to be beyond repair and was broken up at the East India Company's dock at Blackwall thus ending the forty-nine year career of the first *Ark Royal*.

ARK ROYAL II (1914–50)

It was to be another three centuries before the name *Ark Royal* was revived. Her first Commanding Officer, then Cdr R.H. Clark-Hall, claimed the credit for the revival as he recalled in a letter published in the first issue of *Noah's News*: 'Admiral Murray Slatter was trying to think of a name to recommend to their Lordships, and I said *Ark Royal* was a fine historical name and that Captain Noah on Mount Ararat sent out the first air reconnaissance of history – the dove which returned with its olive leaf.' These sentiments were particularly appropriate because the name was to be allocated to a merchant vessel which was under construction at Blyth Shipbuilding Co. in 1913. Once purchased, the Admiralty converted the new *Ark Royal* into a seaplane carrier of 7,400 tons, thus beginning the association between naval aviation and ships of the name *Ark Royal*. She commissioned in December 1914 and later sailed for the Aegean with her aircraft, first seeing action in February 1915. Her aircraft were used for reconnoitring and bombing Turkish ports. By May she had to withdraw from the area, due to the threat from German U-boats operating there, and she spent the remainder of the war as part of the Mediterranean fleet. After the war she was dispatched to the Baltic to support the White Russians but was withdrawn from Sevastopol in mid-1919, complete with refugees fleeing the Russian Revolution. In 1920 she took RAF aircraft to Somaliland to support the operations of the Camel Corps to defeat the 'Mad Mullah'. In 1922 *Ark Royal* was deployed to Kilia Bay to deliver No. 4 Squadron RAF, to enhance the British garrison in the Dardanelles.

In 1934 the Admiralty were planning the construction of a new aircraft carrier which they wanted to name *Ark Royal*. Therefore *Ark Royal II*, in the reserve fleet at Chatham, was renamed HMS *Pegasus* on 21 December 1934. Admiral Cassidi, who commanded *Ark Royal IV*, recalls his visit to *Ark Royal II*, 'I went aboard her when my father had something to do with her when she was in the reserve fleet at Chatham in the 1930s and doing catapult trials, mainly for cruiser catapults – the development of Mr Thomas's "grab" was significant for

Ark Royal II. (FAA Museum)

effective recovery at sea of the Walrus amphibious aircraft.' *Pegasus* (*Ark Royal II*) was recalled for active service to provide fighter cover for nine convoys between December 1940 and July 1941. She was a slow ship, with a speed of only 11 knots, so her presence in these convoys was more of a morale boost for the merchant ships. However, she did have three Fulmar fighters which could be launched against enemy aircraft if necessary and therefore she did offer limited air cover. By the end of July 1941 she had returned to catapult training duties and spent the rest of the war in this role. She was sold on 18 October 1946 and sailed for a further three years under the Panamanian flag as the *Anita I.* By the time she completed her final voyage to Grays in Essex for scrapping in 1950 she had outlived her immediate successor while the fourth ship of the name was about to be launched.

ARK ROYAL III (1938–41)

This was the first of two *Ark Royals* to be built by Cammell Laird and the only one to be known solely as *Ark Royal.* For Cammell Laird, it was a prestigious job to build the 22,000 ton *Ark Royal* because her £2,330,000 contract was the largest post-First World War contract to be awarded, providing much needed employment in Merseyside. With a flight deck length of 800ft, she was the largest ship to have been built in Merseyside at the time of her launching. In a brief, yet successful, war career *Ark Royal* became a household name, thanks to both her success and the taunts of Germany's Lord Haw-Haw asking, 'Where is the *Ark Royal*?' Within eleven days of declaring war the first German attempt to sink the *Ark Royal* was made by U-39 off Ireland on 14 September 1939. The U-boat missed but *Ark Royal*'s destroyers depth-charged the U-boat and claimed the first U-boat kill

Ark Royal III. (FAA Museum)

of the Second World War. Twelve days later one of her Skua fighters had the distinction of being the first British warplane to destroy an enemy aircraft in the war. Later in the same day a Heinkel bomber narrowly missed *Ark Royal*. The resulting wall of water from the explosion and *Ark Royal*'s momentary list led to the first claims by the German Ministry of Propaganda that the Luftwaffe had sunk her. These claims were repeated despite the report of an American Captain about his visit to *Ark Royal* after the alleged sinking. Following this episode she was now a household name and the seeds of the *Ark Royal* legend had been sown. At the beginning of October 1939 she was deployed, in company with the veteran battlecruiser *Renown*, to the South Atlantic to search for German raiders. Although *Ark Royal* and *Renown* did not actually sink the *Graf Spee* they had indirectly determined her fate because her Captain had believed that they were both waiting at the mouth of the River Plate to destroy her.

Ark Royal sailed for Norway at the end of April 1940 to provide air support for British troop landings. This was followed by the provision of air support for the withdrawal of British forces from Norway in June 1940 and the launching of an unsuccessful air strike on 13 June against the German battlecruiser *Scharnhorst* to avenge the sinking of the aircraft carrier *Glorious* five days earlier. At the beginning of July 1940 *Ark Royal* took part in the bombardment of the French fleet at Oran and her aircraft disabled the French battleship *Dunkerque*. Her remaining sixteen months of war service were spent as part of the famous Force H. In the Mediterranean she provided air support for convoys, ferried Hurricane fighters to Malta and launched air strikes against Italian targets; while in the Atlantic she provided air cover for various convoys. At the end of May 1941 she took part

Ark Royal III sinking. (FAA Museum)

in one of the most famous naval engagements of the Second World War. Torpedoes from *Ark Royal*'s Swordfish crippled *Bismarck*'s steering and reduced her speed, thus providing the British battleships with enough time to close on *Bismarck* and sink her. The final months of *Ark Royal*'s service were spent covering convoys to Malta and it was while she was returning from Malta that she was hit by a torpedo from *U-81* on the afternoon of 13 November. Despite the valiant attempts by her Captain and the ship's company, who worked through the night to bring *Ark Royal* into Gibraltar under tow, her list continued to increase. At 6.13 a.m. next day the *Ark Royal* capsized before slipping below the waters of the Mediterranean. The countless German claims had come true and the 'Old Ark' as she was known had gone leaving only the stories of her exploits. Out of a crew of 1,600 men only one life was lost. The Captain had minimized the potential for a large loss of life by transferring most of the ship's company to the destroyer *Legion* soon after the carrier had been hit, leaving a skeleton crew on board to try to save her. The site of her wreck has become a place of pilgrimage for ships of the name *Ark Royal*. Both her successors have held memorial services over her wreck.

ARK ROYAL IV (1955–78)

The subject of this book.

Ark Royal IV. (Rod Lampen via the author)

ARK ROYAL V – 1985–?

Ark Royal V was originally to have been completed as HMS *Indomitable* but, owing to public support for the name to be kept active in the fleet, it was announced three days before *Ark Royal IV* entered Devonport for the last time, that the third ship of the Invincible class would be given the name *Ark Royal* and thus keep the *Ark Royal* legend alive. Like her immediate predecessor, her design was altered from that of her sister ships to incorporate various modifications introduced in the light of operational experience. Perhaps the most noticeable difference was the fitting of the 12 degree ski-jump and the raised fo'c'sle. Other external differences included a greater length, of 683ft as opposed to 675ft for *Invincible*; a beam of 117ft as opposed to 104ft for her sisters; and approximately 3,500 tons greater displacement. She was launched by HM Queen Elizabeth the Queen Mother on 2 June 1981 at Swan Hunter's Shipyard, Wallsend. By the time she was completed in 1985, she had cost

HMS *Ark Royal V* on her moorings in No. 3 Basin Portsmouth Dockyard days before she was moved prior to her five-day tow north bound for Rosyth and a major two-year refit. (Richard Johnstone-Bryden)

£200 million to build. As *Ark Royal* entered her home port of Portsmouth for the first time on 1 July 1985 she was greeted by a flypast from the RN Historic Flight, followed by Sea Harriers and Sea Kings, thus representing the different generations of aircraft to have operated from ships of the same name. The Queen Mother attended the first Commissioning ceremony held in Portsmouth on 1 November 1985, thus continuing the strong links she had maintained throughout *Ark Royal IV*'s service. The links between the two ships were underlined by the appointment of Captain James Weatherall, who was the last Commander of *Ark Royal IV*, as her first Captain.

Ark Royal V was operational for nine years before she paid off into reserve at Portsmouth in November 1994. In July 1986 she visited New York as the flagship of Vice Admiral Sir Julian Oswald for the Naval Review to mark the rededication of the Statue of Liberty. The following year she became the largest warship to pass through the Thames Barrier when she visited London in June 1987. *Ark Royal* sailed from Portsmouth for the start of the Outback '88 deployment in company with the destroyer *Edinburgh*, the frigate *Sirius* and the RFAs *Fort Grange* and *Olwen* in June 1988. This deployment was reminiscent of the previous deployments of *Ark Royal IV* to the Far East, with the ships transiting the Suez Canal, then visiting Singapore, Hong Kong and Australia. In January 1991 *Ark Royal* deployed to the eastern Mediterranean as part of the Allied forces to prevent the Gulf War from spreading outside the Gulf. *Ark Royal* completed two tours in the Adriatic during 1993 in support of UN operations ashore in the former Republic of Yugoslavia. The first tour was in April and was followed by a second stint in July before she returned to Portsmouth to pay off. At the time of writing *Ark Royal* is in reserve in Portsmouth awaiting her modernization which will be carried out in Rosyth from 1999. She is expected to recommission at the beginning of the 21st century.

After her return she was moved into No. 3 basin in Portsmouth Dockyard where she spent the next 4½ years on the moorings that were occupied by *Illustrious* between 1989 and 1991 while she was awaiting her modernization in Devonport.

Ark Royal's return to active service began on 26 April 1999 when she was moved at the beginning of May 1999, prior to her five-day tow north, bound for Rosyth and a major two-year refit. *Ark Royal*'s refit was part of the allocated work program agreed by the Government when Babcock Rosyth Defence Limited purchased Rosyth Dockyard in January 1997. Despite being allocated the work, Babcock still had to meet MOD requirements before the £100 million contract was formally signed in May 1999.

When she emerges in 2001, *Ark Royal*'s appearance will have been changed to incorporate an enlarged flight deck similar in appearance to the new deck recently fitted to *Illustrious*. This enlargement will enable her to take the RAF Harrier GR7 as part of the Royal Navy's move towards joint operations. As part of the preparation work for the flight deck extension, the Sea Dart missile launcher was removed shortly before *Ark Royal* was docked down on 21 June 1999. Other changes will include a new main mast and environmental improvements, in particular to the ship's sewerage treatment plant, refrigeration systems and garbage processing machinery. Unlike her sister ships, *Ark Royal* will not receive the 30mm Goalkeeper CIWS. Instead she will retain her three 20mm Phalanx CIWS which will be upgraded as part of the refit. She will also receive improvements to her command and control sensors and her communications equipment. Another addition to *Ark Royal*'s air group will be the new Merlin helicopter, although it is unclear at the time of writing if she will be the first of the 'Invincible' class to embark the new helicopter operationally.

Interestingly, when *Ark Royal IV* entered Devonport for her Phantomization refit in 1966 it was against the backdrop of political uncertainty over the future of British aircraft carriers after the cancellation of CVA-01. As *Ark Royal V* enters her major refit, Britain is once more looking at the future of the FAA and whether we should be building fixed-wing carriers. Hopefully, when *Ark Royal V* recommissions it will be against the backdrop of an order for two new fixed-wing carriers and a positive future for the FAA.

Chapter Fifteen

DINOSAUR OR PHOENIX?

As we draw towards the close of the century, in which naval aviation was born and subsequently developed into a potent fighting force, we may be about to see the re-emergence of the conventional fixed-wing aircraft carrier at the head of the Royal Navy. Since those dark days of 1966, when Denis Healey so hastily cancelled CVA-01 and sacrificed Britain's fixed-wing carrier force, the Fleet Air Arm has endured mixed fortunes. Within three years of *Ark Royal IV* paying off, Britain fought the Falklands War which relied upon the presence of the two smaller carriers *Hermes* and *Invincible* to provide air power to protect the fleet and back up the amphibious landings to retake the islands. This was the war that we were told only sixteen years before would never happen. It underlined in bold letters exactly why we needed ships of the size and capability of *Ark Royal*. While one can only speculate as to whether the Falklands War would have broken out if *Ark Royal IV* had still been in

An Admiralty model of CVA-01, now at the FAA Museum. (Author)

commission, it is certain that the presence of the venerable Gannet AEW3 would have prevented some of the losses which were suffered. While the Government of the day did not rush out to order new fixed-wing carriers after the Falklands, the lessons learned in the South Atlantic did force them to reconsider the harsh defence cuts they had proposed in 1981.

Indeed, since the Falklands War the smaller and vastly less capable Invincible class have continued to prove the usefulness of the carrier in support of the Government's foreign policy in both the Gulf and off Bosnia. While I have been writing this book it has been very interesting to see the progression of the discussions surrounding the possible replacement for the Invincible class. While a return to aircraft carriers of the size of *Ark Royal* looks unlikely, it is possible that the Royal Navy might get its way and have a larger class of aircraft carriers to replace the current generation of ships. The Government's Defence White Paper of June 1998 has promised that the RN will eventually get two new carriers of 40,000 tonnes, although the fine details including the design and what aircraft will be carried have yet to be agreed. Therefore, there is the real fear that the promise of these new ships might be used as the carrot to get the RN to agree to further cuts elsewhere in the fleet, and at the end of the day these ships may not be built, thus leaving the RN's capabilities further weakened. As the example of CVA-01 and its subsequent cancellation in 1966 by a previous Labour Government demonstrates, the new ships have a long path to navigate before becoming reality and joining the fleet.

One of the designs currently under consideration for the next fixed-wing carrier. (© BAE Systems)

BIBLIOGRAPHY

Reference was made to the following books during my research:

HMS *Ark Royal (IV)* Commission Book (November 1956–July 1958)

HMS *Ark Royal (IV)* Commission Book (December 1959–March 1961)

HMS *Ark Royal (IV)* Commission Book (1961–63)

HMS *Ark Royal (IV)* Commission Book (1964–66)

HMS *Ark Royal (IV)* Commission Book (1970–73)

HMS *Ark Royal (IV)* Commission Book (1974–76)

HMS *Ark Royal (IV)* Commission Book (1976–78)

HMS *Ark Royal (V)* Commission Book (February 1987–December 1988)

Various issues of *Noah's News*

Grant Eustace's Midshipman's Journal

Colin Lawrance's Midshipman's Journal

Tim Lee's Midshipman's Journal

The Ship's Book (*Ark Royal* IV)

Record Books for 801 Squadron, 803 Squadron, 809 Squadron, 824 Squadron, 849 Squadron B Flight, and 892 Squadron

The Four Ark Royals, Lt Cdr Michael Apps RN (William Kimber & Co., 1976)

Royal Navy Aircraft Carriers 1945–1990, Leo Marriott (Ian Allan Ltd, 1985)

The Battle and the Breeze, Admiral of the Fleet Sir Edward Ashmore (Sutton Publishing Ltd, 1997)

The Squadrons of the Fleet Air Arm, Ray Sturtivant and Theo Ballance (Air-Britain (Historians) Ltd, 1994)

Up In Harm's Way, Cdr Mike Crosley DSC*, RN (Airlife Publishing Ltd, 1995)

Vanguard to Trident, Eric Grove (The Bodley Head Ltd, 1987)

Cairnryan Military Port 1940–96, Richard Holme (G.C. Book Publishers Ltd, 1997)

Fly Navy, Ray Williams (Airlife Publishing Ltd, 1989)

Aircraft of the Royal Navy Since 1945, Cdr David Hobbs (Maritime Books, 1982)

The Fleet Air Arm, A Pictorial History, Reginald Longstaff (Robert Hale Ltd, 1981)

Ark Royal. The Admiralty Account Of Her Achievement (HMSO, 1942)

Ark Royal. The Name Lives On, David Hobbs and David Smith (Maritime Books, 1986)

HMS Ark Royal. The Ship And Her Men, David Smith and Andrew Wynn (Maritime Books, 1988)

Ark Royal, Paul Beaver (Patrick Stephens Ltd, 1979)

Encyclopaedia of the Fleet Air Arm since 1945, Paul Beaver (Patrick Stephens Ltd, 1987)

Haul Taut and Belay, Vice Admiral Sir Donald Gibson KCB DCS JP (Spellmount Ltd, 1992)

If Only I'd Seen the Script, Rear Admiral D.R.F. Cambell CB DSC (private circulation, 1994)

Mayflower II, Warwick Charlton (Cassell & Company Ltd, 1957)

Ark Royal, James Dalrymple (Bossiney Books, 1978)

Jackspeak, Rick Jolly and Tugg Wilson (Palamando Publishing, 1989)

Brassey's Annual, 1966, (William Clowes & Sons Ltd, 1966)

Men of Iron, D. Hollett (Countywise Ltd, 1992)

De Havilland Vampire, Venom & Sea Vixen, Phillip Birtles (Ian Allan Ltd, 1986)

Supermarine Attacker, Swift & Scimitar, Phillip Birtles (Ian Allan Ltd, 1992)

Scimitar, David Gibbings and J.A. Gorman (Society of Friends of the FAA Museum, 1988)

Sea King, David Gibbings (Society of Friends of the FAA Museum, 1990)

Gannet, Brian Fiddler (Society of Friends of the FAA Museum, 1988)

Various editions of Janes Fighting Aircraft

Reference was made to various issues of the following periodicals:

Flight Deck, Air Pictorial, Navy News, Fly Navy, Ships Monthly, Classic Boat, 849 Squadron B Flight *Newsletter*

Reference was made to various editions of the following newspapers:

Liverpool Echo, Liverpool Daily Post, Birkenhead News, Shipbuilding News, The News (Birkenhead), *News Chronicle* (Portsmouth), *Illustrated London News, Wirral Grapevine, The Times, Sunday Times, Daily Telegraph, Daily Mail, South China Morning Post* (Hong Kong), *Western Morning News, Western Daily Press, Western Evening Herald, Devonport News, The Fifty Niner* (newsletter of USS *Forrestal* CVA-59)

INDEX

Adams, Lt Terry 147
Aden 84, 93, 105, 114, 122
    Gulf of 94,
Admiralty 1, 7, 8, 10, 14, 17, 60, 71, 77,
    81, 84, 97, 103, 105, 127, 137,
    227, 247
Adriatic 252
Aegean 247
Ahern, CPO Brian 227, 228, 230
Aircraft:
    Aquilon (French Navy) 65, 66
    Badger (Russian Air Force) 122, 179, 191
    Banshee, F2H 48
    Bear (Russian Air Force) 122, 179,
        191, 212, 213
    Bison (Russian Air Force) 122
    Blackburn N39 241
    Buccaneer 68, 69, 109, 126, 236
    Buccaneer S1 95, 96, 97, 98, 99, 110,
        176, 237
    Buccaneer S2 110, 132, 133, 135, 139,
        142, 152, 154, 155, 158, 167, 175,
        176, 186, 187, 193, 195, 199–201,
        206, 214, 217, 219–22, 237, 241
    Cougar, F9F 48
    Crusader, F8U 56
    DH110 37, 39, 240
    Dragonfly 17, 238, 239
    Fury, FJ3 48
    Gannet 206, 220
    Gannet AEW3 62–4, 67, 68, 78, 92,
        99, 104, 109, 112, 113, 119–21,
        135, 139, 142, 152, 166, 167–70,
        172, 173, 186, 195, 209, 214, 221,
        222, 235, 236, 254
    Gannet AS1 21, 26, 44, 234
    Gannet AS4 44, 62, 112, 234
    Gannet COD4 112, 113, 135, 155, 237
    Gannet ECM4 68
    Gannet ECM6 82
    Gannet 044 221
    Gannet XL475 120
    Gannet XL494 214
    Harrier, GR1 133, 148, 149, 242
    Harrier, GR3 133, 176, 242
    Harrier, GR5 133
    Hormone (Russian Air Force) 179
    Hunter 84, 89, 102
    Lightning 196
    N113 37, 241
    P1127 95, 96, 241
    P1154 102

Phantom, F4B 151, 156
Phantom, F4J 238
Phantom, F4K/FGR1 126, 127,
    132–5, 139, 140, 142, 144, 148,
    150, 151, 166, 173, 184, 186, 191,
    193, 195, 196, 199, 212, 214–16,
    220, 222, 238
Phantom 012 222
Scimitar F1 44, 52, 62, 63, 65, 68, 77,
    78, 84, 89, 91, 98, 99, 104, 109,
    112, 120, 123, 236
Sea Dragon 104
Sea Fury 6, 32, 33
Sea Harrier 224, 252
Sea Hawk 21, 24, 26, 32, 33, 35, 44,
    45, 52, 53, 62, 78, 84, 98, 234
Sea Hornet 6, 31
Sea King 252
Sea King HAS1 135, 140, 142, 164,
    166, 167, 171, 175, 183, 188, 203,
    204, 239, 240
Sea King HAS2 135, 207, 208, 209,
    210, 216, 240
Sea King 051 171
Sea King SH-3D 175
Sea Venom 21, 26, 31, 37, 62
Sea Venom FAW20 65
Sea Venom FAW21 31, 44, 235
Sea Vixen 135, 140
Sea Vixen FAW1 52, 62–4, 66, 67, 69,
    72, 73, 78, 84, 85, 87, 89, 94, 95,
    98, 102, 104, 109, 117, 120, 121,
    123, 134, 167, 236, 240
Sea Vixen FAW2 242
Shackleton 26, 121
Sikorsky S51 238
Sikorsky S55 239
Sikorsky S58 239
Skua 9
Skyhawk 56, 104
Skylark 57
Skyraider, AD6 48
Skyraider, AEW1 21, 44, 47, 62, 235
Skyray, F4D 48, 54
Tomcat, F14 191
Tracker, 2TF1 48, 86
Victor (RAF tanker) 140, 212
Vulcan (RAF bomber) 140
Wessex HAS1 77, 78, 83, 84, 93, 94,
    102–4, 109, 116, 120, 135, 142,
    146, 152, 164, 173, 210, 220, 239
Wessex 046 176

Wessex 047 164
Whirlwind 36, 51, 62, 66, 78, 234
Whirlwind HAR3 23, 44, 239
Whirlwind HAS7 63, 68, 76, 77, 239
Wyvern S4 21, 44, 45, 48, 52, 55, 56,
    235
Air Crew Refreshment Bar 171, 172
Albion, HMS 33, 54, 55
Alexander, A.V. (First Lord of the
    Admiralty) 19
Algeria 33
Ambrose Light 153, 154
America, USS 191
Amphlett, Ray 30, 34, 56
Andrea Doria 166
Anita I 248
Anne Royal, HMS 247
Anson, Vice Admiral Sir Edward 26, 32,
    35, 98, 146, 147, 191–3, 201, 202,
    206, 209, 210, 214, 217, 219, 222,
    224, 225, 243
Anymouse system 137
Ark Airways 209
Ark Raleigh 246, 247
Ark Royal I, HMS 246, 247
Ark Royal II, HMS 247, 248
Ark Royal III, HMS 1, 9, 16, 19, 25, 99,
    246, 248–50
Ark Royal V, HMS 227, 251, 252
Ark Royal Preservation Trust 228
Ark Royal star and bar 131
Arko 29
Arran, Isle of 11, 133
Arraxos 216
Arromanches 29
Ashmore, Admiral of the Fleet Sir Edward
    195
Athens 67, 216, 217
Atlantic Fleet Weapons Ranges (AFWR)
    158, 167, 170, 188, 208
Atlantic Ocean 47, 50, 71, 149, 155, 157, 189
Australia 91, 92, 116, 252
Azalea Queen 185
Azores 183, 207

Baillon, Colonel P.F. 199
Ballykelly 112
Barbados 158, 172
Barcelona 65, 156
Barker, PO 94
'Baron RAS' 101
Bay of Biscay 145

BBC 16, 57, 59, 151, 179, 180, 184, 189, 231
Beaverbrook, Lord 16, 25
Bedford, Bill 95, 96
Bedford, RAE 64, 66, 126, 196
Beira 117
Beira Patrol 117, 119, 120, 167
Belize 152
Bell, Cdr Peter 73, 126, 129, 130, 133, 140, 141
Bellamy, Cdr 25
Bergall, USS 182
Bergen 110
Bermuda 50, 152
Bermuda Triangle 209
Bermuda Triangle Crossing Society 209
Bevans, Lt Cdr 62, 73
Bickley, Lt Cdr 167
Bighi Bay 28, 32, 68, 219
Bingley, Vice Admiral A.N.C. 56
Birkenhead 3, 6, 12, 227
Birmingham, HMS 33
Birmingham, HMS (Type 42 destroyer) 195
Bismarck 1, 246, 250
Bizerta 65
Blake, HMS 174, 175
Blue Angels 48
Blyth, Chay 151
Blyth Shipbuilding Co. 247
Bodington, Mr 9
Bond, Lt 67
Bône, Bay of 33
Boscombe Down 44, 110, 134, 150, 242
Boston, USS 48
Brawdy, RAF 206
Brazendale, Lt Cdr Colin 172, 173, 177, 178, 184, 188
Brest 110
Brettle, Ben 178
Bristol Belle 147
Bristol Channel 139
Britannia, HMY 45, 46, 194
British Honduras 152
British Respect, tanker 194
British Steel, yacht 151
Brookes, Cdr S. 63, 243
Brown, Lt 94
Brown Ranger, RFA 106
Browne, Air Commodore 134
Brunsbüttel 201
Budd, Peter 212
Bulwark, HMS 31, 51, 52, 55, 94, 156, 179, 180, 193, 220, 223
Bura 104
Burke, Admiral Arleigh (USN) 48
Burles, PO Harry 171
Burn, Rear Admiral Richard 84, 85, 134, 150, 151

Butterworth 116

Cadiz 247
Caio Duilio 166
Cairnryan 207, 227, 230, 231
California, USS 194
Callaghan, Jim (Prime Minister) 33, 194, 201
Cambell, Rear Admiral Dennis 9, 13–17, 19–24, 26, 28, 29, 33, 36, 193, 238, 243
Cammell Laird 1–4, 6, 7, 10, 12, 13, 15, 16, 19, 137, 227, 248
Campbell, Alaistair 35
Canberra, USS 48
Cannes 29
Canteen Committee 19
Careful, tug 80
Caribbean 167
Carnie, Sub Lt Bob 76
Carrier Borne Ground Liaison Section (CBGLS) 199
Cass, Lt 221
Cassidi, Admiral Sir Desmond 155, 156, 158–61, 164, 174, 206, 243
Cavalier, HMS 139
Cawsand Bay 62, 68
Cecil, Rear Admiral 219
Centaur, HMS 84, 100, 105, 109
CENTO 104
    Military Committee 111
Centurion, HMS 222
Chambre Hardman, E. 3, 4
Changi 116
Chapman, Cdr G.C. 227
Chapman, R. 246
Charles, HRH Prince of Wales 200, 201
Charlotte Amalie 209
Charlton, Warwick 47
Chilcott, Lt Cdr Ben 109, 113, 114, 116, 117, 118
Chilton, Cdr P.C.S. 44
Churchill, Sir Winston 110
Clapham 11, 12
Clarence House 131
Clark-Hall, Cdr R.H. 247
Cleopatra, HMS 233
Clemenceau 191
Cocos Islands 116
Colossus, HMS 29
Connolly, USS 155
Cook, Peter 134
Corsica 156
Cowling, Cdr David 181
Creasey, Admiral Sir George 17
'Creation' by Sam Kotlin 146
Crete 144
Croften, HMS 78

Cromarty 45
Crossing the line ceremony 91, 101
Crowden, Captain Guy 77, 124, 125, 129, 131, 132, 138, 142, 144
Cruddas, Rear Admiral 12, 19, 32, 35
Cudmore, Cdr Mike 163, 214, 217, 224
Culdrose, RNAS 44, 76–8, 109, 192, 224, 240
Cullan, Lt Miles 120, 121
Cumbraes 16
Cunard 124
Curry, Rear Admiral P. 21
CVA-01 102, 117, 253, 254
Cyprus 59, 163,

Daily Express 16, 35
Daily Mail 45
Davies, Lt Cdr Carl 154
Davis Strait 71, 73
Dawson-Taylor, Cdr David 85
Dear, Robert 53
Decimomannu 166, 167
Delimara 34
De Ruyter 64
Devonport 6, 13–15, 19, 20, 22, 36, 39, 44, 52, 55, 56, 59, 63, 67, 73, 75–7, 79, 93, 94, 99, 106, 107–12, 122–4, 126–7, 129, 130, 133, 135, 138, 141, 148–9, 151–2, 155–7, 159–61, 163, 167, 176–7, 179, 189, 191–3, 195, 205–7, 215, 222, 224–5, 227–8, 251
Devonshire, HMS 99, 114, 115, 116
Diamond, HMS 46, 50
Dixon, Rear Admiral (USN) 194
Dobbie, Lt 94
Dobson, Vice Admiral Sir David 84, 87
Docker, Sir Bernard and Lady 29
Donai, MV 93
Drake, HMS 6, 126, 226
Draper, Lt Howard 'Stamps' 147
Dreadnought, HMS 174
Dreyer, Cdr C.W.S. 7–10, 14–23, 28, 42
Dryad, HMS 10
Duchess, HMS 46, 50
Dudgeon, Lt 71
Dunbar-Dempsey, Lt 102
Dunkerque 249
Durrant, Mike 66
Durnford-Slater, Vice Admiral Sir Richard 59

Eade, Sub Lt 61
Eagle, HMS 6–9, 15, 19–21, 39, 52, 55, 56, 60, 75, 81, 102, 107, 110, 115–16, 119, 123, 126–9, 131, 133, 135, 141–2, 149, 152, 155, 191–2, 195, 199, 202, 207, 221, 224, 227–8, 242

Eberle, Rear Admiral 174, 178,
Eccles, Vice Admiral Sir John 16, 19
Eddycliff, RFA 33
Eddystone Lighthouse 52
Edinburgh, HMS 252
Edward, Lt Cdr Robert 55
Elbe, River 201, 202
Elizabeth, HM the Queen Mother 4, 6, 25,
    36, 37, 59, 123, 130–2, 160, 177,
    178, 183, 195, 214, 252
Elizabeth I 247
Elizabeth II 45–6, 194, 195
Endurance, HMS 73
Engadine, RFA 194
Essex, USS 104, 105
Essex Class, American aircraft carriers 35
Eustace, Grant 102–5
Exercises:
    Apex 56
    Cascade 26, 36
    Comman Effort 212
    Corsica 156
    Dawn Breeze 36, 98, 99
    Decex 69
    Display Determination 191, 215, 216
    Dovetail 102
    Fantail 85
    Fantail Two 93
    Febex 33
    Fotex 62 91
    Fotex 63 101
    Hollow Laugh 93
    Isle D'or 204
    Lantreadex 154, 158, 170, 172
    Last Chance 176
    Lime Jug 142
    Longshot 93
    Lymelight 151
    Magic Sword IV 151
    Marjex 56
    Medflex 59
    Med Passex 151
    Northern Merger 164
    Northern Wedding 140, 212
    Ocean Safari 178, 203
    Phoenix 55
    Pilot Light 110
    Pink Gin III 69
    Pintail 92
    Pipedown 54
    Rawfish 89
    Royal Flush II 69
    Royal Knight 151
    Ruler 156
    Safe Pass 183
    Sally Forth 159
    Sardex 156
    Sea Devil 85, 86
    Shotgun 56
    Showboat 91
    Solid Shield 210
    Straight Laced 122
    Strikeback 52
    Strong Express 156
    Sunny Seas 156
    Swordthrust 67
    Teamwork 76 191
    Warrior 115

Falklands War 133, 253, 254
Falmouth 51
    Bay 52, 55
Falmouth, HMS 114
Families Day 112, 138, 139, 159, 176, 206
Far East 76, 79, 81, 84, 85, 93, 97, 99,
    106, 107, 109, 112, 113, 128, 173,
    174, 252
Farquhar, Lt Cdr S.C. 42, 45, 46, 48, 52,
Faslane 191
FDE1 WHAT 39
Fearless, HMS 156, 207
Fell, Vice Admiral Sir Michael 9, 21, 31,
    32, 115, 123, 124, 243
Ferranti 177
Fife, HMS 145, 146
Firth of Forth 200
Fish, Cdre Peter 196, 202, 204, 208, 209, 224
Fleet Air Arm Museum 219, 227, 233
Fleet Maintenance Base 227
Fleming, Rowland 159, 165, 171, 183
Flook 45
Foch 157
Ford, Miss 185, 186
Forrest, Sub Lt Mike 31
Forrest, Rear Admiral Sir Ronald 81, 85,
    86, 93, 96
Forrestal, USS 54, 156, 179, 215
Fort Grange, RFA 252
Fort Lauderdale 150, 156, 158, 188, 211
Franklin D Roosevelt, USS 155, 158
Freemantle 92, 116
Frewen, Rear Admiral John 85

Gallager, Leo 151
Gaunt, J.R., Ltd of Soho 131
Gedge, Tim 148
Genoa 56
George VI 4
Gerard-Pearse, Rear Admiral J.R.S. 161,
    172, 243
Gibraltar 1, 19–21, 25, 26, 36, 54, 56,
    65, 66, 69, 77–9, 97–9, 102, 113,
    122, 148, 152, 156, 163, 167, 176,
    192, 204, 205, 214, 215, 250
    Governor of 21, 23
Gibson, Vice Admiral Sir Donald 76, 77,
    79–81, 83–6, 91, 94, 95, 243
Gillet & Johnston of Croydon 19
Giovanni Assenso 166
Gladstone Dock 10, 16
Glamorgan, HMS 154
Glorious, HMS 249
Gorschov 146, 147
Gosport 17
Graf Spee 249
Graham, Rear Admiral Wilfred 172, 178,
    180, 181, 183, 186, 188, 191, 243
Grantham, Admiral Sir Guy 28
Greece 216
Greenland 71, 86
Greenock 11, 16
Gregale 28
Greta C, MV 164
Griffin, Admiral Sir Anthony 8, 20, 81,
    105, 107, 108, 110, 112, 114, 115,
    243
Guatemala 152
Gunroom 23, 30, 31, 102

Hackett, Lt Ted 160
Hal Far 31, 32, 65, 68, 69, 78
Hamburg 201
Hamilton, Lt Duggie 175
Hamoaze 52, 129
Hampton Roads 46, 48
Hancock, USS 86
Hardy, Lt Cdr Peter 137, 148, 150
Harkness, Rear Admiral J. 60, 61, 63
Harland & Wolf 6, 60
Hart, Sub Lt 102
Harwood, Wally 91, 92, 155
Hawker Siddeley 149
Healey, Denis 117, 253
Hefford, Captain Freddie 63, 68, 126,
    127, 134
Henderson, Admiral Sir Nigel 107
Hermes, HMS 64, 67, 69, 94, 129, 133,
    180, 199, 225, 253
Hermione, HMS 233
Higginson, Leading Seaman 164
Hill-Norton, Admiral of the Fleet the Lord
    60, 61, 65, 67, 71, 73, 75, 76,
    114, 191, 243
Hobbs, Cdr David 166, 168, 175, 176,
    184–6, 188
Holland 134
Holt Hill, Birkenhead 3
Hong Kong 86, 87, 89, 91, 92, 97, 102,
    114, 115, 252
Honnington, RAF 175, 206, 221, 222
Hood, HMS 1,

Hopkins, Admiral Sir Frank 43, 55, 59, 76, 91, 95, 243
Hopwood's Law of the Navy 17
Howard, Lord 247
Howard, William 7
Hudson River 153,
Hughes, Major A.S. 199, 200, 208, 222
Hunt, Cdr N.I.S. 243
Hurricane Flossie 19, 214

Illustrious, HMS 6
Independence, USS 151, 171
Indian Ocean 85, 100
Indomitable, HMS 223, 251
Indonesia 100
International Naval Review 46
Invergordon 45
Invincible, HMS 193, 251, 253
Invincible class 223, 224, 251, 254
Irish Sea 139
Irresistible, HMS 1
Istanbul 59

Jackson, Mr and Mrs 138
Jacksonville 209, 211
Jacksonville Naval Air Station 208
James I 247
Jamestown 46
Janion, Rear Admiral Sir Hugh 111
Janvrin, Rear Admiral H.R.B. 110
Jemitus, Joe 1
Jenkins, Roy 33
Jennycliff Bay 80
Jermy, Lt Mike 120, 121
John, Admiral Sir Casper 70
John F Kennedy, USS 188, 210, 215
Johnson, Sir Robert 4, 16
Judd, Mr Frank 176
Jutland, battle of 126, 139

Kalkara Creek 217
Karachi 104, 105
Karel Doorman 110
Kashin, destroyer 212
Kelly, Lt Cdr 102
Kennedy, President 105
Kerr, Nick 144
Key West 152
Khor al Fakkan 102
Khormaksar 84
Kinch, Cdr Gerry 135, 137, 139, 140, 144, 171, 174
Kitson Vickers 230
Knocknassie Hotel 231
Kolsas 141
Kotlin 141, 142, 144, 145, 147, 151
Kresta II, cruiser 179, 191, 212

Kynda, cruiser 122

Lajes 183
Lamlash 11
Lampen, PO Rod 139
Laos crisis 86, 87, 89
Lawrance, Captain Colin 23–5, 29, 30, 154, 156, 160
Layard, Admiral Sir Michael 85, 87, 89, 202, 208
Leach, Admiral of the Fleet Sir Henry 174–6, 193–5, 215, 216, 228
Lear, Neville 1
Lebanon 59
Leda, MV 141
Lee, Captain Tim 30, 31, 33, 37, 39, 40, 152, 157
Lee-on-Solent 14, 19
Leeds 1, 9, 137, 160
Legion, HMS 250
Leith 200
Lentaigne, Captain Larry 10, 12
Lepard, Keith 180
Leuchars, RAF 196, 206
Leverhulme, Viscount 16
Lewin, Captain 19
Lewin, Admiral Sir Terence 200, 219, 225
Lightfoot, Lt Colin 117
Lion, HMS 95, 110
Lisbon 54, 55, 71, 191
Lithgow, Mike 44
Little, Mr Ronald 25
'Little Wilf' 181, 189
Liverpool 16, 137
Lloyds 9
Loch Ewe 16
Loch Ryan 230
London, HMS 154
Long, Chief Airman Fitter (E) John 25
Lord, Sub Lt James 22, 31
Lossiemouth, RNAS 199
Lossiemouth, RAF 201, 212, 222
Lowestoft, HMS 117
Lowey, Wilf 3
Luce, Admiral Sir David 110
Lygo, Admiral Sir Raymond 24, 32, 35, 124, 127, 129, 130–2, 134, 137, 138, 141, 142, 145–8, 180, 243
Lyme Bay 22
Lyness, RFA 202

McCallum, Lt D. 222
MacDonald, Cdr Douglas 140, 148, 151
McGibben, PO 19
McGrigor, Admiral Sir Rhoderick 6
McIntosh, Cdr 59, 243
MacLeod, Flt Lt M 222

MacPherson, Cdr R.J.S. 124, 243
Madagascar 121
Madden, Admiral Sir Alec 23
Madden, Admiral Sir Charles 77, 110
Madeira 176
Magens Bay 209
Makarios, Archbishop 163
Malacca Straits 85
Malaya 91
Mallard Buoy 80
Malta 26, 28–31, 33, 34, 36, 56, 59, 64, 65, 67, 68, 70, 71, 78, 79, 82, 113, 141, 142, 145–7, 156, 165, 166, 204, 217, 219, 221, 249, 250
Man, Isle of 16
Mancais, Cdr A. 84, 89, 91
Manila 85
Manila Bay 86
Marina, Princess, Duchess of Kent 1
Marjoribanks, Lt 67
Marsaxlokk 33
Marshall, Revd Bernard 189
Martin, Lt Cdr 158
Martin Baker 109
Mathews, A.E. 57
Maund, Rear Admiral 1, 25
May, Lt Cdr 9
Mayflower 47
Mayflower II 46, 47
Mayport 150, 156, 158, 159, 170, 184, 208, 209, 211
MB52, tug 123
Mediterranean 1, 21–3, 36, 59, 65, 68, 79, 99, 106, 141, 151, 155, 156, 165, 174, 180, 191, 204, 214, 215, 250, 252
Medway, River 247
Mersey, River 3, 6, 10, 12, 13
Messina Straits 34, 216
Midway, USS 114
Milford Haven 139
Milne, Lt Cdr Jim 196
Minas Gerais 175
Ministry of Defence (MOD) 86, 180, 189, 190, 228
Mintoff, Mr 219
Mitchell, Able Seaman Edward 19
Mombasa 93, 100, 101, 103–5, 116, 117
Monsell, Cdr Derek 79, 91, 92, 147
Monte Christe statue 174
Moore, Dudley 134
Moore, Geoff 3
Moore, Chaplain of the Fleet the Revd J.W.B. 16
Moore, Ken 15, 34
Moore, Mr 158

Moray Firth 52, 110, 148, 164, 177, 191, 195, 200, 202
Morrison, PO 53
Morton, Captain A 168, 175, 200, 201, 222
Moseley, Lt Cdr C.S. 243
Mountbatten, Admiral of the Fleet the Lord 16, 156, 157
Mountbatten Cliffs 20
Mount Edgcumbe 75
Mount Etna 34, 36
Mount Kilimanjaro 101
Mounts Bay 176, 224
Mountstar Metal Corporation 230, 231
Mozambique Channel 117, 119
Muckle Ossa 55

NAAFI 15, 23, 192
Nabb, Mr 231
Nairobi 104
Naples 34, 35, 57, 65, 79, 148, 151, 179, 205, 216
NATO 167, 179, 180, 194, 199
    Council 159
    Military Committee 159, 191
Navy Days:
    Plymouth 20, 23, 138, 190, 195
    Portsmouth 37, 123
Nelson, Lord 55, 76
Neptune, King 101
New York 48–50, 73, 94, 152, 154
Nicholls, Harry 79, 80
Nimitz, USS 186, 191, 211
Noah's News 14, 25, 28, 247
Norfolk, Virginia, USA 46, 48, 172, 185, 188, 212
Northampton, USS 48
North-East Winter Buoy 80
Northern Shipbreaking 230
North Sea 201
Norway 180
Nuclear weapons 109, 110

O'Brien, Rear Admiral W.D. 122
O'Donnell, Captain Guy 135, 145, 146, 192, 222, 225–7, 243
O'Grady, Harry 154
Okinawa 89
Olmeda, RFA 152
Olna, RFA 165
Olwen, RFA 175, 252
Oman 102
Opalia 194
Operation Antelope 103
Oran 249
Orkneys 55
Ormshaw, Sub Lt Richard 216
Oslo 123, 141

Oswald, Vice Admiral Sir Julian 252
Otus, HMS 151
Outback '88, 252
Owen, Dr David 132

Palma 67, 151, 222
Palmer, Lt 94
Parlatorio Wharf 28
Patrick, Lt James 117
Pearce, Lt Cdr J.H.S. 24, 32
Pebbles, Tony 72
Pedder, Rear Admiral A.R. 32
Pegasus, HMS 247, 248
Penang 84
Pennington, Sir John 247
Pennington, Lt Mike 43, 44, 50, 53, 54, 57
Peppe, Cdr W.L.T 62, 67, 68, 70, 71, 73, 166
Pert, tug 68
Petuxan River 48
Phaleron Bay 217
Phantom OCU 196
Phantom Training Flight 196
Phantomization 123, 132, 236, 239, 241
Philip, Prince, Duke of Edinburgh 45, 46, 105, 194
Pickle, Wilfred 3
Pike, Marine Robert 25
Pilgrim Fathers 47, 150
Plymouth 22, 34, 47, 79, 81, 94, 130, 133, 150–2, 155, 157, 159, 199, 223, 228, 230
Plymouth, HMS 117
Plymouth Sound 39, 47, 75, 77, 92, 105, 106, 122, 132, 134, 137, 139, 148, 151, 155, 159, 161, 192, 230
Pollock, Admiral of the Fleet Sir Michael 94, 95, 97, 99–102, 104–7, 216
Pompeii 205
Pooley, John 181, 182
Portland 9, 22, 77, 132, 133, 164, 204, 206
Port Said 83, 113
Port Said Roads 100
Portsmouth 17, 19, 24, 36, 52, 96, 109, 110, 123, 124, 129, 155, 178, 193, 221, 225, 252
Power, Admiral of the Fleet Sir Arthur 19
Power, Vice Admiral M.L. 45
Priddy's Hard 24
Prison Island 105
Pritchard, Cdr G.I. 243
Puerto Rico 154
Purdie, John 179–83, 189
Puzzuoli Bay 35

QE2 124, 152, 153
Qrendi 147

Queen Elizabeth 39, 54, 152
Queen Mary 49, 54, 152

Raleigh, HMS 139
Raleigh, Sir Walter 246, 247
Ramillies, HMS 126
Ramillies Pumps 125
Rawbone, Rear Admiral A.R. 84, 96
Red Sea 113
Reeve, John 107
Regent, RFA 152, 222
Renown, HMS 249
Resource, RFA 166, 167
Resurgent, RFA 67
Reynolds, Cdr 61, 68
Rhodesia 117
Rhyl, HMS 117
Richardson-Bunbury, Lt Cdr M. 97, 106
Richelieu 110
Riley, Flt Lt Steve 196, 201, 212, 214, 223
Rio de Janeiro 173
Roberts, Rear Admiral John 148–52, 154, 155, 243
Roberts, Owen 6
Roberts, Chaplain Ray 194
Roosevelt Roads 155, 158, 167, 183, 207, 208
Ross, Don 85
Rosyth 67, 110, 179, 227, 252
Rotheram, Captain Martin 112, 117, 119–21, 172, 214, 221
Rothesay, HMS 94
Rotterdam 133
Roxburgh, Vice Admiral Sir John 28, 30, 243
Royal Navy Historic Flight 252
Royal Western Yacht Club 79
Russell, Lt 71
Russell, Cdr Desmond 77

Sailor, BBC series 179, 182, 189, 191
St Allen, RAF 222
St Brandan, MV 139
St Thomas 151, 158, 209
Salter, Ben 164, 178, 186, 187
Salvador 175
Sampson, Nikos 163
Sandown Bay 22
Saratoga, USS 48, 54, 65, 127
Sardinia 148, 166
Savile, Jimmy 178
Scharnhorst 249
Scott, Captain David 145
Scott, Sir Peter 42
Sea Slug, missile 146
SEATO 86
Sembawang 85
Sergeants' taxi 19

Sevastopol 247
Shackleton, HMS 80
Shepherd, David 219, 220, 222
Sherman, MV 167
Shipbreaking Queensborough Ltd (SQL) 230, 231
Ship's Flight 51, 78, 81, 135, 141, 152, 164, 173, 176, 195, 210, 220, 238, 239
Sicily 34
Sievewright, Lt Cdr George 8, 13
Sigonilla 216
Singapore 85, 91–3, 100–2, 114–16, 119, 123, 252
Sirett, Lt 94
Sirius, HMS 252
Skinner, Captain A. 77–9, 82
Slade, Lt 221
Slatter, Dick 72
Slatter, Admiral Murray 247
Smeaton Pass 79, 80, 206
Smeeton, Vice Admiral Sir Richard 63, 76, 228
Snotties' Nurse 31
Solent 19
Somaliland 247
Somerville-Jones, Lt Cdr Keith 184
Southampton 54
Southsea 17
Southwick 110
Speedwell 47
Spithead 19, 36, 39, 54, 193, 233
Spithead Fleet Review 192–5, 215, 233
Staten Island 153
Statue of Liberty 153, 252
Staveley, Rear Admiral 202, 211
Stewart, Captain 10
Strensal camp 160
Stretton, RNAS 6
Stutchbury, Lt John 121
Subic Bay 86, 114
Suddenham, Mr 83
Suez Canal 81–4, 94, 97, 99, 100, 113, 114, 122, 252
Sunday Express 16
Superman, tug 80
Swan Hunter 252

Tagus, River 191
Ta' Qali 147
Tarseus III, tanker 207, 208
Tarver, Lt Cdr Alan 121, 150
Tew, Mechanic (E) 1st Class Gordon 25
Thames Barrier 228, 252
Thurley, Patrick 233
Ticonderoga, USS 35
Tidespring, RFA 115

Tintagel Castle, HMS 9
Tofts, Captain 68, 115, 116
Torishima range 89
Torrey Canyon 155
Toulon 29, 68, 191, 192, 204, 205
Trafalgar, battle of 54, 76
Treacher, Captain John 127, 129
Tristrum, Lt Cdr 150
Triumph, HMS 23, 30
Truscott, Lt Cdr L. 63
Twiss, Vice Admiral Sir Frank 114
Typhoon Dinah 92

U-39 248
U-81 1, 250
United States 39

Valetta Harbour 79
Valley, RAF 139
Vanguard, HMS 6, 23
Van Zelm bridle arresting gear 127
Vatcher, Mr 19
Venerable, HMS 110
Vernon, HMS 36
Vickers, Barry 231
Victorious, HMS 68–70, 77, 79, 102, 114, 127, 236
Vietnam War 114, 140
Virgin Gorda 154
Virginia Capes area 152, 184
Voi National Park 104

Waite, Captain C. 224
Walker, Lt Cdr E.M.C. 79–81
Wallsend 252
Warship Week 1
Watkins, Cdr John 8
Wattisham, RAF 196
Wave Sovereign, RFA 21
Weatherall, Vice Admiral Sir James 205, 210, 211, 214, 224, 227, 252
West Indies 157
Westland Helicopters 238, 239
Weston, Rear Admiral 16
Weymouth 22, 77
White, Captain Robert 81
Whitehead, Lt Cdr 44
Wigg, Cdr J 102
Wiggin-Fanshawe, Admiral Sir Godfrey 57
Wight, Isle of 24
Wilcock, Cdr Graham 66, 161
Wilkinson, FMAA Tom 177, 178, 181, 182, 187, 188, 231
Wilson, Charles 48
Wilson, Jack 2
Wimbledon, Lord 247

Woodard, Rear Admiral Sir Robert 76–8, 83
Woollen, John 13, 60, 61, 63, 72
Woolley, Cdr W.J. 10–12, 14, 19, 22
Wreford, Lt Cdr Peter 92, 103
Wright, Admiral Jerauld (USN) 48

Yeovilton, RNAS 140, 200, 215
Yugoslavia 252

Zanzibar 105

FAA/RAF squadrons:
  1 Squadron (RAF) 148, 176
  4 Squadron (RAF) 247
  701 Squadron B Flight 44
  800 Squadron 24–6, 35, 44, 63, 68, 78, 82, 84, 89, 91, 109, 234, 236
  801 Squadron 98, 132, 237
  802 Squadron 44, 234
  803 Squadron 9, 109, 123, 236
  804 Squadron 44, 57, 234
  807 Squadron 63, 68, 236
  809 Squadron 132, 135, 154, 155, 158, 167, 168, 173, 175, 184, 200, 206, 217, 221, 237
  815 Squadron 44, 77–85, 87, 93, 94, 102, 103, 105, 109, 112, 115, 123, 234, 239
  819 Squadron 109, 112, 239
  820 Squadron 63, 68, 239
  824 Squadron 44, 63, 68, 135, 140, 155, 164, 166, 167, 171, 175, 176, 188, 195, 196, 208, 209, 216, 224, 234, 239, 240
  826 Squadron 224
  831 Squadron 42, 44, 45, 52, 55, 68, 82, 235
  848 Squadron 76
  849 Squadron 95, 109, 206; A Flight 63, 67, 68, 236; B Flight 44, 135, 155, 166, 168, 172, 204, 209, 214, 221, 224, 235, 236, 237; C Flight 78, 82, 105, 109, 112, 123, 236, 237
  890 Squadron 78, 79, 82, 84, 85, 91, 94, 105, 109, 123, 236
  891 Squadron 31, 235
  892 Squadron 63, 65, 67, 68, 127, 134, 135, 137, 140, 155, 163, 166, 171, 172, 188, 191, 196, 200, 206, 236, 238
  893 Squadron 44, 69, 71, 235, 236
  898 Squadron 24, 25, 35, 44, 51, 53, 55, 234
  899 Squadron 95, 135, 202, 242